The Magic of a Common Language

Current Studies in Linguistics
Samuel Jay Keyser, general editor

The Magic of a Common Language

Jakobson, Mathesius, Trubetzkoy, and the Prague
Linguistic Circle

Jindřich Toman

The MIT Press
Cambridge, Massachusetts
London, England

Set in New Baskerville by Vail Composition.
Printed and bound in the United States of America.

Library of Congress Cataloging-in-Publication Data

Toman, Jindřich.
 The magic of a common language : Jakobson, Mathesius, Trubetzkoy,
 and the Prague Linguistic Circle / Jindřich Toman.
  p. cm. — (Current studies in linguistics ; 26)
 Includes bibliographical references and index.
 ISBN 0-262-20096-1
 1. Pražsky linguistický kroužek. I. Title. II. Series:
Current studies in linguistics series ; 26.
P147.T66   1994
410'.72043712—dc20   94-17845
                                                              CIP

Contents

Preface

He said that when one went to an exhibition and looked at the pictures of other painters, one knows that they are bad, there is no excuse for it, they are simply bad, but one's own pictures, one knows the reason why they are bad and so they are not hopelessly bad.

Gertrude Stein on Picasso

Leafing through the accounts of the Prague Linguistic Circle by some of its members, I occasionally had the odd feeling that the writers perhaps had not been there at all or did not want to tell us—the accounts were canonical, the piety overwhelming, the dynamics of history and its occasionally loud laughter all securely purged. That this impression was not really frivolous became obvious to me in the 1970s, when I used to see Roman Jakobson. With him, by contrast, the picture was never grey. In the end, I realized that Jakobson himself was the best historiographer of Prague linguistics. But he was also an ideologue, a true whig historian, inviting another historian's scrutiny.

It thus seemed natural to reopen the case at a new level, and so I began to read. I decided to start with what everyone had relegated to footnotes: all the articles listed in an old bibliography of Jakobson's work under the rubric Miscellanea. What could be more detached from the topic than Jakobson's numerous columns for Czech newspapers, such as *Lidové noviny* and *Prager Presse?* And what could be more irrelevant than to continue with Vilém Mathesius's miscellanea, such as the proposal concerning a systematic reorganization of

Czechoslovak tourism? In short, the margin soon moved into the center. Although the procedure was idiosyncratic, at least a color picture was emerging. Well, if pictures such as these could be had, why not face the challenge and arrange them into a new album; why not organize them into a new argument?

Although a number of problems arose, certain aspects of the approach remained fairly clear and unproblematic. There was little doubt in my mind about how to arrange the new album, or about what the new argument was and was not going to be. The book was not intended to deal with the internal development of Prague linguistics—in other words, it is not an introduction to structural linguistics or to structural aesthetics. Although technical questions of linguistics had to be incorporated, they are meant to form a part of a larger picture. The focus is on the embedding of the Prague Circle into the broader cultural ambience of the 1920s and the 1930s. Thus, I pursue the differences in the conditions and the style of research between Russia and Czechoslovakia, the relationship of the Circle to Prague's multicultural society, the special role of Russo-Ukrainian and German scholarship in Prague, the relations between the Circle and the Czech avant-garde, and the impact of the guiding images of contemporary social thought on linguistics. The last point seems especially fascinating, both because of the way it is obvious and because of the way it was neglected. Much in the thought of Mathesius, Trubetzkoy, and Jakobson can be understood only if data from the margin are moved into the center. The interwar ideal of collective work, the idea of a synthesis of knowledge, and the emphasis on socially defined commitment to scholarship all left visible traces on the Prague Linguistic Circle, but all are missing from the standard accounts.

I also had few doubts as to how to put the album together. Because of the marginality of a great deal of the material, it seemed to me that I should present it as undiluted as possible; hence the large number of quotations. In retrospect I realize that the method may have gotten out of hand a little bit, but I am still willing to defend it. Owing to the relative inaccessibility of certain materials and the unwillingness of previous historiographers to deal with them, the factual basis remains crucial. The method is by no means sophisticated, and in retrospect I wish there had been more time and space to discuss the selection of data and to scrutinize the status of a number of the sources more carefully. After all, most of them were conceived as texts and remain texts. Yet I believe that in the end there is more than rich documentation—there are also a few arguments, and where there are arguments there is room to argue about them.

As with any other album, the reader should feel free to leaf through this volume. For those who like a story, however, I can recommend several paths. Chapters 2 and 3, section 5.1, chapter 11, and section 12.1 can be read as a fragment of Roman Jakobson's intellectual biography. Chapter 4 and section 5.2 provide a sketch of Vilém Mathesius's intellectual vita, and chapter 10 is a self-contained discussion of N. S. Trubetzkoy. Chapters 7–9 are devoted to the guiding cultural images of the interwar period and to their co-creator and executor, the Prague Linguistic Circle. Chapter 6 addresses the important and little-studied subject of interwar Prague as a multicultural center of learning. Chapter 1 was written on Samuel Jay Keyser's advice to "say everything that you want to say right at the beginning"; I apologize to him if it came out a little bit short.

My interest in the Prague Circle began as a hobby. Although I certainly felt happy to be in privileged company, I regarded conversations in the 1970s with Roman Jakobson, Vilém Fried, Petr Suvčinskij, and Jiří Veltruský mainly as civilized discourses on Czech and Russian cultural history. This was quite natural in view of my East European background; for me, knowledge of important things was almost always a combination of oral history and antiquarian enterprising. I especially enjoyed listening to Roman Jakobson, whom I saw for the last time in September 1981. After a long afternoon of his reminiscing about his days in Prague, I left his house in Cambridge, Massachusetts, with a lighthearted remark: "So long—next year, same time, same place." Jakobson replied with a smile that he might be dead by then. Sadly, he was right. It was only after he and other contemporaries of the Circle were no longer here that I decided to professionalize my hobby and go ahead with a book. Soon, innumerable questions of detail arose, especially when I began to work with Jakobson's archives. Although I had a strong supporter in the late Krystyna Pomorska, time could not be defeated. The number of persons of whom I could ask questions was diminishing. The lenses were in order, but some pictures could simply no longer be taken.

Acknowledgments

The present study concludes a part of a project on the history of the Prague Linguistic Circle. Research on some sections was made possible through a grant by the Deutsche Forschungsgemeinschaft (Bonn–Bad Godesberg) to the author in the 1980s; further research was done in the early 1990s while the author was on the faculty of the University of Michigan. The help of both institutions is acknowledged with much gratitude.

In addition to institutional support, a major factor in completing this part of the project was the continued interest of teachers, colleagues, and friends. The author is particularly grateful to Elmar Holenstein, Ladislav Matejka, Stephen Rudy, Jarmila and Jiří Veltruský—and, extra-alphabetically, Morris Halle—for their interest and encouragement. He is also grateful to his colleagues in the Department of Slavic Languages and Literatures of the University of Michigan—particularly to Michael Makin, Omry Ronen, and Benjamin Stolz—for their readiness to discuss idiosyncratic issues and to help with pedestrian work. The staff of the Institute Archives and Special Collections at the Massachusetts Institute of Technology is also warmly thanked.

It is a sad fact of life that a number of friends from whom a great deal of inspiration came at various points cannot take the results under their critical scrutiny—Vilém Fried, František Galan, Roman Jakobson, and Krystyna Pomorska are no longer with us. It is to their memory that the book is dedicated.

The Magic of a Common Language

1

Mathesius's Problem

In May 1911, after arriving in Prague to take up his appointment to the physics department of the German University, Albert Einstein wrote to his friend Michele Besso: "Incidentally, the city of Prague is wonderful, so beautiful, that it alone would be worth a journey." (Einstein and Besso 1972: 20) Moreover, Einstein seemed to be in good company in his new environment. Historians have noted with interest that he was a welcome guest in a number of local circles, and that Franz Kafka's friend Max Brod even made a literary character of him—the astronomer Johannes Kepler in Brod's *Redemption of Tycho Brahe*, a novel set in Prague around 1600, was inspired by Einstein's personality. But, beautiful as the ambience was, Einstein did not conceal from Besso in the same letter that Prague was also "an intellectual desert without conviction." He left after three semesters.

Had such a linguist as Ferdinand de Saussure, Antoine Meillet, or Baudouin de Courtenay come to Prague in the same years as Einstein, he too might have left quickly—the provincialism of the city was pervasive. But when another foreign scholar, Roman Jakobson, was fleeing Czechoslovakia on the eve of the Second World War, he confessed to his friend Jaroslav Seifert, a Czech avant-garde poet and future Nobel laureate: "I was glad to be in this country and I was happy here too." (Seifert 1981: 323) And in 1943, addressing an audience of New York Czechs worried about the fate of their occupied homeland, Jakobson said: "I do not think that there is any doubt about the nature of the intellectual legacy with which the Czechoslovak resistance has to identify itself today and tomorrow. Above all, it is the legacy of the avant-garde, or more precisely, revolutionary cultural development of the first twenty years of the Czechoslovak Republic."[1] Turning to his farewell with Seifert, he continued: "Saying goodbye to me in Prague in the days of April of 1939, a great Czech poet put it very well: 'There is only one thing you must not forget—these twenty years were immensely beautiful. Remind everyone of how much work we managed to do.'"

The radical shift from Einstein's "intellectual desert" to Jakobson's "revolutionary cultural development" owes much to one man: Vilém Mathesius, a far-sighted Czech linguist whose determination to modernize Czech culture and scholarship had been formed well before the First World War. Mathesius had been educated at a time when historicism was losing its appeal as a sole model of explanation and when German scholarship was ceasing to be the primary point of orientation for Czech scholars. But, for all his determination and organizational efforts, Mathesius's early efforts bore little success.

The outcome of the First World War promised to change all this. Old Austria broke apart, and an array of new states, including Czechoslovakia, arose within its former territory. The new state was able to assert its borders easily, suffered no major economic problems, and was sustained by an atmosphere of enthusiasm and optimism. After centuries of troubled dependence on the Habsburgs, the Czechs were independent again. This was a hopeful time for Czech scholarship, which seemed poised to transform the momentum into splendid results. Some non-academic segments of the intelligentsia had already done very well in transforming themselves. The young artists and poets of the Czech avant-garde quickly accepted the ideology of modernism and energetically jumped on its international bandwagon. In 1922, Jaromír Krejcar, an avant-garde architect who would later belong to Roman Jakobson's circle of friends, edited a collection, entitled *Život* [*Life*], which included not only poetry and texts of the Czech avant-garde but also essays by Le Corbusier, Ilya Èrenburg, Adolf Behne, and other representatives of the European avant-garde, generously interspersed among which were pictures of ocean liners, airplanes, Charlie Chaplin, Mary Pickford, and other icons and heroes of the Roaring Twenties. This embrace of modernism extended beyond avant-garde book-making: Krejcar and other Czech avant-garde architects embellished Prague's suburbs with constructivist villas well before the new state managed to erect its banks, ministries, and libraries. The avant-garde did not discuss province and fatherland very much—the modern spirit was international.

Czech academics were considerably slower to change, thus showing that political independence and intellectual productivity do not automatically go hand in hand. Czech scholars seemed at first to be preoccupied with odd questions. In *New Athenaeum,* a journal co-edited by Mathesius, many pages were devoted to discussions of whether one should publish in Czech or in German. Mathesius was soon forced to conclude that scholarship was even more provincial in the new state than it had been under the Austro-Hungarian monarchy.

Under these circumstances, Mathesius's personal qualities proved crucial. He believed in rationally organized work and in the active involvement of intellectuals in public affairs. He pursued the idea of "constructive work," a notion that for him stood in opposition to Romanticism. *Kulturní aktivismus* [*Cultural Activism*] (Mathesius 1925a), a collection of essays, is the most explicit source of his personal philosophy, but his ideas can also be conveniently gleaned from small journalistic pieces, such as the brief reflection on Czechoslovakia's Independence Day that he published in the cultural weekly *Přítomnost* [*Present Times*] in early November 1926. He noted that the anniversary celebrations were visibly lacking in spirit and were ultimately wasted on petty political campaigning. In this way, a major psychological mistake was being committed: "We are not using this exceptional occasion to educate our citizens and to reinforce all their creative efforts." (Mathesius 1926: 673) For Mathesius, a clear alternative was to "convert [Independence Day] to Construction Day, a day on which a working program for the coming year would be announced and explicated in detail." The program was not to consist of bombastic undertakings. Instead, small concrete projects were to be pursued, leading to results which could be seen and evaluated: improvements in the organization of public transport or of tourist facilities, for example. This new conception of Independence Day would have immense consequences for the self-education and self-awareness of the new Czech society:

We shall learn to think in concrete and practical terms and gain confidence in our initiative. Moreover, we shall learn not to leave things half done simply because the new Independence Day will be back in just a year, bringing the need to check what has been accomplished, what remains to be done and who is guilty that not everything has been done. Such an Independence Day will teach us to work constructively, and work constructively we must, unless we want to decay. (ibid.)

Considerations such as these prove that Mathesius was the right man in the right place. Driven by an ethos of consciously planned work, he was keen to identify problems and search for solutions. Yet, despite all the calls for a restructuring of the new Czech society, it was an outside event that allowed Mathesius to fulfill his desire to turn Prague into a world center of linguistics. The event in question was the October Revolution of 1917, which unleashed a flood of émigrés from the Soviet Union, many of whom began to arrive in Czechoslovakia in the early 1920s. As a result, for the first time in its history, Prague became a major focus of East European emigration. Although postwar Berlin was briefly the capital of Russian culture abroad, and Paris was to become a huge center for Russians and Ukrainians in the 1920s and the 1930s, neither Germany nor France offered government-sponsored institutions and grants for individual academic and literary figures. All this was available in the Czechoslovak Republic, which quickly declared it a matter of principle to subsidize free Russian and Ukrainian culture and scholarship. The personal initiative of Czechoslovakia's first president, Tomáš G. Masaryk, was crucial, but the move was also supported by a broad range of politicians.

The Russian and Ukrainian scholars were a crucial ingredient in Mathesius's attempt to create a linguistic society. Reminiscing about the entry for March 13, 1925, in his notebook, Mathesius later wrote:

The lack of lively scholarly contact with the Prague philological community which used to depress me, was now felt very intensely by Jakobson, who came to Prague from quite different circumstances. We often used to talk about the need for a debate and study center for young linguists, and it was quite natural that we looked for a remedy among ourselves. I have noted that on March 13, 1925, I invited Jakobson and Trnka and also Karcevskij, later a lecturer in Russian at the University of Geneva, but then a master of the Russian gymnasium in Prague. . . . (Mathesius 1936b: 138)

One may wonder in retrospect how these four men got along at all. Mathesius was a professor of English and apparently a somewhat dry Protestant; Bohumil Trnka was his disciple and devoted assistant; Sergej Karcevskij, a Russian émigré, had been a social activist and a student of linguistics in Geneva; and Roman Jakobson, an avant-gardist and a Formalist, was now an employee of the Soviet diplomatic mission in Prague and, in the eyes of many, a Soviet spy. How did they communicate? Did Mathesius and Trnka speak Russian, and did Karcevskij know Czech? All we know is that the four shared a passionate dissatisfaction with the old linguistics and a vision of an alternative. The evening of March 13, 1925, was the first recorded gathering of the group that later became known as the Prague Linguistic Circle.

The evening at Mathesius's home did not immediately bear fruit. Determined as Mathesius was, and devoted as the members were, no strikingly new quality was apparent when the Prague Circle began to function publicly in 1926. At this point the Circle was still a discussion society. The process of amalgamation required yet another ingredient. This was fortuitously supplied by the zeitgeist, and its name was collectivism. The First World War had radically changed European attitudes toward individualism, a social value that was strongly visible on the turn-of-the-century intellectual scene. Mathesius had even argued that the Czechs, rather than being original individualists, were better at collective work. In "Czech Science," one of the essays in *Cultural Activism,* he criticized everything he saw in the Czech academic community: Bold attempts at synthesis were not appreciated, narrow-minded specialization prevailed, and Czech scholars did not participate in the international circulation of ideas. He argued that a collective approach would solve many of these problems:

This is not a situation which could not be changed. It is true that we are not distinguished by individual courage. Our courage is of a more corporate character. . . . But given the fact that we were not endowed with individual courage, or perhaps that its tradition has not evolved here, one cannot say that it is impossible to create conditions for fostering it in research, for instance, by creating a favorable atmosphere or by supplementing it with our corporate courage. (Mathesius 1925b: 89)

A desire for ideologies transcending the liberal "free play of interests" was common in this epoch. A society with meaningful goals, one in which individuals would renounce personal whims in favor of higher interests, was a topic of wide discussion. The Circle followed this trend in its own way. When the First Congress of Slavic Philologists met in Prague in 1929, the Prague Circle presented its famous Theses (a comprehensive program of research) as a manifesto worked out collectively by its members and not signed with any individual name. A year later, the Statutes of the Circle defined its activities as the collective work of a group of scholars united by a common scholarly worldview. It was in the drafting of the Theses that a radically new quality began to emerge. Jakobson, full of excitement, reported to Trubetzkoy on April 6, 1929:

The active core of the circle has concluded that in its function as a parliament of opinions, as a platform for free discussion, the circle is a relic and has to be transformed into a group, a party, which is tightly interlocked as far as scientific ideology is concerned. . . . This process is taking place at present with much success. An initiative committee of sorts has established itself in the circle, including Mathesius, the very able linguist Havránek, Mukařovský, Trnka, and myself. This transformation of the circle literally inspired its members; in fact, I have never seen such a degree of enthusiasm in Czechs at all. (Jakobson to Trubetzkoy, RJP b. 123, f. 51. The word "party" is omitted in Jakobson 1975.)

Thus the ingredients that helped motivate the step from the periphery to the center are known: Mathesius's determination, the presence of East European émigrés, and the liberal atmosphere of Masaryk's Prague (which made it possible to transform a multinational pool of scholars into a true republic of scholars). The result was a solution to a specific academic problem, but also a unique form of cross-cultural dialogue. The degree of integration achieved in the Prague Circle was unprecedented. The Circle became a meeting ground for Czechs, Russians, Ukrainians, and Germans, for traditional scholars and for leftists. The long and sometimes difficult process by which this integration was achieved forms the subject matter of this volume.

2

The Linguist Is a Futurist: Roman Jakobson's Formative Years

Reminiscing about Jakobson's early participation in the Prague Linguistic Circle, Mathesius said that Jakobson came from "other circumstances." The usage was positive, referring to Russia's vibrant intellectual atmosphere in the first decades of the twentieth century. One way of reconstructing these "other circumstances" is to survey the formative years of the man who helped solve Mathesius's problem by transmitting the news about this intellectual paradise.

Roman Jakobson was born in Moscow on October 10, 1896 (N.S.); his father was a merchant. In 1915, as a first-year student at Moscow University, Jakobson belonged to the initiators of a group later known as the Moscow Linguistic Circle, and around the same time he also became friendly with a group of young St. Petersburg intellectuals who formed OPOJAZ, a circle that played a central role in the development of what came to be called Russian Formalism. Jakobson's early interests mirrored in many ways the breadth of topics with which OPOJAZ and the Moscow Linguistic Circle were concerned. But besides pursuing Slavic philology and folklore at Moscow University, he was involved in the Russian avant-garde. He might thus seem to have had an unusual dual loyalty: to scholarship and to art. As we shall see, however, the duality was only apparent. The attempt to maintain a single, unified intellectual worldview was actually the cornerstone of the avant-garde program. This chapter describes the details of the ambience in which this program flourished, focusing on Roman Jakobson.[1] Chapter 3 will provide a broader context to Jakobson's biography.

2.1 Scholarly Beginnings: Dialectology and Folklore

In his autobiography, Charles Darwin recorded an episode that reveals the intense curiosity and the passion for nature that apparently were inscribed early in his personality:

. . . no pursuit at Cambridge was followed with nearly so much eagerness or gave me so much pleasure as collecting beetles. . . . one day on tearing off some old bark, I saw two rare beetles and seized one in each hand; then I saw a third and new kind, which I could not bear to lose, so that I popped the one which I held in my right hand into my mouth. Alas it ejected some intensely acrid fluid, which burnt my tongue so that I was forced to spit the beetle out, which was lost, as well as the third one. (Darwin 1983: 34f.)

The passion underlying the emotionally intense episode and the desire to retain it in a narrative elevate this experience to a constitutive element of Darwin's intellectual biography.

Leafing through the numerous retrospectives and conversations Roman Jakobson published in the last decades of his life,[2] one is also tempted to search for a central theme—and it seems that there is one. Jakobson stated in 1966 that a "passion for gathering proverbs possessed [him] as soon as [he] learned to scrawl letters" (Jakobson 1966: 637), and that he began to preoccupy himself with "phantasmagoric vocabulary, vacillating between sense and nonsense" (ibid.: 639). His universe was language, and his beetles were proverbs and the characters populating them. Consider, for instance, the enigmatic Makar from the Russian proverb "Na bédnogo Makára vse šíški váljatsja" ("It is upon the poor Makar that all the cones fall"):

The childish concern for Makar has never been forgotten; I used to mumble *kára Makára* 'Makar's penalty' and to yell a byword devoted to the same hero—*kudá Makár telját ne gonjál* 'so far away that Makar never drove his calves there'—with an unwittingly hammering stress on its four oxytone *á*. Why was the ill-fated fellow expected to roam around the world? (Jakobson 1966: 638)

Arcane as this preoccupation might appear, Jakobson himself took off the veil of mystery by making his childhood idiosyncrasies more transparent—in Russia, proverbs were simply everywhere: "But proverbs themselves are actually not the point. Folklore is an essential force in Russian society and life." (Jakobson 1984b: 6)

Jakobson's first school was the Lazarev Institute of Oriental Languages, which had played an important educational role within Moscow's Armenian community since the early nineteenth century[3] but had by the end of the century been more or less assimilated into the Russian system of gymnasia.[4] The Armenian connection seems to have had little impact on the young Jakobson; he never brought it up in later years. More important was the fact that the institute taught languages and employed a number of first-class professors, some of whom also had appointments at the university; among them were the classicist F. E. Korš, the folklorist A. N. Veselovskij, the folklorist and linguist V. F. Miller, and the folklorist V. V. Bogdanov. Not surprisingly, the theme of folklore appears in this environment again:

Miller impressed us, and his works interested me since childhood: at the age of eleven or twelve years, or so, I already had read his studies on epic poetry and its history. . . . Under the influence of Miller and Bogdanov,[5] and other teachers, I also took interest in another question: how to collect folklore? Spending the summer in the country, in the village, I began to transcribe folklore texts. What was the easiest for me was of course the folklore of children. . . . I recorded texts of Russian children and also of Gypsy children. (Jakobson 1984b: 7f.)

Collecting folklore and dialect data remained Jakobson's favorite preoccupation during his Russian years. As we shall soon see, this hunger for raw data was not unique—a whole generation of modern Russian poets, artists, and linguists had become fascinated with folk art. And this interest was in no way in conflict with the interests of the emerging avant-garde.

Jakobson graduated from the Lazarev Institute, with a Silver Medal, in May 1914; he then enrolled in the Russian department of the historical-philological branch of Moscow University.[6] In his conversations with L. Dezső, Jakobson (1973) recalled that soon after entering the university he happened to attend a session in the memory of F. F. Fortunatov (b. 1848), a senior professor who had reigned over Moscow linguistics and Slavic philology until his death on September 20, 1914. The memorial address given by the classicist F. E. Korš impressed him so much that he instantly submerged himself in the *Russkij filologičeskij vestnik* [*Russian Philological Reporter*], the main philological journal of the time, right from its first issue. He also recalled running into a statistical study on Pushkin's language by the famous mathematician A. A. Markov which, he admitted, he did not understand much (ibid.).

All this early preoccupation with linguistics occurred in an atmosphere characterized by a marked interest in dialectology. Jakobson later emphasized that this was the field in which he received his basics: "This was what we were schooled on." (ibid.) By contrast, his knowledge of modern developments in linguistics does not initially seem to have been very profound. Neither the St. Petersburg professor of linguistics Jan Ignacy Niecisław Baudouin de Courtenay (who represented the most advanced linguistics to be found in Russia around the turn of the century) nor the handful of younger scholars around him left a very deep impression on Jakobson. During the semester he spent in St. Petersburg in 1917 he occasionally attended lectures by one of Baudouin's disciples, the early phonologist Lev V. Ščerba, whose work he knew, but he was mainly attracted by lectures by A. A. Šaxmatov. This scholar combined unusual charisma with a good understanding of students[7]; however, his primary specialization, Russian historical philology, did not reflect any change in the scholarly paradigm. L. P. Jakubinskij, another important linguist in Baudouin's St. Petersburg circle and later a member of OPOJAZ, nicknamed Jakobson an "armored Muscovite" in reference to his traditional schooling—a characterization with which Jakobson (1973) essentially agreed.

The picture that emerges is one of a student fascinated by dialectology and the language of folklore. In 1916, Jakobson was awarded the Buslaev Prize for his work on the language of North Russian *byliny* (folk epics). A year before, he presented an essay on the influence of folk poetry on V. K. Trediakovskij, an eighteenth-century poet and style theorist who played an important role in the formation of early modern Russian literary language. While the Buslaev Prize essay is not extant, the paper on Trediakovskij has been preserved.[8] One finds in it passages that document Jakobson's fascination with the formal aspects of folk poetry, including parallelism, meter, sound structure, and the occurrence of "unintelligible" words. Analyzing a poem by Trediakovskij, Jakobson also remarks upon the repetition of sound groups, later a favorite area of interest among the Formalists:

Most interesting are examples where one word (emphasized by capitalization) seems to contaminate sound groups of two or three words in its environment: *valit - LISTIK - lisički; zimu -i uš - šumit - mašut.* (Jakobson 1915 [1966: 617])

In several places Jakobson used the term "formal analysis," noting at the same time that "the investigation of formal aspects of Russian poetry has not yet begun" (ibid.: 613). He also took the occasion to criticize Valerij Brjusov, a Symbolist poet and verse theorist, for his lack of understanding of the inspiration Pushkin's verse drew from popular poetry. Brjusov was to remain a representative target of Jakobson's attacks in later essays.

Jakobson soon became an active member of the Moscow Commission for Dialectology (see chapter 3 below), and he took part in its dialectological and folklore expeditions in 1915 and 1916. In the summer of 1915, together with two other students (Petr Bogatyrev, Jakobson's close friend, and Nikolai Feofanovič Jakovlev, later a renowned Caucasiologist and member of the Moscow Linguistic Circle), he did field work in the Moscow region. In a report on this trip he stated that besides dialect data he had collected from the peasants an ancient lamp, a dress, and a shirt (Jakobson 1916b: 147). He entitled a presentation about his trip "Miracle Stories of Peasants in the Vereja Region." [9]

While participating in the work of the Moscow Commission for Dialectology, Jakobson proposed an ambitious program to "represent cartographically the characteristics of Russian dialects." [10] According to Kasatkin (1977: 201), he also prepared, together with his teacher, the philologist D. N. Ušakov, a monograph on dialects in the Moscow administrative region. Jakobson considered his student work interesting enough to publish in Prague in the late 1920s (Jakobson 1927a). This publication shows no trace of modern linguistics or phonology.

Jakobson's attachment to dialect research was very strong. Moreover, his loyalty to his teachers and peers in the Commission is striking. He particularly esteemed the scholarship of the philologist N. N. Durnovo, a major figure in the Commission, despite the fact that Durnovo was initially not enamored of linguistic theorizing. To the extent that one can generalize from scattered remarks, it even seems that Jakobson's understanding of dialect research was at first also traditional. Consider this, from the opening chapter of his first book, a study of Velimir Xlebnikov:

Dialectology provides the main impetus for the discovery of basic linguistic laws, and it is only through the study of the processes of living speech that we can penetrate the mysteries of the frozen language structure of earlier periods. (Jakobson 1921a: 3)

The argument is not original—European linguists had begun to place technical value on the role of dialectology in language recon-struction as early as the 1870s.[11] However, in evaluating this compo-nent of Jakobson's education we have to understand that in Jakobson's youth the status of dialectology differed from the percep-tion many linguists now have. Despite a strong historical underpin-ning, dialectology had a modernistic flavor because it dealt not with texts but—as a ubiquitous phrase of the period went—with "living language." This is clearly visible in Jakobson's reflections from the 1920s on the status of dialectological and ethnographical work done by the Commission:

Our excursions were a sort of reaction to the romantic enthusiasm of the older generation of ethnographers who studied isolated places, "un-touched" sites of the ancient—an enthusiasm which led to a situation in which ethnography of provinces furthest from the cultural centers had been studied in more detail than, for example, the immediate vicinity of Moscow. (Jakobson 1927a: 78)

And two years later, on the occasion of the First Congress of Slavists, Jakobson raised dialectology to nothing less than "avant-garde schol-arship which did away with romantic dreaming of things Slavic":

This avant-garde scholarship . . . , [these] positivist Slavists, had within half a century completed admirable critical and positive work in collecting and classifying an enormous amount of material, with which we are now work-ing. (Jakobson 1929g: 11)

Jakobson's use of the term "avant-garde" is evidently intended to refer to value-free data collecting and to a preoccupation with living material.

But while dialectology was typical of Moscow's philological ambi-ence of the period, Jakobson actually learned a little bit more than was usual for the discipline, and this "little bit more" makes it impos-sible to reduce him to a plain dialectologist. The first chapter of his Xlebnikov study, the main parts of which were written in 1919, closes with the assertion that a theory of poetic language can be developed only if "a poetic dialectology of its own" is worked out. Jakobson elucidated this idea with reference to Pushkin's poetic language:

Pushkin is the center of the poetic culture of a particular time with a particular area of influence. From here one can distinguish the poetic dialects of an area which tend toward the cultural center of another, like the dialects of practical language. (Jakobson 1921a: 5f.)

An inventory of such poetic dialects follows, including transitional dialects, dialects with a tendency toward transition, mixed dialects, and archaic dialects. Most significantly, these are not terms Jakobson invented himself; they are categories developed by the Moscow Commission for Dialectology. A narrow-minded expert in dialectology is bound to overlook this passage, as it is contained in a study of an avant-garde poet and does not offer any specific analyses of dialect data. And yet it is clear that the passage offers an extraordinary insight into the mechanics of Jakobson's scholarly imagination. He is transferring the perspective used in dialectology, including some very specific concepts of dialect theory, to literary history—an area rather removed, at first glance. For the first time in Jakobson's writings, linguistics is raised to the level of a model of research.

It is hard to judge at this point whether this is just scientism invading one more territory or whether there is also a touch of Romantic liberty in this approach. One is in any case reminded of early German Romantic poets and philosophers—particularly Novalis and Friedrich Schlegel, who also drew unusual parallels between fields traditionally not thought to belong together. In Jakobson's case, however, the Romantic mystique of this procedure is relativized somewhat by the fact that the linguistics that is elevated to the role of model is essentially positivist dialectology. This conclusion is confirmed by a glance at the minutes of the meeting at which the Xlebnikov study was originally presented to the Moscow Linguistic Circle. In the discussion that followed his lecture, Jakobson made clarifications that point to Neogrammarian concepts. Responding to Bogatyrev's doubts about whether it is appropriate to invoke dialectology when one single author is studied, he said: "The only source of scholarly knowledge is individual language. Dialect is always, more or less, a fiction." (Šapir 1991: 45) This down-to-earth statement points to standard Neogrammarian opinions rooted in an emphasis on individual speech as well as in a disinclination toward grand generalizations.

Thus, the execution of what one might term a romantic synthesis remains rudimentary. Yet at the same time romantic figures of thought are visible. The conjunction of disjoint disciplines returns in Jakobson's reasoning in this period, most strikingly in his 1919 essay on Futurism.[12] Here, Jakobson links some aspects of the theory of modern painting with the pre-phenomenological psychology of Carl Stumpf. Despite their rudimentary nature, these attempts to cross disciplinary boundaries indicate a transition from data surveys to a scholarly vision, from collecting to theorizing—be it conducted in the spirit of scientistic monism or in that of Romantic chaos.

2.2 Avant-Garde Beginnings—Goodbye to Words . . . and More Folklore

Folklore and dialectology were not the only important elements in the formation of Jakobson's intellectual profile. As Jakobson repeatedly suggested, the emerging modern art and literature were also important. It is hard to determine the key moments on his path to modern poetry with precision, but again all indications lead to his childhood. As for those who were instrumental in this development, Genrich Edmundovič Tasteven (1881–1916),[13] a teacher of French at the Lazarev Institute, deserves special attention. Jakobson (1974) recalled that Tasteven, an admirer of French Symbolism, showed him *La poésie de Stéphane Mallarmé* by Albert Thibaudet, an influential French critic committed to Symbolism, and encouraged him to write an essay on Mallarmé. Under Tasteven's tutelage he also translated "Une dentelle s'abolit," a highly challenging example of Mallarmé's hermetic art.[14]

Tasteven himself was an influential participant in Russian modernism, acting among other things as the managing editor of the Symbolist journal *Zolotoe runo* [*Golden Fleece*]. During a trip to Paris in 1913 he contacted the Italian Futurist F. T. Marinetti and subsequently organized his tour to Russia (Markov 1968: 147ff.; Michelis

1973: 133), on the occasion of which he published a study entitled *Futurism—On the Way to a New Symbolism* (Tasteven 1914). The title may indicate that Tasteven was not entirely at the forefront of the radical post-symbolist avant-garde; nonetheless, besides translations of five manifestoes by Marinetti, the book contains a basic description of the aesthetics and language of Italian Futurism. Among other things, Tasteven described the Futurists' interest in neologisms and in the disruption of syntax.

Jakobson, however, was no passive recipient of literary education. An interesting set of documents from his Lazarev Institute period shows that as a schoolboy he wrote poetry and published some prose. One might argue, of course, that literature was an integral part of humanist education in those days, and that a student was almost expected to write some poems. Nonetheless, one would be ill-advised to relegate these early texts to the margin as they show the emergence of themes that accompanied Jakobson virtually all his life. The following poem (RJP, box 31, folder 21) is selected here from a small group of poems written in 1908, the earliest known material from Jakobson's hand. In June 1908, when it was dated, Jakobson was not quite 12 years old.[15]

Смерть

В поле былинка,
В море песчинка
Счастливей меня.
Детство промчалось,
Юность отдалась
Лишь отблеском дня.
Все мои силы
Скроет могила
Как темная ночь[.]
Не за горами
Смерть, за плечами[,]
"Так прочь же ты, прочь!"
Жизнь обрывалась[,]
Смерть приближалась,
А хочется жить[,]
Жизнь хоть и бремя . . .
Жизни в то время
Порвалася нить[.]

Death

Grass in a field,
Sand in the sea
are happier than I.
Childhood rushed past,
Youth resounded
with only a glint of a day.
All my powers
A tomb will hide
like dark night.
Death is not over the hills
but over my shoulder
"Away with you, away!"
Life was stopping,
Death was approaching,
But I want to live
Although life is a burden . . .
Life's thread was broken
off at that time.[16]

Details of Jakobson's early poems will certainly be more adequately resolved by specialists in Russian poetry of this period, but even a layman will note the influence of folklore. The opening exploits parallelisms, typical of Russian folk poetry. At the same time, however, one is surprised by a distinctly articulated subjective-existential vision, something that cannot be understood in exclusively folkloristic terms.

Although there are no data that would allow us to document the transition from this style to the poetical experiments Jakobson conducted in 1913 and 1914, it is well established that he was seeking contacts with the most radical Russian artists during his final years at the Lazarev Institute. In 1911 or 1912 the painter Adol'f Mil'man took him to the gallery of Sergej Ivanovič Ščukin, a Moscow businessman who had amassed a major collection of modernist paintings, mostly French. Further important acquaintances were forged in 1913 and 1914. Jakobson's avant-garde heroes and friends now included the poets Alexander Kručenyx and Velimir Xlebnikov. He also communicated with the painters Kazimir Malevič, Pavel Filonov, and Ol'ga Rozanova, and he knew Michail Larionov and Natalia Gončarova, an artist couple who made fundamental contributions to the Russian avant-garde. One is tempted to speculate that Jakobson's abilities as a "practical linguist" must have contributed to his popularity among the artists. In early 1914 he acted as interpreter during Marinetti's visit to Moscow, a function probably mediated by Tasteven. But Jakobson was certainly more than a linguistic wunderkind tolerated among artists who were on the average somewhat older than he. When Malevič invited him in 1913 for a trip to Paris that he planned for the summer of 1914 (Jakobson 1980), he saw in him more than a linguistic assistant—here is a plan of how Paris was to be conquered: "Malevič would exhibit his experimental paintings and I would lecture on them because he did not know any French and in any case regarded me as a theoretician." (Jakobson 1974) A relationship such as this is certainly remarkable (Malevič was almost 20 years older), but, again, not completely singular in those days. Note, for instance, that the "official" theorist of the avant-garde painters Gončarova and Larionov, both born in 1881, was the poet Ilia Zdanevič, who was 19 years of age when, in 1913, he supplied an introduction to a catalogue of these artists. Jakobson himself later noted: "A peculiar phenomenon emerged here, which is interesting sociologically, so to say, namely the problem of the youth. . . . This was really a period in which the youth stood in the center." (1974: 22) Jakobson further suggested that generations enter the public arena in different periods at different ages, and that his was an epoch in which the entrance age was low. However, I tend to see here an example of the general trend toward emancipation of marginal groups rather than an isolated "youth cult." Clearly, an increase in the social acceptability of adolescents in "functions of authority" was not at odds with this general trend.[17]

Jakobson's desire to participate in the radical discourse of the avant-garde is particularly well illustrated by a letter to Kručenyx from February 1914.[18] In it, he takes leave from the ideals of Symbolist poetry, which up until then was, as he put it, merely a romantic "stained-glass window." Things had changed:

The glass is blown up, and from the fragments—in other words, pieces of ice—. . . we create designs for the sake of liberation. From demonism, from null, we create any convention whatsoever, and in its intensity, its force, is the pledge of aristocratism in poetry (here I'm at my peak). . . . And as to the human speck, I spit on it! (Jakobson 1985b: 3; Jakobson's own translation)

Probably in the same year, 1914, and in any case not substantially earlier, poems came from Jakobson's pen that matched the programmatic desire for the revolt (RJP, box 31, folder 22):[19]

Прощание слов

По всей вселенной сквозняк ужасный
Пустоты домы пронзают сквозь
Мой шато валок устой опасный
Не трахнусь в пусто пока авось
 Вот пустогрезой пустот распутных
 Восходят домы кричащей кручей
 Маячат домы средь долов мутных
 И город снится гнетущей тучей
Она - мапа, вкруг туман вода
Везде немножечко продувает
И протянулися провода
Всем спешно сплетни передавая
 Тень мелотелого телефона
 Спасла от ужаса нежных урн
 Хоть трубка косная злей пифона
 Но я держусь (не вися) за шнур
Среди трезвона тредлинный сон
Стаканчик чаю и в нем лимон
Я за кулисами куст в пыли
Да вдруг директор театра рек
Куда зашли посмотри издали
А лезть за сцену какой же прок
 Да хорошо коли есть кулисы
 Спасут смолчат о пустот позоре
 Но все кулисы изгрызли крысы
 Про них написано в "Ревизоре"
Подобны связке гнилых грибов
Слова на проволоку нанизаны
А прежде город на тверди слов
Висел как занавес на карнизе.

Words' Farewell[20]

Throughout the Universe blows a dreadful draft
Voids are piercing right through houses

The Linguist Is a Futurist

My chateau is unstable, the foundations dangerous
I shall not burst into the void for a while perhaps
 Like an empty dream of dissolute voids
 Houses arise like a crying cliff
 Houses loom among dull valleys
 And the city is dreamed as a lowering cloud
The cloud is a lure, mist and water around
Everywhere a little breeze
And the wires have been stretched
Hurriedly transmitting rumors to everyone
 The shade of a chalk-bodied telephone
 Has saved from the horror of tender urns
 Although the staid receiver is fiercer than a python
 But I hold on without hanging to the cord
During the thrice-chime comes a thrice-long dream
A glass of tea with a lemon in it
I'm in the wings a dusty bush
And suddenly the theater director proclaimed
How come you're here, watch from a distance
What's the point of creeping backstage
 Yes, it's good if there are wings
 They'll save, say nothing of the shame of voids
 But all the wings have been gnawed away by rats
 They are written about in Gogol's Inspectors
Like a string of rotten mushrooms,
Words are threaded on a wire
While earlier the city hung on a firmament of words
Like a curtain on a rod

The overall mood is visibly dynamic, if not apocalyptic, and some-what reminiscent of early German Expressionism. A deliberating, in-trospective poetic ego is also present, sustaining a link with the poem "Death." As in other early poems by Jakobson, one might speculate about the influence of the Ego-Futurist Igor' Severjanin, very popular then, who also liked the instrumentarium of modern technology side by side with an inventory of aristocratic props. But perhaps the most interesting part in view of Jakobson's future development is the motif of the telephone and telephone wires which introduces a reflection on words, and, in some sense, language.

The details of this poem reveal some curious analogies. The phrase *gnilýe gribý* (rotten mushrooms) would seem to echo *modrige*

Pilze (moldy mushrooms) from "A Letter" by the Austrian author Hugo von Hofmannsthal.[21] In this prose Lord Chandos, the fictitious writer of the letter, makes a famous confession that also establishes a poetic link between rotten mushrooms and words: ". . . the abstract words that the tongue must by necessity make use of in order to make articulate judgments collapsed in my mouth like moldy mushrooms." (Hofmannsthal 1902 [1979: 465]) The Chandos Letter was not only the work of a widely known author; it was also one of the central pieces of the Viennese Sprachkrise of the turn of the century. But whether one really wishes to assert an instance of direct influence is of course a different matter—a common third source seems more probable. Nonetheless, despite the folkloristic quality of Jakobson's image of threaded mushrooms, a very specific decadent image occurs in both texts: words—and, by implication, language—are characterized through images of rotting.

But, probably more important, the language of the poem shows traces of the experimentation that ultimately led to nonrepresentational phonetic poetry, known in the history of modern Russian poetry as zaum'. The first examples of this poetry, which was embedded in a broader European trend toward nonrepresentational art, are generally associated with Aleksej Kručenyx, in whose 1913 collection *Pomada*[22] the following page appears:

3 poems
written in
a special language
It differs from others!
Its words have no
definite meaning
*
No. 1 dyr bul ščyl
ubeš ščur
skum
vy so bu
r l èz

Although Jakobson's "Words' Farewell" is not as radical as Kručenyx's zaum' poetry, the exploitation of sound clusters, a stage that paved the way to zaum', is quite prominent. Some of Jakobson's lines

are genuine tongue twisters; alliterations and consonances, both vocalic and consonantal, dominate. Besides *gnilye griby,* there are

Vot **pust**ogrezoj **pust**ot ra**sput**nyx,
No vse ku**lisy** iz**gryzli** kry**sy,**

and

Sre**di tre**zvona **tred**linnyj son.

While "Words' Farewell" was only an approximation to zaum',
Jakobson's real "goodbye to words" is found on the last page of a
thin brochure entitled *Zaumnaja gniga* [*Transrational Pook*[23]] (Kručenyx and Aljagrov 1915[24]):

Aljagrov[25]

mzglybžvuo jix″dr'*ju* čtlěščk xn fja s″p skypolza
a Vtab-dlkni t'japra kak*a*jzčdi evreec černil'nica

RAZSEJANOST'[26]

*u*duša j*a*nki ark*a*n
kank*a*n arm*j*ank
duš*j*anki kita*j*anki
k*i*t y t*a*k i n*i*kaja
arm*j*ak
ètik*é*tka t*i*chaja tkan' t*i*k
tk*a*nija k*a*ntik
a o orš*a*t kj*a*nt i t*j*uk
t*a*ki mj*a*k
†mj*a*nty chnj*a*ku škj*a*m
anm*j*a kуk'
atr*a*ziksiju nam*ě*k um*ě*n tamj*a*
mj*a*nk - uš*a*tja
ne avaopostne peredovica
perednik gublicju stop
tljak v vago peredavjas'

One may speculate that this arrangement followed the pattern Kručenyx used in his *Pomada*—that is, the top "prose" lines may be
viewed as an introductory gloss. If so, Jakobson proved more radical
than Kručenyx, who had still been using straight Russian in introducing his zaum'. But whatever the function of the gloss in Jakobson's
text might be, there is no doubt that it itself is "more zaum' " than

the poem following it—if we assume, somewhat simplistically, that "more zaum' " means "more remote from the structure of Russian." With the exception of the last two words, the gloss violates the constraints on the sound shape of Russian words considerably by focusing on illicit consonant clusters.[27]

The poem itself reads as a relatively reasonable approximation to Russian, at least from a phonological point of view. Some of the words actually qualify as well-formed Russian.[28] However, as far as meaning is concerned, one is left with only educated guesses. A major reason for this is the lack of forms that one could naturally associate with finite verbal morphology, hence the poem remains rather impenetrable if one looks for potential predications. Lines such "ètikètka tichaja tkan''—for which Rudy (1987: 280) suggests the reading "a label is a quiet fabric"—are an exception. Syntax remains rather opaque throughout this poem, and one has to agree with Rudy (ibid.) that "the poem's global meaning lies in its destructive structure."

In addition, Jakobson heavily exploits a feature that was characteristic in "Words' Farewell": the repetition of sound clusters. In fact, one might well claim that consonantal clustering is the main theme of the poem.[29] One may also speculate that "*janki* ark*a*n," "arm*ja* nk," and "arm*jak*" are variations on Jakobson's own name.

Jakobson's progress toward zaum', a nonrepresentational, "pure" poetry paralleling the experiments of abstract painting, was in no way incompatible with an interest in folklore. In his later recollections Jakobson did not really place his experiments into the context of modern "isms," but stressed the proximity of unintelligible texts to children's babbling, tongue twisters, folk incantation and glossolalia:

We knew very well that there were children's folktales that contained sounds without meaning; we were aware of incantations and glossolalia. And this played a great role. My first conversation with Xlebnikov occurred when I brought him texts that I collected for him of children's folklore and incantations that were completely zaum', without any words. (Jakobson 1980)

Xlebnikov was profoundly interested in Jakobson's folkloristic expertise and used his excerpts from I. Saxarov's *Skazanija russkogo naroda* [*Russian Popular Narratives*] in his own "Noč' v Galicii" ["Night in

Galicia"], a poem dated November 1913. Jakobson also discussed with Xlebnikov the language of the Xlysty, a sect of religious ecstatics who spoke in tongues (Jakobson 1988: 445).[30]

Although this was an interest that brought Jakobson close to Xlebnikov (and to Kručenyx), the "we knew" passage with which the above quotation begins should be understood rather broadly. All the phenomena Jakobson names impressed a great number of Russian artists and poets in the first decade of this century very strongly. "The Poetry of Spells and Exorcisms" (Blok 1908) stands out. The interest in Xlysty and other sects was also strong. Symbolist authors such as Konstantin Bal'mont and Andrej Belyj exploited the Xlyst culture and language in their writings a number of ways (see Ivask 1976). Thus, in this respect there is no basic rupture between the Symbolists and the avant-garde.[31] The difference lay in the approach. The avant-garde, in contrast with the Symbolists, exploited these unusual linguistic phenomena in a very technical way, emphatically underscoring a strong element of anti-psychologism. Rather than treating *zaum'* words as ungraspable emanations of mysterious spiritual powers, the avant-garde poets and literary theorists tended to emphasize their value as technical clues to the nature of poetical construction.[32]

Viewed in a broader perspective, the folkloristic underpinning of Russia's avant-garde demonstrates a specific instantiation of the attraction to the exotic that was prevalent in those days in European art. But while a variety of exotic or noncanonical art forms (including things as different as industrial products and the drawings of children and the mentally ill) were objects of much fascination all over Europe, the folkloristic trend seems to have been especially strong in Russia. Statements such as "The path of art leads through nationalization to cosmopolitanism" (N. and D. Burljuk 1914 [1988: 84]) seem to indicate some awareness of this fact. The trend was lasting. The abstract painter Lissitskij went so far as to establish links between Suprematism and Russian folklore.[33] Russian artists thus differed from their French counterparts who mostly emphasized genuine transcultural exotism (such as generated in the encounter with African art). The Russians were ultimately closer to the German artists of Der blaue Reiter, who, among other things, admired folk art. However, verbal folklore remained a rather inconspicuous source of inspiration in the Western avant-garde. The kind of interest that Jakobson took seems to have been specifically Russian.[34]

2.3 Early Methodological Commitment

Toward a Synthesis

It would be quite inadequate to conclude that Jakobson simply participated in a number of distinct enterprises, or that he was educated in a specific scholarly field and had modern art as a hobby. The attitude that made little fundamental distinction between art and scholarship was prominent and fully sanctioned. Science had made inroads into arts and letters in the era of Positivism and sustained its influence on the emerging European avant-garde around the turn of the century. To many European artists science seemed to provide instruments for tackling a domain that had seemed to be the prerogative of poetic introspection. Not only the painting of analytic Cubism but also such scientific developments as the discovery of x rays, progress in photographic techniques, and (above all) the unveiling of the so-called fourth dimension were believed to offer new insights into the substance of things. Russia, in part owing to a strong tradition of esotericism, responded to this trend positively.

At the same time, science was moving from the Newtonian worldview to an Einsteinian universe, and it seemed to be assimilating to art in many ways:

Science, it was felt, had just broken through its deterministic constraints, and in view of the seeming radicality of some of the new ideas to the lay mind . . . anything was now possible. Such a situation lent itself readily to a holistic view of the universe; all types of information now seemed legitimate: rationalistic, intuitive, mystical, artistic. Because the scientists were busy rearranging their visions of the universe, artists suddenly felt free to do the same. (Douglass 1980: 361)

Jakobson followed this development keenly, as is witnessed by a very important document of his Russian years: a 1919 essay on Futurism in which he explicitly treated modern painting in connection with the revolution in modern science.[35] Denouncing the art of the

previous era, Jakobson asserted that the artist used to be a slave to
routine, consciously ignoring "both everyday and scientific experience" (Jakobson 1919a [1981: 717]). He recognized that the Impres-
sionists were applying the results of science in their technique of
decomposition of color, but he thought that a genuinely fruitful relation between science and art was not to be asymmetrical. Following
Gleizes and Metzinger's influential 1912 essay "Du cubisme,"
Jakobson suggested that creative work with color led to the formulation of a law of interdependence between form and color. Thus,
laws could also be discovered independently of, or in parallel to,
science.[36]

Besides its factual content, the proposition that art and scholarship—painting and psychology, or, dialectology and literary theory—
can be discussed with the same language manifests a basic step toward a synthetic worldview. Jakobson's devotion to art and scholarship is thus by no means an odd alliance of two distinct loyalties: a
drive for a unified worldview was clearly the main factor. In the essay
on Futurism, Jakobson perceives the contemporary epoch as one of
unity, extending the monistic vision to a whole historical period:

The overcoming of *statics,* the discarding of the absolute, is the main thrust
of modern times, the order of the day. A negative philosophy and tanks,
scientific experiments and deputies of the Soviets, the principle of relativity
and the Futurist "Down With!" are destroying the garden hedges of the old
culture. The unity of the fronts of attack is astonishing. (Jakobson 1919a
[1981: 719])[37]

He then makes the idea of an overall attack against the old palatable
by means of a collage of excerpts from popular accounts of modern
physics. The long quotations in the Futurism essay are mostly taken
from Nikolaj Alekseevič Umov and Orest Danilovič Chvol'son, two
Russian natural scientists concerned with the impact of modern science on culture; in addition, there are some references to the social
reformist Alexander A. Bogdanov. All these sources combine to
yield an ultimate impression of a unity of a revolution at all levels,
including art, scholarship, and politics. And the epoch has style:
"the leitmotifs of the present are visible in all areas of culture."
(ibid.: 720).

Relativism and Valuation-Free Scholarship

The period between 1918, when Jakobson graduated, and 1920, when he left Russia, are primarily documented by the essay on Futurism, the Xlebnikov study, and an article on Brjusov's poetology (Jakobson 1919a, 1921a, 1922). The last two were presented as lectures to the Moscow Linguistic Circle. These texts touch on a variety of themes, some of which are complicated and murky both in their genesis and in their implications. One such theme is that of relativism, or, perhaps better, cultural and historical relativism. Clearly, the Formalist doctrines themselves are among its sources. Although it is not common to invoke relativism in connection with the Formalist school, a large body of Formalist work, especially as regards literary history, can be seen at the conceptual level as an attempt to introduce a relativistic perspective into diachronic literary studies. The idea that each epoch has its own system of intrinsic values and norms is quite transparent in this respect. But there is evidence pointing to yet another kind of source that is interestingly connected with the assertion of relativism. In his Futurism article, Jakobson (1919a) takes up Einstein's theory of relativity. His discussion, which is not technical, is typical of a sentiment that saw in Einstein's theory something basically congruous with the feeling that seemingly eternal truths and values were crumbling. This was a popular way in which change in the natural sciences was related to the widespread feeling of a crisis of values—indeed, of cultural decay.

In the period under consideration, the relativistic discourse typically converged with an emphatic refusal to pronounce value judgments, especially in matters of culture and history. Historically or culturally defined systems ceased to be evaluated. This attitude, fundamental to N. S. Trubetzkoy's work, is also prominent in Jakobson's:

Scholars who study the poetry of the past usually impose their own aesthetic customs on the past, they project current modes of poetical production into the past. . . . The past is regarded, or even more, evaluated from the point of view of the present. But scientific poetics will be possible only then, if it renounces any sort of evaluation; after all, isn't it absurd for a linguist, as a linguist, to pass value judgments on dialects in accordance with their relative value. (Jakobson 1921a: 5)

Clearly Jakobson speaks here as a relativist in matters of historical aesthetics, and his reference to dialectology represents one more instance of linguistics' being elevated to the position of a model discipline.

The theme of relativism returns in Jakobson's 1921 article on Dada, passages of which touch upon the issue of cultural ranking. Reporting on the "great historian" Oswald Spengler, Jakobson wrote:

According to Spengler, when Kant philosophizes about norms, he is sure of the actuality of his propositions for people of all times and nations, but he does not state this outright, since he and his readers take it for granted. But in the meanwhile the norms he established are obligatory only for Western modes of thought. (Jakobson 1921d [1987: 430]) [38]

Although this is stated in the form of a report, one plausibly concludes that Jakobson actually identified himself with Spengler's relativistic judgment. The inference is justified because Jakobson reminded the reader that his friend Xlebnikov had expressed similar ideas. Xlebnikov had said: "Kant, intending to establish the boundaries of human reason, determined only the boundaries of the German mind. A slight professorial lapse." (Jakobson 1921d [1987: 431])

While the rejection of ranking and other value-based judgments remains a constant theme in Jakobson's thinking and repeatedly appears in the 1920s and the 1930s, particularly in connection with literary history,[39] the theme becomes murky once the confines of scholarship are crossed. Evidently, Jakobson (and Trubetzkoy, for whom the issue was very important) soon arrived at a serious impasse; valuation-free scholarship was hard to convert to an instrument of action, and action had become imperative at a number of points.

Trubetzkoy was aware that valuation-free scholarship cannot be used as a political tool without a change in substance. In his private correspondence he admitted to Jakobson that, while evaluation must be driven out of scholarship, elsewhere matters might be different:

In matters of culture—in art, politics, in all sorts of *activity* (and not *theory*, which is what scholarship is), one cannot do without evaluation. Obviously, some degree of egocentricity is necessary, but this must be enlightened egocentrism rooted in reflection and linked with relativism, rather then with absolutism. (March 7, 1921; Jakobson 1975:13)

Anti-Psychologism and Husserlianism

Another methodologically important issue that marked linguistics in the first decades of this century was the question of psychology as a tool of explanation. It is common knowledge that a rigid belief in psychologism, especially in association psychology, was among the prominent features of Baudouin de Courtenay's circle. For Baudouin, association psychology represented a basic achievement of modern science, providing an indispensable grounding for linguistics. Not surprisingly, Baudouin's disciples followed their teacher in this respect. In an encyclopedic dictionary of linguistics, Polivanov wrote under the entry "association":

The role of association as such in linguistics is so strong that one could say our whole language (language-process) represents merely a sum [*sovokupnost'*] of associations. (Polivanov 1960: 122) [40]

In contrast to this, a reserved attitude toward psychologism reigned in Moscow. Looking at the years of his studies in Moscow before the First World War, the Russian philosopher Henry (Gustav) Lanz[41] wrote:

Edmund Husserl's attack on psychology and Emil Lask's theory of 'Geltung' were the philosophical sensations of the day. "Truth" got loose from psychological slavery. "Beauty" was expected to follow it. (Lanz 1931: ix)

Some of these "philosophical sensations" were available in Russian translation. The first part of Husserl's *Logical Investigations* had been translated (Husserl 1909), and a number of further texts (including Husserl 1911) appeared in *Logos*, a journal devoted to the theory of epistemology.

As a result of this intensive reception of Western literature, the anti-psychologistic trend, especially in its Husserlian version, gained momentum. When Jakobson began his university studies, it was possible to pursue this trend in an academic setting. Indeed, Jakobson stressed its impact on his early scholarship repeatedly,[42] among other things underscoring his participation in the psychology seminar of Gustav I. Čelpanov, originally a disciple of the German psychologist Wilhelm Wundt. Although Čelpanov has often been described as an eclectic (probably an accurate assessment), he embodied an important scholarly ideal. As an experimental psychologist he insisted on keeping psychology and philosophy strictly separate, yet as a humanistically oriented scholar he insisted on a permanent dialogue between psychologists and philosophers (Joravsky 1989: 107f.). In effect, he played a "cultural" role in psychology, much as Umov and Xvol'son did in their disciplines.

Jakobson recalled Čelpanov in a biographical statement in 1974. He described him as an outstanding teacher, liberal and open to new directions. He got acquainted in his seminars with the foundations of Gestalt theory and wrote a term paper about word images in the manner of Kurt Koffka. However, the essential thing he found in Čelpanov's seminars was "Husserl's psychology, a discipline that impressed and influenced students in Moscow in those days very much" (Jakobson 1974: 21).

But Jakobson had praised Čelpanov in more specific terms as early as 1936, upon his death. He portrayed him as a fighter against "misguided metaphysics of mechanistic materialism":

Čelpanov vigorously fought his whole life against the mythology of this anti-scientific naive materialism in all its variants. . . . He further denounced Sečenov's demand that psychology be replaced by physiology, something Pavlov and Bechterev also demanded fifty years later; he further criticized positivist slogans about the so called objective psychology and, finally, all advances of mechanists in Russian Marxism. (Jakobson 1936h: 42f.)

Most important, Jakobson noted,

[Čelpanov's works convincingly] defended the thesis of complete reality and independence of mental experience and of autonomy of psychology with respect to philosophy and natural sciences. Čelpanov's undoubtedly has his share in the overcoming the mechanistic factions among Soviet Marxists and in purging naturalistic relics from Russian scholarship, linguistics included. (ibid.)

The atmosphere of Čelpanov's seminars was obviously stimulating: "The debates in his seminars were on a high level: passionate

psychologists and militant Husserlianists were equally welcome."
(ibid.) Among the latter was Gustav Gustavovič Špet, a Russian philosopher who had studied with Husserl in Marburg before 1914 and
who had a certain impact on Moscow's linguistic community in the
early 1920s, contributing to the abandonment of naive psychologism
in linguistics.

Given the intensity of Moscow Husserlianism in those years, one
cannot regard Jakobson's exposure to it as surprising or in any sense
improbable.[43] In the subsequent years, however, several factors con-
spired to obscure this intellectual link; in fact, some students of structuralism had difficulties to believe that Jakobson's early commitment
to Husserl was more than mere name-dropping. Probably the most
fundamental confusion has arisen from the fact that well into the
1930s there are virtually no explicit references in Jakobson's writings
to Husserl. Moreover, for a long time Husserl appears in Jakobson as
a simple anti-psychologist. The language of Jakobson's recollections
about Čelpanov's seminars is instructive in this respect: the seminar
introduced "Husserl's *psychology*" and was a battleground of "passionate *psychologists* and militant Husserlianists." There is no mention of
phenomenology here, no explicit reference to specific phenomenological techniques, and no reference to the Logic of Parts and
Wholes (an important descriptive discipline expounded in the second volume of Husserl's *Logical Investigations* and a tool on which so-
called eidetic analysis—i.e., analysis of essential structural properties
of objects—was based). Thus, Husserl appears mainly as an authoritative fighter against the naive psychologism of the preceding era.

When Husserl came to Prague in 1935 and lectured before the
Prague Linguistic Circle, Jakobson greeted him precisely in this legendary capacity, underscoring "the fundamental importance of his
logical research for the modern development of general linguistics,
especially syntax, semantics, and noetics, *and for the liberation from the
stifling impact of psychologism*" (Husserl 1936: 64; emphasis added).
Jakobson added that Husserl's *Logical Investigations* was a quasi-Bible
for young Moscow linguists, who had to use illegal methods to obtain
this book in its original during the war. Husserl seemed surprised by
this introduction—he had no knowledge of his research's profound
impact on modern linguistics:

[Husserl] on his part surprised his audience by making virtually no reference to his *Logical Investigations;* instead, in a fascinating way, he turned to the history of his dialog with Dilthey and sketched the integration of linguistics into a general *Geisteswissenschaft* from this perspective. (L. S.[44] 1935)

It would seem that Husserl was at this time far remote from his Russian image of 20 or 25 years earlier.

Jakobson refers to Husserl in his Xlebnikov study from 1921, the most advanced reflex of his Moscow years, invoking the lack of "what Husserl calls *dinglicher Bezug*" in certain neologisms (Jakobson 1921a: 47). However, this early, and probably first, documented exploitation of Husserl does not really show any specific appreciation of Husserl. It is a reference to an element of a theory of reference which, although discussed in *Logical Investigations,* is perfectly neutral with respect to anti-psychologism (or phenomenology).

To make things more difficult, we also find passages in the Xlebnikov study that are hard to reconcile with anti-psychologism in the first place. When embarking upon technical questions of sound structure, Jakobson uses the psychologistic language throughout; witness the phrase "language thinking," a hallmark of Baudouin's terminology, widely disseminated beyond the confines of his circle. Terms such as "association" and "dissociation" are also used in a manner that does not make them very different from the contemporary standard. And Jakobson's first usage of the "phoneme" notion, also in the Xlebnikov book (Jakobson 1921a: 48), is psychologistic in the sense that it exploits the notion "image," the standard terminological counterpart of French *image* (commonly used by Saussure) and German *Vorstellung* (as in *Lautvorstellung,* "sound image"). This terminology recurs as late as in the phoneme definition in Jakobson's 1929 *Remarques* and remains effective in a major piece of the Prague School phonology, the Projet terminologique of 1931 (Circle 1931a). It was only in the early 1930s that the Prague phonologists abandoned this vestige of psychologistic language.

However, Jakobson did criticize psychologism in the early 1920s. He and Bogatyrev wrote in a 1923 report on the state of Russian linguistics that G. G. Špet was justified in criticizing "the fatal effect of illegitimate mixing of linguistics and psychology" (Jakobson and Bogatyrev 1922–23: 458), typical of scholars such as Steinthal and

Wundt. Moreover, Jakobson derived some anti-psychological ammunition from avant-garde art criticism. He disliked Kandinsky's art because of its psychic "depth" and the attempt to work out a psychology
of colors based on associations between colors and emotions; witness
his critical remarks on the address of this pioneer of abstraction
(Jakobson 1920a).[45]

But despite all these vacillations there are important passages
that—although they do not bear Husserl's name—eventually lead to
Husserlian methodology in technical respect. As was noted above, in
his Futurism essay Jakobson discussed a law of interdependence of
form and color, originally discussed by Carl Stumpf. Let us now consider the passage explicitly:

The creative mastery of color [by the Impressionists] naturally led to a realization of the following law: any expansion of form is accompanied by a
change in color, and any change in color generates new forms (a formulation of Gleizes and Metzinger).

In science this law was first advanced, it seems, by Stumpf, one of the
pioneers of the new psychology, who speaking about the correlation between color and colored spatial form stated that quality participates in
changes of extension. When extension changes, quality is also transformed.
Quality and extension are by nature inseparable and cannot be imagined
independently of one another. This necessary connection differs from the
empirical connections of two parts lacking the character of necessity, e.g., a
head and body. Such parts can be imagined separately.

In painting the set [ustanovka] toward nature created a necessary connection precisely of such parts which are in essence disconnected, whereas the
mutual dependence of form and color was of course not recognized. And
vice versa: the set toward pictorial expression resulted in the creative realiza
tion of the necessity of the latter connection, while the object was freely cut
into pieces (so-called Divisionsim). (Jakobson 1919a [1981: 718])[46]

This central passage can, after all, be related to Husserl's Logic of
Parts and Wholes because it focuses on independent [selbstständig]
and dependent [unselbstständig] elements in perception, and, in
general, on the idea that a complex whole cannot have an arbitrary
constitution. Recall here that the Logic of Parts and Wholes provides
for two relations that hold for constituents within a complex whole:
A selects B, and B selects A (mutual dependence), or, A selects B,
but B does not select A (one-sided dependence—einseitige Fundier-

ung). This is, to simplify somewhat, the "technical" language into which an anti-psychologistic, noncausal, static description of perceptual phenomena is translated. Whenever such language can be detected, it is justified to invoke Husserlianism. Whether one might also want to invoke Husserl, or *Logical Investigations,* is of course another matter. After all, it is Stumpf's and not Husserl's name that Jakobson mentions, and Jakobson might have read Stumpf directly. (Rudy (1978) solves this question by suggesting that Jakobson's account of Stumpf actually stems from those sections of *Logical Investigations* where Husserl discusses Stumpf.) But whatever the ultimate "influencological" solution is, it must be borne in mind that Husserl's Logic of Wholes and Parts is an explicit execution of Stumpf's earlier ideas, especially those put forth in Stumpf 1887. In this sense, there is no contradiction.

Thus, while Jakobson was obviously familiar with certain elements of phenomenology at a technical level, the subsequent absence of references to Husserl is puzzling. Until the second part of the 1930s, Jakobson makes virtually no reference to Husserl that would indicate a return to the Logic of Parts and Wholes.[47] It is also unexpected that Jakobson apparently did not seek contact with any Husserlians — especially not Boris Jakovenko, the most active propagator of Husserl's phenomenology in pre-1917 Russia and an émigré in Czechoslovakia in the 1920s (see Jakovenko 1929–30). No contacts between the two are known. Furthermore, although strongly attracted by Hegelian dialectics in the 1930s (see below), Jakobson did not attempt to marry Hegel and Husserl, as was quite typical of the Russian philosophical tradition, nor did he make any references to these syncretic attempts. However, when he referred to Husserl in his *Kindersprache, Aphasie und allgemeine Lautgesetze,* a book written in 1940, the link was significant—here empirical content of Jakobson's linguistic analyses is presented in the language of Husserl's Logic of Parts and Wholes. At this point everything fell into place.

These inconsistencies and mismatches between conceptual commitment and analytic practice are interesting in that they lead to the conclusion that incompatible positions can well coexist in initial stages of a paradigm—one should simply not expect perfection in a newly born research project. While Jakobson's discussion of the nature of perception in his 1919 Futurism essay was a non-accidental attempt to assimilate modern psychology and appreciate its analytic content,[48] it was simply still very difficult to come up with detailed linguistic analyses. For a long time Husserl's doctrine did not itself provide much in terms of exemplary analyses besides a non-psychological account of certain mathematical and logical notions. We thus have to accept a situation, perhaps a fairly typical one, in which an instance of thematic commitment (such as anti-psychologism) does not coincide with the actual analytic practice, where notions of thematic commitment and analytic practice are understood in the sense of Gerald Holton (1973).

2.4 Radicalism

. . .we are not on Don Quixote's side, but with the muzhiks and hooligans beating him. . . .
Roman Jakobson, early 1915

Above I sketched what I believe are obvious parameters of Jakobson's formative years. The enterprise has been riddled with pitfalls: although Jakobson has documented his biography abundantly, he also was a grand whig historian and myth-maker—and perhaps understandably so. The world of his comrades and peers, artists and scholars, perished in political upheavals well before one could realize that it might one day represent the most enigmatic period in Russia's modern history. Moreover, in the West, where he spent most of his life, this culture appeared marginal to non-specialists, and, hidden under a language barrier, often only provoked a patronizing attitude. But, Jakobson's partisanship notwithstanding, I find his account of Moscow's intellectual climate generally convincing. We thus see elements of a biography which, with all respect for the individual, was expressive of the time and place. But one element is still missing: Jakobson's radicalism.

Jakobson's education in linguistics does not really point to anything very radical—we have in fact seen a number of sober, positivistically oriented moments. But his poetry represented an extreme even within the frame of the Russian avant-garde, and so did the choice of some of his research topics after he graduated—Xlebnikov's poetry above all. Two factors have clearly reinforced this radical attitude: the ambience of avant-garde circles and the atmosphere of the Bolshevik Revolution. As for the first, recall the radical words, quoted above, with which Jakobson sought Kručenyx's acclaim; further, compare the intensity of the hatred for the old in the following passage from a letter to Matjušin:

> It seems to me that we are not on Don Quixote's side, but with the muzhiks and hooligans beating him; he is a Romantic, on his knees, celebrates the old and the deceit which elevates us. . . . (to Matjušin; not before January 1, 1915; Jangfeldt 1992: 75) [49]

The assimilation of scholarship to the radical mores of the avant-garde emerges rather soon. It was noted above that as early as the Trediakovskij essay the Symbolist poet Brjusov received some negative attention. Though in his university paper Jakobson merely spoke of Brjusov's lack of insight into Pushkin's art, when he lectured before the Moscow Linguistic Circle in 1919 he called Brjusov a charlatan and subjugated his poetology to merciless thrashing. Not surprisingly, after Jakobson submitted the lecture for publication, V. I. Ivanov severely criticized it in an internal review for the publisher, essentially stating that this was a collection of invective. [50]

As for the role of the Bolshevik revolution, some groundwork is necessary. Most accounts of Russian Formalism, including Jakobson's reminiscences, are silent on this most important political event in modern Russian history. This is especially disappointing in the case of Jakobson, who otherwise even had some childhood memories of the Revolution of 1905:

> 1905, the year of the first Russian revolution! I was a school beginner, we were children, suddenly the teacher walked in and said: "Everyone get home! Cautiously and immediately!" We had no idea what was going on. It was the beginning of the revolution in Moscow. We went and saw the older classes—everything was upside down, benches and desks, and on the blackboard we could read: "Down with aristocracy! Down with exams!" We stayed at home for weeks. Shooting was heard again and again, and one could see red banners from the window. For school-children who went through these events it was impossible to forget. (Jakobson 1974: 13)

Jakobson's restraint in matters of 1917 is not entirely surprising. During his years in emigration, beginning with the 1920s in Czechoslovakia and then continuing in the United States, he was often targeted by zealous anti-communists who tried to prove his association with Bolshevism and who would have been grateful for anything that might help them construct a case. Moreover, Jakobson may have felt, in some sense correctly, that his activity in 1918–1920 was not particularly important in a political sense. In comparison with his close associates Vladimir Majakovskij and Osip Brik, his public engagement was incomparably smaller. Ultimately, however, his avoidance of the subject is unfortunate.

There is only fragmentary information about Jakobson's political engagement in the relevant years. For instance, Golanov (1925: 753) lists a lecture by Jakobson before the Moscow Linguistic Circle entitled "On the Question of National Self-Determination" (given not later than 1919). The title sounds political, but since the text does not seem to have been preserved one can only speculate about its contents. There is, however, no doubt that in the years after 1917 Jakobson found himself among a leftist segment of the young intelligentsia that was attracted by the possibilities that the new state seemed to open to art and scholarship. He was in constant contact with Brik and Majakovskij, both of whom had moved to the new capital (the latter in March 1919) to become active members of the Moscow branch of IZO (the Division of Visual Arts of the People's Commissariat for Education). It is at this time that Jakobson appears on IZO's staff as Brik's scholarly secretary. The following passage from the memoirs of the artist V. O. Roskin describes the atmosphere:

[Majakovskij and Jakobson] lived together—a poet and a theoretician. The times were difficult. A former employee of the Jakobsons baked rolls for them and helped to feed them. In the evenings they would write, during the day they would walk to the offices of the Division of Visual Arts, which were located at Crimea Square in the building of a former lyceum. This branch was initially directed by the artist V. Tatlin, who came from revolutionary Petersburg in the uniform of a Baltic sailor, hung all over with grenades and ammunition belts. All this was quite entertaining, to administer art in such an outfit. (quoted from Parnis 1987: 410)

Among the articles Jakobson wrote during his IZO period was a declaration entitled "The Tasks of Propaganda in Art" (Jakobson 1919b), published on the occasion of the Day of Soviet Propaganda (September 7, 1919) under his Futurist pseudonym, Aljagrov. The statement is brief and fully congruous with the sentiment prevailing among the young intelligentsia. The main argument is a denunciation of liberalism in art and in the domain of aesthetic norms. Jakobson denounces liberal pluralism and argues for a radical replacement of old art forms with new ones. Art, he suggests, is not a market governed by the law of supply and demand:

Forms in art are not chosen in the same way a buyer chooses gloves in a store.

It is often forgotten that the life of art consists in the replacement of the methods of forming, that for all forms there comes a moment when they "turn from the forms of development of means of production into the shackles of these means" (Marx).

New art form is a deformation of the old, a protest against it. Peaceful coexistence of two art forms at the same time is as impossible as the simultaneous existence of two geometrical bodies in the same space. . . .

Insofar as the task of revolutionary artistic enlightenment is a revolution in cultural, and in particular in aesthetic customs, enlightenment must demolish and annihilate the remnants of the past in culture. In other words, continuation of the static in the arts, the fight with epigonism—this is the task of enlightenment in the arts. (Jakobson 1919b)

There is nothing about politics here, no explicit statement in support of the new regime, nothing about the political and social forces behind the revolution; there is only denunciation of the liberal art market. Yet the passage has the quality of Milan Kundera's "lyricism of the youth" in showing a radical art theorist demanding a total unity of the present. It is significant that Jakobson explicitly asserts a deeper congruence, rather than a coincidental similarity, between developments in art and society:

The apology of eclecticism and artistic conformism represents creative impotence. The epidemic blooming, the outbreak of such a conformism coincides with moments of social decline. (Jakobson 1919b)

Obviously, this is a judgment about the previous epoch which is seen as characterized by disconnectedness and by the lack of a unifying stylistic gesture. Also note Jakobson's judgments about naturalism in the Futurism essay, where naturalism, the style of the second part of the nineteenth century, is represented as a style that creates inessential connections.

In the language, the hand of a zaumnik is easily detected. There are a number of alliterations and sound repetitions. Consider the beginning of the above quotation:

vybiraet **p**okupatel' **p**erčatki v **m**odno**m m**agazine
(buyer chooses gloves in a fashion store)

Further:

bystryj **sb**yt neobchodimo sozdat' **to**my **to**varu, ko**to**ryj. . .
(quick marketing must be provided for those goods that . . .)
[perežitki] **ot**ličajutsja **ot**sutstviem vsjakoj inoj **t**endencii . . .
([remnants] stick out because of absence of all other tendencies . . .)

Clearly, the spell of sound stands in the service of the revolution. But which revolution: in politics? in art? or just with a capital R?

Jakobson's association with the Division of Visual Arts of the People's Commissariat for Education was not a long one. But this was in part so because the Revolution offered alternatives to scholarship—at least temporarily. In early 1920, Jakobson was assigned to the post of the director of the press office of the newly established Soviet diplomatic mission in Estonia's capital, Tallinn (Reval). Since in the immediate post-revolutionary years the Soviet foreign service was practically beginning from scratch, this was an incomparably more important position than that at the Division of Visual Arts. Moreover, the Soviet representation in Tallinn was one of the few posts through which travel to the Soviet Union was possible at all.[51] However, Jakobson was called back to Moscow in April when a commission was formed to work out a proposal that would provide guidelines for negotiations about the new Russo-Polish border. The commission, which included linguists and ethnologists, was led by Academician Speranskij and involved Jakobson's teachers Durnovo, Ušakov, and Sokolov. However, the outbreak of the Russo-Polish war on May 4, 1920, made this assignment an episode.[52] In June 1920, another diplomatic assignment followed: the Soviet Red Cross mission in Prague.

We have no information with which to determine whether Jakobson's diplomatic assignments should be interpreted as instances of "soft emigration." Evidence in either direction is elusive. Clearly, the political situation was worsening rapidly, and emigration was taking place not only among the anti-Bolshevik opposition but throughout the progressive intelligentsia. Moreover, Jakobson's parents and brothers moved to the West—to Berlin. Jakobson himself may have had reasons to flee. He at least suggested so in a letter, dated November 28, 1950, to the Czechoslovak politician Petr Zenkl,[53] then in exile in the United States:

In 1917–1918 I was a member of the Executive Committee of the student section of the Russian Constitutional Democratic Party led by Miljukov, and to stay in the Soviet Russia became more dangerous for me. I succeeded to leave it as a member of the Red Cross Mission for Prague with warmest letters of recommendation from such expressly anti-Soviet Russian leading scholars as Šaxmatov and Speranskij to their Prague colleagues and friends. (carbon copy, in English, in RJP, box 47, folder 32)

Scholarly considerations aside, the fact that Šaxmatov provided Jakobson with a letter of recommendation would make sense under the circumstances Jakobson names: Šaxmatov was a member of the Central Committee of the Constitutional Democrats, the Kadets. But although this important piece of information may speak for "soft emigration," caution is recommended in taking the letter at face value. We have to bear in mind that it was forwarded to Zenkl with a single purpose: to withstand the inquisitorial practices of the early 1950s in the United States.[54] The circumstances in which it was written were very special, and the distance from the post-revolutionary events considerable. Another of Jakobson's letters, sent from Prague to Vladimir Majakovskij and dated February 8, 1921, does not really read quite the same:

To Vladimir Majakovskij

A governmental newspaper besmirched you severely today. "Son of a bitch" was the mildest expression. Your popularity grows in leftist circles. The local Bol'shoi will stage a translation of your *Mystery Bouffe*—there will be an awesome uproar around it. Whenever the best dramatist here, Dvořák, now a Communist, writes about a play in a left-wing Prague newspaper, he invariably asserts that it is bourgeois filth in comparison to you. The best Czech leftist poet Neumann is translating your *150,000,000*.[55]

And after imploring Majakovskij to send more news including his newest works, Jakobson concludes the letter with this announcement: "In a few days there will be a reading of your poetry for workers at the Czech industrial center Brno." Again, there are no explicitly political statements here, but the overall tone is one of assertion and loyalty to the upbeat revolutionary spirit. There are no hesitations, no doubt about the potency of the revolutionary culture—workers listening to revolutionary poetry seems to be the right thing. And indeed, some 50 years later, back in Czechoslovakia, this time as a visitor from the United States, Jakobson was looking back at his coming to Prague in 1920 as a moment in his biography:

. . . when the revolution—a genuine and pure revolution then—brought me as its diplomatic representative and faithful fighter to [Czechoslovakia]. . . . And it was precisely here that I realized how necessary this revolution was for the country I was born in, and, also, to what degree the fate of the revolution was an expression of Russia's crude and sinister historical traditions. (Jakobson 1969b [1988: 181])

I shall continue my survey of Jakobson's radicalism in subsequent chapters, but it might be useful to underscore at this point that there will be no "case" and that no record of "bad points" will be kept. It is sufficiently clear—and by no means new—that the zeitgeist produced a generation of intellectuals who operated within the confines of an anti-liberal reaction to the nineteenth-century culture. Their searches were supposed to change the world radically, while their lives were radically dismembered by social chaos. No document expresses this atmosphere better than the following passage from a letter by Jakobson to his dame de cœur, Elsa Triolet, written from Prague in September 1920, two months after his arrival:

Every one of us has lived not one but ten lives in the last two years. I, for instance, have been in recent years a counterrevolutionary, scholar (not a bad one), scholarly secretary of the Director of the Department of the Arts Brik, deserter, card player, irreplaceable specialist in a heating enterprise, man of letters, humorist, reporter, diplomat, typecast as a romantic lover, etc., etc. Believe me, this all is an adventure story and that's all that there is to it. And so it is with almost every one of us. (Jangfeldt 1992: 77)

Jakobson's later statements from the 1920s and the 1930s were generally progressivist, in crucial points often diplomatic. Rather than remaining a "faithful fighter" of the revolution, he eventually became an enlightened Russian patriot, his radical attitude primarily absorbed by scholarship.[56] In a letter of recommendation dating from 1939, Mathesius attributed to Jakobson "an insatiable thirst of knowledge so characteristic of the best Russian scientists,"[57] and in his commemorative remarks after Jakobson's death in 1982 Noam Chomsky spoke of the "seriousness of endeavor" that he encountered when meeting Jakobson at Harvard in the 1950s (Chomsky 1983: 81). Obviously, these characterizations go hand in hand—perhaps Jakobson's radicalism was not what it had been in the 1920s, but his radical commitment to scholarship was still evident.

3

"The Other Circumstances": Moscow, St. Petersburg, and the Revolution

Because the Prague Linguistic Circle owes its uniqueness to an encounter of Czech and Russian scholarship, it is important to have a clear picture of the conditions under which research was conducted in these two countries prior to the encounter. The present chapter therefore complements Jakobson's early biography with a somewhat broader picture of the Russian circumstances. After all, it was not a single person but a score of unusual thinkers and artists that contributed to the intensity and diversity of Russian intellectual life at the beginning of the century. Among the most assertive groupings in which young literary scholars and poets aggregated were the St. Petersburg OPOJAZ (Society for the Study of Poetic Language) and the Moscow Linguistic Circle. Despite the extensive literature on these two circles, many details of their structure and work remain to be described. I will show that despite their radical image, the new circles blended well into the Russian tradition of scholarly societies. I will discuss some differences between Moscow and St. Petersburg as regards attitudes toward theoretical approaches to language, as well as some organizational and political factors (including the impact of the revolutions of 1917), and I will show that the work of the Moscow Linguistic Circle was institutionally dependent on the new regime, a point largely ignored in the literature.[1]

3.1   The Tradition of Moscow

Societies and Circles—The Moscow Commission for Dialectology

In Russia, the overall expansion in science and education that took place in Europe in the second half of the nineteenth century manifested itself in, among other things, the growth of universities. Up until the early twentieth century, however, the government denied them an autonomous status and exercised tough control in all respects.[2] Curricula were typically handled in a rigid, schoolmasterly way, and professors' scholarly duties were very elementary. The situation was described by G. O. Vinokur, a prominent member of the Moscow Linguistic Circle:

Until now the scholarly life of a professor has usually taken place outside of the general norms of university life, since a professorial position was, strictly speaking, tied to a university almost exclusively by pedagogical activity. (Vinokur 1921)

Vinokur's description of the nature of professorial assignment in Imperial Russia is essentially correct: being primarily responsible for lecturing and examining, a Russian university professor did not have to engage in research at all.[3] Under these circumstances the institution of academic or learned societies [akademičeskoe or naučnoe obščestvo] represented an important alternative. Vinokur continues:

As far as an individual professor could also try to link his scholarship to his university, he could only resort to working in various, far from numerous societies attached to universities. But they almost always represented more or less casual discussion groups, and never had any clear program of research. (ibid.)

Although one may raise objections to Vinokur's assertion that learned societies were merely random discussion groups, there is little doubt that they gained considerable importance in the second half of the nineteenth century. These new institutions were better able to react to the dynamics of scholarship and to respond to the needs of young academics than the university and the Academy.[4] Although learned societies were in no way immune to changes in the political climate, they ultimately functioned as alternative communication centers, blending with the Russian tradition of intellectual circles.

Although independent, the learned societies were usually associated with universities. The major university centers, St. Petersburg and Moscow, had the greatest concentrations of such societies. At the turn of the century, 70 learned societies resided in St. Petersburg alone; 30 of them pursued medicine, 16 natural sciences, and 11 in the humanities; the rest were technical and pedagogical (Soboleva 1983: 150f.). The societies typically resulted from private initiatives, often had access to independent funding, were able to pursue their own publishing, and followed the overall trend toward specialization and professionalization. Typically, professors and experienced researchers would merge in them with enthusiastic beginners, including students. Another prominent feature of these societies was discipline; it was the rule to keep and print minutes of meetings and to publish annual reports.[5] Of course, this kind of discipline was in part built in for legal reasons, making a closer supervision possible. Let us not forget that the Imperial authorities were very apprehensive about student activities and suspected, often with reason, all sorts of revolutionaries among the academics.

The Moscow Linguistic Circle was closely connected with a learned society that faithfully reflected this late-nineteenth-century form of research, namely the Moscow Commission for Dialectology [Moskovskaja dialektologičeskaja komissija]. The Commission was formed in January 1904 on the recommendation of the leading Russian philologist, A. A. Šaxmatov,[6] and subsequently played a major role in Moscow linguistics. As was common, a senior scholar was appointed head of the group: the classical philologist Fedor Evgenevič Korš. However, all major work was conducted by younger academics, primarily N. N. Durnovo, N. N. Sokolov, and D. N. Ušakov. Seventy-two lectures were given before the Commission between 1904 and 1914; of these, Durnovo alone gave 24, Sokolov 18, and Ušakov 7 (see Ušakov and Sokolov 1914). These three researchers were responsible for the scholarly concept of the Commission and for the theory of dialects to which the Commission subscribed. The group, which existed under its original name into the 1920s, was eventually "reorganized," like other academic and artistic institutions, with the onset of Stalinism. It discontinued its activities in 1927.[7]

Besides young academics, students played an important role in the work of learned societies. The Moscow Commission for Dialectology is a good example of this tendency, since a large proportion of its work served the purpose of training the students. Thus, the commission effectively integrated a whole generation of young linguists, assuming a dominating position in Moscow linguistics of the period. The prominent Russian phonetician R. I. Avanesov later asserted that the Commission was the only linguistic society in Moscow in prewar times (Avanesov 1973: 202). Indeed, some papers with general linguistic themes were read at the Commission's meetings; the emphasis, however, was on dialectology.[8]

A Realistic Approach to Language

In sketching Jakobson's formative years, I have noted the attraction of the younger linguists to dialectology. Recall that there were elements in this discipline that were perceived as modern—above all in the sense of fulfilling the need to consider the "real" situation of language, to examine it in its everyday forms of existence. This attitude did not exclude a historical point of view, but the traditional emphasis on ancient written sources was now rendered abstract and speculative. The Commission responded to this new realistic sentiment by developing its own concept of dialect, in which a purely linguistic approach was combined with what might now be termed sociolinguistic concerns. Of primary theoretical importance was N. N. Sokolov's (1908) theory of "transitional dialects," further developed by Durnovo (1917). Transitional dialects contrasted with "mixed dialects" [smešannye govory]: the former showed genuine internal change, while the latter were characterized by borrowing from other dialects without actually changing their structure. These distinctions were elaborated in part as an alternative to Johannes Schmidt's Wellentheorie [wave theory], a popular model of the spread of linguistic innovations.

An important expression of realism characteristic of the Commission's approach was the emphasis on field work. The Commission carried out a number of expeditions to various parts of European Russia even during the war years—thus, in the summer of 1916, twelve persons, including Jakobson and Bogatyrev,[9] were able to conduct field research in nine governmental districts (Ušakov 1922: 288). Much of what was later done in the Moscow Linguistic Circle was strongly influenced by this empirically oriented style of work. For instance, Jakobson's (1920–21) and Karcevskij's (1923a) studies of lexical changes in the Russian vocabulary after the revolution are rich in data amassed through field work. A typical continuation of this empirical approach was the "Program for the Collection of Data on the Folk Theatre" (Bogatyrev and Jakobson 1923), probably worked out in the Moscow Linguistic Circle. This is a questionnaire that pays attention not only to traditionally recognized peasant folk theatre but also to popular urban plays. Interest in the latter kind of phenomena documents the extended force of a valuation-free positive scholarship—urban dialects and folklore were perfectly admissible objects of inquiry; they in no way represented "degraded cultural objects" [gesunkenes Kulturgüter], as Jakobson and Bogatyrev repeatedly stressed.

Although closely affiliated with the university, the Moscow Commission for Dialectology was defined as an independent project. Its work had a systematic and to some extent collectivistic character, which certainly contributed to its success. But this alone does not account for the fact that mainly young academics or students were active in the Commission. More likely, the younger generation was fascinated by the topicality of dialectology itself, by its realistic point of view.

3.2 The Moscow Linguistic Circle: Beginnings and Early Goals

Despite the image of radical innovation, the Moscow Linguistic Circle was in all respects a legitimate offspring of the Moscow Commission for Dialectology; hence, it blends well into the tradition of Russian learned societies. It originated within Moscow University, some of whose students applied in late 1914 for an authorization to form a student group within the Commission for Dialectology. The permission was granted on March 1, 1915 (N.S.), and the circle met for the first time the very next day. It functioned as an integral part of the Commission for the next four years.[10]

According to Jakobson, one of the reasons why the circle wished to be associated with the Commission, rather than be autonomous, was the fear that student associations alerted the police. Although this aspect certainly carries some weight, the students, mostly pupils of Ušakov, Durnovo, Ščepkin, and Speranskij, may well have striven after a group more uniform in age. In matters of research, however, the goals of the Moscow Commission for Dialectology and the newly formed student circle hardly differed: both primarily carried out empirical studies on Russian dialects. The question of whether the founding of the circle represented a genuinely new departure must be thus answered in the negative as far as the period 1915–1918 is concerned. However, the picture changed substantially in subsequent years.[11]

The students who formed the basis of the new group included Fëdor Nikolaevič Afremov, Petr Grigorevič Bogatyrev, Aleksej Aleksandrovič Buslaev, Roman Osipovič Jakobson, Sergej Iosifovič Ragozin, Petr Petrovič Svešnikov, and Nikolaj Feofanovič Jakovlev. Buslaev, Jakobson, and Ragozin were first-year students who entered the university in the fall of 1914. Whereas Jakobson, Bogatyrev, and Jakovlev subsequently became highly visible scholars,[12] the careers of the remaining original members cannot always be clearly documented. A. A. Buslaev is recorded in 1921 as a member of a lexicology team preparing a new dictionary of Russian (Bulaxov 1978: 39); in the 1950s he also helped Jakobson to compile materials on the history of the Circle (Buslaev et al. 1958).[13] P. P. Svešnikov appears as a co-author of a text book of Russian for speakers of English, published in 1935 (Bulaxov 1978: 199). S. I. Ragozin emigrated to Czechoslovakia (presumably in the early 1920s), where he produced a thesis on Czech-Russian relations; he moved to the United States after 1945, and he was at Harvard in the 1950s.[14] Afremov disappeared without trace during the period of the Civil War.[15]

A survey of extant documents suggests several distinct periods in the work of the Moscow Linguistic Circle. As indicated, there is an initial student group with strong ties to the Moscow Commission for Dialectology. This group existed from 1915 to 1918 and does not seem to have carried any specific name. A major change occurred in the fall of 1918, when the group was recognized as an autonomous research organization under the name Moscow Linguistic Circle and received financial support from the People's Commissariat for Education (Narkompros). This marked the onset of a period of an expansion of membership that covers the winter of 1918–19. According to Gornung (ca. 1970), the decisive break, and the beginning of the main, third period, occurred on May 11, 1919, when Jakobson gave a lecture on Xlebnikov's poetic language.

An important document of the Circle's early activity is a report by the Circle's secretary G. O. Vinokur (1922). Besides a list of lectures for the period 1918–19, the report also explicitly states the early aims of the Moscow Linguistic Circle:

Among the collective projects carried out during the first period of existence of the Circle, the following should be noted: 1) collecting of additions and corrections to the map of the Russian language edited by the Moscow Commission for Dialectology, 2) collecting of material for the study of the Moscow dialect, 3) study of the language of the *byliny*, 4) research trips for dialectological and ethnographic purposes. (Vinokur 1922: 289) [16]

According to this report, the Moscow Linguistic Circle made a proposal in 1918 to commence work on a dialect atlas. Folklore—especially the ongoing innovations in the oral traditions, such as the integration of news about war events into popular narrative patterns—was also investigated. In any case, the difference from the Moscow Commission for Dialectology was still relatively small at this stage. Even the autonomous Circle was in its beginnings strongly dependent on the Dialectology Commission.

This basic chronology indicates that the "real" Moscow Linguistic Circle was a child of the Revolution in a number of respects. It was cemented through the recognition as an independent research group by a new institution, the Commissariat of People's Education, and its reputation reached its peak in the years 1919–1923, not earlier. Another major factor in the Circle's development, the influx of St. Petersburg scholars, was also a result of the changes unleashed by the Revolution. In fact, the peak of the Circle's activity is defined by the integration of a number of persons from St. Petersburg and cannot thus be studied as a purely local, Moscow-based event.

3.3 The Avant-Garde of St. Petersburg

OPOJAZ[17]—Biographies of Movie Heroes

While it is not easy to distinguish the activity of the Moscow Linguistic Circle from that of the Commission for Dialectology until mid-1919, there is plenty of evidence of the vibrant and in all respects independent activity of what was then the most important group devoted to literary theory and modern linguistics: the OPOJAZ group in St. Petersburg. This circle became visible through its publications as early as 1916, generating a wealth of studies that proved fundamental for the development of Russian Formalism. As there is a rich literature dealing with OPOJAZ and its theories of literary structure,[18] I shall present only a very selective account here, concentrating on the initial years and underscoring the fact that there was a very strong theoretical momentum within OPOJAZ, a feature not so clearly present in the early Moscow Linguistic Circle precisely because the latter was an offspring of a positivistically oriented tradition. I shall also draw attention to certain internal characteristics of the group, specifically its composition and the spirit of nonconformism and radicalism with which its leading members were imbued.

Viktor B. Šklovskij, the co-founder of OPOJAZ, referred to this group as "a circle of philologists"[19]—a description that must be taken seriously, since a part of the circle was recruited from among the pupils of Baudouin de Courtenay, a group that included L. P. Jakubinskij, E. D. Polivanov, and, very briefly, V. B. Šklovskij himself. Thus, the group provided a meeting ground for linguists and literary theoreticians whose personalities and intellectual interests were quite unusual. A brief survey of the biographical data speaks for itself. Let us begin with the linguists.

Evgenij Dmitrievič Polivanov began to lecture at the university in 1914. At the time OPOJAZ was forming he had already taught general linguistics and oriental studies, and he had experience in research. In 1914–1916 he carried out field work in Japan and visited Korea and China. As with Jakubinskij, the other prominent linguist in OPOJAZ, Polivanov's main reason for taking part in the work of OPOJAZ was his interest in poetry.[20] He pursued formal analyses that focused mainly on the sound organization of poetic language; alliteration was among his main interests.[21] He worked on traditional poetry and folklore, but he also dealt with Majakovskij's verse (Polivanov 1980). It is obvious that, although he was a highly technical linguist, Polivanov regarded the study of the language of poetry as an integral and theoretically relevant part of language studies. The second volume of his unpublished Introduction to Linguistics for Orientalists included a section entitled "Linguistics and Poetics: A Phonetic Theory of Bound Speech" (Leont'ev 1983: 48). Moreover, V. V. Ivanov (1957: 65) reiterates Šklovskij's statement that Polivanov was compiling a universal "Corpus poeticarum," a survey of sound devices exploited by the languages of the world. While the latter two studies have not been preserved, Polivanov's early work from the OPOJAZ time is available. It includes "On Sound Gestures in Japanese" (Polivanov 1916b) and "Formal Types of Japanese Riddles" (Polivanov 1918). All this points to an interest in "word art," an approach typical of OPOJAZ and sharply contrasting with the socially and nationally defined concerns of earlier Russian literary criticism.

A list of academic interests and achievements, however, gives only an imperfect picture of Polivanov. He was a radical and a nonconformist, little fitting the usual stereotype of the professor. His rumored mannerisms and mystifications found an indirect way into *The Scandalist,* a parodistic roman à clef by his contemporary Venjamin Aleksandrovič Kaverin. This fiction incorporates a number of participants in the literary life of Petersburg, including the Formalists, the former Futurists, and Polivanov himself, who appears as one of the leading characters under the name Dragomanov (Kaverin 1928 [1980]). Although Kaverin treated Polivanov with the utmost respects in his more recent memoirs (Kaverin 1985), the portrayal of Dragomanov in *The Scandalist* is far from complimentary. There are allusions of dark dealings and obvious references to Polivanov's dependence on drugs. Dragomanov maintains, among other things, that he used to work in the Hagenbeck Circus as a trapeze artist. His lectures are obscure, and his students quite peculiar (Kaverin 1928 [1980: 422]). Interestingly, Kaverin lets Dragomanov explain his complicated linguistic views in a fairly detailed and coherent manner. Thus, Dragomanov rejects traditional opinions and puts forward his view of a development of languages from numerous original tongues into a single world language (ibid.: 424). Most likely this is a parody of Marr's (and Baudouin's) theory of linguistic convergence. At another point Kaverin obviously parodies the theory of functional dialects (ibid.: 558f.).

Another member of the early OPOJAZ, Lev Petrovič Jakubinskij, also took an interest in poetics while a student. Like Polivanov, he

conducted part of his studies with Baudouin de Courtenay, whose
favorite pupil he apparently was. He was among OPOJAZ's most prolific authors, contributing numerous articles to its publications
(Jakubinskij 1916, 1917a,b, 1919).

Among the non-linguists,[22] the most prominent member of the
early OPOJAZ was Viktor Borisovič Šklovskij. He was an active participant in the Russian Futurist scene before 1914, and his Futurist inclinations had profound consequences for the evolution of the
OPOJAZ doctrine. A number of his theoretical ideas developed as
early as 1913, directly from the movement known as the Cubo-
Futurism, and his manifesto *The Resurrection of the Word* is an important document of compatibility between the early Russian Futurism and OPOJAZ. A glance at Šklovskij's biography between 1914
and 1922 shows a personality that does not lag behind Polivanov in
its nonconformism and lack of orthodoxy. His scholarly output during the war years is in any case astonishing, especially since he repeatedly spent extended periods of time in combat. The end of the world
war found him in Persia, yet in the early months of 1918 he was back
in Petrograd working on literary theory and participating in an anti-
Bolshevik revolt prepared by the Social Revolutionaries (the so-
called SRs). The conspiracy was uncovered, and Šklovskij had to flee
and hide—among other places, in a psychiatric asylum in Saratov.
He recalled this time with characteristic irony:

The doctor warned me: "Just don't pretend anything. Pretending a mental
illness always shows. But if you try to look *comme il faut,* you'll make a truly
psychotic impression." So I lived normally. I wrote. (quoted from Čudakov
1990: 95)

Returning illegally to Moscow, Šklovskij worked intensively on his
analytic studies and even lectured in the Moscow Linguistic Circle.
But this episode was also a brief one. The year 1918 saw him again
fighting against the Bolsheviks in the Ukraine. It is here that his
character inspired the famous Russian novelist Michail Bulgakov, in
whose *White Guard* Šklovskij turned up as Špoljanskij—orator, bomb-
thrower, philologist, and defiant adventurer (see Čudakova 1988:
263). This period of Šklovskij's biography, which might even have
made Marinetti envious, peaked in March 1922 when Šklovskij had

to flee the country. He spent the years 1922 and 1923 in Berlin but subsequently was able to return to the Soviet Union.

Many of these details, including the apparently anecdotal fact that Polivanov and Šklovskij inspired unorthodox literary characters, may now have an unreal touch of cinematic fiction. But the protagonists were quite real and were all equipped with a remarkable capacity to perform under the most adverse circumstances—unwavering commitment to scholarship was common to Šklovskij, Jakobson, Polivanov, and, beyond the confines of OPOJAZ and the Moscow Linguistic Circle, Trubetzkoy. Trubetzkoy's wanderings through the Russian provinces during the months of Civil War is an example of scholarship flavored by utmost hardship. And even later, Jakobson's escape from Nazi-occupied Europe was likewise characterized by feverish scholarly work in the face of a political cataclysm. Jakobson's statement that while he was on the run his only wish was to complete his *Kindersprache* "before they [the Nazis] come [to Sweden]"[23] is another variant on work between the trenches and the writing desk.

Not every OPOJAZ member lived under circumstances such as Šklovskij's. Nonetheless, the gallery of members-radicals can be easily continued. Boris Anisimovič Kušner was a poet associated with Futurism, and had one or two collections of poetry to his name. In 1918 he published a booklet of prose which Majakovskij considered an unsuccessful but nevertheless unique attempt at Futurist prose. Although Kušner is generally regarded as a minor character, his intellectual biography yields rewarding insights into the Zeitgeist—in a span of not quite 20 years, he was involved in almost all phases of the Russian avant-garde: Futurism, Komfut, OPOJAZ, Proletkult, IN-XUK, LEF, Novyj LEF. It is deplorable that, with a few exceptions (Bowlt 1976; Lodder 1983) little information about him exists. References to Kušner's death in 1938 give neither the place nor the date— a sure indication that he had perished in the Gulag.

Finally, Osip Maksimovič Brik—after Šklovskij the most important driving force within OPOJAZ—was a dilettante in the classic sense of the word; his subject at the university was law, his hobby was poetry. Born of a well-to-do merchant family, he turned into a patron of artists and financed a number of publications, including those of OPOJAZ. In his later career, he was also involved very actively in a number of radical literary groups (Komfut, INXUK, LEF, and Novyj LEF), sharing in this respect some similarities with Kušner's career. His writings from the 1920s—better-known than those from the period of our concern—show him as a veritable crusader against anything remotely traditional in culture and art, endorsing a strictly functional and utilitarian approach to the arts, calling for an entire reshaping of the received system of genres (jazz replacing classical music, newspapers replacing novels, etc.), and denying the role and value of individual artistic personality (". . . there are no poets and writers, there is only poetry and literature" (Brik 1923: 213)). Because this course conflicted in the late 1920s with much that purported to be new socialist art (his critique of Gladkov's *Concrete,* a catechism of socialist realism, stands out), Brik and the group around *Novyj Lef* eventually became officially unacceptable. He renounced most of his views under political pressure in 1936 (Brik 1936).

Within OPOJAZ Brik gained recognition for his study "Sound Repetitions: An Analysis of Sound Structure of Verse" (Brik 1917), a piece that in retrospect reads as a somewhat mechanical articulation of OPOJAZ's interest in sound patterns. Nonetheless, his involvement in the group was crucial. His style gave OPOJAZ a touch which was very different from the Moscow academic ambience—the term "avant-garde salon," rather than "scholarly society," comes to mind first. It was in Brik's apartment that OPOJAZ usually met, and it was Brik's wife Lili who played the dame de salon.[24] The Briks moved to Moscow after the Revolution, and he became a radical cultural activist.

OPOJAZ—Early Interest in Theory

A brief look at the three OPOJAZ volumes[25] and related publications clearly reveals that the St. Petersburg members were more enterprising than their peers in Moscow and took interest in more complex theoretical questions than the latter did in their formative years. As was pointed out above, certain key notions of OPOJAZ were direct imports from heated Futurist proclamations of 1913 and 1914, includ-

ing Šklovskij's essay *The Resurrection of the Word*. Šklovskij also deserves
attention because of his pronounced anti-psychologism, as witnessed
by his critique of Aleksander Potebnja, a Ukrainian linguist and folklorist who subscribed to psychological explanations. In the following
I shall not, however, aim at a full exposition of OPOJAZ doctrine, but
proceed selectively simply to document the level of theoretical discussion that characterized the group.

In general, OPOJAZ was more aware of developments in the West
than was the case in Moscow, where folklore and dialectology usually
did not lead beyond the limits of Russian scholarship. Thus, Jakubinskij (1916) was establishing the difference between poetic and practical language with reference to, among others, Charles Bally, Maurice
Grammont, and Antoine Meillet. Also, the translations of Grammont
and Nyrop in the first volume of the *Sborniki* indicate that the St.
Petersburg group was familiar with French linguistic literature. This
background was partly the result of the openness of the circle
around Baudouin, which also included L. L. Ščerba, a young lecturer
who had studied in Paris for several years. In short, an important
characteristic of Baudouin's circle was an interest in theory, which is
also the impression gained from the *Sborniki;* questions of dialectology did not play any role.

Some of the approaches employed in the *Sborniki* make a remarkably "Saussurean" impression. This is of course not a direct result of
Saussure's influence, but grows out of a convergence of theories that
arose from the general intellectual climate of the period. (That these
themes may today appear "Saussurean" follows from an ahistorical
reading that recognizes them through the prism of Saussure's
Cours.) One theme of this type is the reexamination of the role of
material, or substance, in language and art. This is a topic familiar
not only from Saussure's theory of value but also from other writers,
including some turn-of-the-century art critics and philosophers such
as Ernst Cassirer (see his *Substanz- und Funktionsbegriff* (1910)). Kušner's work is a remarkable example in this respect. While he recognizes certain features as characteristic and constitutive for a given
kind of art (e.g., theme, its interpretation, the kind and form of execution), material is important only to the extent it exercises influ-

ence in the last point. Thus, although in Gothic architecture material was selected in consonance with the task underlying the solution,

chiseled sand-stone and bricks are merely characteristic of the construction technology of the time. *A Gothic building is quite conceivable made of concrete, cast in bronze, or erected in any other material without any detriment to the architectural-artistic essence of the structure involved.* (Kušner 1916: 42; emphasis added)

This treatment of the substance of art tends in the same direction as, for instance, Saussure's anti-essentialist discussion of the figures in chess. Saussure suggests that a figure, e.g. the knight, can be replaced by an arbitrary character, made of arbitrary substance, as long as the replacement is attributed with the same value as the figure it stands for. This is so because "dans les systèmes sémiologiques . . . la notion d'identité se confond avec celle de valeur et réciproquement" (Saussure 1916 [1974: 154]).

Closely connected with this anti-essentialist approach is the establishment of the proper subject of inquiry. It is not the material but the principles of its organization that define the undertaking:

Although the nature of the material is not characteristic of art, the principle of its organization is, for on this depends the form of the work, i.e., one of the constitutive aspects of art. (Kušner 1916: 45)

These selected quotations illustrate a theme that was intensively pursued in the early OPOJAZ. Quite typical were attempts to show that, while practical and poetic language were identical in substance, they "organized" the substance differently. In other words, poetic language had its own laws.

As was noted in the chapter on Jakobson, however, St. Petersburg linguistics was split in that it pursued very modernistic perspectives while subscribing to psychologism. The following passage from Polivanov's clearly written introduction to linguistics may serve as an example of this:

Those sound images of a given language which are capable of establishing an association with sense images and different words will be called phonemes.

Those diverse kinds of sounds which can represent a physical, i.e. articulatory, realization of a particular phoneme (a psychic entity) are called variants. Variants of a phoneme that depend on combination, i.e., cooccurrence, with particular sounds or particular phonetic moments (e.g., stress), are called combinatorial variants.

Unconditioned variants, which can but need not occur, are called facultative variants. (Polivanov 1916a: 55)

Although this is one of the first clear definitions of the phoneme, it has a distinctly psychologistic flavor, thus pointing to the presence of Baudouin.

A. A. Šaxmatov

To see another aspect of the St. Petersburg scene, let us examine the following passage from reminiscences by V. V. Vinogradov, a Slavist who was in the early 1920s associated with the Moscow Linguistic Circle and who later became one of the most prominent members of the Soviet academic establishment:

Academic scholarship, that is, that type of philology taught and presented in university seminars, did not satisfy us, especially after the departure of Baudouin de Courtenay and the death of Šaxmatov. Why? Because it seemed that we were being taught a subject that did not interest us. The teaching of linguistic disciplines essentially reduced to a standard scheme with historical illustrations or—which was in fact the strongest aspect—to the presentation of historical phonetics. (Vinogradov 1975: 258)

A resentful tone might have been a topos by the time Vinogradov wrote these lines, but less so the inclusion of two St. Petersburg professors who certainly did not belong to the young generation yet who seemed not to be considered dust-covered academics: Šaxmatov and Baudouin de Courtenay.

Aleksej Aleksandrovič Šaxmatov, an academician and a specialist in the history of Russian but also a member of the Central Committee of the Constitutional Democrats, might seem an unlikely focus of identification for the young generation of linguists. Trubetzkoy, for instance, sharply criticized the methods of language reconstruction that Šaxmatov practiced. Yet Šaxmatov played an important role in both Trubetzkoy's and Jakobson's intellectual development.[26] A closer look reveals that his personality was unusual and his research unorthodox and little worried about authority, his own included. The atmosphere around him is echoed in reminiscences of the prominent Russian historian G. Vernadskij, who was present in 1914 when the young historian M. D. Priselkov defended his doctoral dissertation. In the ensuing disputation Šaxmatov raised objections to certain points concerning Priselkov's reconstruction of the text of the old Russian chronicles:

[Priselkov:] "Forgive me, Aleksej Aleksandrovič, ... but I took this from your textual reconstruction of the chronicles."
    The audience burst into laughter.
    "That is precisely what you should not have done," Šaxmatov answered firmly. "You should have used the text as it is preserved in the manuscript. After that you should have proceeded critically to examine my conclusions and either to support them with your own arguments, or else to reject them." (Vernadskij 1970: 216)

Important evidence of Šaxmatov's role as a model for the young generation is found in the remarkable obituary Jakobson wrote for him. This text from September 1920—published by Jakobson in Czechoslovakia—portrays the grand man of Russian philology in glowing, almost Futuristic colors:

Šaxmatov truly loved only his future work. His past merits were of no interest for him, he did not know of them. Thus there was in Šaxmatov not the slightest trace of arrogance, not the least suggestion of the bureaucrat resting on his laurels. . . .
    Remembering Šaxmatov one does not know whether he charmed one more as a scholar or as a person. The most surprising thing about him was the dynamism of his thought. He never stood still; he was never satisfied with a "definitive" solution. When he was once shown that his statements of 1915 were not compatible with those of 1912 he simply answered: "That is why I have written a new book, in order to nullify old statements." Šaxmatov always searched for the answer to all questions; he could never accept the existence of the unresearched; he would always rather construct a daring set of hypotheses. Šaxmatov knew no rigid systems; all material was constantly subject, in his eyes, to the attack of scientific thought. (Jakobson 1920c) [27]

J. I. N. Baudouin de Courtenay

No less important than Šaxmatov was the charismatic Jan Ignacy Niecisław Baudouin de Courtenay (1845–1929), a number of whose students became active in OPOJAZ. Baudouin was born in Warsaw, then the capital of a Russian province, and spent a considerable part of his life in professorial positions at Russian universities—including St. Petersburg, where he arrived in 1900. He was not only a prominent linguist but also a political activist strongly involved in anti-authoritarian and emancipatory causes.[28]

It is quite in line with Baudouin's profile that the radical Futurist Šklovskij would bring his literary experiments to Baudouin's attention and attempt to involve him in Futurist activities. There are contradictory accounts of the extent to which this was successful, but it seems that Baudouin presided over a wild Futurist evening on February 11, 1914 (O.S.), during which he got involved in a discussion with the zaum' poet Kručenyx.[29] The event was not entirely to Baudouin's liking, and his later intervention in the discussion of *zaum'* poetry (Baudouin 1914a,b) resulted in a rejection of this experiment. Yet his statements show so much personal involvement that one is left with the impression that the Futurist undertaking was important to him and that he felt he had to give his judgment.[30] According to Toddes et al. (1977), Baudouin was interested in zaum' because he hoped to gain insight into the productivity of certain suffixes. He, at any event, had introduced Šklovskij to his student Jakubinskij and thus indirectly contributed to the formation of OPOJAZ.[31]

Baudouin was not only an inspiring linguist but also an outspoken dissident who made himself very unpopular with the authorities, partly because of his active support for the introduction of a federal system of government in Russia.[32] Polivanov wrote in the 1930s: "From the second year of my university studies, my worldview was determined in a great number of ways by the influence that my teacher Baudouin de Courtenay, an internationalist and radical by conviction, had on me." (quoted from Polivanov 1968: 8)

How Baudouin saw the relationship between Russian and Western scholarship is exemplified by his remarks on N. P. Nekrasov's 1865 essay "On the Meaning of the Forms of the Russian Verb." This essay, which is important for its fundamental insights into the morphology of the Russian verb—not recognized and in fact obscured in earlier analyses by Western linguists—met with sharp criticism in Russia. But Baudouin did not bring up the case to assert that Russian grammar is something that foreigners have no right to discuss:

The special reason for which I am bringing this up is that I do not accept nationalization of logic—I assert the same laws of human thinking for everyone. There is no European, no American, no French no English, no German, no Russian, no Polish science, there is only one science—universal science. And just for this reason I assume that the right of making scientific discoveries and generalizations is not forever leased by Western scholars and that independent original ideas can originate in Russian or Polish heads. There is not the slightest need to be a servile slave of so-called "European scholarship" and repeat nonsensically and uncritically what has been borrowed from it. (Baudouin 1901 [1963, volume 1: 363])

Baudouin's style of teaching, too, showed few signs of orthodox academism. His practice book, a collection of 337 linguistic exercises, provides insight into his dissident pedagogy. The first part is especially worthy of note. In it the students were asked to comment on certain passages which Baudouin (1912: 5) collected under the inconspicuous section title "From Textbooks Approved and Recommended by Academic Committees" and accompanied by devastating remarks. For example, he comments on a passage from a textbook in which the German declension system is given: "And this is followed by a whole mass of completely absurd and indigestible rules about what belongs to which declension." (ibid.: 13) And in the afterword Baudouin speaks of dozens of passages that "do not help develop the intelligence but serve to obscure and stultify it" (ibid.: 91).

Baudouin's students also testify to his informal style of teaching and its effect on the students:

[His] lectures differed from those of other professors not only in content, . . . but also externally, in the fact that his students saw for the first time a professor who did not sit at the lectern reading his lectures from a notebook, but who stood at the blackboard with chalk in hand, explaining his subject orally and writing examples on the board. (Bogorodickij; quoted from Rothstein 1975: 465f.) [33]

To conclude, we see that personalities of only very few charismatic seniors could well provide a point of identification and exert a considerable influence on a whole generation of students.[34] This was particularly visible in St. Petersburg, where attraction for nonconformism and Brik's willingness to funnel it into a salon had profound consequences. The Muscovites Trubetzkoy and Jakobson, curiously

enough, were slow in appreciating Baudouin's scholarship. In Trubetzkoy's case, Baudouin's radical cosmopolitanism may have been a
retarding factor.

3.4   After 1917

Moscow—The Super-Circle

As was pointed out above, it was only in the fall of 1918 that the
Moscow Linguistic Circle emerged as an independent body; it existed until November 1924, when it formally dissolved itself. From
Gornung's (ca. 1970) account and other printed and archival
sources, the following periods of the Circle's activity can be distinguished: (1) fall 1918–May 1919; (2) May 1919–late 1922; (3) spring
1923; (4) 1923–November 1924. The account below is, in its main
points, organized in this manner.

In the fall of 1919 the Circle was recognized by Narkompros and
was included in the net of research institutions Narkompros was
managing and financially supporting. But although this change was
fundamental in institutional terms, it is not easy to determine exactly
what the difference between the activities of the Circle and the Commission for Dialectology was.[35] Gornung (ca. 1970) suggests that initially there was no fundamental difference. This might be close to
true—in 1918 the Circle proposed to the Dialectology Commission
to work jointly on a dialect atlas, something the Commission otherwise specialized in (Vinokur 1922: 290).

Vinokur, the secretary of the Circle, compiled an activity report
which includes, among other things, a list of lectures given in the
Circle in 1918 and 1919:

1) Jakovlev: Russian oral historical poetry of the 16th and 17th centuries;

2) Brik: On the poetic epithet;

3) Bogatyrev: On folk anecdotes;

4) Bogatyrev: On Pushkin's "Hussar";

5) Bogatyrev: Poznanski's work on incantations;

6) Jakobson: On poetic language in the works of Xlebnikov [May 11,
1919[36]]

7) Brik: On the rhythm of verse;

8) Report by Ing. Gursky on abbreviations in factory terminology [May 2, 1919[37]]

9) Jarxo: On the so-called trochaic tetrameter in Carolingian rhythms;

10) Tomaševskij: On iambic pentameter in Pushkin [June 8, 1919];

11) Bogatyrev

12) Vinokur

13) Buslaev ⎫ On Gogol's "Nose"

14) Jakobson

15) Brik

16) Sokolov: Contemporary folk legends and *častuški*;

17) Kušner: Sound Elements [Èlementy zvučanija];

18) V. Šklovskij: History of the novel;

19) V. Šklovskij: Composition of the *sujet* in cinematographic art;

20) S. Bobrov: On determining influences in poetry. (Vinokur 1922: 290) [38]

As we know on independent grounds that Jakobson's lecture on Xlebnikov took place on May 11, 1919, and represented a major turning point, the five lectures preceding it could be understood as a document from very early in the first phase. Since they all revolve around folklore and oral tradition, they would argue for Gornung's position. However, it is unclear whether this conclusion is permissible—although the list is not alphabetized, we cannot automatically assume that the lectures are ordered chronologically, see, for instance, the order of (6) and (8), for which independent dating is available.

Whatever the details might be, the first six or eight months do not really speak for the vibrant and aggressive Circle we know from the legend. One of the potential reasons might be the competition. In its initial phase, the Circle competed with other foci of interest, including the Dialectology Commission and the University. The Commission was, for instance, the ground for Karcevskij's often recalled "Verb Talks" in 1917–18. According to Jakobson and Bogatyrev,

De Saussure's pupil S. I. Karcevskij presented a number of lectures on the Russian verb in the Commission for Dialectology which showed the use of the static method; they provided a decisive impetus for linguistics in Moscow. The Commission organized a series of "Verb Talks" in 1917 and 1918 in which important methodological problems were the subject of discussion." (Jakobson and Bogatyrev 1922–23: 180)

Other competing centers are also recorded: Gornung (ca. 1970) reports that in the fall of 1918 another Moscow linguist, professor M. N. Peterson, organized a postgraduate seminar on syntax, and that several of the Circle's members participated (Gornung, Jakobson, Buslaev, Vinokur, Dinges, Jakovlev). And, finally, another University-based circle, the Linguistic Society [Lingvističeskoe obščestvo], was founded in April 1918 (Peterson 1922: 287).[39]

Languid as the first post-Revolutionary phase might have been, it is important to stress again that the Circle now existed as an autonomous, state-recognized, and state-supported institution, thus transcending the pre-revolutionary norms of academia. Its membership quadrupled since 1915,[40] and the Circle began to elect officers, including a chairman, a deputy chairman, a secretary, an assistant secretary, and a librarian. The officers received remuneration. Likewise, speakers received honoraria (Buslaev et al. 1956). The Circle also had a headquarters, located in the apartment of Jakobson's parents in Ljubjanka Passage [Ljubjanskij proezd] no. 3,[41] a building in which Majakovskij also lived. The Circle's library was there, too:

The Circle obtained the library of the late Professor Duvernois. In order to buy this library, funds were allocated by the library section of the Narkompros. The library contains a rich collection of ancient authors, a valuable selection of Sanskrit texts and of dictionaries and various linguistic works. (Vinokur 1922: 290)

(In view of the aims of the Circle, it is somewhat surprising that the collection contained such materials.)

While some of the above listed institutional changes cannot be reliably dated, there is little doubt that the Circle's spirit changed in May 1919 with Jakobson's lecture on Xlebnikov (later published as Jakobson 1921a). This presentation evidently transformed the atmosphere in the Circle substantially. Gornung (ca. 1970) reports that the lecture generated intensive discussions that went on for a while and that, subsequently, the Circle was meeting intensively during the

summer of 1919, sometimes even twice a week—the frequency resulting in part from the circumstance that the Civil War was raging
"and people did not leave for the summer vacations." On the basis
of Gornung's testimony and other documents, one may conclude
that this was the beginning of the core period of the Circle's activity, which lasted until late 1922 or early 1923. That period is characterized by a high number of lectures and by a merger of the OPOJAZ
core with the Moscow Linguistic Circle. The Briks and Majakovskij
moved from St. Petersburg to Moscow in 1919, and Šklovskij and
Kušner were there for extended periods of time. The merger is evident from the above list of lectures, which contains the names of
lecturers otherwise known from the OPOJAZ publications. The influx of St. Petersburg participants proved vital in any case.

Why and exactly how Jakobson's lecture marked such a sharp turn
will probably never be explained in all details. The minutes of the
meeting (Šapir 1991: 45–48) paradoxically show that almost nobody
agreed with the lecturer: Brik simply stated that neither the theme
nor the results were clear to him; Bogatyrev objected to Jakobson's
idea of "poetic dialectology" (see above), and Buslaev and Nejštadt
also voiced criticism. Since the audience consisted of only six persons, this represented a lot of dissent. Jakobson defended himself
adamantly, though. The following was his answer to Brik:

> The report *does* have a precisely defined topic and goal. The goal is this—it
> is the goal of a poetic dialectology, which means a description of poetic
> linguistic facts and Xlebnikov's poetic procedures. It is of course well possi-
> ble that this description turned out not to be exhaustive, but criticism
> in matters of completeness is not substantive. What does such description
> lead to? It leads to the establishment of poetic language on the basis of facts,
> and to the statement of its laws, with a projection into history. (Šapir 1991:
> 45)

Maybe it was the topic—Xlebnikov—or the obvious theoretical inspiration of the lecture, or the opportunity to engage in a discussion,
the feeling of participating in an open enterprise, or the sum of all
these, that generated so much enthusiasm. Discussions were in any
case a characteristic feature of the meetings. Note, for instance, the
following important passage about the working mode of the Circle
in Vinokur's report:

The main aim was to collect new material and analyze old material from new points of view. The work of the Circle was defined as laboratory work. The Circle never insisted that its members produce fully complete pieces of academic work. Methods of analysis were worked out in collective cooperation. (Vinokur 1922: 289)

The final lines, characterizing the Circle's work as "laboratory work," the appeal to the collective spirit, and the negative view of authoritative academic work all can be interpreted as signs of the radical spirit of the Circle. Aggressive language was certainly a part of it, too—Jakobson did not hesitate to call Brjusov a charlatan. The expression "laboratory work" relates to meetings in which a common theme was chosen and each participant took 10–15 minutes to present and defend his analysis. The discussion on Gogol's "Nose" (see the list above) may have been such a "lab exercise."

A number of materials document the dynamism inherent in the internal work of the Circle—above all, the minutes of the Circle's meetings (reproduced in Flejšman 1977, Šapir 1991 and Toddes and Čudakova 1981)[42] which give an impressive picture of the working methods of the Circle and which include lists of discussants and summaries of contributions. The latter tend to be brief, but are occasionally very informative.

Other documents from the second phase of the Circle attest to a high level of activity. An activity report for the period March 1921–March 1922[43] lists 35 lectures, plus two meetings organized jointly with the Commission for Dialectology. In view of the fact that the Circle had 39 members at that point, this is really a remarkable performance. Moreover, there were eight business meetings, 14 meetings of the executive committee, and 23 informant sessions to collect folklore data. The members also continued to do dialect field work outside Moscow, and they participated in the work of other research groups, such as the group preparing a new dictionary of Russian. There is little reason to suspect that this activity was blown up in the report for bureaucratic reasons.

The list of lectures for 1921–22 is also significant in that it shows a general widening of the direction—by now a great variety of literary and linguistic themes is discussed by a group of scholars that is no longer so homogeneous as in the initial stage. Among the lectures listed are six by Jakovlev on Caucasian themes, four by Maze on Hebraic themes, five by Šor on a variety of themes, and three by Durnovo (including one on N. S. Trubetzkoy's work). Thus, whereas Jakobson (1925c: 753) later claimed that in its early days the Circle "was also concerned with a detailed analysis of the problems of language, as dependent on its various functions, and especially with an analysis of the problems of Russian poetic language," and that "particular emphasis was placed on rhythm and on the stylistics of folklore," such a program is not readily recognizable in the early 1920s.

Relying on Gornung's account, one must conclude that, despite the astonishing volume of activity, the Circle was losing its original vigor by late 1922. When Vinokur returned from his diplomatic assignment in 1922, he revitalized the group for several months, organizing mainly lectures on Saussure. This might well be regarded as the third period in the Circle's activity. It is best documented by Bernštejn's lectures on Saussure, the first systematic Russian account of *Cours de linguistique générale* (Sljusareva and Kuznecova 1976).

By January 1, 1923, the Circle had lost its financial support. It dissolved itself in a meeting in November 1924, transferring its library to GAXN. GAXN also absorbed some of the members (Gornung, Buslaev, Žinkin), who joined the project Problems of Art Form directed by G. G. Špet. This group, it might be added, distanced itself from the original Formalist doctrine.[44] This circumstance is among the reasons that one must agree with Jakobson that the Circle's end "was caused partly by outer and partly by inner factors" (Jakobson 1981: 287).

By way of conclusion, a feature often highlighted in the literature (e.g., Pomorska 1968)—the participation in the Circle of a number of contemporary poets—will be mentioned briefly. Two poets are recorded as members in the very early days: Vladimir Majakovskij and Sergei P. Bobrov.[45] In 1922, Boris Pasternak, Nikolai Aseev, and Osip Mandel'štam also became members. This fact has become a legend in and of itself, and it might be difficult to keep Dichtung separate from Wahrheit by now, especially as far as the level of active participation of these poets is concerned. Gornung, who seems reserved with respect to Futurism and thus perhaps with respect to

Majakovskij too, notes that Majakovskij participated only in two meetings, yet adds that he was always around and was well remembered for playing cards with the Circle's members.[46] Gornung also recalled that Xlebnikov was present at one of the early meetings. But there is actually nothing wrong with the semi-apocryphal nature of the poets' participation. Much as in Prague, as we shall later see, the personal link between scholars and poets had a great symbolic value and marked yet another difference between traditional academia and the new avant-garde scholarship.

Linguists and the Revolution

. . . a revolution . . . then genuine and pure. . .
Jakobson (1969 [1988])

I touched upon the impact of the Bolshevik Revolution on the Moscow Linguistic Circle and OPOJAZ in the previous chapter, treating it mainly from the perspective of Jakobson's biography. Jakobson's case, however, was one of many. A closer look shows, not surprisingly, that the lives of a great number of young linguists changed as a result of Russia's political transformation. These changes followed various patterns, advancement often inviting vulnerability and degradation.

One pattern is represented by what we might call "group jumping." Thus, Brik and Kušner shifted the focus of their work from OPOJAZ to the Communist Futurists (Komfut), a group in which Majakovskij was also prominent. The Komfuts had to be members of the Bolshevik Party (which was the case with Brik and Kušner) and follow the principles of Communist cultural ideology.[47] Komfut activities are primarily documented in *Iskusstvo kommuny* [*The Art of the Commune*], a radical journal with anarchist undertones which first appeared in the winter of 1918–19 and in which Brik and Kušner published often.

A less frequently noted but very obvious pattern resulted from fact that the new regime provided linguists with new careers, among other things contributing to the weakening of OPOJAZ. Thus, Polivanov and Jakubinskij accepted positions in new institutions or worked in the highest offices of the new administration. Jakubinskij concentrated on the reorganization of higher education for a while; he was among the driving forces behind the Institut živogo slova [Institute of the Living Word], an institution designed to serve teacher training. The institute opened in November 1918, Lunačarskij being its main supporter in the new bureaucracy (see Leont'ev 1986). On the whole, Jakubinskij subscribed to the directives of the new regime from this point on. In contrast to Polivanov, who often openly opposed Marr (the official representative of Marxist linguistics) Jakubinskij became closely associated with Marr's Institute of Language and Thought during the 1920s and began to attack structuralism in linguistics severely. Among other things he wrote a critique of Saussure, which in some places must be regarded as burlesque (Jakubinskij 1931).

Polivanov's career changed profoundly after the October Revolution. Leont'ev (1983) reports that he began to cooperate with the Bolsheviks after the February Revolution and was assigned important functions in the reorganization of the Russian Foreign Office. Among his responsibilities was the deciphering of encoded messages and secret treaties of the Imperial government. In February 1918, he was made a political supervisor in St. Petersburg's Chinese community, which is said to have numbered more than 300,000. He was in charge of political propaganda in this group, but his position might also be seen against the background of the drug trade. In 1921 he moved to Moscow, where he became an assistant in the Far Eastern Division of the Komintern. On the whole, his posts were compatible with his Far Eastern and Central Asian linguistic expertise, and did not remove him from teaching entirely. His association with the new regime was quite conscious and extensive. He became a party member in 1919. Since he vigorously opposed Marr, he was eventually removed from Moscow and ultimately perished in a concentration camp in 1938 after a peregrinage through a variety of academic positions in Soviet Central Asia.[48]

Jakobson's involvement with the new authorities was in part rooted in his linguistic, or more precisely dialectological, expertise. In 1919, when Soviet authorities were negotiating with the then independent Ukraine, complicated border issues had to be solved and answers were sought in dialect maps. Jakobson happened to be around when questions about the border and the dialects were posed by the Soviet diplomats, and thus he became involved in diplomacy, where linguistic expertise was a major asset. In early 1920 he was appointed director of the press office of the newly established Soviet diplomatic mission in Tallinn (Reval), and later he became an interpreter for the Soviet Red Cross mission in Prague.

While it is certainly possible to see Russia's transformation as a process that offered careers, there is of course a sobering reminder—the overriding characteristics of a career in those days were instability, unpredictability and fragmentation. Recall Šklovskij, Bulgakov's man of many identities. His zigzagging between the front lines and the rear eventually resulted in emigration. In 1922 he even considered staying abroad, but eventually he returned to Russia. Trubetzkoy's biography, too, turns into a fragmented sequence of unclear goals—Sofia, Vienna, . . . Brno? And the same holds for Roman Jakobson. His diplomatic career in Prague was uneasy, as we have seen above, and alternatives, including a return to Moscow, were considered repeatedly.

4

Vilém Mathesius: In Search of a New Linguistics

In this chapter I focus on the early work of Vilém Mathesius, the founder of the Prague Linguistic Circle. I survey his formative years and show that, in favoring a realistic, common-sense approach to language, he was addressing questions that had not been previously considered traditional—such as the study of language as a means to an end. Early in his scholarly career he rejected historical and psychological causalism, ultimately favoring synchronic analysis of contemporary language. The most visible component of his linguistic thinking, anti-historicism, was congruent with Realism, which was a major trend in Czech social thought. Mathesius was well acquainted with this current and with the work of its advocate Tomáš G. Masaryk.

In portraying Mathesius's formative years, I also touch briefly upon the state of linguistics in Bohemia before the First World War. This review makes it clear that the most important Czech linguists from the period before 1918 did not have a particularly strong effect upon the later structuralists, either through their works or through their personalities. Their main concern was solving puzzles within the framework of historical linguistics. A contemporary characterization of Czech linguists as "collectors and observers," originally intended as a compliment, seems an apt description of the style of work prevailing in Mathesius's student years. Interest in theoretical problems, in daring syntheses, was very limited. This penchant for normal science ultimately provided a background against which Mathesius and his circle became active.[1]

4.1 Mathesius's Formative Years

Vilém Mathesius was born in 1882 in the East Bohemian town of Pardubice; he spent his youth and attended a gymnasium in nearby Kolín. Mathesius later remarked that being a gymnasium student in a small town such as Kolín was "almost something privileged; on occasions, there was a distinct feeling that the whole town felt and lived with the students" (Mathesius 1936a [1982: 410]).

Greek was Mathesius's favorite subject; he described the classes taught by Jan Němec as "exercises in clear thinking" (ibid.: 413). Another person whom he valued in particular was his teacher of philosophical propaedeutics, Otakar Kádner: ". . . during our gymnasium time, [he] showed us better than anyone else that there are problems in science whose solution is yet to be found" (ibid.: 414). Kádner would lend Mathesius books which he himself had borrowed from the University Library in Prague. For his German-teacher, Ignác Kadlec, Mathesius in retrospect also had only words of admiration—Kadlec subscribed to *Mind,* the British philosophy journal, visited art exhibitions in Prague regularly, and, most important for Mathesius, was a fervent Protestant with inclinations toward the Church of Scotland: "I shall never forget how his face began to shine, when he could talk to us about things which had moral beauty." (ibid.: 413)

That the impact of Protestantism on Mathesius was so strong and lasting[2] is to a great extent due to Čeněk Dušek, a pastor in Kolín, who taught Mathesius not only religion but also English:

Dušek's was a proud, dauntless and deeply honest personality; his Anglo-Saxon schooling only enhanced these traits and gave him a rich, non-bookish education and a free vision. Nowhere could we breathe in an atmosphere so full of culture and free spirit as in his classes. (Mathesius 1934a [1982: 423])

He impressed us as a cultured personality with a broad horizon and a free vision. He educated himself mainly abroad, especially in Scotland, and his uninhibited lectures on history and occasional political remarks conveyed a spirit much freer than we were used to. His physical appearance was in consonance with this. (Mathesius 1936a [1982: 414f.])[3]

Dušek's admiration of English culture, love of the English language, and adherence to Protestantism had a certain "dissident" flavor under the officially Catholic and culturally Germanocentric Austro-Hungarian monarchy.

Mathesius's progress at Charles University was fast—he began his studies in 1901, his doctoral dissertation went into print in 1907, and his habilitation (second doctorate) was awarded to him in 1909. He then immediately began to teach English philology at Charles University, effectively becoming the founder of English studies in

Czechoslovakia. Measured by Russian standards, there are no unusual associations, no avant-garde inclinations, no participation in radical circles. The fact that Mathesius mentions some youthful "attempts in verse" (1942 [1982 : 436]) makes him in no way unusual—this was close to a norm. However, measured by the standards of Czech chauvinism of the turn of the century, there is one unusual detail: Mathesius also attended lectures at the German branch of the university.

In 1921 he began to lose his sight, which impaired his scholarly work and made him depend on the help of assistants. The condition was a symptom of a severe disease that later disabled him for extended periods of time. In view of these personal circumstances, Mathesius's scholarly activity and organizational performance are awe-inspiring. Clearly, his determination, backed by a firm Protestant discipline, played a major role in coping with his physical handicap.

4.2 Normal Science

Mathesius's reminiscences contain a number of passages about his university teachers, but in comparison with what he could recall about his gymnasium years there are not very many passages that reveal genuine excitement and attraction. Although he appreciated some of his professors as personalities, one looks in vain for signs of strong identification with them.[4] However, there is evidence that he envied one of his fellow students for being able to study such an advanced discipline as biology:

I visited him in order to breathe the air of science in his presence, as I used to say. In view of the lively research activity in modern plant physiology, it seemed to me that what the School of Arts[5] could offer me in philology was dull and showed little evidence of a clearly defined goal. (Mathesius ca. 1942 [1982: 436])

Indeed, the turn of the century was characterized not only by a lack of spectacular results in Czech linguistics but also by a fairly unattractive state of university teaching. Contemporary critics pointed out that the attitude in the School of Arts at Charles University was too schoolish, and that the atmosphere was determined by students studying for their teaching certificates (Janko 1911). This state of the university can to a certain extent be explained by the fact that for long periods of time, Charles University, the only university in Bohemia and Moravia, was simply a small provincial institution. Moreover, in the second half of the nineteenth century Czech linguists were able to follow the newest developments only in a receptive way. The emergence of the Neogrammarian School in Germany had an impact, though, and was felt strongly in Slavic philology, especially in the area of Czech studies. At the turn of the century, the most productive and esteemed personality in Czech linguistics was a Slavist, the preeminent Czech Bohemist Jan Gebauer. His strictly historical and data-oriented approach is particularly manifest in his major projects, often considered monumental by his contemporaries—a historical grammar of Czech and a dictionary of Old Czech. Both remained unfinished at his death in 1907.

Some of Gebauer's prestige was based on his involvement in the only spectacular event in Czech linguistics of the 1880s and 1890s: the so-called Manuscript Controversy.[6] A group of Czech philologists and historians headed by Tomáš G. Masaryk (1850–1937), then a newly appointed professor of philosophy in the Czech section of Charles University, had unmasked two presumably medieval manuscripts (allegedly found in 1817 and 1818, respectively) as forgeries. The proof was a splendid scholarly achievement. However, many Czech patriots, and the majority of cultural opinion-makers, received the learned arguments with little enthusiasm, and some with fury. The Manuscripts were regarded by the general public and by many historians and philologists with utmost reverence, and the songs telling of the heroic deeds of the Czechs against the Germans were most influential in fueling Czech nationalism. At a time when the Czech national consciousness was on the rise, doubts about their authenticity met with great hostility.

The exposure of the Manuscripts and the detailed socio-historical and philological analyses that were involved strengthened the scientific prestige of Czech historiography and philology considerably. Czech scholars had finally succeeded in raising their scholarship to a European level and were now listened to by their European peers.

Perhaps no document conveys the grandeur of this achievement more cogently than a letter from the German Slavist August Leskien to Jan Gebauer, dated December 30, 1887:

Your name will always be known as one of a genuine and courageous defender of scholarship and truth. . . . Will the public never become smart enough to realize that in scholarship only one single thing matters—the pursuit of truth under all circumstances; and that it is of little concern whether feelings of some kind will be hurt in such endeavor; and that patriotic fuss has no place in scholarship either. Men like us—Slavs or Germans—will not forget that there is a realm of humanity high above all the nationalistic hatred and that scholarship makes out a large part of this realm. We want to keep this realm free of all forgery and falsehood. (Gebauerová 1926 : 359f.)

Noble and rewarding as these words may have been, they do not alter the fact that the exposure of the Manuscripts did not so much involve conceptual questions as the application of available scientific means and methods; strictly speaking, this was an exercise in what Thomas Kuhn has called "normal science." And since the normal science of the day was Positivism, the Manuscript Controversy reaffirmed support for a strictly data-oriented, programmatically anti-speculative attitude in the social sciences, thus representing a dramatic climax of Czech Positivism.

When Mathesius began his studies, the excitement over the Manuscripts had receded, and Jan Gebauer struck Mathesius as merely an authoritative, if not authoritarian, professor:

In his explanations Gebauer was strict. He could not bear empty talk and insisted mercilessly that the very formulation that he himself had arrived at should be used. I can remember how he once rejected several basically correct attempts at the interpretation of a word because the interpreters were not using exactly the wording "the word lost the characteristics of its formal category and was thus subject to exceptional changes." From single facts and rules for interpreting such facts one did not proceed to formulations of a general nature. This was an atmosphere in which the rigor of scientific method could be clearly sensed, but in which no new thoughts were born. (Mathesius 1937 [1982: 419]) [7]

In an evaluation of this epoch in which "no new thoughts were born," assessments of Gebauer seem particularly important, for he held, as a leading scholar in Czech studies, a key position in the School of Arts. Syllaba (1983: 86) estimates, on the basis of enrollment lists, that during his teaching career at Charles University his lectures were attended by a total of about 3000 students. Gebauer's own records show that he issued certificates of participation to 643 students in his seminars (ibid.). In view of the size of the School of Arts at that time, these are very high numbers.

After Gebauer, the most important linguist at the university was the Indo-Europeanist Josef Zubatý. Zubatý's influence became more visible after Gebauer's death in 1907 and owed a great deal to Zubatý's increasing interest in Czech. He was without doubt affected by the "individualism" that had become influential in linguistics around the turn of the century. He also attracted a certain amount of sympathy as an independent scholar who did not allow himself to be particularly influenced by any specific doctrine, that of the Neogrammarian infallibility of sound laws included. Also, his fine taste and his friendship with the composer Antonín Dvořák made him an intriguing personality. Nevertheless, there were similarities between Zubatý and Gebauer. The obituary Mathesius wrote for Zubatý is of some interest:

Any abstract generalization went against Zubatý's feeling for reality, and if he had been more familiar with modern phonological theories he would certainly have regarded them with the same mistrustful rejection with which he treated the Neogrammarian theories. . . . Zubatý did not, in his whole life, write a book. His work on Czech is extensive, but it consists of a long series of specialized contributions to Czech lexical history and syntax. (Mathesius 1931a: 242f.)

These characterizations largely correspond to those of the younger generation. Miloš Weingart, a member of the Prague Linguistic Circle, wrote:

Zubatý was a typical *empiricist* who never started his investigation with general considerations and general sentences, but took particular facts as a point of departure. . . . Focusing his observations on analyses of particular facts, he had no interest in classifying and defining them precisely. *He was neither a synthesizer, nor a systematizer.* Thirty years ago, in 1901, he wrote something quite typical of him in his programmatic article on syntax: "Content is always more important for me than the system." (Weingart 1931: 290; emphasis in original) [8]

In Search of a New Linguistics

As we shall later see, aversion to theorizing, the absence of system and synthesis, deplored in Weingart's statement, alienated the old school from the new generation that demanded bold visions. Ultimately, Weingart's judgment was a judgment about a new culture of linguistics.

4.3 Early Themes—Linguistic Realism, Language Optimization

Mathesius's linguistic writings from 1906–1914, his early period, reveal a definite wish on his part to change the subject matter and the methodology of linguistics.

The first point emerges clearly in Mathesius's first published work, a review of Otto Jespersen's 1894 *Growth and Structure of the English Language* (Mathesius 1906). Mathesius focuses on Jespersen's idea that linguistic analysis must start from the spoken form of language, "from the truly living language" (ibid.: 316). As we have seen, this realistic slogan was often heard in the late nineteenth century and was quite typically understood historically—the study of the present, especially in the area of dialectology, was merely to provide a key to the understanding of language change. However, the interest in the "living word" was becoming increasingly acceptable without any diachronic legitimization, also. In addition, the so-called modern philologies, which were closely connected to practical language teaching and which emphasized descriptive fields such as phonetics, were also abandoning historicism. Thus, a different variant of the study of the "living word" was emerging, one in which diachronic motivation was no longer respected.

For Mathesius, who was educated in the first decade of this century, the ahistorical variant of linguistic realism became guiding. Practical pedagogical concerns also had some influence. Before the First World War, he frequently wrote on new, pedagogically applicable linguistic literature in the *Gazette of Czech Gymnasium Professors*. He spoke with great sympathy, for example, of the Association Phonétique Internationale, originally a teacher's organization, characterizing it as a "powerful front of supporters of the method that aims to teach language as it is really spoken, not just the language of literature" (Mathesius 1909: 206). Although not shocking by our contemporary standards, the concern for modern language posed a fairly radical demand for quite a long time and was strong enough to drive reform movements in the field of teaching. To appreciate the change of atmosphere, recall that by the middle of the nineteenth century the German linguist Karl Weinhold still demanded that the teaching of Middle High German be mandatory in grammar schools in Germany (Weinhold 1850).[9]

Mathesius's emphasis on contemporary spoken language went hand in hand with a number of approaches that previously had not been considered traditional. One of these was the study of language as a means to an end. In his review of Jespersen, Mathesius agreed with Jespersen's advocacy of the economy of expression based on the premise that language serves a specific purpose: "Language fulfills its purpose the better the *simpler* the means for communicating a *complete* message." (Mathesius 1906: 313; emphasis in original)[10] Although this was Mathesius's rendering of Jespersen's position, he tried to show that this view stood in complete opposition to the generally accepted approach. He also quoted the dialogue-oriented and—to use today's terminology—pragmatically based approach of Philip Wegener (1885) as evidence of this modern means-to-an-end position. We shall see below that the idea of optimal functioning, including attempts at intentional optimization (such as in man-made auxiliary languages), was a very important reaction to the earlier conception of language as a natural rather than a cultural phenomenon.

Mathesius's emphasis on those aspects of language use in which intention of the speaker was visible—that is, on style—was quite in line with this orientation. Karl Vossler, the German stylist-syntactician who drew inspiration from Benedetto Croce's subsumption of linguistics under aesthetics, is mentioned only briefly in Mathesius's early writings, but the presence of his ideas is actually quite apparent.[11] Mathesius's interest in stylistic questions, often referred to as an interest in syntax and word order, is central. As we shall see below, he explicitly stated that word order is modified by aesthetic considerations—a wording that is strikingly Vosslerian. It represents not only one more point of difference from the Neogrammarian canon but also one of the sources of the linguistic interventionism later so prominent in the Prague Circle.

Mathesius explained his seemingly contradictory emphases on the "living word" and on the study of the language of poetry as follows:

Poetic language is in no way artificial, it is not a genuine language with an admixture of something foreign—it is only another aspect of the multifaceted linguistic production. . . . Linguistics must draw upon all of these rich sources of information which linguistic creativity provides. (Mathesius 1907–1910, pt. 1907: 270)

Thus an approach emerges here that is characterized by a balanced, if not "ecumenical" approach to data—Mathesius sought to study the whole spectrum of language, all data were essentially equally authentic.

4.4 Against Taine and Determinism

One might assume that the new themes that were emerging around the turn of the century ("living word," "conscious use of language," "study of literary language") would have produced nothing more than a new type of descriptivism which differed from the old simply in that it studied a new kind of data: "real," "contemporary," "more comprehensive" facts. It is thus important to ascertain whether Mathesius's work also reveals methodology that would match the new understanding of the field. Some such endeavors are expressed in his dissertation, although it is devoted to a literary topic.

Mathesius's doctoral dissertation (1907–08) is a lengthy analysis of Hippolyte Taine's 1856 study *Shakespeare, son génie et ses œuvres*. While the heavy, almost pedantic style of certain sections might seem to point to a diligent beginner, Mathesius's overall position is actually iconoclastic. There are passages which are very self-confident and coherent from the methodological point of view. Mathesius is critical of the fact that Taine systematically ignores Shakespeare as a poet by not paying attention to his verbal art: "[Taine] leaves aside the formal beauty of Shakespeare's language, its rhythm and melody" (Mathesius 1907–08, pt. 1908: 233). It is even more peculiar to Mathesius that "the construction [stavba] of Shakespeare's plays, his art of composition and drama—this all does not exist for Taine" (ibid.). In criticizing Taine, Mathesius further sees an overemphasis on psychological and historical aspects as one of the reasons for his failure: ". . . the literary work is not analyzed [by Taine] for its literary qualities but only as a symptom of the life of a particular individual, a particular epoch and a nation." (ibid., pt. 1908: 239) This is at variance with Mathesius's interest, namely to investigate "what the integrating elements of a work of art are and how they can be determined" (ibid., pt. 1907: 228). Mathesius defends the unconventionality of his question in a brief discussion of the German linguist and literary historian Wilhelm Scherer, objecting to Scherer's concern with "causes and consequences." What Mathesius has in mind is something different—he aims at "establishing literary-historical facts, i.e., basic elements of a given work of literature without reference to the author" (ibid., pt. 1907: 228).

Mathesius's remarks thus clearly aim at a non-historically rooted methodology that regards literary texts as autonomous objects.[12] From this point of view, of course, Taine, the major representative of the nineteenth-century Positivism, was a logical target. Taine's approach to literary history and criticism was a consequential application of a rigorous determinism. Taine's main concern was search for causes at all levels; a creative personality, however ingenious, was always a result of a particular instance of historical causation—art, and its language, had no special status. Hence, the very idea of criticizing Hippolyte Taine, an articulate determinist, shows Mathesius's methodological audacity.

4.5   Tendencies

Important as the rejection of Taine's determinism might have been, it merely led to a general position with little indication of how to proceed in concrete analytical work. A partial answer to this crucial question is Mathesius's first extensive linguistic work, "Studies on the History of English Word Order" (Mathesius 1907–1910). The title is somewhat puzzling—a reader seeking elucidation on the history of English word order will find little relevant information on this subject. The final two chapters actually deal with "Word order and rhythm in *contemporary* English of educated London speakers." But, as we have already seen, this attitude is by no means surprising, in light of Mathesius's reluctance to deal with diachronic topics.

Mathesius embarked here on a difficult subject, one that intrigued him all his life. He sought to establish principles of word order from an interplay of rhythmic and grammatical factors. In this research tradition the rhythm of prose was seen as the major determining factor of word order. The study reveals Mathesius's methodological coordinates, especially where he deals with earlier opinions on the matter. Among the scholars whose analyses he rejects are representatives of psychologism. He quotes Misteli:

Let us not deceive ourselves about the value of psychology in grammar. Psychology does not provide any new explanations and does not introduce any new causes which would be unknown or inaccessible in grammar. Psychology only shifts the focus and yields new points of view. What is not explained in grammar will also remain a problem for psychology. (Mathesius 1907–1910, pt. 1907: 263; originally in German)

Mathesius also appreciates the opinions advanced by Philip Wegener, who is for him a representative of research pursuing "a precise analysis of living language":

To him [Wegener], a sentence is not only a series of words, but also the tone with which it is pronounced, and the expression of the eye and the facial gesture which accompany it. (Mathesius 1907–1910, pt. 1907: 264)

Facing the richness and complexity of facts, which he obviously values highly, Mathesius eventually embarks upon the method of inductive generalization, the validity of which increases with the volume of material under investigation:

. . . linguistic creativity, by its very nature a psychic phenomenon, is of a subjective nature, and what appears relatively stable in it is merely tendencies. They are sustained by analogical creation and gradually pass into different tendencies. The real word order which is to be studied is a result of a conjunction, or compromise, or competition, of these two factors, which are moreover modified by aesthetic, especially rhythmic, considerations. It is thus obvious that the real word order will be maximally subjective, changing from an individual to an individual, from a period to a period, from a nation to a nation, and that its general laws will be broad abstractions whose validity will be the higher the richer the material under study is. (Mathesius 1907–1910, pt. 1907: 270)

In the course of the study, the notion "broad abstraction" is replaced by "tendency":

The word tendency as used in these chapters does not mean an evolutionary direction but a constant drift in linguistic activity *(Geschehen)*, as determined by a static analysis of the material and hence valid only for the period or dialect selected. (ibid., pt. 1910: 130, n. 5)

We thus see that individual speech and the overall diversity of material are still the guiding images that must not yield to idealizations. Given these goals, the result Mathesius envisions is logical—it is the statement of tendencies, essentially an inductive typological generalization concerning a particular state of language. Numerous tables with statistics indicate that tendencies will ultimately be found statistically.

Mathesius further exposed his ideas about tendencies in his often-mentioned work "On the Potentiality of Language Phenomena" (1911).[13] In respect to this work, it is of great importance to clarify Mathesius's rather unusual use of the concept of potentiality. In the first lines of the treatise, he says "I take it as meaning static variation, that is, instability in a given period, in contrast to dynamic mutability which manifests itself as change over a span of time." (Mathesius 1911 [1982: 9]) With potentiality so defined, a link with Mathesius's preceding work emerges, as does a link with his later projects. As late as 1932, the information bulletin of the International Phonological Association (an offshoot of the Prague Linguistic Circle) announced the following project by Mathesius: "Oscillations dans la pronunciation, leurs types et leur importance pour l'analyse phonologique" (Association Internationale . . . , no.1, 1932: 61). The choice of the term "oscillation," rather than "potentiality," might have been appropriate already in 1911.

In the 1911 treatise, Mathesius again struggles with data. Owing to the enormous richness of data that a linguist was facing when studying potentiality, selective idealization was ultimately necessary. Concluding that the linguist had no choice but to concern himself only with the main characteristics of the language, Mathesius stressed that it would be a mistake to identify these apparent simplifications of linguistic phenomena with the actual nature of language:

... the apparent simplicity of linguistic phenomena is often understood not as a result of the linguistic method but as a real characteristic of language, which frequently gives rise to unfortunate mistakes. It is in the nature of the matter itself that besides a common scientific quest for laws as general as possible, an ever stronger opposition against an exaggerated mechanical simplification of the facts must exist in linguistics. (Mathesius 1911 [1982: 9])

Obviously, an essential part of Mathesius's methodology is extreme wariness—the complexity of the facts must always be in the foreground. Mathesius sees language as an essentially complex, immeasurable, and daily increasing accumulation of phenomena to which one cannot really do full justice.

All in all, the "Potentiality" essay leaves one with the impression that Mathesius embarked upon an ambitious synthesis of facts brought together from different areas to be scrutinized from a single unifying point of view. But methodologically, his views are not especially sophisticated. One is almost tempted to say that, in opposition to his own exhortations to scholarly courage (see below), he was himself somewhat reluctant to put such courage into practice. He had not entirely shaken off the scientistic paradigm of the nineteenth century—data rather than theories were his central concern and statistics was the magic key. Others have noted this attitude, too. Bohumil Trnka, a loyal disciple and collaborator, tried several times to characterize Mathesius's methodology, ultimately reaching a somewhat ambivalent conclusion:

Mathesius stuck to facts, which he constantly collected and tried to understand in their broadest context. He believed neither in the uniformity of events nor in general laws and thus rejected psychological explanations of literary development, whether individually or collectively oriented. His own theories . . . do not show the daring one-sidedness characteristic of other scholars, but are remarkable for their overall solid character and sound judgment, something that he admired very much in the nation whose culture he represented at the university [i.e., England]. . . . His point of view was that of common sense which does not stray too far from "facts" and flexibly takes over from theory anything that contributes to an understanding of observed reality. (Trnka 1946: 4f.) [14]

Among the younger members of the Circle, this methodology did not carry much weight. It was rather foreign to Jakobson and

Mukařovský, not to speak of Trubetzkoy. It thus appears that the central pieces of Mathesius's work, such as the "Potentiality" essay, did not impress so much by their method as by the fact that they forcefully shifted interest to the synchronic point of view.

4.6 Mathesius's Ahistoricism and Masaryk's Realism

In the final sections of his "Potentiality" essay, Mathesius backs his preference for the static view with a reference to *Foundations of Concrete Logic* (Masaryk 1885),[15] thus making Masaryk one of the conceptual fathers of the Prague linguistic doctrine. This genealogy is by no means accidental. Although not a linguist, Masaryk included in his architecture of the sciences a section on linguistics, something that makes *Foundations of Concrete Logic* quite unusual. For this he consulted a number of authorities, including H. Paul, W. D. Whitney, A. Marty, H. Steinthal, and J. Gebauer; yet his treatment of linguistics contains a trait which is not to be found in these authors—an extension of Comte's notions *statique sociale* and *dynamique sociale* to linguistics:

The abstract study of language and the concrete language history have two main tasks, respectively, which correspond to those of social dynamics and statics, namely to explain not only the origin and evolution of language, but also its nature. . . . Projecting this perspective to an abstract level, we are dealing with statics and dynamics of the laws of language: statics represents a general grammar, which accounts for rules according to which a particular language formed its sounds, roots, forms, syntax, etc. Abstract philosophical dynamics explains the origin, development and decay of language. And projecting this perspective to concrete language history, we also assume statics and dynamics—the former is simply grammar, the latter the so-called historical grammar. (Masaryk 1887: 191)

Masaryk was further placing visible emphasis on non-historical research. This was what he called "preoccupation with close and accessible phenomena":

. . . genuine scientific method—also in linguistics—consists in the study of those phenomena that are closest and most accessible to us; more distant phenomena are measured by reference to the closer ones. . . . Thus the investigation of a living language will be more rewarding from the scholarly point of view than the study of a dead or even some primeval language. . . . We thus once more underscore that the study of the evolution of a thing must be connected with the study of the thing itself—a rule that cannot be repeated emphatically enough. . . . (Masaryk 1887: 192f.)

It is hard to decide whether Mathesius's reference to Masaryk directly initiated or merely reinforced Mathesius's ahistoricism. Yet it is clear that he found his conceptual support in Masaryk, a philosopher and sociologist whose influence on Czech culture and society was considerable.

While works such as *Foundations of Concrete Logic* were addressed to an academic audience, the end of the century witnessed Masaryk also addressing a broader audience with a political program called Realism. Certain details of the Realist doctrine are actually of paramount importance in the present connection. Masaryk constructed in his Realism a general framework for all non-historically oriented projects in social sciences. Repudiation of historicism was one of his most noticeable demands:

This demand concerns not only political views—it is general in its nature, and is intended to govern all of the human thought and action, thus forming a philosophical basis of what can be called Realism. I have expressed it in an abstract form in my *Concrete Logic* [Masaryk 1885]. The central rule can be formulated as follows: always and everywhere recognize things and their core. The evolution of things is not of central importance to the mind, but rather to the things themselves; clearly, evolution also belongs to the nature of things, but knowledge and attention must not be allowed to remain stuck with historical change. (Masaryk 1908: 132)

Realism must oppose historicism, or rather, an exaggerated historicism. Things—not history, things—not evolution, are the watchword of Realism as I understand it. This is not only the base of the national view, but of course of a philosophical view and a philosophical method. (Masaryk 1908: 141)

In an atmosphere in which national pride had been expressed by the constant concern with national history, Masaryk's emphasis on "things," rather than their history, was of immediate political value. But these thoughts were also, as Masaryk repeatedly emphasized, philosophically based, or, at least, based on a general worldview, and thus could serve as a framework for scholarly programs. We shall see in the next chapter that Mathesius took this precept very seriously and tried to implement the Realistic program in all respects.[16]

Thus, the study of contemporary language and its rooting in an overall drive against historicism are the most fundamental characteristics of Mathesius's early work. Interestingly, in 1945, a month before his death, the edge of the synchronic challenge no longer appeared so decisive to him. Writing to Havránek, his combatant from the Prague Linguistic Circle, he confessed:

I have finally reached the conclusion that in life there are often two forces, or movements—almost contradictory, yet equally justified as such—that permanently fight for superiority. But a total rule of any of them means that the evolution of life will stop or be put in danger. In linguistics, for instance, the forces are the diachronic and the synchronic approach. When I began with my own work as a linguist, the diachronic approach was in such preponderance that it was destroying the possibilities of further development. I thus stood up against it and worked systematically in a synchronic manner, not denying, however, the justification of the diachronic approach. (Mathesius to Havránek, March 5, 1945; Havránek family archives)

In the same passage, Mathesius described himself as a "dynamic classicist." He also added that, had he lived in England around 1750, he would have certainly had joined the pre-Romantics, "who advocated theories destroying Classicism." Remarkable as this confession sounds, the element of balance was not so obvious when Mathesius began to teach at Charles University in 1909. Suffice it to take a glance at the calendar of lectures for the winter 1909–1910 term. It includes a "Historical Grammar of [English] Contemporary Language: I. Introduction via Analysis of the *Present* State of the Language" (*Seznam* 1909–1910; emphasis added). The title almost sounds like a joke, but Mathesius was a serious man.

5

An Intermezzo: Jakobson and Mathesius in the Early 1920s

This chapter bridges the time span between 1920, when Jakobson left Russia, and 1926, when the Prague Linguistic Circle formed. The bridging approach is not so arbitrary as it might seem—the main actors were present in the early 1920s and worked intensively, yet the path to the creation of the Circle was still long. Jakobson came to Prague on July 10, 1920, and quickly began to publish in Czech journals. (In fact an interview with him appeared as early as July 21, 1920.) Czech language and culture gradually began to attract him; this is reflected in his study of Czech verse, in which he made important steps toward structural phonology. The first part of this chapter sketches this work. The second part of the chapter traces Mathesius's thinking during the same time. Mathesius also worked on linguistic topics in the early 1920s, but in the long run his organizational activity turned out to be more important. He soon developed into a cultural activist and a commentator on Czech public life, essentially following Masaryk's ideas about the role of scholarship and education in the new Czechoslovak society.

5.1   Jakobson in Prague, 1920–1925

The Early Years

In the early summer of 1920 Roman Jakobson left Moscow for the West. After a brief stop in Tallinn, he proceeded via Germany to Czechoslovakia to serve in the Red Cross mission the Soviets were opening in Prague. However, the idea of studying in the Czech capital was also a possibility—a letter of recommendation from Šaxmatov was in his suitcase.[1]

There were some "poetic" moments on this trip. On the boat to Danzig a Czech passenger recited to Jakobson works by the great Czech Romantic K. H. Mácha (see Jakobson 1976c).[2] Jakobson himself befriended the diplomatic courier of the Prague mission, Theodor Nette,[3] and recited some of Majakovskij's poetry to him. In Germany, Dadaism must have attracted Jakobson; this is witnessed by his survey article "Dada" (Jakobson 1921d). Since he arrived in Prague on July 10, 1920, it is tempting to speculate that he was lucky enough to see the scandalous Dada-Messe that opened in Berlin in late June.

Jakobson arrived in Czechoslovakia as a member of a mission that was supposed to handle the repatriation of Russian prisoners of war.[4] Not surprisingly, anyone's association with a Soviet institution aroused a great deal of suspicion. The mission was not regarded as very efficient in fulfilling its task and was apparently detested as a Bolshevik outfit staffed by Jews.[5] Jakobson left it after several weeks and began to study at Charles University, probably in a state of shock at the scandalous echo that the arrival of the mission caused. Some Czechs apparently even thought that the Jakobson who had arrived in Prague was not the same Jakobson who had been recommended by Šaxmatov—that the real Jakobson had been murdered and Šaxmatov's letter stolen.[6]

Jakobson's state of mind is reflected in the following passage from a letter to Elsa Triolet, probably dating from November 14, 1920:

You are asking me what I am doing in Prague. I don't know whether you know it or not, but I was heavily targeted here in September because of the Red Cross. The press was yelling about "a snake firmly embracing our professors" (that was I) etc., the professors were hesitating whether I was a bandit or a scholar or an illicit bastard, songs were sung about me in cabarets, all this was not very witty. The situation was complicated—it seems that my destiny is to balance in unthinkable circumstances. As a result, I left the service—no tears, no bad words—and turned to the university. (Jangfeldt 1992 : 80)

The subsequent letters to Elsa Triolet indicate hard work: Jakobson begins to publish a lengthy article on the language of the Russian Revolution (Jakobson 1920–21), succeeds in getting the Xlebnikov book published (as early as January 1921), and requests French books (among them Saussure's *Cours*). A year after his arrival, a Czech reviewer hinted at the existence of earlier unfavorable reports about the "young Russian Slavist" before finding reasons to absolve him:

R. Jakobson came to Prague as the official translator of the first Soviet mission headed by the ill-reputed Dr. Gillerson.[7] No wonder then that he aroused mistrust at the beginning, despite bringing with himself a warm recommendation of the famous Petersburg Slavist, the late academician Šaxmatov, and despite the fact that reputation of a gifted Slavist preceded him. R. Jakobson however got rid of the odium cast on him by the association with the Soviet mission, left its service, and having returned to his scholarship, he is now fully dedicating himself to Slavic studies in Prague. (Červinka 1921)

Well intended as the final lines of this portrait may have been, the protagonist in the "adventure story" (recall his letter to Elsa Triolet) was hard to convert to a brave student. Jakobson returned to his work for the mission, which continued until late 1928.[8] Not surprisingly, his political background remained a recurring issue during his entire Czechoslovak career. For instance, the daily *Národní listy* published the following lines in 1929, when Jakobson no longer was with the mission and the Prague Circle was already in full swing:

Nobody is so naive in the whole Czechoslovak republic as not to see quite clearly that Mr. Jakobson's Slavic activity in Prague is nothing but a disguise under which Mr. Jakobson fulfills his true mission—the mission of a communist agent. Nobody will believe that Mr. Jakobson lives here in Prague the way he does just on honoraria from the *Slavische Rundschau*. . . . (Kramář 1929)

The allegations made in this anonymous article, generally attributed to the conservative politician Karel Kramář, were taken back after Jakobson sought legal redress.[9]

Jakobson did not make it easy for his Czech defenders. In his first public appearance, answering questions about the state of the Soviet culture and scholarship, he underscored the positive value of the ongoing changes. In another appearance, a public discussion about proletarian art, he denounced a panelist for lacking competence on the subject; the panelist was an émigré (Weil 1921). Also, his loyalty to Majakovskij and the leftist avant-garde remained unbroken. His letter to Majakovskij, quoted above, makes him appear comfortable with the spread of anti-capitalist sentiment in Czechoslovakia, and a polemical defense of Majakovskij which he published in February 1921 stresses the fact that the Futurist poet was no political opportunist in the service of the new regime—he had simply always been a Bolshevik (Jakobson 1921c). Moreover, Jakobson associated himself with S. K. Neumann, an important modernist poet with an anarchist background who was now essentially a Communist agitator.

Nonetheless, balancing the unthinkable seemed neither improper nor impossible—the social space was apprently non-Euclidean. Jakobson also met Vilém Mathesius, who invited him for a "briefing" as early as September 1920, and gradually became interested in the type of Czech intellectual life that was associated with T. G. Masaryk's program. Within two months of his arrival he published an obituary to Šaxmatov in *Čas,* a newspaper representing President Masaryk's Realists.[10] Another obituary, commemorating the Russian Slavist V. N. Ščepkin—Jakobson's and Trubetzkoy's teacher—appeared in *Čas* in February 1921 (Jakobson 1921b). And an article on the language of the Revolution (Jakobson 1920–21) began to appear in installments in *Nové Athenaeum,* a journal co-edited by Mathesius and continuing the tradition of Masaryk's *Athenaeum* of the 1880s.

Although all this engagement made him highly visible, Jakobson remained for years an émigré not integrated in his new environment. His correspondence with Elsa Triolet, with Šklovskij and with Durnovo (1924–1927) shows that "distant horizons" rather than the new base still occupied a large proportion of his mind in the 1920s. Visits to Germany, where he was meeting Majakovskij and Šklovskij, were also important. His correspondence with Trubetzkoy, which begins in 1920, represents a discourse that was not dependent on Prague. By the mid-1920s, Jakobson's letters to his former teacher Durnovo, then also in Czechoslovakia, do not indicate that he finds the Czech academic environment particularly stimulating. His scholarly horizons are still defined by international journals and by the work of his colleagues in the Soviet Union. As late as 1927 Jakobson refers to the Prague Linguistic Circle as "Mathesius's Circle"—not "ours," as might be expected (to Durnovo, February 4, 1927; Toman 1994). Occasionally his writing appears a little bit patronizing with respect to the Czechs. Parts of an essay on modern Czech poetry in the Czech avant-garde journal *Pásmo* (see below) are reminiscent of recommendations administered to a backward cousin.

Throughout his early years in Prague, Jakobson kept track of conditions in the Soviet Union. Writing to Durnovo in November 1924, he gave the following bleak description:

On the whole, the situation in Moscow is more and more depressing. . . . Jaroslav Francevič [Papoušek][11] returned from Moscow full of dark pessimism. Sonja [Jakobson's wife] yesterday received a letter from her family—things are bleak: some have died, some are ill, some were kicked out of jobs, some were arrested. (Jakobson to Durnovo, November 19, 1924; from Toman 1994)

Would he return to the Soviet Union? Certainly not:

At work: a request came again from Moscow to remove me; P[apoušek?] reports the same. Antonov[12] is resisting, but this cannot go on forever. I will not go to Russia; if things do not succeed here, one will have to go to the garden and bite into the sour apple, as the English say. (ibid.)

But even in this fundamental matter of the return, Jakobson remained indecisive for a long time. In 1927 he disclosed to Durnovo that he had a plan to return to the USSR with his friend Bogatyrev if a professorial position were to materialize (to Durnovo, February 4, 1927; Toman 1994).

Steps toward Phonology—*The Foundations of Czech Verse*

The first longer work Jakobson published in Prague was his study of Xlebnikov (Jakobson 1921a); a booklet on Czech verse followed two years later (Jakobson 1923a). The style of these books was raw. Trubetzkoy was shocked at the organization of the Xlebnikov study (Jakobson 1975: 17). The book on Czech verse lacked a table of contents, chapter titles, and section heads; only in the later Czech translation from the original Russian (Jakobson 1926a) was the text divided into chapters.

But deficiencies of presentation and style should not detract from the fact that, in his early days in Prague, Jakobson was engaged in important work. Not only does the study on Czech verse contain a number of observations relevant to Czech versology; it also represents Jakobson's first steps toward structuralist phonology. In fact, Jakobson calls his approach to the Czech verse, and to poetic language, "phonological," thus reminding the modern reader that the first treatise from the Prague ambience that invoked phonological perspective was written several years before the emergence of the Circle. Jakobson was developing phonology—a hallmark of Prague linguistics—singlehanded, outside any group and without any substantial participation by Trubetzkoy or Mathesius. The conceptual influences that can be found in the book stem mostly from the Geneva linguists Sechehaye and Bally, while further elements point to work done in OPOJAZ and the Moscow Linguistic Circle. The overall topic of Jakobson's *Czech Verse* is versology, a theme clearly relating to his Russian years. The point of departure was whether Czech poetry could adequately follow the meter of the classical chronometric systems, based on Greek and Latin, or whether a syllabotonic interpretation of classical patterns was more natural. That controversy was historical in nature and was no longer acute in the 1920s; however, much of the book was shaped by Jakobson's actual exposure to Czech, in both its poetic and its everyday modes. Throughout the book he reports his subjective reactions to the sound properties of Czech:

... normal Czech speech, because I was unfamiliar with it, gave me the impression of a sermon intended to convince one of something at all cost, to hammer something into one's head. . . . Because of the high number of quantitative pauses, the speech of Prague women made the impression of lamentation and whining on me—as if they were lamenting—and several other Russians whom I asked. . . . Incidentally, melodic patterns of Czech also leave an emotional impression in a Russian. . . . Czech emotive speech differs from its equivalent in Russian so profoundly that a Russian who is not familiar with it perceives it, both on stage and in practical life, as something artificial, mannered, if not pathological. (Jakobson 1923a [1969: 40f.])

Differential observations such as these are characteristic of the relativism that was discussed in chapter 2 above. They exploit reactions that are natural from the point of view of an external observer, whereas they are "false" from the point of view of the speaker whose language is observed. This effect fascinated a number of contemporary scholars who made it a prime element in early structuralist analyses. For instance, in one of his contributions to the OPOJAZ collections, Jakubinskij also focused on reactions to foreign languages or to nonlinguistic material (Jakubinskij 1916: 21).

Although one can clearly see that Jakobson was aware of this phenomenon, ways of exploiting this insight in concrete analytic work were by no means obvious. In order to explain the difference between native and non-native judgments, he made use of Sechehaye's distinction between "grammatical" and "extragrammatical" elements (Sechehaye 1908), arguing that the definition of what is grammatical and what is extragrammatical was language-specific, hence relative, hence not a matter of linguistic substance. A specific sound property may function as a grammatical element in one language while being perceived as "extragrammatical" in another—grammatical sound properties of Czech may count as extragrammatical in Russian.

At this point Jakobson assumed, like Sechehaye, that grammatical elements constitute an organized system in a given language. But he also attempted to translate the dichotomy grammatical/extragrammatical to more specific notions, namely phonological/nonphonological:

Alongside the sound phenomena that enter the phonological system of a given language, i.e., alongside the signifying elements whose replacement may result in a change of meaning, every language has a number of "non-signifying," i.e., extragrammatical, elements. (Jakobson 1923a [1969: 37])

The question Jakobson now raised was whether the extragrammatical domain can also be organized, and, if so, in what way. He argued that the answer is in the positive and that the principles of poetic language must be listed among the organizing principles of the extragrammatical domain. In other words, the idea was that the extragrammatical domain was free to be structured by poetic language.

A similar line of argument was used for the analysis of emotive language. The result was the same: the denial of the idea of intrinsic emotivity. Jakobson emphasized that it was not possible to define extragrammatical factors by means of a substantive definition, i.e., without knowing what the grammatical factors of the given language were. The relation between grammatical and extragrammatical was not a matter of substance:

The exploitation of extragrammatical elements by emotives is not determined by some natural expressivity, occasionally ascribed to these elements

in the literature, but by the fact that these elements are not exploited phonologically in the language under consideration. Thus extragrammatical elements—just like a phonological system—have a local, national or
traditional character and their range is determined by the phonological
frame of the given language. This is the reason of why a foreigner typically
interprets phonological elements of a foreign language as expressive means
and the expressive ones as phonological. (Jakobson 1923a [1969: 40])

Thus, a purely relational, or "structural," concept of sound structure
is asserted in Jakobson's book on Czech verse—phonology is a matter of form, not substance.

Considerations of this kind place Jakobson into proximity with Edward Sapir's (1925) often-quoted study "The Sound Patterns of Language." Although Sapir did not deal with emotivity, a topic popular
among French and Russian linguists, he took a strictly nonessentialist
position. In his view, two languages may possess identical sound substance yet show different phonological patterns and, vice versa, the
same phonological pattern may be executed in a different sound
substance in different languages—pattern formation is all that matters. Naturally, this all sounds very Saussurean; however, one would
be ill-advised to try to establish a direct link—the overall frame of
reference is a tendency toward a "desubstantivization," a search for
organizing principles, so clearly visible in the philosophy of the turn
of the century (see, for example, Ernst Cassirer's 1910 book *Substanz-
und Funktionsbegriff*).

The factual value of Jakobson's analyses of Czech might be disputed in details, yet the overall approach represented an important
step forward. Turning to conceptual borrowings from the early Geneva doctrine, especially Sechehaye, we also note that Jakobson explicitly acknowledges the idea of the phonological system:

By phonological system I understand the same thing as modern French linguists, namely *une collection d'idées de sons* (see, for instance, Sechehaye, Programme et Méthodes de la Linguistique théorique, Paris 1908: 151).
(Jakobson 1923a [1969: 21, n. 24])[13]

The Czech edition of 1926 further expands on this idea:

A phonological system is a set of all the sound images that are capable of
associating with distinctions in meaning in a given language. Phonology is a

discipline of articulatory actions seen from the point of view of their tasks. (Jakobson 1926a: 122, n. 15) [14]

The added assertion that phonology deals with articulatory gestures in view of their task reveals the increasing emphasis on the conception of language as a tool—as we shall see in the next section, the mid-1920s were characterized by interest in goals, tasks, tools, functions, and the like.

In view of future developments we note, however, that although the idea of the system is acknowledged and exploited in *Czech Verse,* a full-fledged theory of sound structure is still far away. Jakobson says little about the structure of phonological systems (notions such as phonological correlation are not discussed yet). The only important exception is this generalization:

. . . a language with a phonologically functioning dynamic accent permits of a change of distinctions in both quantity and tone, i.e., extragrammatical elements, but does not permit of changes in patterns of expiration. A language with a musical accent functioning phonologically does not permit of metatony within the boundary of a word. (Jakobson 1923a [1969: 44f.])

This passage points to a more sophisticated understanding of the concept of structure in that it introduces a restrictive condition stated in the form of a conditional. From this point on in the history of structural phonology, sound structure cannot consist of an arbitrary set of elements. It can be argued that this figure of thought continues Jakobson's Futurism article, where Stumpf's law of interdependence between form and color was discussed in similar terms.

The Concept of Language in the *Pásmo* Essay

While *Czech Verse* is a major work giving insight into pre-Circle phonology, there are also minor yet by no means insignificant texts from the pre-Circle period in which Jakobson expounds his ideas about the nature of language. I shall concentrate here on a little-known essay that appeared in the Czech avant-garde magazine *Pásmo* [*The Zone*] in 1925. The forum demonstrates that scholarly discussion of new trends was still underdeveloped in Czechoslovakia and that poets and artists were perhaps more curious than professors. The date of publication is equally interesting. The article appeared in May 1925, and the informal pre-Circle meetings at Mathesius's home had begun in March.

The general topic of the article is the state of contemporary Czech poetry, but in order to analyze this area Jakobson has to expound some elements of his linguistic theories. First, the nineteenth century gets some bashing—something that will later become a rule:

In studying the phenomena of language, the linguistics of the second half of the last century asked the question "How did they come about?" and largely ignored the question "What were they for?" But elementary language consciousness asks the question about problems, about goals. I am listening to someone speak and I ask "What are you telling me this for?" and the speaker can answer "If I speak, then I know what for." This "what for" of every act of speech, its task, is clear to the speaker as well as to the listener, as long as the one can understand the other. Language, according to the apt definition of contemporary French linguists, is a system of conventional values, just like a deck of cards, and therefore it is an error to give an analysis of language without regard for the multitude of possible tasks outside of which no such system actually exists. (Jakobson 1925a: 1)

The central category in this passage is that of "task." For Jakobson, task is *the* constructive factor in language: the system of language does not exist independent of purpose, or function. In fact, he goes so far as to say that a general notion of language does not exist— there are only specific functions and specific functional dialects:

A concept of language as such is a fiction. Just as there do not exist laws of a general card game equally applicable for blackjack, poker, and for building a house of cards, so, likewise, linguistic laws can be established only for a system determined by a specific task. (ibid.)

And, again, the second part of the nineteenth century is exposed as the dark age of linguistics that did not realize this fundamental fact:

The nineteenth century scholarship was not concerned with these things; sporadic attempts to take language function into consideration turned out to be unhelpful inasmuch as the multitude of functions was artificially restricted to one. But today we know: communicative language with its orientation toward the object of the utterance and poetic language with its orientation toward the expression itself represent two different, in many respects opposed, language systems. . . . (ibid.)

The rest of the passage indicates interest in the study of functions, clearly in continuation of the Moscow Linguistic Circle and OPOJAZ.

The idea of functional languages and the idea of verbal creation as a task-oriented activity recur at a number of places in the *Pásmo* essay. Jakobson views modern Czech poets as consciously working on a big linguistic task: creating the modern Czech poetic language. This is essentially an assignment, something to be worked on in an organized manner. The essay was also an exercise in militant rhetoric, in some ways resembling Jakobson's revolutionary "Tasks of Artistic Propaganda" (1919b). The place of publication was certainly fitting—the avant-garde in art and the avant-garde in scholarship shared the rhetoric with which the past was aggressively denounced and new goals projected.

5.2 The Legacy of Realism and Mathesius's Activism in the Early 1920s

While Jakobson might have experienced a conflict resulting from his two images, the scholar and the radical, Mathesius was in some sense also in an unclear position: that of an organizer who was still miles away from his goal.

With the emergence of the new state in October 1918, higher education and university based research in Czechoslovakia changed considerably. In Prague, Charles University became purely Czech; its German section was superseded by an independent German University, which existed in Prague until 1945. In addition, two new universities were founded in 1919—one in Brno [15] and one in Bratislava. An important moment in the new development was the presence of a set of ideas revolving around the role that scholars and scholarship were to play in the new state. Much of this cultural ideology had been envisioned in Masaryk's doctrine of Realism, discussed in the preceding chapter. Recall that Realism was not only a point of reference as regards the analytic dimension of research but also, and primarily, an overall cultural vision that also included what might be called the culture of scholarship.

The socio-cultural component of Realism appears somewhat vague today, partly because of Masaryk's emphasis on very general educational and moral ideas and partly because Masaryk merely wanted to establish a framework for national revival without giving specific directions for putting his views into practice. Nonetheless, the nucleus of Masaryk's thoughts can easily be reconstructed. In *Česká otázka* [*The Czech Question*] he sketched Realism as follows:

Our primary concern is how to extend and deepen literary, scientific and philosophical education. This is the main task for all thinking minds. Owing to its anti-historicism, Realism pays more attention than the past to the extension of our scientific education in the area of natural and, in particular, social sciences. This kind of education, with the exception of historiography and language and literary studies, has not yet become a property of the nation. . . . Realism is an attempt to render the whole of science and philosophy the property of the nation, without ignoring the standards of scientific rigor. Realism wants to make science available to all levels of the nation; it is a protest against the monopoly of education, an attempt to socialize scientific and philosophical education. (Masaryk 1895 [1908: 142f.])

There is no plan for a program of a political party within the framework of which the roles of education and science would be defined— it is the other way around. As Masaryk often asserted, reforms in political life should be consequences of the deepening and democratization of general education. The frame of reference naturally included the idea of progress, manifesting itself in (among other things) a consistent and systematic application of the discoveries of modern science to all areas of everyday political life.

At the beginning of the 1920s Masaryk's intellectual disciples tried to put into practice projects for which Masaryk had set an example 30 years earlier. In 1920, Mathesius and Emanuel Rádl founded *Nové Athenaeum* [*New Athenaeum*], a journal intended to carry on where Masaryk's *Athenaeum* (1883–1893) had left off. Like Mathesius, Rádl, a biologist with strong philosophical interests, followed the direction that Masaryk had embarked upon. For Rádl there were no doubts that the future of the Czech state depended on the introduction of scientific thought into its public life. In a lecture on the tasks of philosophy in the new state (Rádl 1922), he stated that philosophy should be able to establish principles of open, rational, and objective criticism in public life. These principles—and not nationalism— ought to be the main force behind the new state. Pronouncements such as these were characteristic of the early 1920s, critically reminding the Czech society of its pragmatism and its lack of interest in theory. At the same time, the ideals that were invoked were clearly rationalistic, and wholly compatible with those of the scientistic enlightenment of the nineteenth century. Science was the discovery of truth, and the general public was directed to share it.

This encompassing function of Realism represented a guiding point of orientation for Vilém Mathesius, for whom, moreover, the idealistic and moralistic elements in Realism must have been inherently attractive. It would almost appear as if the founding of the Prague Linguistic Circle had been a well-conceived attempt on his part to organize a specific segment of Czech scholarly life and thus to implement Masaryk's program in the area of research and education.

Mathesius himself was certainly captivated by the élan of the period immediately after 1918. He took on the activism and optimism of the younger generation:

As seems to be clear from the discussion about the state of Czech science, the younger generation has more optimism and more courage. I sympathize with their optimism and believe that a better organization of academic life will release a great deal of energy from which our national culture will benefit and which will prove to be strong enough in international competition. (Mathesius 1920: 6)

This enthusiasm represented something of a change. In 1914 Mathesius published a somewhat pessimistic analysis entitled "On Some Deeper Causes of Our Present Situation" in which he sharply criticized not only the state of Czech cultural and academic life but also what he would later call "intellectual culture" [myšlenková kultura]. He was of the opinion that Czech intellectual culture had not yielded any lasting results, and that Czech cultural traditions were disbalanced and had no continuity, changing abruptly from generation to generation. A cult of unconsidered immature activism ruled. Public life was dominated by commonplaces elevated to political logans instead of by planned action. All in all, there was a lack of English common sense.

This kind of criticism, which shows clear correspondences to Masaryk's Realism, was intensely pursued by Mathesius after World War

I. Now there was a real opportunity to draw practical consequences from earlier analyses. In a number of essays and articles in journals written in the early 1920s, Mathesius expressed his views on the situation in science and scholarship and related problems. Some of these essays appeared in the collection *Cultural Activism—English Parallels to Czech Life* (Mathesius 1925a).[16] The collection was attentively received, but the essay "Czech Science" (Mathesius 1925b) attracted particular attention.[17] Written in the mid-1920s, "Czech Science" is no longer concerned with general considerations; the discussion is now much more pragmatic, more analytical and, more disillusioned than ever before. Mathesius deplores the lack of creativity and the mediocre output of Czech science and comes to the conclusion that this sterility has not been greatly affected by any university reform. He goes so far as to give the following devastating characterization of Czech academic life:

If we look at the last 120 years of Czech cultural development . . . we almost get the feeling that the entire development of the Czech scientific tradition has not brought with it an adequate increase in scientific creativity. (Mathesius 1925b: 87)

In the independent state, Mathesius maintained, Czech science had become even more isolated than it had been before the war; Czech scholars were now left too much to their own company and would publish little in major languages, including German.[18] But most of all he regrets the complete absence of an atmosphere conducive to "scientific courage." He speaks of "ultrapositivism," narrow-mindedness, and general pettiness:

The Czech scientific climate suffers above all from excessive skepticism. The Slavic tendency toward negative criticism has merged with positivistic narrow-mindedness. It is not the positivistic approach, a necessary condition in scientific study, which is at fault, but the positivistic fear of a daring idea or an untried path, a positivistic fixation with singular facts which lacks any attempt to unify these within a larger conception in order to arrive at genuine insights. (Mathesius 1925b: 89)

In a remarkable passage that anticipates the Kuhnian notion of "normal science," Mathesius conveys the impression that for Czech scholars science does not represent search for knowledge, but "task-solving according to given rules in return for grades and awards for the neatness and orderliness with which they are carried out" (ibid.: 90). He repeatedly emphasizes that scientific activity is a pioneering task, based on personal courage, but that "it is precisely this kind of courage that is lacking in our academic life" (ibid.: 88).

Clearly, seven years after the inception of the new state, Mathesius was in a state of disillusion.[19] Yet with all that we know of his frame of mind, we would not expect him to have been passive. In view of the existing lack of initiative, he sketched the following solution:

This is not a state about which nothing can be done. True, we do not show a great deal of individual courage. Our courage is based in organizations. . . . Even if individual courage is not one of our gifts, or has not had any tradition, this does not mean that it cannot be replaced in science and elsewhere by fostering an adequate climate or by our courage to organize. (Mathesius 1925b: 89)

In retrospect, thoughts leading to the formation of the Prague Linguistic Circle can be recognized here. Yet the concept that is supposed to be the driving force of Czech science is perhaps unexpected: collectivism. Although not unknown before the war (Masaryk, and Mathesius also, campaigned against the romantic individualism that they believed to be typical of the Slavs), the force with which this guiding image was asserting itself was new.

6

A Republic of Scholars: Cross-Cultural Integration in Interwar Prague

There is an old image of Prague in which the city figures as an urbane center of culture and learning. This is the Prague of Charles the Fourth, Prague the promised land of medieval Jewry that Roman Jakobson and Morris Halle wrote about, the Prague of the Hapsburg emperor Rudolph the Second, the Czech-German-Jewish Prague of circa 1900. With Masaryk's Prague, liberal and integrating, one more instance of this image of ethnic symbiosis and intellectual tolerance was added. The Linguistic Circle was a product of this unusually rich era and a reminder that symbiosis proceeds best with artists and scholars.

In this chapter I shall review some aspects of Prague's multicultural academia after 1918 and, with the founding of the Linguistic Circle in sight, examine what intellectual resources were at Mathesius's disposal. I shall also introduce the future members of the Circle, both as independent scholars and in terms of their compatibility with the Circle. With this scheme of presentation, strict chronology may occasionally be abrogated, and brief portraits may extend well beyond the interwar period. Technical as these portraits may appear, they are important for a detailed understanding of the genesis and the functioning of the Circle.[1]

6.1 Russian and Ukrainian Prague

Institutions

Scholars and Students

It was only a matter of coincidence that the new state, and its intellectual life, would not become the exclusive domain of the Czechs and the Slovaks. Soon after 1918 Prague (and Czechoslovakia), for the first time, turned into an important center of East European emigration. The extent of the support offered by the Czechoslovak government to Russian and Ukrainian émigrés is unique in the history of emigration from the Soviet Union. Czechoslovakia offered government-sponsored institutions and grants for individual academic and literary figures, which would enable, in turn, the publication not only of a number of important literary reviews, but also of academic writing in Russian and Ukrainian. In all these matters, the personal initiative of T. G. Masaryk stands out.

Some knowledge of the Russian emigration seems particularly important to the present study, since this emigration involved many members of the academic intelligentsia and produced scholarly institutions which formed a pool of potential participants in Czech academic life. A Russian émigré wrote in the *Prager Presse* in September 1924:

Of all the Russian academic centers abroad, Prague is today the leading one. This is amply illustrated by the number of Russian professors (94) and students (3,500), by their schools and scholarly performance, by the administration of their pedagogical activities, and, finally, by the existence of their own academic press. Prague's unique position within the Russian scholarly community abroad is widely recognized—a report by a Russian professor has recently called the city "a Russian Oxford." (Michailovskij 1924, pt. 1) [2]

Among the most important of the academic institutions that soon formed was the Russian National University, active from 1923 until the end of the Second World War. In the area of research, the Kondakov Institute, which pursued Old Russian art history and Byzantinology, was noteworthy. The Russian Historical Archives Abroad housed the most extensive collection in the West of documents pertaining to the years of revolution and civil war. The Russian Law School, under the formal auspices of Charles University, set forth to educate and prepare lawyers for the time when Russia would again be a "legal state." (However, by the end of the 1930s the law school's graduates still had no chance to work in their field; see Novikov 1938: 49.)

Most of these institutions reached peaks of activity in the 1920s and began facing difficulties in the 1930s. None survived 1945. The Ukrainian Pedagogical Institute was closed in the early 1930s. The fate of the Russian Historical Archives was sealed after the Second World War—the collection was ceded to Soviet authorities in 1945, officially as an expression of Czechoslovak gratitude toward the Soviet Union. But, despite the fact that in the 1930s émigré cultural activities were slowing down, there still was much to report. Alluding to the Prague Dostoevskij Society (see below), the Russian poet and critic Vladimir Xodasevič wrote in 1934 that Paris unjustly claimed cultural priority of the émigré cultural life, while serious work was actually being done outside Paris—particularly in Prague.[3]

In view of what we know about the Russian propensity for academic societies, it is by no means surprising that a number of émigré circles and societies sprang up. For example, a Philosophical Society was active under the aegis of the Russian National University from 1925 on.[4] The society was primarily the home of Russian philosophers J. J. Lapšin, S. J. Hessen (Gessen), and N. O. Losskij, then all in Prague. Younger scholars, some of them later members of the Prague Linguistic Circle (D. Čyževśkyj, P. N. Savickij, and S. Karcevskij), participated in this society too (Karcevskij lectured on the "Nature of the Word" on May 18, 1926). The list of lectures given before the society (Čyževśkyj 1927) indicates interest in the theory of knowledge and also in the philosophy of Edmund Husserl. Boris Jakovenko, mentioned above as a propagator of Husserl's phenomenology in pre-revolutionary Russia, was also active in this society.

The Ukrainian emigration also developed a great number of very active institutions. Among them were the Ukrainian Free University (in Prague), the Ukrainian pedagogical Drahomanov Institute (in Prague, from 1923), the Ukrainian Sociological Institute (in Prague, from 1925), the Ukrainian historical-philological Society (in Prague, from 1923), and the Ukrainian Commerce Academy (in Poděbrady). Ukrainian archives and museums were also organized.

Meeting Places
Since institutions engaged in instruction were naturally oriented toward the émigré population, we assume that there was little interaction between the émigrés and the Czechs in such places, and that the main foci of exchange were scholarly societies. One such society was the Dostoevskij Society, founded in 1930.[5] The activity of this society is firmly associated with Al'fred Ljudvigovič Bem, a Russian

literary historian and also a member of the Circle (see below). The history of this society is of some interest as it is an example of a group that attempted to transcend the émigré ambience. Established by Bem as a purely Russian circle in 1925, the society made a step out of the Russian environment after several years and was officially established in March 1930 with ostensive support of prominent Czech intellectuals. Besides Otokar Fischer, also a member of the Circle, the membership list of the founding committee reveals an intriguing mix of names, including Max Brod, a Prague Jewish author; Emil Filla, a Czech modernist painter; Gerhard Gesemann, a Slavist from the German University; Zdeněk Nejedlý, a Czech Russophile and professor; J. Hromádka, a Protestant theologian; Vasil Škrach, Masaryk's personal secretary; Anna Tesková, a translator from Russian and a friend of Marina Cvetaeva(see Makin 1993), and many others. The activities of the society were, however, of a relatively short duration. The Dostoevskij theme may have been of limited interest for the broader academic community.

A review of contemporary documents also reveals moments of disappointment that Russian and Ukrainian émigrés experienced in Czechoslovakia. Clearly, they found themselves in a very different culture in which appeals to Slavic brotherhood were often of little use. M. Novikov addressed the issue in his later reminiscences, noting occasional reservation on the part of the Czechs toward the Russians. The attitude, in his words, derived from "the differences in character and Weltanschauung of the two nations" (Novikov 1957: 250). Although the details of the new symbiosis remain to be described, one may conclude that the integration into the new environment was slow. In view of this, the Dostoevskij Society and the Linguistic Circle represented the two major integrative instruments little concerned with problems resulting from differences in worldview. The degree of integration in the Circle is particularly remarkable since not all Russians and Ukrainians in Prague were émigrés in the usual sense of the word: the status of Jakobson and Bogatyrev, to name two, was ambiguous. Jakobson was an employee of the Soviet diplomatic representation in Prague until 1928, and Bogatyrev lived in Czechoslovakia with the official consent of Soviet authorities. (He returned to the Soviet Union in 1940.) Also Durnovo traveled to Czechoslovakia officially. On the other hand, scholars such as Sergej Karcevskij, Dmitrij Čyževśkyj, Alfred Ljudvigovič Bem, Lenontij Vasilevič Kopeckij, Petr Nikolaevič Savickij, and Agenor Artymovič were closely associated with émigré institutions and were vocal critics of the Soviet state. That all these scholars— and local Czechs and Germans—were able to work together in the Circle represents a remarkable accomplishment which was not replicated by any of the remaining academic institutions of the period.

The Contribution of the East

The scholars from the Russo-Ukrainian community played a prominent role in the work of the Circle—Jakobson, Bogatyrev, and Karcevskij were present right from its beginnings. But the Circle gradually attracted other East European scholars as well. The following subsections survey the backgrounds of those who were most active, showing in what sense they represented an intellectual asset for the Circle's activity.

Sergej Karcevskij

One of the most important members of the early Circle was Sergej Karcevskij. I have already pointed out his role as a mediator between Geneva and Moscow, noting in particular that after his return from Switzerland in 1917 he introduced Saussure to Moscow linguists.

Born in Tobolsk, Siberia, in 1884, Sergej Karcevskij[6] left Russia after the revolution of 1905, emigrating to Geneva, then an important center of Russian political emigration. As his enrollment record shows, he was a student of French language and literature at the University of Geneva from the summer of 1909 until early 1915.[7] From the summer term of 1913 on, he mainly took courses with Charles Bally. The record further indicates that he also took one course with Saussure, namely Sanskrit, in the winter term of 1911– 12. Although his participation in Saussure's lectures on general linguistics is not documented, Karcevskij, counted Saussure among his mentors: "The formation of my linguistic ideas was strongly influenced by lectures and works of my teachers, F. de Saussure, Ch. Bally, as well as by A. Meillet." (Karcevskij 1924: 48) His loyalty to his Genevan teacher is also documented by a number of references; for instance, a motto from Saussure introduces Karcevskij's article on the Russian verb (1923b).

In 1920 Karcevskij emigrated again, this time for good. He first taught at the University of Strassburg, but in 1922 he moved to Prague, where he was appointed to the Russian Pedagogical Institute. Here he edited together with S. J. Gessen (Hessen) and V. A. Rigan the pedagogical journal *Naša škola za rubežom* [*Our School Abroad*]. Like Bally, Karcevskij was interested in pedagogical work, and Prague, then a center of Russian pedagogical organizations, provided a conducive environment. Importantly, *Our School Abroad* preserved a number of contributions by Karcevskij which, although mostly reviews, give a rather clear picture of his linguistic thinking, thus providing information about ideas he contributed to the formation of the Circle's doctrine.

Karcevskij's earliest publications in *Our School Abroad* document his efforts to pursue Genevan themes further. Intonation, the logical and emotive nature of language, and constituent structure *(syntagmatique)* are the topics in which he was most interested. These interests make him appear a close follower of Charles Bally. His reviews and polemics relate in part to the so-called Formal-Grammatical Movement, a current in Russian syntax and language instruction that became especially visible in the early 1920s. These Formal-Grammatical debates (which have no relation to Formalism in poetics) reflect the impact of the Russian grammarian A. M. Peškovskij on Russian linguistics and on the teaching of Russian in schools. Karcevskij recognized Peškovskij's merits, but regarded the current applications of his system in school grammars written by the Formal Grammarians as an unacceptable vulgarization. Criticizing the Formal Grammarians for what he thought was a mechanical approach to language, a disregard for language as a functioning system, and an identification of synchrony with staticity (immovability, *nepodvižnost'*), he noted:

. . . one can see, particularly in Peterson's case, that before approaching the living language, a formalist has to put it to death; he is able to handle only a language that is dead, easy to chop into pieces. (Karcevskij 1924: 61)

In another discussion of the Formal Grammarians he wrote:

The point thus is that a static analysis of language does not mean cutting the tissue of language mechanically into dead pieces. Language is a functioning mechanism and it is necessary to study particularly its functioning, and only under this aspect is it possible to select from it particular elements, or more precisely, parts of the mechanism. (Karcevskij 1923c: 194)

In general, Karcevskij appears to be a dissident from the Saussurean canon. He entertains a preference for processual aspects—for language seen from the perspective of "functioning," "tension solving," and the like. Thus, he makes a distinction between the emotive and intellectual functions of language and argues that the two functions are in a conflict that resolves itself permanently. This is a perspective that became associated with the Prague doctrine. Since Karcevskij's formulations are among the earliest of this kind, it seems logical to conclude that he was instrumental in developing this approach.

In summary, Karcevskij emerges as one of the most experienced and theoretically minded linguists in Prague in the early 1920s. He was familiar with devices of grammatical analysis on a level that, perhaps with the exception of Mathesius, was not achieved by any of the "candidates" of the Circle at that time. He also had an interest in syntactic problems, a field that was not absorbed by the Prague doctrine in any significant degree.

Karcevskij moved back to Geneva in 1927, i.e., after the first year of the Circle's activity. He published in the Circle's publications, but, obviously, his personal engagement in the Circle could no longer be so intensive.

Petr Bogatyrev

The Russian folklorist Petr Grigorjevič Bogatyrev (b. 1893, Saratov; d. 1971, Moscow) came to Prague in 1921, apparently at the suggestion of Jakobson, a close friend from his student days. I have no information about his educational background, but his participation in the Moscow Commission for Dialectology and the Moscow Linguistic Circle is well attested. In Czechoslovakia, he was first active as an archives researcher for the Soviet authorities and later was appointed to the University of Bratislava, where he obtained his habilitation in 1930. Bogatyrev was among the earliest members of the Circle; he began to participate in its meetings as early as December 1926.[8] In 1940 he returned to the Soviet Union, where his adherence to structuralism, especially after attacks denouncing him as a bourgeois ethnologist in the late 1940s,[9] made his position rather precarious for years to come. Rehabilitation came in the late 1950s.[10]

Bogatyrev's bibliography contains more than 300 titles, the bulk stemming from his Czechoslovak period. Surveying his titles from between 1915 and the early 1920s, and thinking about him as a future member of the Circle, one is not likely to foresee a future theoretician of structural ethnography. This is so because many writings up until the late 1920s contain very little in terms of an explicit theoretical discussion, but, rather, show an emphasis on methods of collecting and presenting data. For instance, in a review article (Bogatyrev 1916), which also addresses a study by V. F. Čiž entitled "The Psychology of Village *častuška*," Bogatyrev has no argument with the apparently psychologistic approach of the author, but shows a concern for detailed and accurate registration of ethnographical data. This approach is also exemplified by his (and Jakobson's) project to design a questionnaire for the collection of data on folk theatre (Bogatyrev 1923: 91–121). In all these respects, Bogatyrev's scholarly style reveals the style of his Moscow education.[11]

The fact that Bogatyrev's early studies make somewhat plain reading does not, however, mean that no methodologically interesting premises are implied. For Bogatyrev, there are no unworthy, "low" data; to use later terminology common to Bogatyrev and Jakobson, there is no gesunkenes Kulturgut. Contemporary folklore represents a legitimate, in fact preferable, object of inquiry. Bogatyrev, for example, advocated the study of folk narratives inspired by the World War and demands more recording of such material:

This would give us an opportunity to examine how quickly oral narratives spread in Russia in *our time* and how old legends surface in the memory and assimilate to *present* events. (Bogatyrev 1916: 341; emphasis added)

It would be hard to find themes more typical of Bogatyrev than those just quoted: city folklore, the ongoing transformation of patterns in

A Republic of Scholars

popular narrative, and the process of exchange between the past and the present and between "high" and "low" culture.

While in Czechoslovakia, Bogatyrev entertained friendly scholarly contact with Czech folklorists—among them Jiří Polívka, the specialist in Slavic folklore mentioned above. A fragment of their correspondence published by Kolár (1972) documents Bogatyrev's continued interest in field work, especially his trips to the Carpatho-Ukraine, then within Czechoslovak territory. We see here that he engaged in "total" field work, at the same time amassing data on oral culture, material objects (such as embroidery), and dialects. Thus, he comments on details of pronunciation and tries to relate dialect boundaries to the boundaries of ethnic regions.

In the mid 1920s, references to Saussure start to appear in Bogatyrev's writings. Having compiled an extensive documentation on the belief in supernatural beings in Carpatho-Ukraine, he remarks that this "living material" makes it possible to undertake a synchronic study of superstitions. And as for the synchronic method in linguistics, he explicitly qualifies it as "susceptible of being extended to folklore" (Bogatyrev 1926: 54). In other words, his reference interprets Saussure's synchronic linguistics as an approach that has general applications in cultural studies (see also the introduction in Bogatyrev 1929).

Most of Bogatyrev's work that qualifies as structural-functional ethnology stems from the late 1920s and the 1930s. At this time, he also had intensive contacts with a number of Czech theatre artists belonging to the avant-garde left (E. F. Burian, J. Honzl), and his increased attention to problems of theatre, theatre semiotics, and the relationships between theatre and folklore ranks him among the instigators of a structuralist theory of theatre. This subfield, which began to emerge in the 1930s in the Prague Circle, is mainly represented in the work of Jan Mukařovský and Jiří Veltruský. After 1937, Bogatyrev was active at the University of Bratislava, where he had a number of disciples who pursued the type of ethnographical work he had introduced. Andrej Melicharčík was the most prominent among them.[12]

Bogatyrev returned to the Soviet Union from Slovakia in 1940. Among the work from the post-1940 period, relating to Czech and

Slovak matters, are a collection of Slovak fairy tales, a Russian-Czech dictionary, and a translation of Jaroslav Hašek's *Good Soldier Švejk* into Russian.

Dmytro Čyževśkyj

Born in 1896, the Ukrainian scholar Dmytro Čyževśkyj[13] considered himself a philosopher in the early years of his career, and his peers indeed mentioned him repeatedly in this capacity (Trubetzkoy 1936: 5; see also Toman 1992d). He escaped from Russia in 1921 and came to Prague from Freiburg im Breisgau, an old German university town, where he studied philosophy in the early 1920s. His appointment in Prague (1924–1932) was to the Ukrainian Pedagogical Institute where he taught among other things philosophy and logic. Furthermore, he was active in the Russian Philosophical Society in Prague, one of the numerous Russian circles that sprung up there in the early 1920s. Here, besides making a number of presentations, including a lecture on phenomenology (in 1926) and one on Kant as a logician (in 1927), he met not only with émigré Russian philosophers but also with S. Karcevskij. The fact that he taught logic is particularly interesting, and the way he went about it can be reconstructed in part from the course syllabus *L'ogika* (Čyževśkyj 1924), written in Ukrainian. The book, mimeographed from handwritten stencils, reflects his interest in general questions of methodology and the theory of knowledge. In the 1920s Čyževśkyj also published a number of articles and reviews concerned with problems of contemporary philosophy and with the Soviet philosophical scene.

Although Čyževśkyj lived in Prague from 1924 to 1932, there is no positive evidence of his direct participation in the early activities of the Circle. Nonetheless, he emerges as an important member of the Circle around 1930. His authority derived in all probability from a lecture aimed against psychologism in phonology that he gave on January 27, 1930, and later at the first phonological conference (Réunion phonologique), organized by the Circle in December 1930 (Čyževśkyj 1931). In this presentation Čyževśkyj maintained his role as a philosopher and spoke on general methodological questions, criticizing psychologistic approaches in linguistics strongly. Later, in a contribution to a festschrift for Vilém Mathesius (Čyževśkyj 1932), he pointed briefly but clearly to conceptual links between the evolving theory of markedness and certain ideas in the work of the Russian philosopher and grammarian Konstantin Sergeevič Aksakov, which were relevant in this connection (see Holenstein 1984). He was also one of the first philosophers to review the phenomenological work of the Czech philosopher Jan Patočka in the publications of the Circle (Čyževśkyj 1936).

Čyževśkyj was a specialist on Hegel, and the fact that he announced a book to be written with Roman Jakobson on the "Dialectic of Language" makes one believe that Jakobson hoped Čyževśkyj's philosophical expertise would make the investigation into the "dialectic of language" more than mere essayism. As we shall see below, the dialectical approach to language appeared rather suddenly in the writings of the Circle in the early 1930s and in many instances smacked of a somewhat superficial assimilation of current philosophical fashion. Čyževśkyj, in any case, studied problems of dialectic very critically on the basis of his commitment to Hegel, and, among other things, exposed the vulgarization of dialectic in official Soviet publications of that time (Čyževśkyj 1928, 1930).

Čyževśkyj left Prague in 1932, shortly before the Ukrainian Pedagogical Institute was dismantled. He went to the university of Halle, fleeing to the American zone of Germany in 1945. He was subsequently a professor of Slavistics at Marburg. After a stint at Harvard (1948–1956), he returned to Germany. He died in Heidelberg in 1977.

With Čyževśkyj we encounter a scholar who represented the Circle's link to philosophy. He also represents one of the East European émigrés who, although unambiguously rooted in his own culture, involved himself in Czech matters strongly as his numerous studies on Czech literature show. He truly immortalized himself in 1934 by discovering in Halle a manuscript of a major work by J. A. Comenius, a Czech philosopher of the Baroque era.

Nikolaj Durnovo

The Russian linguist Nikolaj Nikolaevič Durnovo, one of the organizers of the Moscow Commission for Dialectology, is usually not listed among the early members of the Prague Linguistic Circle; however, his impact on the Circle is detectable. Durnovo, born in Moscow on October 23 (November 4 O.S.), 1876, spent the years 1924–1928 in Czechoslovakia with a Czechoslovak study grant arranged by Jakobson for him,[14] working mainly in Brno, where he hoped to obtain a professorial position. None of the records available indicate that he lectured before the Circle or ever was a formal member, but he did participate in several meetings in 1926 and 1927, and he contributed to the Circle's Theses a section on the study of Old Church Slavonic. He returned to the Soviet Union in February 1928, where he was soon accused of participation in the so-called "Slavists' Plot," a completely fabricated anti-Soviet conspiracy allegedly directed from abroad. The accusations and the evidence against him included contacts with Jakobson and Trubetzkoy, possession of Trubetzkoy's publications, and a photograph in which he appears with Bogatyrev, Jakobson, and Trubetzkoy.[15] Clearly all these charges were arbitrary, but they amounted to damning evidence in the years of the Stalinist purges. Durnovo was first sentenced to five years, but then executed on October 27, 1937.[16]

In consonance with his fairly traditional background, Durnovo was initially not convinced of the merits of structural phonology. Publications from his Czechoslovak years show that he gradually accepted certain premises that characterized the new paradigm, such as the distinction between synchrony and diachrony (see Durnovo 1924: 3), although he stressed the importance, if not the priority, of historical and dialectological studies at the same time. Despite reservations, he converged with the Circle through his criticism of Saussure's conception of "fortuitous linguistic history":

I envisage [linguistic] evolution as a series of changes which, although seemingly affecting only individual linguistic facts, are inevitably connected with the entire linguistic system and have its motivation within this system. Thus history of language is not a discipline about separate individual changes in the language, but a discipline about the changes of the language as such, as a system. They are therefore no less an important part of the science of language than synchronic investigations because they are also concerned with language as a whole. (Durnovo 1927: vi)

This is a clear assertion of the idea—also evident in Jakobson's *Remarques*—according to which the history of language is a history of a system, i.e., a history of transformations of systems into systems. I do not believe that Durnovo initially attempted to execute this idea on an analytical level. Many of his writings from the Czech period leave the impression of meticulous data reviews with only little desire to proceed to conclusions worded in the manner of structuralist theories (e.g., phonology). This attitude is clearly visible in his review of Karcevskij's 1927 *Verbe Russe*. Although Durnovo concedes that this is a major study, he dislikes the introductory chapter, in which much of Geneva structuralism is expounded—this chapter, he says, is worded "dogmatically and very abstractly" (Durnovo 1931: 140).[17] However, his opinion changed later, and he actually did work out brief phonological analyses in Trubetzkoyan style after he returned to the Soviet Union. They were, however, published as late as 1975 in the appendixes to Jakobson 1975.

Other Russian and Ukrainian Scholars
The Russian and Ukrainian communities included a number of scholars whose participation in the Circle was perhaps not so prominent, yet whose presence formed an important element in the everyday work of the Circle: Savickij, Bem, Artymovič, Symovič, Kopeckij.

A good illustration of the cross-disciplinary cooperation that evolved in the ambience of the Circle is the work of the Ukrainian geographer Petr Nikolaevič Savickij. Although Savickij was neither a linguist nor a literary scholar, his contribution to the Circle was very important. Born in Černigov in 1895, Savickij emigrated in 1920 to Bulgaria, where he met N. S. Trubetzkoy and other so-called Eurasians. In 1922 he moved to Prague where he lived until his death on April 13, 1968 (excluding the years of his forced deportation to the USSR: 1945–1956).

Savickij's geographical theories cannot be dealt with adequately here, but the basic idea upon which Eurasianism and Savickij's "geosophy" rested is relatively simple. Eurasia, a territory more or less identical to that of Imperial Russia, was understood as an autonomous entity—neither a part of Europe nor a part of Asia. The reasons adduced for this position were geographical, climatological, historical, political, economical, and even linguistic. Savickij's central notion was that of *mestorazvitie*, a term intended to mean "a place of development." Eurasia was one such place of development—a macro-region in which a variety of entities, some genetically related and some unrelated, would enter a law-governed symbiosis. Significantly, Savickij attempted to deemphasize the agency of causal laws within such regions, replacing them with all sorts of rather ornamental considerations about symmetry of regions, soil structure, etc. In working on his Eurasian interpretation of Russia, Savickij found two very attentive listeners in N. S. Trubetzkoy and Roman Jakobson. His expertise in geography, history, and economy was highly esteemed, especially by the Russian members of the Circle, and contributed to his authority within the Eurasian Movement (of which he was practically the leader in the 1930s).[18]

The Circle also included a number of scholars whose background was quite diverse both in terms of education and age. They did not bring structuralist ideas to the Circle; rather, it seems, they accepted them while in the Circle. One of these scholars was Al'fred Ljudvigovič (Alexej Fedorovič) Bem, born on April 23, 1886, in Kiev, and unaccounted for since May 1945.[19] A literary scholar who taught Russian at Charles University from 1922 and received his doctoral degree from the German University in 1932, Bem was the driving personality behind the Prague Dostojevskij Society.

Bem's record in the Circle's activities begins in February 1928. One of his lectures bears the elaborate title "The Method of Detail Observations in Literary Science" (February 3, 1936), and some formulations from the summary indicate that, despite his primary interest in literary history, he accepted certain tenets of Structuralism:

A work of art has a closed unified structure toward which all its components gravitate. There is therefore nothing accidental in it: each component is motivated by the whole. (Bem 1936: 133)

On December 10, 1934, Bem participated in a discussion on methodological problems, objecting to what he perceived as a shift from structuralism to sociologism in Mukařovský's work:

. . . I cannot imagine the development of evolutionary dynamics without teleology: in what direction does all this dynamics aim? Yes, it is immanent to the literary domain, I completely agree, but I cannot understand evolution without goal. If we understand literary evolution teleologically, as unfolding progression toward a certain goal, not only as grouping and re-grouping of individual phenomena, we shall finally arrive at a direct evaluation, not a relative one as required by Mukařovský's method. (Bem 1935: 331)

The Ukrainian scholar Agenor Artymovič was a generation older than the core members of the Circle. Unfortunately, only scant information on his scholarship is available, although his participation in the Circle was important. Some details can be retrieved from Jakobson's obituary (which, however, may be more authentic as a source of scholarly criteria Jakobson himself propagated):

Just like the greatest representative of Ukrainian scholarly tradition, Potebnja, Artymovič fought against the narrow-minded, chauvinistic seclusion of domestic scholarship and insisted on close cooperation of modern Ukrainian scholarly work with the world of Russian, Slavic and international scholarship. . . . He was exposed to the strict Neogrammarian school, yet he was able to cast off the habits of psychologism and naturalism, not only superficially, but also in substance. (Jakobson 1936e: 63)

Artymovič gave several lectures, including two on the theory of written language [20] and one on the "Potentiality of language." [21] (The latter deals with Saussure's dichotomies and the relation between sounds and phonemes.)

Among the Ukrainian names we also find Vasyl Simovyč. He worked as a professor at the Pedagogical Drahomanov Institute, where he eventually became a rector. He was active in the Circle and remained a member after leaving Prague for Lemberg in the mid-1930s. [22]

Finally, mention should be made of Leontij Vasilevič Kopeckij. Kopeckij received his habilitation in 1930 and became a professor at the Commerce Academy in Prague in the same year. His early publications reflect some interest in the functional stratification of language, in particular as familiar from the Russian context (Vinokur, Vinogradov, Seliščev). Yet on the whole, Kopeckij is primarily representative of a pedagogy-oriented applied linguistics. [23] His main field was lexicology; his Russian-Czech dictionary became the basis of modern Czech-Russian lexicology and was used especially intensively after 1948.

In summary, the Russian and Ukrainian scholars—diverse by generation, presuppositions, and interests—represented by far the largest non-Czech contingent in the Circle. The Circle integrated them most easily and benefited from their scholarship most directly.

6.2 German Prague

Slavists at the German University

By no means did Czechoslovakia's achieving independence in 1918 imply the end of German cultural life in Prague. Although a part of the German speaking intelligentsia was attracted by German cultural centers outside Czechoslovakia (a process that actually began long before 1918), Prague remained a prominent locus of German academic life.

The Circle clearly benefited from this fact, establishing a good relationship with the Slavic Department of the German University.[24] The German Slavists, in turn, emulated the Circle. In December 1930, the Deutsche Gesellschaft für slavistische Forschung was founded at the German University. Among the goals of its five "circles" (!) was "to organize and carry out research projects which can only be approached *collectively*, i.e., in cooperation with researchers in other fields" (Frinta 1931: 474f.; emphasis in original). The language of this program converges with the Prague Linguistic Circle's rhetoric of collective work (see below) quite visibly.

Among the Prague German scholars who participated in the Linguistic Circle most actively were Eugen Rippl, Gustav Becking, and Friedrich Slotty. Rippl (b. 1888), initially an instructor in Czech at the German University, obtained his habilitation in 1929. He began to participate in the Circle's meetings as early as October 1928 and continued to be the most active German member until 1938. Becking,[25] a musicologist, gave several lectures at the Circle's meetings and greatly influenced Jakobson (see below). He does not seem to have attended many meetings otherwise; a language problem might have been the reason. Slotty, an Indo-Europeanist with a strong interest in Etruscan studies, held the chair in historical linguistics at the German University and published a number of articles in the publications of the Circle. He began to attend the Circle's meetings in December 1928.[26]

German scholars were not among the members of Mathesius's initial group (around 1925–26), nor had many of them pursued questions relating to Mathesius's or Jakobson's quest for a redefinition of linguistics and literary studies. Like a number of other scholars who participated in the Circle at a later point, they were gradually attracted to the Circle, although none of them could be even remotely regarded as a structuralist. Slotty, for instance, was traditionally educated and basically maintained this line, yet he was a very active member. Jakobson had to mobilize some of his rhetorical skills to define Slotty's scholarly profile when he wrote on the occasion of Slotty's fiftieth birthday: "Slotty casts away the tradition of Positivism; he remains, however, a strictly empirical scholar." (Jakobson 1931j) This evaluation resembles the obituary (quoted above) in which Jakobson underscored Artymovič's ability to transcend older linguistic views. Jakobson in any case highlighted Slotty's organizational work for the Circle with a remarkable wording that elevated organization of scholarly work to an element of a modern scholarly worldview: "It is characteristic of Slotty's scholarly Weltanschauung that he recognizes the topicality and importance of the international organization of collective scholarly work." (Jakobson 1931j) Among Slotty's functions in the Circle was the chairmanship of the bibliographical commission, one of the Circle's four commissions.

Jakobson and the German University

The Prague Linguistic Circle, and Roman Jakobson in particular, benefitted a great deal from contact with the Prague Germans. A particular source of fascination for Jakobson was Gustav Becking's work on rhythm, a subject which had brought Becking together with Eduard Sievers. With Gerhard Gesemann, another professor in the Slavic Department of the German University, Becking worked on folk songs from Montenegro (see Becking 1932). All these fields were also of interest to Jakobson (see, e.g., Jakobson 1925b), but the impact of Becking's lecture "Musikwissenschaft und Phonologie" stands out. Jakobson reported this lecture in the *Prager Presse* with a great deal of enthusiasm, counting it among the most important events of Prague scholarly life in recent years.[27] The lecture presented musicological evidence in support of the Sprachbund idea (see chapter 10 below).

When the prospect that Jakobson might receive a doctorate from Charles University diminished, the links with the German Slavists opened an opportunity for him to submit a thesis to the German University in 1930. As the title "On Comparative Study of Slavic Decasyllabic Verse" indicates, the thesis must have appealed to the German University's numerous specialists in Southern Slavic folklore.[28]

Jakobson, like Mathesius, received a great deal of stimulation from the earlier linguistic tradition at the Prague German University. In particular, Jakobson was among the few who frequently reminded his colleagues of the work of the Swiss philosopher of language Anton Marty, who taught at this university from 1885. Marty was among the early advocates of a strict division between "genetic" and "descriptive" approaches; the two categories are essentially synonyms for "diachronic" and "synchronic," respectively. Marty was also functionally inclined and had an impact on the philosophers Oskar Kraus and Ludwig Landgrebe, active in the Circle in the late 1930s, especially as regards questions of semantic analysis.[29]

The Circle and Rudolf Carnap

An interesting episode in the relations between the Prague Circle and the German University is the guest lecture of Rudolf Carnap, who taught in Prague between 1931 and 1935. The summary of Carnap's lecture, given on May 20, 1935, reads as follows:

R. Carnap: On Logical Syntax. Carnap summarized basic ideas of his book *Logische Syntax der Sprache,* gave a definition of the sentence, touched upon sign systems that operate with sentences and can therefore be defined as "languages." Among such languages are, besides "verbal languages," languages of formulae and the like. He treated laws according to which signs must be combined in order to yield a sentence which has a meaning; he also treated laws according to which a sentence can be derived from another sentence. He especially dwelled upon a special class of signs—connecting signs, the meaning of which can be determined through an immediate analysis of the form of their combination and through transformation. ([Carnap] 1935: 256) [30]

A report in the *Prager Presse* adds further details:

Under no circumstances does [Carnap's] "logical semasiology" aim at replacing the methods of modern linguistics. Its function is limited in that it wishes to help linguistics only in the study of the cognitive function [darstellende Funktion] of historically given languages. This was the question Professor Carnap directed at linguists. (–SS–[31] 1935)

Some of the topics Carnap treated might have appealed to the semiotic trend that was evolving in the Prague Circle in the 1930s, but, on the whole, the linguists were divided as far as Carnap's offer was concerned. The report in the *Prager Presse* notes that R. Jakobson, E. Otto, and R. Wellek reacted positively. A. Isačenko, Seidel, and some of the philosophers present (S. Hessen and O. Kraus) were negative.

There were basic differences between Carnap's position and that of the Prague Circle; the shared ground was limited, despite the positive reactions of some Circle members, and Carnap's ideas had little impact on the Circle. Later remarks by Mukařovský (1940) seem to confirm this assessment. Mukařovský takes pains to define a basic difference between his own conception of language and that of Carnap's, among other things criticizing Carnap's reduction of the multitude of language functions to one. He also objects that Carnap's theory has no application for the study of poetic language: where the aesthetic function dominates, the question of truth has no sense. Of course, in view of the fact that Carnap explicitly limited himself to the cognitive function, the force of this critique seems hard to maintain.

Jiří Veltruský (personal communication) has explained that Carnap was invited as a result of a controversy that arose in the 1930s between "Logism" and phenomenology—a controversy in which the Prague Circle took the Husserlian position.[32] The incongruity between Carnap and the Circle seems fairly natural for other reasons as well. Since Carnap's foremost task was to drive out metaphysics, it is hard to imagine how he would react to the Circle's proclivity for dialectics, particularly strong at the time of his lecture.[33]

Tensions

The nature of the participation of German scholars in the Prague Circle was changing. In the 1930s scholars who could no longer work at universities in Germany started to move to Prague, and some of them became professors at the German University. The Decennial Report (Circle 1936) lists two scholars who moved to Prague from Germany: Ludwig Landgrebe[34] and Emil Utitz.[35] Landgrebe had to leave Halle, Utitz Rostock. In all, the Decennial Report lists eight scholars who were in one way or another associated with the German University: Becking, Landgrebe, Rippl, Ružičić,[36] Savickij,[37] Slotty, Utitz, and the philosopher Oskar Kraus.[38]

Political developments in Germany in the 1930s gradually affected German scholars in Czechoslovakia and had a certain impact on the Circle as well. Indicative of this development was a sharp controversy about the work of the historian Konrad Bittner, who received his habilitation from the German University in Prague in 1931 and who specialized in Slavo-Germanic relations. The members of the Circle vehemently criticized his monograph *Germans and Czechs* (Bittner 1936), pointing out that it depicted Czech-German relations in the light of German superiority and advanced judgments favorable to contemporary German ideology. Bittner's book was the subject of a special meeting of the Circle on December 7, 1936, and it was severely denounced.[39]

In the tense atmosphere of the late 1930s, the attitudes of some of the German members of the Circle began to change. In November 1936, Gustav Becking, then dean of the philosophy faculty of the German University, signed an official greeting to the Circle on the occasion of its tenth anniversary; in early 1939, he and Rippl renounced their membership.[40] It is generally assumed that Becking was lynched in the final days of the war in the streets of Prague by a mob of vengeful Czechs. And although Slotty was an outspoken anti-Nazi, he shared the postwar fate of many Germans who, like him, had not participated in Nazism but were discriminated against severely on grounds that they were Germans.[41]

In sum, the role of German-speaking scholars in the Prague Circle had a somewhat different character than that of Prague Russians and Ukrainians. Their scholarly pursuits were mostly traditional, and largely defined by topics rather than by methodology. Also, the institutions of these scholars were different from the émigré institutions of the Russians and the Ukrainians. (The German University was a relatively stable state institution, while Russian and Ukrainian institutions in Czechoslovakia were vulnerable.) Nonetheless, their participation in the Circle was significant.

6.3 The Czechs

Besides Mathesius, about half a dozen young Czech academics were active in the Prague Circle from the very beginning. The participation of some (e.g. Bohumil Ilek, an assistant to Mathesius) was episodic, but others (e.g. Bohumil Trnka, Bohuslav Havránek, Jan Mukařovský, and Jan Rypka) remained core members of the Circle practically until its demise. What assets did they bring?

Bohumil Trnka
Bohumil Trnka was born on June 3, 1895. After graduating from Charles University in 1919 with the completion of a historically oriented thesis on the origin of weak verbs in Germanic languages, he was appointed lecturer in English philology in 1925. His habilitation dealt with Old Saxon syntax (Trnka 1925). Much of Trnka's scholarly development was closely linked with Mathesius, who was Trnka's teacher beginning 1913 and for whom he served as private secretary beginning 1923, when Mathesius's sight began to deteriorate. Indeed, a number of similarities exist between the two men, ranging from their admiration for Jespersen to their conviction that they, as modern philologists, should be able to master their field completely by virtue of having competence in both English linguistics and literary history.

Among Trnka's very early works are several publications on shorthand systems for Czech. This interest, in which historical aspects were absent and which combined an applied perspective with elements of quantitative linguistics, contributed to Trnka's later development as a phonologist. He asserted this connection in the 1920s and continued to publish in this area well into the 1930s (Trnka 1937).

His early publications, mostly reviews, indicate an interest in literature aimed at transcending historicism. A mix of Humboldtianism and Vosslerianism was certainly among the earliest points of orientation on this path, as is suggested by some reviews from the very beginning of the 1920s. Writing on a French author, J. Epstein, Trnka states in 1922 that language is a mirror of the national soul, history, science, arts, and customs (Trnka 1922). A year later, in a review of a study by F. Schürr, a disciple of Vossler, Trnka has little argument with Schürr's basic tenets, namely an explanation of language change by at least a partial appeal to the Geist: "That the spirit is active in sound change is certain. . . ." (Trnka 1923: 165) He also finds that the revolution that originated under Vossler's influence in Romance linguistics is now spreading into English and Germanic philology, thus closing the gap that kept linguistics in isolation from the Geisteswissenschaften. He does not contest the tendency to explain language through national psychology, but, significantly, he adds:

If our aim is to explain a language by recourse to the psychology of the nation that speaks it, we have to attempt a detailed static analysis of this language in a given period of its evolution first, in order to be then able to proceed to questions of dynamics. The conviction that proceeding from statics to dynamics is in linguistics the safest way is expressed by Prof. V. Mathesius in his study "On the Potentiality of Language Phenomena." . . . A practical attempt to focus upon the statics was also undertaken by Jespersen in his *Modern English Grammar,* vol. 1 (Heidelberg 1900): he treats all sounds in particular centuries separately. This has the advantage that all facts which belong together are now connected, whereas otherwise they would have stayed torn apart. (Trnka 1923: 166)

Articles in which more clarity and explicitness in matters of methodology are visible begin to appear in 1924. Not surprisingly, one of them is a lengthy survey of Jespersen's grammatical system (Trnka 1924). Trnka was familiar with Saussure at that point, and several times he measured Jespersen by Saussurean criteria. The verdict was not always in Jespersen's favor.[42] A discussion of the complementarity of diachronic and synchronic linguistics is also a part of the review, but the final judgment is clearly a call for a more intensive cultivation of the static method—which "in the present time will be a healthy reaction against the one-sided emphasis on the study of sounds and against the dynamic method which some scholars erroneously believe to be the *only* acceptable method of linguistic research" (Trnka 1924: 39; emphasis in original). Trnka had no qualms about repeating some of these formulations almost word for word in his contribution to the first volume of the *Travaux,* the official publication of the Circle, where they still sounded iconoclastic (Trnka 1929). The fact that he could use his 1924 formulations about synchronic study of language in the later publications of the Circle is an important indication that the Circle cultivated ideas that had emerged independent of it.

Trnka soon became one of the core members of the Circle, and his loyalty to the group was proverbial. Much of the information on the early activity of the Circle is preserved due to his function as secretary, and thus chronicler, of the group. Also, some of his later activity reports, including those from the 1940s, contain historiographically important information. His obituary for Mathesius (Trnka 1946) gives very interesting insights into the thinking of his teacher and is probably the most important source on him.

Trnka's entire career was intimately connected with the English Institute of Charles University. In the 1930s, he concentrated on the phonology of English and other Germanic languages; among the results is the first phonological description of English ever (Trnka 1935). The anti-structuralist campaigns of the 1950s left little impression on him; the kind of political opportunism he tolerated can be gleaned from titles such as "How to Render Cyrillic Script on Our Typewriters" (Trnka 1955). He died in 1984 after an accident.[43]

Bohuslav Havránek

Bohuslav Havránek, one of the most active Czech members of the Circle, was born in Prague on January 30, 1893. He received his doctoral degree from Charles University in 1917, but was active as a researcher for the Czech Dictionary Office, a lexicological institute within the Czech Academy, prior to his graduation. Many of his early publications appeared in *Our Language,* a journal whose puristic tenets will be discussed below. But rather than purism, matters of lexicology and applied linguistics were among Havránek's earliest interests. He reviewed terminological dictionaries and presented analyses of "odd" words and idioms. (This is reminiscent in many ways of Zubatý's style, and indeed Zubatý was among Havránek's teachers.) Havránek's interest in terminology, which characterizes his entire work, had thus begun very early.

Theoretical questions are not discussed systematically in his early publications but there is a clear awareness of current methodological issues. In a review of a Czech grammar by the French Slavist André Mazon, Havránek (1923) reacts positively to Mazon's discussion of contemporary language, including spoken language. He identifies in Mazon's observations about "the system of contemporary language" a typical trait of the "French school" (ibid.: 305), and he deplores that "in the static study of contemporary language we have not done much so far" (ibid.: 306). This must be interpreted as expressing opposition to the predominant historicism and interest in what was discussed above under the heading "living word." In general, a certain familiarity with French developments can be traced in Havránek's early work. (Mathesius and Trnka seem to have turned to French authors somewhat later.)

Havránek also seems to have been the first Czech linguist to refer to Saussure's *Cours* in a significant manner. The first Czech reaction to this book—a brief mention that appeared in 1920—was profoundly misleading in that it left the impression that the *Cours* was principally a work on comparative historical linguistics.[44] Havránek's reaction, also brief, was certainly more insightful. He stressed the idea of autonomous linguistics in Saussure and quoted a supporting passage from the 1922 edition of the *Cours:* "la linguistique a pour unique et véritable objet la langue envisagée en elle-même et pour elle-même" (Havránek 1924b: 218).[45]

At an early point, Havránek also voiced skepticism toward elevating Schleicher's Stammbaum model to the only possible model of linguistic diachrony. He held the view that West Slavic languages particularly clearly display linguistic transitions, showing how language change spreads across linguistic boundaries from one historical area into another; evolution of languages could not thus proceed only by genetic splits (Havránek 1919: 233).

Havránek's interest in modern developments is easily documented. This interest, however, is not really matched at the analytical level. Saussure is primarily referred to as an authority justifying the study of contemporary language. Also, the foreword to his habilitation (Havránek 1928), which outlines briefly new developments and is laden with "modern names," is more of a background statement. The study itself, historically oriented to a large extent, does not match the introduction.

Like Trnka, Havránek remained a core member of the Circle. His scholarly career lead him to Brno in the 1930s and back to Prague after World War II. His opportunism under the Communist regime made him controversial in his later years, raising fundamental questions about the character of scholarly work in a totalitarian state. And as for his major concern, a functional theory of language culture, this is what he conceded in one of his last publications: "The notion 'language culture' has been, as recent studies show, in flux; it has not been satisfactorily worked out either theoretically or practically. This work is still ahead of us." (Havránek 1979: 10) He died in Prague in 1978.[46]

Jan Mukařovský

Jan Mukařovský was the only non-linguist involved in the earliest activities of the Circle. (He attended the second meeting, in December 1926.) Born in 1891, he studied at Charles University and subsequently spent 10 years in Pilsen as a grammar school teacher. In 1925 he returned to Prague. In 1931 he began to lecture at the University of Bratislava, where he was appointed professor in 1934 and where he taught until 1937. Subsequently he became a professor of aesthetics at Charles University in Prague.

Literature on Mukařovský and his contributions to the development of structural aesthetics is plentiful and typically lacks a historiographical perspective—practically up until now, Mukařovský has been regarded as a theoretician whose work has continued to inspire literary theorists. From this perspective, Mukařovský's writings from the 1930s and 1940s, rather than those from the 1920s, stand out.[47]

Mukařovský was not visibly influenced by nineteenth century positivism in literary scholarship and aesthetics. A look at his formative years reveals a great deal of interest in individualistic versology of the turn of the century. The most important early publication, his dissertation "A Contribution to the Aesthetics of the Czech Verse" (Mukařovský 1923), focuses on prosody, yet a closer look shows that the actual aim was to determine poets' individual characteristics: Why is it that we immediately perceive the pentametric iamb of one poet as strikingly different from the same meter of another poet? Mukařovský held the position that "the pronunciation of verses of a particular poet has certain permanent properties" (ibid.: 6) and that the goal was to identify these properties. This concern with the auditory aspect of poetry was certainly influenced by Eduard Sievers, in particular by his *Rhythmisch-melodische Studien* of 1912.

Mukařovský's interest in actual recitation and listening is, of course, consonant with the tendency to study language in its most realistic manifestation and not on paper. This might appear as a purely descriptivistic approach, but the idea of a "unifying force"—a higher-order quality inherent in style (see also Mukařovský 1985)— opened ample space for theorizing. This concern prefigures Mukařovský's notion of "semantic gesture," which became prominent in his later writings and which was aimed at describing a holistic quality characterizing the styles of particular authors (see Jankovič 1965).

Mukařovský became a core member of the Circle. He was very productive in the 1930s and then, especially, in the 1940s (a period which is somewhat erroneously regarded as a dead spot in the activity of the Circle). After Jakobson, he is the most important representative of Czech structuralism. His essays cover a broad range of themes, including general aesthetics, Czech literature, visual arts, and drama. In comparison with the work of Jakobson, Mukařovský's writings are systematic and exhaustive. His renunciation of structuralism after 1948 (when the Communists seized power in Czechoslovakia) and his active participation in prominent political functions remain enigmatic. His political malleability allowed the new regime to make important inroads when imposing Stalinist standards on Czech culture and scholarship (see chapter 12 below). It was only in the 1960s that his structuralist works were again published. Mukařovský died in Prague in 1975.[48]

Miloš Weingart

Although Miloš Weingart (b. 1890) began to publish in 1912, his scholarly output became more visible after he received his habilitation in 1919. A notable title among his early publications is a contribution to *Nové Athenaeum* that shows a keen understanding of the ideals of science put forward by Masaryk. Although Weingart seems to accept the general program of Realism, he judges the orientation of Masaryk and his *Athenaeum* as the orientation of a generation whose "mental abilities and sentiments were above all analytical" and whose worldview consisted in data recording:

This sober and cautious interest in practical matters led the generation of the 1880s above all to precise facts—examination and collection of individual facts was everything. Correspondingly, the publication of results usually had the form of specialized monographs. This generation distrusted grandiose conceptions, syntheses and all-inclusive pictures, for it was afraid of losing reliability and exactness, and felt, moreover, these were just empty words. By contrast its own style was consciously plain, even sometimes sparse and dry. There were exceptions, to be sure, but even broadly based works of this generation, such as [Gebauer's] *Historical Grammar of Czech,* were actually really a collection of monographs. (Weingart 1919: 92)

We have already encountered this type of criticism in Mathesius, and the alternative Weingart put forward also sounds familiar. He refers to an alternative whose origins he explicitly locates at the turn of the century and which in his view gained weight in the years immediately before the war—the new generation of scholars is no longer positivistic, but holds views of a type which he calls idealistic, a term which clearly echoes Vossler's "idealistische Sprachwissenschaft." For Weingart, the future of scholarship is a synthesis:

It seems that the new generation of scholars that has succeeded the generation of the university founders, or is just waiting to enter scholarly life, will again be a little bit nearer to the Romantics or, to be more exact, that it will strive for a synthesis of scientific realism with scientific Romantism. (Weingart 1919: 93)

Weingart's position is indicative not only of the fact that the young generation did not fully adopt the methodological approach of the old generation but also of the desire for comprehensive accounts.

Despite dissatisfaction with previous scholarship, Weingart's emphasis on historical method remained quite strong. In a period in which the future members of the Circle were fascinated by a nonhistorical approach, Weingart argued not only for the traditional unity of philological disciplines but also for its foundation in the comparative-historical method (Weingart 1924). Thus, a set of brilliant assesments and a desire for synthesis stand out, while references to specific categories of the new methodology (e.g., static method) cannot be documented in the early period. Despite his critical view of the previous style of scholarship, Weingart shows little inclination to depart from the traditional historicism.

In view of his early position, it is not very surprising that Weingart clashed with the core of the Circle in the 1930s and that the conflict eventually lead to his abandonment of the Circle. In the long run, his work on Old Church Slavonic might well be the most appreciated segment of his scholarship today. Weingart died in 1939.[49]

Jan Rypka

One of the names that appear in Mathesius's recollections of the early days of the Prague Circle is that of Jan Rypka. Mathesius lists him as one of the six participants in the first official meeting of the Circle, on October 6, 1926. Jan Rypka, born in 1886 in Kroměříž, was an Oriental philologist, educated in Vienna and specializing in Iranian and Turkish. Besides translations from Turkish, his major publications from the early 1920s include studies of classical Ottoman poetry (e.g., Rypka 1924). He defended his habilitation in 1925, and subsequently he held a number of leading academic positions in Oriental studies practically until his death in 1968.

Although Rypka was one of the most loyal members of the Circle, acting among other things as the treasurer, he was not a structuralist linguist. The major common denominator between him and some other members of the Circle was in all likelihood an interest in metrical problems. His metrical studies of classical Ottoman poetry were his most visible contribution to the Circle's publications (Rypka 1936). Rypka also took interest in questions of contact between languages, as is witnessed by his lecture "On Mutual Interpenetration of Major Islamic Languages" (October 2, 1927). As we shall see below, language contact was an important topic in the early phase of the Circle.

The nature of Rypka's later scholarly activity in the Circle is somewhat unclear.[50] While he produced translations from Islamic languages,[51] his philological works, including textbooks of oriental languages, indicate that linguistic structuralism left no marks whatsoever on him. After the Second World War, Rypka rarely mentioned his membership in the Circle and his linguistic interests. In a conversation from his last years, published posthumously, we only find a laconic statement: "I was never disinterested in linguistic work" (Kubíčková and Veselá 1969: 130). Rypka died in Prague in 1968.

6.4 A Republic of Scholars

The present chapter may have stretched the reader's patience to the maximum—a great number of little-known names were presented and obscure details of interwar Prague addressed. Considered in isolation, many of these facts may well seem to deserve the peace of historical oblivion. Nonetheless, they command our attention here because phenomena such as organization of scholarship, emigration, and multicultural symbiosis shed light on the formation of the Prague Linguistic Circle.

Clearly, the participants in the Circle were in many ways disparate and characterized by diverse backgrounds. There were great differences in experience and expertise—in their capacity as analytic researchers, Mathesius and Karcevskij stood in contrast to the relatively inexperienced scholars of the younger generation. There were considerable cultural differences in orientation—the anglophile attitude represented by Mathesius and Trnka was not matched by the Russians and Ukrainians, while the interest in the francophone literature only slowly made headway among the Czech linguists (Havránek was an exception to this). There is also a rather clear feeling of an initial lack of methodological radicalism among the Czechs, due in part to the fact that they had been exposed to such turn-of-the-century developments as Vosslerianism (itself a major critique of nineteenth-century linguistic methodology). Recall that Mathesius, Trnka, and Weingart all show familiarity with Vossler.

Despite these and other differences, there was obviously a vast scholarly potential and basic presuppositions for cooperation. If we look for common denominators in matters of scholarship, we find that a nonhistorical approach, combined with a healthy regard for the dynamism of language evolution, dominates. This was a perspective that characterized nearly all the future participants in the Circle well before the Circle itself became reality. Attraction by previously uncommon models of historical evolution, such as linguistic convergence, ties in with this perspective. The interest in phenomena not acknowledged by historical grammar (literary language) is also congruent with this trend.

Seen in broader cultural terms, the departure from historicism (especially on the part of the Czechs) was related to the desire to transcend dependence on German scholarship, which was still historically oriented. It was a remarkable coincidence, then, that the émigrés from the Soviet Union aided the Czechs in this enterprise and helped them surmount the danger of provincialization looming after the demise of the Austro-Hungarian monarchy. One might think that the price the Czechs had to pay was unacceptable—the emergence of a "circle culture" might, after all, be viewed as an instance of Russification of Czech scholarly life. However, as we shall see in the following chapters, the ideals of collectivism that the Circle represented were rather general, and in any case they were independent of local Russian developments.

It would appear that the cultural symbiosis that resulted from the post-1917 migrations was only possible against the tolerant atmosphere of Masaryk's Czechoslovakia, which opened a space for integration and provided the local Czechs, Germans, Russians, and Ukrainians with a way to transcend their local or émigré-rooted ambience. But it may well be that the spirit of cooperation that the Circle radiated was not the rule—the basic image of cultural harmony that we nowadays attribute to Czechoslovak interwar society may not be correct across the board. If this is a correct assessment, an important lesson results—namely, that cooperation and integration proceed best among scholars. Although the concept of cooperation was elevated to an element of the scholarly worldview (recall Jakobson's charcterization of Slotty), the primary driving force on the part of the core members was a very specific commitment to redefining the nature of linguistics and literary studies. In this sense the Prague republic of scholars benefitted greatly from the spirit of symbiosis, but it may have ultimately succeeded in transcending the destructive character typical of a great number of East European multicultural communities precisely because it was a community of scholars.

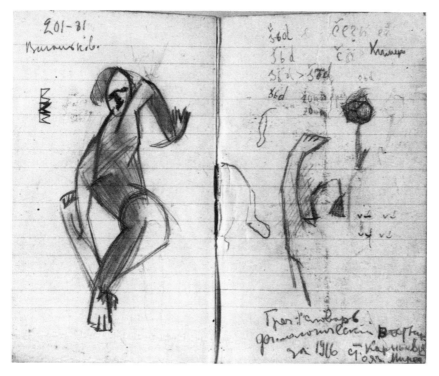

Avant-garde and Russian philology: a spread from one of Jakobson's notebooks from his student years in Moscow. Jakobson's notes include bibliographic references (lower right) and metrical schemata (upper right). The artist is unknown. Source: RJP, box 31, folder 25. Courtesy of Roman Jakobson and Krystyna Pomorska Trust.

Members of the Soviet Red Cross mission to Czechoslovakia, 1920. The bearded man in the middle is Dr. Gillerson, head of the mission; Roman Jakobson is to his right. Courtesy of Roman Jakobson and Krystyna Pomorska Trust.

A page from the Circle's attendance book showing the entries from the first two meetings. Photograph by Hana Hamplová. Courtesy of Archives of Czech Academy of Sciences.

<u>I.</u> schůze.　　6. X. 1926.

Dr. Heinrich Becker:
　　Der europäische Sprachgeist.

Přítomni: Jos. Rypka　Henrik Becker
　　Roman Jagodson　Trnka
　　+ Boh. Havránek　Mathesius

<u>II.</u> schůze.　　3. XI. 1926.

Přítomni:　　　　　Mathesius
　　+ Boh. Havránek
　　R. Jagodson
　　B. Trnka

Přednáší Dr. B. Havránek:
　　Gramatické kategorie pasivní.

A meeting of Russian linguists in Brno, late 1926. From left to right: R. Jakobson, N. S. Trubetzkoy, P. G. Bogatyrev, N. N. Durnovo. Courtesy of Roman Jakobson and Krystyna Pomorska Trust.

Vilém Mathesius (center) and Bohumil Trnka (right), 1928. Source: *Vilém Mathesius: Jazyk, Kultura a Slovenost* (Prague: Odeon, 1982).

Petr Bogatyrev in the 1930s. Courtesy of Roman Jakobson and Krystyna Pomorska Trust.

Vitezslav Nezval, Karel Teige, and Roman Jakobson (left to right) at the Krohas',
Brno, 1933. Photograph by Jirí Kroha. Courtesy of Roman Jakobson and Krystyna
Pomorska Trust.

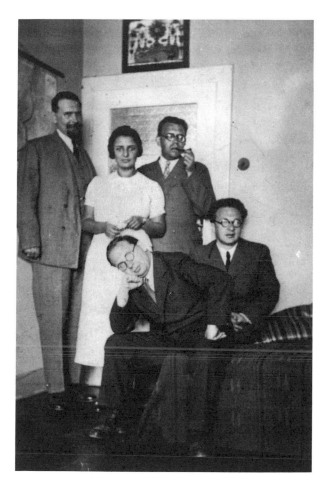

In Brno, 1933: (standing) N. S. Trubetzkoy, Sonya N. Jakobson, Dmytro Cyzevs'kyj; (sitting) P. G. Bogatyrev, Roman Jakobson. Courtesy of Roman Jakobson and Krystyna Pomorska Trust.

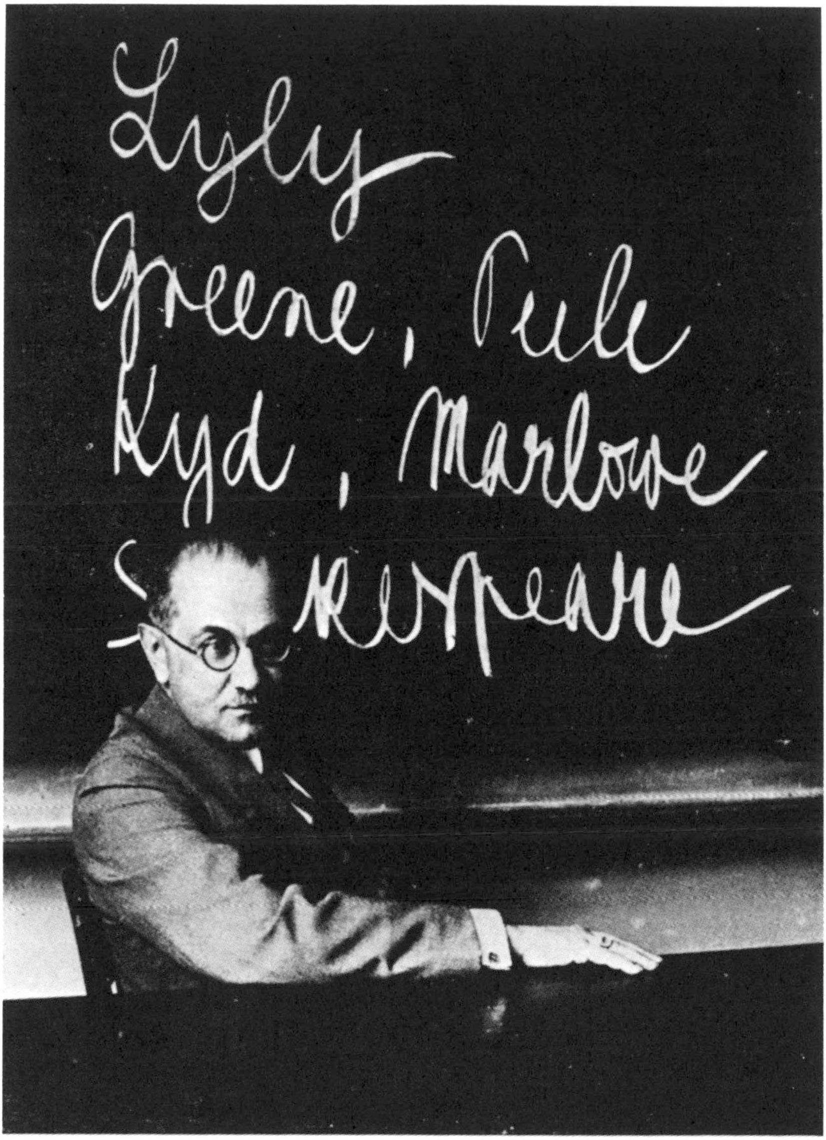
Lyly
Greene, Peele
Kyd, Marlowe

Vilém Mathesius lecturing in the 1930s. Source: *Vilém Mathesius: Jazyk, Kultura a Slovenost* (Prague: Odeon, 1982).

Jan Mukařovsky in the 1930s. Source: *Studie o Janu Mukarovském* (Prague: Univerzita Karlova, 1990).

Roman Jakobson in New York: a drawing by Antonín Pelc, published in the London magazine *Obzor* in 1942.

The Czech avant-garde in New York. 1942. At top: Jaroslav Jezek. Standing below, left to right: Jan Werich, Jirí Voskovec, Bohuslav Martinu, Egon Hostovsk'y. Sitting: Hugo Haas, Adolf Hoffmeister, Jan Loewenbach, Antonín Pelc, Adler, Jakobson, Kopf. Drawing by Pelc, published in *Obzor* in 1942.

The Eurasian horse.

Trubetzkoy's *ex libris* from the 1930s (artist unknown).

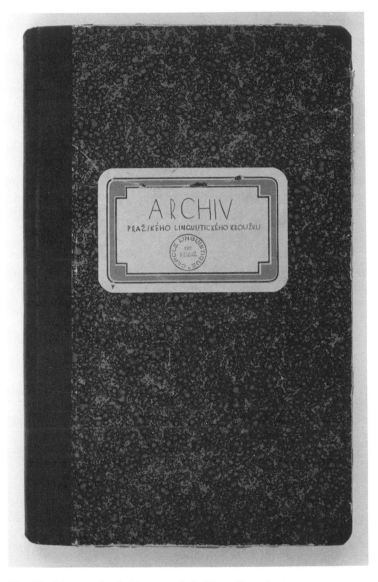

The Circle's scrapbook. Photograph by Hana Hamplová.

The Magic of a Common Language

The Prague School's doctrine developed as a syncretic doctrine—as a veritable receptacle of approaches that were perceived as alternatives to the traditional comparative-historical linguistics of the nineteenth century. These alternatives included synchronic analysis, anti-psychologism, anti-causalism, and the idea of contacts and mergers between languages. They also included the understanding of language as a social institution, which implied the possibility of conscious intervention into language. The most important of the Prague School's technical innovations was the concept of an internally structured whole—a structure based on implicational laws.

The 1928 Congress of Linguists in the Hague and the writing of the Prague Circle's Theses illustrate how these themes were articulated and how they formed the basis of a bold program of synthetic research that was quite in consonance with the contemporary ideals of an overall synthesis in cultural and social thinking.[1]

7.1 Early Lectures

It is often said that the activities of the Prague Linguistic Circle began on October 6, 1926, with a lecture by Henrik Becker, a young Leipzig-based linguist passing through Prague. However, as has already been noted, Vilém Mathesius held informal meetings at his home as early as March 1925. He recalled:

On March 13, 1925, I invited Jakobson and Trnka and also Karcevskij, later a lecturer in Russian at the University of Geneva, then a teacher at the Russian gymnasium in Prague. On October 14, of that same year, I again invited Jakobson, Trnka, Karcevskij, and also B. Havránek, who was then preparing for his habilitation in Slavic philology. (Mathesius 1936b: 138)

It was only after this private prelude that the Circle began holding "official" meetings, in the autumn of 1926. Mathesius heard from

Trnka that Henrik Becker was in Prague[2] and wished to present his ideas to local scholars. He decided to give him a chance:

I organized such a meeting in my office, which was then at 4 Veleslavín Street. On October 6, 1926, in the afternoon, six persons attended: besides Becker and myself, there were of course Jakobson, Trnka, Havránek, and also Rypka, an Orientalist, then a university docent [lecturer]. We attentively listened to Becker's lecture entitled "Der europäische Sprachgeist" and then discussed its theses very thoroughly. We all liked the meeting and started to organize further meetings with enthusiasm. (Mathesius 1936: 138f.)

Mathesius's language is amusing: the audience listened "attentively," the discussion proceeded "very thoroughly," and the organization of further meetings continued "with enthusiasm." With the exception of Mathesius and Rypka, the audience was young, although no students were involved (as used to be the case in Moscow): Trnka was 29, Jakobson 28, and Havránck 31. Becker himself was 24.

At subsequent meetings some new faces appeared (Bogatyrev, Mukařovský, Oberpfalzer, Sedlák, Weingart), however, the group remained quite small. In the academic years 1926–27 and 1927–28 the attendance rarely exceeded 10; it rose somewhat in 1928–29, but it never exceeded 15 even then. Trubetzkoy's "Alphabet and Sound System" (February 6, 1928), a lecture that today might be perceived as important, was attended by only seven persons, Trubetzkoy included.[3] Not only were the Circle's early meetings small, but many of them (perhaps more than half) took place at members' homes— a practice that lasted until 1930 and in the case of business meetings well beyond.[4] Larger meetings were not held until the early 1930s; among those, the lectures on language culture in January 1932, which drew audiences of 100 and more, stand out. The important guest lectures of the 1930s were also relatively large; for example, Edmund Husserl's (November 18, 1935) attracted an audience of 45.

Despite its small size and its relatively private character, the Prague Circle had a formal structure right from the start. A list of participants was kept, there were numerous business meetings, and minutes of both the lectures and the business meetings were kept.[5] Although no formal list of members from the early period was preserved, the notion of membership was evidently well defined; formal votes were taken on the admission of new members. The Circle obtained formal status in December 1930 when it registered as a society and passed its by-laws.[6]

There were 34 lectures in the first three academic years (1926–1929).[7] The range of interests was broad, with linguistic topics clearly dominating.[8] But the main feature of this early period are state-of-the-art surveys focusing on current research abroad.[9] Particularly prominent is the attempt at filling the francophone, and especially the Genevan, gap. Not only work by Saussure, but also work by Sechehaye and (most of all) Bally was studied with much interest in the Circle.[10] The prominence of Bally indicates that the breadth and explicitness of his analyses made him more accessible than Saussure. In any case, Geneva linguistics was certainly not seen as restricted to Saussure, as is typically the case today. The Genevan influence became less prominent in the 1930s, primarily because it did not provide much new inspiration for the emerging phonology, but it rebounded in the late 1930s and the early 1940s—particularly in Jakobson's work, where references to Saussure are frequent.[11]

7.2 The Magic of Shared Themes

The common language that was developing in the early meetings of the Circle revolved around a handful of themes, each of which had a certain dissident flavor when considered against the late-nineteenth-century background. Some of them—anti-historicism, anti-causalism, anti-psychologism, interest in the "living word"—have already been discussed in the sections on Jakobson's and Mathesius's formative years and thus will be treated only briefly. Others—especially the new concept of structure—deserve more explicit discussion.

Synchrony and Diachrony

One of the early private meetings at Mathesius's home (on October 14, 1925) was devoted to "New Currents and Tendencies in Linguistic Research," a survey paper Mathesius was preparing for presentation to the Czech Academy. In its printed form (Mathesius 1927), the paper begins with a sharp distinction between the past and the present—between the historically inclined nineteenth-century linguistics (which Mathesius called "genetical-comparative linguistics") and contemporary searches for an alternative ("analytical-comparative linguistics"). Mathesius listed points he regarded as weak in the older approach, but did not wish to abandon historical linguistics entirely. Instead, he envisioned a synthesis of the two rival currents, "which should combine their advantages without sharing their weaknesses" (ibid.: 189). Despite this synthetic-sounding assertion, the rest reads anti-historically; thus, no fundamental corrections to the picture of Mathesius's linguistic worldview given above in chapter 4 are necessary.

By 1927, of course, driving out historicism had become a widespread theme. The First International Congress of Linguists, held in the Hague in April 1928, reinforced an overall change in theoretical attitudes, especially among the younger participants. Jakobson reported from the Congress that

there was a widespread feeling that *comparative Indo-European linguistics,* in the past century the core of linguistics, was driven out of its dominant position—as a *science démodée* as Meillet half-jokingly noted. (Jakobson 1928c)

Weingart reported:

Section One, General Linguistics, was in the foreground both in terms of contents and attendance, by all means overshadowing the Indo-European Section. This was ironically acknowledged by Meillet, who jokingly excused himself saying that there was nothing so "demodée," "passé de mode," as Indo-European comparative linguistics. This attitude was one of the typical signs of the present state of contemporary linguistics: after the previous lack of interest in general linguistics, as it was fashionable in the time of our studies, when university institutes were dominated by positivistic members and epigones of the Leipzig school, a lively change in favor of general linguistics has been taking place in the last ten years. . . . (Weingart 1928: 473) [12]

Mathesius himself contributed to the demotion of historicism at the Congress with his paper on "Linguistic Characterology" (Mathesius 1928a), a discipline that he conceived of as an alternative to historical linguistics.[13] He had already stated that linguistic characterology "will play a first-rate role in the linguistics of tomorrow" (Mathesius 1927: 191).

The interest in alternatives to historical linguistics was the least controversial element among the members of the emerging Circle.

Anti-Psychologism

Another element that was smoothly absorbed was anti-psychologism. There is ample evidence that the issue of psychological explanation came up frequently in the Circle's discussions and that this avenue of research was rejected. In an informal meeting on March 23, 1928, Jakobson and Mathesius cricticized Louis Brun, an early member of the Circle, for a psychologistic explanation of metaphors. On April 30 of the same year, Mukařovský stressed in a discussion that subjective lyric was not a psychological notion; it had syntactic correlates—"psychology is left behind." [14]

The rejection of psychologism was linked with an insistence on the autonomous status of linguistics. Mathesius's "proto-lecture," for instance, contains not only an explicit rejection of psychologism (especially the Wundtian kind) but also an assertion that linguistics is not reducible to psychology:

If language, instead of being simply a result of reflex processes, is ... a system of conventional signs, then psychology cannot be expected to offer easy and direct help to linguistics. Consequently there is no chance of linguistics' ever becoming a mere branch of psychology. (Mathesius 1927: 203)

Trnka, in his "Semasiology and Its Importance for Linguistics" (1927), underscored that diachronic and synchronic semasiology should aim at wider perspectives rather than deal with particularities, and that psychology was inadequate for this purpose. Progress would be achieved only when facts were examined "without any aprioristic psychological theories" and the autonomy of linguistics was observed:

... in semasiology, which is so close to psychology, the principle holds, stressed in Saussure's well-known book *Cours de linguistique générale,* that in studying language phenomena it is necessary to stand on the ground of language itself. (Trnka 1927: 41)

Chapter 7

"Social Conventionalism"

Although there is no record of an extended discussion in the early years in which the idea of language as a social phenomenon was asserted, it is not difficult to conclude that this was the guiding position. Jakobson (1928b: 184) briefly stated that the acoustic image produced by the speaker is a "social fact," essentially implying that phonemes are social values.

This position was compatible with the idea that linguistic entities are social conventions. Mathesius (1927) fully subscribed to the idea of language as a system of conventional signs, a proposition that was a permanent feature of his understanding of language. A somewhat more elaborate version can be found in one of his essays from 1935:

> Language is essentially nothing else but a very complicated convention of customs that is not fundamentally different from signaling on railroads. Words that we use in order to be understood, their shape and the way in which they are combined into sentences—all this arose by way of a spontaneous linguistic convention. (Mathesius 1935: 369)

This approach was shared by other members of the Circle, too. For example, Trubetzkoy asserted that language is a system of conventional signs that serve communication within a given speech community.

Linguistic Activism, Teleology, *volonté obscure*

One of the most remarkable developments of the post-Neogrammarian period was the idea that language might be considered as a domain of human action rather than as a natural object evolving indpendent of human will. We read the following in *Vie du langage*, a popular introductory book by the French linguist Albert Dauzat:

> When one speaks . . . , one pursues a goal, namely to be understood. In order to achieve this goal, each person, individually, modifies and corrects one's language *consciously* so that perfection is achieved. (Dauzat 1910: 100; emphasis added)

The idea of a conscious modification of language was popular not only among those who were perfectioning existing languages in the domain of style, but also among those who were inventing new perfect languages—an approach that was sanctioned within the Prague Circle. The question of an international auxiliary language was on the program at two Circle meetings in early 1929 (March 1 and April 9), and Roman Jakobson, reporting on the International Congress of Linguists (Geneva, 1931) noted approvingly:

Finally, the congress unconditionally accepted the idea of a *conscious and intentional* intervention into the life of language, as well as a closely related plan of an international artificial auxiliary language—something that was regarded as heresy by earlier representatives of linguistics. (Jakobson 1931i; emphasis added)

In retrospect, a number of variants of activistic attitudes toward language can be identified.[15] In his *Pásmo* article, Jakobson already was explicit about the impact of speakers' communicative intentions on the properties of language. His wording resembles the above passage in Dauzat. Another member of the Circle, Miloš Weingart, also explicitly discussed the importance of speakers' intentions:

According to Neogrammarian and Positivist teaching, the communicative intention of the speaker is excluded from linguistic activity; conscious linguistic creative activity by the speaker is rejected. . . . But just as in psychology, this positivism is not sufficient for the understanding of all phenomena in linguistics. As far as language is concerned, a glance at word-order phenomena will suffice to make it clear to everyone that intentional and expressive moments, i.e., conscious creative activity, is decisive in constructing the sentence. (Weingart 1928: 481)

This variant of linguistic activism clearly echoes the position of the Vossler School.

Yet another variant of linguistic activism appears in Jakobson's work under the label "teleology"—among other places, in his lecture "Concept of Sound Laws and the Teleological Principle" (Jakobson 1928b), read on January 13, 1927. Here Jakobson speaks about "teleological sound-study," claims that the social character of sound change can be explained only "if posed in teleological terms," and asserts that the interpenetration of language systems can be fully understood "only from the teleological point of view." Related notions include "goal-oriented" (as in "goal-oriented interpretation of sound phenomena"). Another term that Jakobson used around that time is "finalism" (Jakobson et al. 1928a: 33).

It has often been pointed out that Jakobson's recourse to teleology is hard to interpret, and it may well be that several competing meanings are involved. If so, one of them is clearly activistic. Jakobson understands language as a social phenomenon and speakers as concerned with tasks, e.g., with maintaining a certain acoustic output. The teleological nature of language change can then be understood as the result of the speakers' conscious and permanent "maintenance work" with respect to the system.[16]

The idea of linguistic activity as work on a task is pervasive in Jakobson's thought of this period. One domain in which conscious action upon language is particularly visible for him is poetic language, with "its obvious and manifest intentionality, its undisguised teleology" (Jakobson 1929f: 593). Of course, the "modern French linguists" to whom Jakobson referred in his *Pásmo* essay come to mind.[17] Dauzat's name has already been mentioned, but more important linguists should be cited: Meillet, Sechehaye, Bally, Vendryès, and perhaps Brunot. In his "Langage naturel et langage artificiel," Bally—inspired by the French linguist Victor Henry—argued that the role of intentionality was more substantial than was generally believed. He repeatedly underscored that, if languages that serve à la grande communication, such as French, English, German, are studied from the perspective of their functioning in communication,

they will not perhaps appear to us to be entirely natural organisms, functioning automatically, evolving slowly and regularly, with reflexion and will not intervening; quite the contrary, one will see that the "artificial" element, so to speak "conscience," plays a real role in them. (Bally 1921: 626)

On the whole, Bally clearly underscored that language was not only an instrument of communication, but also a highly pliable one:

it is probable that languages, in their permanent process of adapting themselves to the needs of communication, are giving way more easily to conscious changes. (Bally 1921: 637)

Although the above position is conceptually akin to the idea of linguistic activism, we also find attempts to equip the language itself—not necessarily its speakers—with teleological power or with "intentions." Jakobson, who often invoked Anton Marty in this context, asserts:

> There are linguistic changes which, similarly to moves in the chess game, have "the intention to exercise action on the system." (Jakobson et al. 1928c: 35)

By and large, these intentions—characteristically flanked by quotation marks—are situated on a somewhat different level than human intervention in language, thus reminding us somewhat ironically of the notion *volonté obscure* discussed in Bréal's *Essai de sémantique.* (Bréal assumed that language evolution was shaped by an active, sui generis force.) In Prague, such notions were essentially reduced to the idea that language development is governed by laws, and that these laws are autonomous laws of language rather than of psychology or sociology. The idea of such internal laws was contrasted with Saussure's idea of fortuitous sound change, a concept that seemed quite unacceptable.[18] Later work often invoked the idea of dialectic, or intrinsically determined movement, in comparable contexts.

Language Contact and Convergence

Reminiscing about Becker's first appearance before the Prague Circle, Mathesius recalled that the young linguist had speculated about "how European languages converge under the influence of a common culture, how they get 'Europeanized'" (Mathesius 1936: 138). Some clues to the contents of Becker's lecture can be found in Trnka's published summary:

> H. Becker treated the question of mutual influences of European languages as conditioned by shared cultural life. These influences are manifested by semasiological borrowing (Calques linguistiques, Lehnübersetzungen), as well as by lexical, syntactic and morphological borrowing; under longer contact of two languages, parallel sound changes also appear. (Trnka 1928–1936(i): 182)

Whereas these introductory lines point to a rather technical treatment of language contact, the remainder of the summary is phrased entirely in terms of cultural history. For Becker, it appears, the relevant factors in European linguistic development included a medley of components, ranging from Völkerwanderung to German Romanticism.

Language contact, or language convergence, represented an alternative to the Schleicherian Stammbaum model. Other lectures on linguistic convergence attest to the fascination this alternative held for the early Prague Circle. On October 6, 1926, Jan Rypka lectured on cultural convergence of languages influenced by Islam (October 6, 1926). Trnka too had some interest in the topic of convergence. The term Sprachbund also appeared relatively early in Trubetzkoy's brief note in the Hague, where he defined the contrast between Sprachbund and Sprachfamilie (Trubetzkoy 1929b).

Phonology and a New Concept of Structure

In August 1944, Mukařovský and Trnka visited Mathesius in Kolín. Afterward, Mathesius wrote to Havránek:

My visitors will certainly tell you what we talked about. Trnka took with him the savings book of the Circle. On the third page of the binding inside, you will find a note pointing to the password of the savings book. I forgot to look at the exact wording, but I think it says "The Main Area." If so, you will easily understand that this means the discipline represented by N. S. T.'s name. (Mathesius to Havránek, August 17, 1944; Havránek family archives)

Mathesius's cryptic wording here is actually easy to understand: The undisputed "main area" of the Circle's work was phonology, the discipline associated with N. S. Trubetzkoy. It quickly became a model discipline, and it was widely believed to provide basic concepts for research in other areas, including those outside linguistics proper. Though much is known today about the history of Prague phonology,[19] certain aspects still need to be highlighted. Among the most interesting facets of the evolution of phonology in the late 1920s are the emergence of a new concept of structure and the somewhat unexpected circumstance that the initial progress in this area took place outside of the group proper.

Phonology as a Private Discourse

The latter point can be dealt with rather quickly. As we have seen, phonology was not really the most popular theme in the earliest days of Circle. Lectures on arguably phonological topics began to appear only in 1928, in connection with preparations for the congress in the Hague (Trubetzkoy's "Lautsystem und Alphabet," February 6, 1928; Jakobson's draft of "Proposition 22," February 14, 1928). It was only in December 1928 that the Circle did its first "phonology-storming": on the fourteenth Mathesius lectured on English phonology, and on the eighteenth Trubetzkoy lectured on "Comparison of Vocalic Systems." This chronology reflects the fact that within the Circle phonology was for a relatively long time Jakobson's private project, as is witnessed by the singularity of the phonological perspective he introduced in his study of Czech verse (Jakobson 1923a). Trubetzkoy joined the phonological enterprise only around 1926–27. An important document of this development is the extensive correspondence of the two scholars (Jakobson 1975), yet the fact itself that we have to resort to epistolary sources in order to pursue the history of Prague phonology strongly indicates that the discourse on phonology was initially not shared within the group. Mathesius's phonological work was conducted in so different a style that, in view of later developments, one might doubt that it belonged to the Prague paradigm at all.

This situation began to change with a number of publications that appeared around 1929—in particular, Trubetzkoy's "Vokalsysteme" (1929a) and his *Polabische Studien* (1930)—in which all the main notions of Prague phonology appear. Although their origin does not really make them an invention of the Circle, the Circle became their collective custodian and user. The lesson is obvious: Whatever emphasis on collective work there might have been in the Circle, inventions occurred in individual heads.

A New Concept of Structure

The congress in the Hague consolidated the consensus on the core notions of structuralism, those of system and structure. References to these concepts once again appear in reports from the Hague as if masterminded from a single press bureau:

The notion system has been gaining an ever increasing significance in linguistics, and the conviction is growing that neither specific sound changes nor speech sounds . . . can be treated without reference to the system of linguistic values. (Jakobson 1928c)

This [new] approach does not aim so much at an analysis of individual phenomena . . . , but rather at a whole linguistic system at a chosen point in time, present or past. (Weingart 1928: 480)

Not only the elements as such are interesting, but also the whole in which they appear in a specific language at a specific point. It is this union of elements that is currently becoming the center of research interest. (de Groot 1928: 424)

At this point the idea of a structured whole had been evolving for a considerable time among influential philosophers, sociologists, and linguists. (Wilhelm Dilthey, for example, made very frequent use of notions such as Struktur and Strukturzusammenhang.) Although Saussure's ideas were clearly inspirational to the Prague linguists, the concept of structure that emerged in the Circle represents an important change that involves a perspective completely different from the Geneva understanding of this concept. As has been noted above, the early phonological theories did not address the internal structure of the phonological system. In contrast, the essence of the new approach was the study of relationships between the constitutive elements of a system. The first documented source in which this innovation can be found is the 1927 monograph on the Russian verb in which Karcevskij voices explicit criticism of the Saussurean notion of structure, noting right at the start that this notion is based on premises that are simply absurd:

It has become a commonplace to assert that linguistic values exist only by virtue of their mutual opposition. In this form, of course, this idea leads to an absurdity: a tree is a tree because it is neither a house, nor a horse, nor a river. . . . A simple and pure opposition necessarily leads to chaos and cannot provide any basis for the system. (Karcevskij 1927: 13f., n. 2)

Karcevskij rejects the concept of system as a set of elements that merely satisfy the criterion of contrast and proposes an alternative conception:

Genuine differentiation presupposes simultaneous similarity and difference. Mental facts form sets based on a common element; they do not establish oppositions except within such sets. In their turn and by the same principle, these sets are then members of higher-order sets, and so on. (ibid.: 14)

This conceptually significant statement underlies the theory of the hierarchical (or layered, or implicational) nature of the language system. The asymmetric interpretation of phonological correlations is one of its consequences.

To my knowledge, the above passage was never quoted by the Prague researchers and Karcevskij has never been explicitly credited with this innovation. One cannot therefore confidently claim that the theory of layered linguistic structure was later erected upon this very passage; but whatever questions of priority may arise here, the spirit of this wording is characteristic of the Prague approach. For instance, Trubetzkoy's 1931 discussion of the notion "structure" echoes the very same idea:

If a language were characterized only by disjunctive phonological oppositions, i.e., if each phoneme of this language would relate to all remaining phonemes in the same disjunctive way, this language would have no phonological system at all. (Trubetzkoy 1931a: 96)

Karcevskij introduced his critique of Saussure with a reference to Ernst Cassirer's *Substanz- und Funktionsbegriff* (1910). Cassirer discussed issues involved in discrimination and comparision of perceptual data presented in series [Reihe]. Among other things, he noted that in this type of classes one observes "a gradually firmer and firmer ordering and articulation of the being as regards the gradation of material *similarities* characterizing the individual objects under comparison" (Cassirer 1910: 5). At a later place, "series of similarities" [Ähnlichkeitsreihen] are accounted for by a principle that generates such class formations:

This transition from one element to another . . . obviously presupposes a principle according to which the transition progresses and by means of which a kind of dependency is determined which holds between each element and its neighbor. It thus becomes apparent that all notion-formation is linked to a certain *form of series-formation*. . . . We regard a perception-complex as *notionally* apprehended and ordered when its members do not stand side by side without any relationship, but originate in a necessary order from a basic member in conformity with a fundamental generating relation. (Cassirer 1910: 19f.)

Cassirer's theory—which echoes Husserl's *Logical Investigations*—rests upon the idea of "ordered complexes of individuals" [geordnete Mannigfaltigkeiten] rather than on domains characterized as sets of "disconnected particulars" [unverbundene Besonderheiten—Cassirer 1910: 22]. In comparison with this, Saussure's theory of structure appears simplistic in that it only provides a criterion for the membership in the set of elements that form some particular structure.

Karcevskij's recourse to Cassirer is interesting for other reasons as well. The laws of concept formation that Cassirer's theorizing involved were purely static laws, and they were not linked to, or translatable to, the mechanism of causation—they were simply assumed to apply. This approach corresponded perfectly to the methodological sentiment of the Prague Circle, as is witnessed by the desire to leave the causalism and evolutionism of the nineteenth century behind. This tendency, of course, was consonant with the Circle's later appreciation of Husserl and of such notions as Stumpf's Strukturgesetz.[20] Thus, the new concept of linguistic structure ultimately relates to the turn-of-the-century epistemological discussions in European (pre-)phenomenological psychology and varieties of gnoseologically oriented philosophy, rather than to Saussure.[21]

The new concept of structure quickly found its way into phonology in the form of a technically articulated theory of phonological correlations. The idea of organizing sound inventories in a manner resembling correlations had probably been around for some time in one form or another. In a 1922 study, the Norwegian linguist Alf Sommerfelt—later an advocate of the Circle's ideas and Jakobson's personal friend—suggested that the consonantal system of Old Irish was characterized "par deux grandes oppositions qui le traversent tout entier" (Sommerfelt 1922: 7). Sommerfelt visualized one of these grandes oppositions—that between palatals and non-palatals—in the following way:

k k'
g g'
b b'
t t'
d d'

L L'
R R'
N N'
m m'
s s'
f f'

But Sommerfelt does not say how each of the classes of sounds represented here relates to the other, let alone that they form a correlation. On the Prague view of structure, however, the sounds listed in
the right column relate to the sounds in the left column in a specific
way: the right column depends on, or is implied by, the left column.
It was only in the Prague phonology that this relationship became
subject of interest and was ultimately made the basis of the theory of
markedness.

Much of the relevant inquiry stems from Jakobson and from the
discourse between him and Trubetzkoy. Their discussion on the
topic begins—at least in its documented epistolary form—with the
publication of Jakobson's *Remarques,* to which Trubetzkoy reacted
with exaltation in a letter dated November 2, 1929. On July 30, 1930,
he added:

Obviously every (or, perhaps not every?) phonological correlation assumes
in linguistic consciousness the form of a contrast between the presence or
absence of some feature (or the maximum or minimum of a feature). In such
a way, one of the members of a correlation inevitably appears as "basic," "active," and the other as the "negative," "passive." (Jakobson 1975: 162f.)

Jakobson's reaction to Trubetzkoy's remarks has been preserved.
He responded to Trubetzkoy on November 26, 1930, just weeks before the Reunion phonologique, the first conference dedicated to
phonology:

Your idea that correlation is always a relationship between a marked and
unmarked series is one of your most brilliant and productive thoughts. I
think that it will be of importance not only for linguistics, but also for ethnology and history of culture, and that historico-cultural correlations such
as life-death, freedom-lack of freedom, sin-virtue, festive days-workdays, etc.,
always reduce to relationships of the type *a/non-a,* and that it is important
to establish for each epoch, group, nation, etc., what precisely constitutes
the marked series. (Jakobson 1975: 163)

Whereas Trubetzkoy's remarks were restricted to a linguistic discussion, Jakobson's reply is almost shocking in the way it demonstrates his unrestrained readiness to transpose linguistic notions to a general level, to raise linguistic methodology to a general model of research.

7.3 The Courage to Synthesize

So far, we have seen that the Prague doctrine accumulated a number of "dissident" themes which, although discussed by other linguists, were still new. The Circle added relatively few new concepts, such as those of layered structure and mark. In view of this it might seem that the doctrine was essentially syncretic, merely accumulating themes rather than developing new ones. But before we draw that conclusion, let us go back some two decades and briefly touch upon certain judgments that Czech linguists made on the style of their discipline.

One year after Gebauer's death, Josef Janko wrote in a survey on the state of Czech linguistics:

Under the aegis of Gebauer there was a great deal of very diligent work done in Old Czech grammar, mainly by the present or past members of his seminar. . . . This is not the place to name all these eager collectors and observers, monographists in the true sense of the word. . . . (Janko 1908: 273)

The eager collecting and the small-scale puzzle work (monographism) that Janko held in high esteem were no longer universally appreciated after World War I. Oldřich Hujer, another of Gebauer's students, was obviously dissatisfied when he found in a survey of Czech linguistics in 1922 that "among the works written on the Czech language there is not yet a study of a synthetic nature to provide a comprehensive view; the monographic type of work is the most common here, dealing with particular phenomena and special questions" (Hujer 1922: 115). And remarks such as these were not restricted to linguistics. Commenting on the work of Otakar Hostinský, a Czech philosopher and an influential student of aesthetics, one of his disciples wrote: "Hostinský was not a *systematic scholar* in the genuine sense of the word, he was a born monographist instead." (Nejedlý 1921: viii)

Presenting the terms "monograph" and "monographist" and the phrase "work on a particular phenomenon [Einzelerscheinung]" in a negative light was a final act of distancing from the era of Positivism. The new discourse that was forming was meant to stand in contrast with the old ideals. It created its own vocabulary, introducing, among other things, a set of topoi that highlighted the courage to synthesize and to give a bold vision to the field. Inability or unwillingness to write a work of synthetic nature was thus perceived as an instance of scholarly impotence or of the lack of scholarly courage.[22]

It is against this background that the emergence of what appears to be a mixed doctrine must be understood. The doctrine was actually synthetic rather than syncretic. Correspondingly, it sought adequate forms of expression—one of which was the *program*, understood as a label for a genre (similar to a manifesto). The major example of this genre are the Theses Presented to the First International Congress of Slavists (Circle 1929), a program of linguistic research unveiled before a rather conservative community of Slavists convening in Prague in the autumn of 1929.

Perhaps inspired by the publishing format of programs distributed at the Hague congress, the Theses (originally in Czech) had the form of loose leaflets.[23] There are ten in all, some of them brief statements not exceeding several paragraphs and some of them several pages long.[24] The topics range from methodology to the application of functional linguistics to school instruction. Thesis 3 has a subsection on poetic language. The first Thesis, which is on methodology, restates points that are by now familiar: Language is defined as a system of goal-oriented means of expression. The role of speaker's intention is stressed. A synchronic approach with an emphasis on typology and a provision for a synthesis of synchronic and diachronic points of view is envisaged. Subsequently, much emphasis is placed on phonology. Some points are fleshed out more completely than before; in particular, the section on the functions of language and standard literary language in Thesis 3 is the most explicit statement on the so-called language functions up until that point. Although only two functions are still recognized (communicative and poetic), other concepts, such as internal, external, emotive, and intellectual speech, are introduced. On the whole, however, one has the feeling that the impact of the Viennese psychologist and student of mental functions Karl Bühler (see especially Bühler 1909) and the line of research he represented had not yet entered the Prague doctrine. Some themes appear only in the form of anticipatory notes. Of these, at least one became a full-fledged project in the 1930s. This was Trubetzkoy's morphophonemics, a profound innovation in linguistic theory.

Naturally, the Theses did not provide the sort of detailed perspective that an encyclopedia or a textbook provides, yet they embodied the spirit of synthesis in articulating a comprehensive project. Like the brief programs from the Hague, they had the demonstrative effect of a manifesto. With them, the earlier self-indictments about the lack of courageous scholarly vision were finally transcended. In retrospect, much in the Theses appears too heterogeneous to yield adequate results; however, it is important to realize that they were directed against the atomistic character of the nineteenth-century linguistics and that they expressed dissatisfaction with the "monographism" and affirmation of "normal science." Moreover, not only do the Theses radiate the magic of a common language; besides that, they are imbued with a collective spirit—they were signed by the Circle, not by individual authors.

8

Un'organizzazione combattiva

The early years of the Prague Circle can be chronologically summarized as follows:

1925—private meetings at Mathesius's home

1926—formal meetings begin

1928—Mathesius, Jakobson, Karcevskij, Trubetzkoy, and Weingart participate in First International Congress of Linguists, held in The Hague

1929—the Theses are prepared, and the Circle presents itself as a group to the Congress of Slavists

1930—the Circle becomes a registered society, and the Reunion phonologique (the world's first conference on phonology) is held in Prague

1932—lecture series on language culture ("Purism Debate")

Some of these events are particularly important from the viewpoint of group dynamics. This chapter discusses the stages of the group process and establishes the role of collectivistic ideals.[1]

8.1 The Group's Dynamics

The Fusion

Despite the fact that the Circle "was no product of chance," as Mathesius later put it,[2] visible results were somewhat slow in coming. In 1928 the Circle was no more than a discussion group,[3] but during its preparations for the First International Congress of Slavists (to be convened in Prague in December 1929) a significant change took place. The Circle decided to work out a comprehensive program of its work and present it to the Congress collectively. In the few months during which the Theses were being drafted and discussed, a deep restructuring of the Circle's group dynamics occurred—as is evident from the following passage in a letter from Jakobson to Trubetzkoy dated April 16, 1929:

The initiative core of the circle has now concluded that the circle in its function as a parliament of opinions, as a platform for a free discussion, is a relic, and that it has to be transformed into a group, a party, which is tightly interlocked as far as scientific ideology is concerned. This process is taking place at present with much success. An initiative committee of sorts has established itself in the circle, including Mathesius, a very able linguist Havránek, Mukařovský, Trnka, and myself. This transformation of the circle literally inspirited its members; in fact, I have never seen such a degree of enthusiasm in the Czechs at all. (RJP b. 123, f. 51)

Jakobson and Mathesius seem to have shared the leadership of the group, Mathesius occupying the senior position because he had natural authority as an instigator of the Circle, was academically well established, and enjoyed general recognition. Jakobson, the vice president, complemented him as "the cementing force of the Circle":

[Jakobson] knew everyone and he knew how to make everyone interested in the activities of the Circle. When by chance he was not present because he was detained by his University duties in Brno, the usual zest of the meeting was missing. It seems to me that the audience was waiting for him, especially for his part in the discussion which followed every lecture. (Součková 1976: 2)[4]

In moments of crisis, not surprisingly, Jakobson's role was described in negative terms. After leaving the Circle in 1934, Weingart saw in Jakobson only a big manipulator. The value judgment removed, this opinion upholds Jakobson's crucial role.

The feeling that the Circle was unique in its group dynamics is well documented in contemporary sources, including this lengthy passage by Mathesius:

With the Prague Linguistic Circle an institution came into existence which in a number of respects represents something new in our scholarly life.

First of all, one must stress that the heart which drives and regulates the entire activity of the Circle is scholarly discussion. If we look around in Prague's academic ambience, we soon see that it does not provide many opportunities for scholarly discussion in general and linguistic in particular. Neither learned societies nor scholarly groups were able to create an atmosphere in which discussion could flourish. . . . The Prague Linguistic Circle is an exception to this. In its meetings, which take place twice a month, and are alternately located at the English Department of Charles University and at members' homes, more than half of the time is reserved for discussion; and it is usually quite difficult to make the participants part, notwithstanding the late hour. In my opinion, there are two reasons for this: first, the intimacy of the atmosphere, which is a result of the fact that the Circle is a closed society whose members have grown together through frequent contact; secondly, there is identity of intellectual interests which exercises mutual attraction. (Mathesius 1929: 1130)

While using many group-dynamically relevant key words—"intimacy of atmosphere," "mutual attraction," "closed group," "identity of intellectual interests"—Mathesius emphasizes discussion, thus revealing that he may have been a little surprised by the fusion and by the subsequent low priority attached to a "parliament of opinions."

In the same connection, Milada Součková recalled that "seldom was a Czech without an accent heard," and that "even those who hardly knew how to speak any other language but their native Czech acquired a kind of queer pronunciation after some time" (Součková 1976: 2).[5] This is an important indicator of the group's cohesion.

The Clashes

The evidence available indicates that the Circle was rather radical in the way it enforced its requirement of loyalty. Paragraph 9 in the by-laws of the Circle (which date from late 1930) states:

He who is excluded from the Circle ceases to be its member. Each member of the Circle has the right of proposing to the executive committee the exclusion of a member whose conduct is at variance with the purpose of the Circle. (Circle 1930)[6]

This clause is based on the first paragraph of the Statutes, which explicitly names the purpose of the Circle as "to work on the basis of functional-structural method toward progress in linguistic research" (ibid.) Since new members had to affirm their conformity with the Statutes in writing, they were also effectively underwriting this first point. Apparently, some newcomers had reservations about an explicit declaration of loyalty—René Wellek, for instance, reacted with enthusiasm to the news of his admission to the Circle, and expressed his complete agreement with the by-laws, but then added:

I would only like to remark that the admiration I have for structural methods does not exclude that I should work in literary history with other, especially ideographic methods, as follows from my entire previous research. (to Mathesius, September 21, 1934; APLK) [7]

Wellek's case is singular, though. An unreserved assertion of methodological conformity was a part of the Circle's scholarly culture. This is witnessed by a portrait of the Circle that Roman Jakobson wrote for the Italian review *La Cultura* in 1933:

. . . already in 1929, during the Congress of Slavists in Prague, [the Circle] presented itself as *a militant and disciplined organization,* with precise programmatic theses. The novelty of the structure of this Circle, in contrast to the traditional type of scholarly society, appears in the fact that the Circle renounces carrying out the task of a parliament containing diverse currents and proclaims openly in its statutes that it aims at collaborating in the progress of linguistic research on the basis of the structural functional method, and that the activity of any member of the Circle which shows itself in opposition to this program will result in his *expulsion.* (Jakobson 1933a: 636; emphasis added)

Both the Statutes and this passage, which echoes Jakobson's letter to Trubetzkoy quoted above, raise the question of discipline and, ultimately, exclusion. Whereas members of a non-radical group may become passive or simply lose interest and leave the group once they feel a dissonance between their work and that of the other members, a radical group often reserves the right to punish by means of expulsion. In view of this, two conflicts in which members left the Prague Circle under conditions approaching expulsion should be reviewed.

The first case is that of the literary historian J. V. Sedlák. Sedlák was one of the most regular participants in the Circle's meetings between April 1927 and January 1930, and on February 8, 1929, he delivered a lecture entitled "Literary History and Literary Science."

However, his approach was apparently geisteswissenschaftlich—he did not hold formal analysis, particularly in the area of prosody, in high esteem. Vojtěch Jirát, another member of the Circle, noted that Sedlák's approach was somewhat one-sided and claimed that for Sedlák pure spirit and its laws provided the only basis of explanation. The mechanics of the clash are not documented, but it is known that two members of the Circle soon attacked Sedlák's work fiercely. Jakobson (1929f) published a scathing review of *On the Problem of Poetic Rhythm* (Sedlák 1929), and so did Mukařovský (1929). Jakobson called the book "catastrophic," "childish," and "fatally confused," and he branded Sedlák's approach *pavěda* [pseudo-science, degenerate scholarship]. No formal record of his expulsion is known, but Jakobson wrote to Trubetzkoy on May 28, 1930: "We have managed to exclude Sedlák." (RJP box 123, folder 51) Sedlák was last recorded as attending a meeting of the Circle on January 13, 1930. The Decennial Report simply states that he ceased to be a member in 1930 (Circle 1936a, p. 13).

The second case, which involves Miloš Weingart, cannot be documented accurately either, but the basic facts are clear. Weingart was a very active member of the Circle, served on one of its committees, and participated in a 1932 discussion about purism that caught the attention of the general public (see below). He disliked the positivistic spirit of nineteenth-century Slavic studies, and he had no inhibitions about criticizing Gebauer and his generation as empiricists, monographists, and the like. However, his traditional personal profile and inclinations suggest that he was one of the more conservative members of the Circle—for example, he was once cited as evidence that not all members of the Circle liked modern art and literature. It is also obvious from Weingart's publications that, although he was well familiar with the structural-functional framework and with its intellectual context,[8] he was not really using it analytically; he tended toward traditional philological positions. Only after Weingart's departure from the Circle (in September 1934) did an open conflict flare up. This culminated in an open critique of Jan Mukařovský in which Weingart (1935–36) described the Prague Linguistic Circle as too easily manipulated by Jakobson and as forgetful of the Czech tradition in formal studies of literature. Weingart portrayed

Mukařovský as a gifted but superficial and impressionistic scholar who naively followed fashionable Soviet imports, including dialectic and such related notions as Hegelian Selbstbewegung.[9] On the basis of an open letter in which the Circle responded to Weingart formally in October 1934, one may conclude that Weingart was not excluded but rather left on his own (see Weingart 1935–36: 208). The letter expresses hopes for friendly relations in the future, but obviously no such friendliness was in the cards. On December 17, 1935, the Circle condemned Weingart's scholarship in extenso at a meeting convened solely for that purpose. Thus, although he was not formally excluded, the desire of the Circle to distance itself from him in a dramatic collective action was very clear—one almost has the feeling that the Circle was disappointed that an opportunity to apply paragraph 9 had slipped away.[10]

8.2 The Ideal of Collective Work

The Prague Circle explicitly and consciously emphasized collective work. In this respect, it is instructive to compare the Circle with the group of German linguists known as the Neogrammarians. They too were a highly visible group within the linguistic community; indeed, they were accused of forming a faction. Hugo Schuchardt called them a "school," and Adalbert Bezzenberger called them a "closed party." However, Hermann Paul (a Neogrammarian) protested that he merely shared certain goals with Karl Brugmann and Hermann Osthoff. Paul was also unwilling to accept the accusation that he and Eduard Sievers associated with Osthoff and Brugmann "for party purposes" [zu Parteizwecken]. Speaking about the use of the term "Neogrammarian" by Osthoff and Brugmann, Paul added:

A name such as this could nourish the idea that a closed clique exists with a set of definite beliefs and a party discipline—something one is unfortunately used to in scholarly life. Such an idea is, however, not justified. . . . (Paul 1886, column 3)

Paul argued that he was merely part of a community of scholars who felt "a certain coherence among themselves and a certain opposition against the older and backward ones." "However," he continued, "it does not follow from this that they are bound to feel solidarity among themselves, be accountable for one another or that each of them cannot pursue his own independent way in research." (Paul 1886, column 3) Paul clearly felt uneasy about the idea that scholarship could be influenced by matters not intrinsic to research. Evidently he was using the expression "party discipline" with a negative connotation and was rejecting the concept of solidarity—perhaps out of embarrassment at the idea of presenting scholarly work in a collective context.

Whereas some degree of loyalty is an automatic component of the group process, collective work was a value per se in the Prague Circle. This is the basic difference vis-à-vis earlier group formations, such as the Neogrammarians. Contemporaries noted that in its conscious display of the collective spirit the Prague Circle was unusual among schools. Reporting on the Circle to an Italian newspaper, the Italian Slavist Renato Poggioli listed several characteristics of the Prague doctrine and added:

What is important in our connection are not so much the results but the system of work. This consists—as laid down in the first article of the Circle's Statutes—"in collective activity aimed toward the resolution of current linguistic issues." . . . Whenever a group of the Circle's members participates in an international congress, they present a collective scholarly memorandum to which—in accordance with the ancient principle of the division of labor—each member has contributed with his own bit of scholarship. And also in the normal yearly work, the group always embarks, with zealous discipline, upon a sole and specific topic, which the research of all the members will settle with a maximum of pedantic accuracy. (Poggioli 1937)

Poggioli further noted that the Circle was able to proceed in a premeditated manner "as if this was a kind of spiritual Taylorism or Stakhanovism"—something that the Slavs and the Germans were particularly good at, in contrast with the Italians. (Poggioli's (1962) description is interesting if only for the fact that he later wrote an important interpretation of twentieth-century avant-garde movements in which group dynamics played a significant part.)

Of course, in view of contemporary attitudes there is nothing very mysterious about the Prague Circle's conscious cultivation of collectivism. Recall Mathesius's remarks on collective courage in the essay

"Czech Science." Consider also the wording of Jakobson's letter to Trubetzkoy (quoted above), and compare it with the following passage from an essay by F. X. Šalda, a prominent Czech critic and later a member of the Circle:

Parliamentarianism, which is so intimately connected with democracy, is today in decline everywhere. The competition among parties cripples its activity, thus making it a clumsy machine which permanently stumbles and produces phrases instead of work. (Šalda 1927 [1963: 263])

This is quite consonant with Jakobson's contrast between a "parliament of opinions" and a "combat organization."

In general, the epoch disfavored what was termed "excessive individualism" and placed much confidence in the collective. Scholars were in no way exempt from this admiration of collective values. In September 1929, Logical Positivists from Berlin and Vienna organized a joint meeting—curiously, in Prague—on the occasion of which the Viennese Ernst Mach Society produced a small brochure entitled *Wissenschaftliche Weltanschauung—Der Wiener Kreis*. The preface asserted that the Vienna Circle consisted of "men of identical scholarly attitude" and that each of them "strives after integration, each foregrounds the unifying aspects, no one will disturb solidarity by individualism" (Carnap et al. 1929: 14). In the preface to *Der logische Aufbau der Welt*, Carnap described collective research as follows: "The individual does not aspire at constructing the entire edifice of philosophy in a single bold throw. Instead, everyone works in his specific place within one single science" (Carnap 1928: iv). Thus, the Viennese philosophers were embarking not only upon what was believed to be a radical rejection of metaphysics, but also upon a redefinition of the place of scholars in research and in society. That even geniuses agreed on the idea that scholars no longer were individualists is not surprising. In 1930, Albert Einstein wrote the following in a letter to *Literaturnaja gazeta,* which he addressed to the people of the Soviet Union:

The tragedy of the European character since the Renaissance times consists in a disproportional emphasis of one's own "ego". . . in a detachment of an individual from from the collective, something foreign to the world of Classical Antiquity and to the nations of the East. (Einstein 1930: 316) [11]

8.3 Collective Statements, Collective Actions

Collective Texts, 1928–1930

Although the collectivistic perspective was certainly not unique to the Circle, it would be a mistake to think that the Circle was just blindly following an intellectual fashion. Mathesius, Jakobson, Trnka, and other members repeatedly mentioned the collective nature of the Circle's work and asserted it very seriously. Correspondingly, the number of texts and actions conceived collectively was quite large. Consider these, listed in chronological order:

"Proposition 22" (Jakobson et al. 1928a)

"Geneva-Prague Declaration" (Bally et al. 1928)

"Theses Presented to the First Congress of Slavic Philologists" (Circle 1929)

"Projet de terminologie phonologique standardisée" (Circle 1931a)

"Principes de transcription phonologique" (Circle 1931b)

"Theses on Language Culture" (Circle 1932)

"A Reply to J. Haller" (Circle 1933) [12]

Among these texts the Theses stand out.

On the basis of documents available today, individual sections of the Theses can be associated with particular authors.[13] However, Mathesius described the process by which they were written as follows:

This program presented to the Prague Congress of Slavists in the form of theses . . . is a result of genuinely collective scholarly work. The participants of the congress may of course say that one chapter is worked out according to suggestions of a certain member of the Circle and the other according to those of another, yet the final formulation is the result of joint work in which individual authorship gave way to collective effort. (Mathesius 1929: 1131)

Thus, the force of the Theses derives from the merger of two distinct perspectives: the idea of a synthesis of knowledge and its execution by collective means.

Further texts were worked out by the members of the Circle on the occasion of the Réunion phonologique: "Projet de terminologie phonologique standardisée" (Circle 1931a) and "Principes de transcription phonologique" (Circle 1931b). In form, these publications do not resemble manifestos; nonetheless, they are collective works. Publishing a list of definitions and a system of notation can be seen as an attempt to control the discourse, but in this case the general focus was on a planned, systematic approach to research. Standardization, in any case, was one of the key words of the period.

Collective Actions: The Purism Debate (1932)

The Prague Circle as an "organizzazione combattiva" came to the foreground with the Purism Debate, a public lecture series on language culture held in January 1932. This debate, which took place before a domestic audience, established the Circle on the Czech cultural horizon much more forcefully than its international success had. Moreover, it gained the attention of some prominent literary authors.

The "combat action" was directed against *Naše řeč* [*Our Language*], a Prague philological journal devoted to questions of good Czech. The editor-in-chief, Jiří Haller, was the main target of criticism. Haller, not quite 40 years old when *Naše řeč* was entrusted to him, soon gained a reputation for pedantry. He also clearly disliked functional linguistics:

There are people who one-sidedly regard language as a mere tool of communication. They are fully satisfied if language fulfills its communicative function. But they are not worried about what language is like. To them, correctness of language is reduced to mere comprehensibility. They are materialists whose approach is a direct consequence of their attitude to spiritual values of human life in general. But he who understands that language is more than a tool of communication, that it is the most characteristic means by which we express our national, artistic, and personal culture, recognizes that one cannot only avail oneself of language, one has to serve it, too. (Haller 1931a: 204)

In 1929, when Vítězslav Nezval, a leading avant-garde poet,[14] published a novel entitled *A Chronicle from the End of a Millennium,* Haller decided to examine it in *Naše řeč*, although it was not really customary to review literary works there. Haller took a normative linguistic point of view and suggested that there were strong reasons for doing so. His characterization of Nezval is revealing:

Nezval is an adherent of new poetry which sees its task not in a stylistically perfect presentation of beautiful ideas, but rather in an arbitrary depiction of the world of images and impressions. For this it suffices to put together singularities, petty ideas and unusual metaphors in loose complexes which cohere only by means of untamed associations of memories and impressions. (Haller 1930: 153)

He then went on to suggest that an author of this type must fail when confronted with the task of writing a novel. Such an enterprise requires a serious and concentrated approach to language and a firm command of the mother tongue. Nezval possessed none of these qualities. This introduction was followed by an enumeration of mistakes in which Haller listed morphological forms which he thought were wrong, examined Nezval's phraseology, and found a number of typographical errors.

In early 1931, *Naše řeč* published a similar analysis of *Duše a slovo* [*Soul and Word*], a book of literary essays by Otokar Fischer, a literary scholar and a member of the Prague Circle.[15] Haller (1931b) again evinced a list of mistakes, of which he said there were at least 200—many of them German corruptions.

Among the first to respond was the novelist Ivan Olbracht, a leftist in politics but a relatively conservative stylist. His critical remarks on Haller (Olbracht 1931) started an avalanche of further essays and glosses. Olbracht was willing to accept the existence of a journal concerned with normative problems in the domain of official and commercial documents, but he disputed Haller's right to evaluate the language of literature in such a manner:

. . . literary language is much more complicated than the primitive language of administration. . . . It has a different function. . . . In matters of linguistic expression a creative person cannot confine himself to what is regarded as correct by official authorities. . . . For the writer language is merely a tool, not material as it is for the philologist. (Olbracht 1931 [1958: 103f.])

Amid the discussions prompted by Olbracht's comments on Haller, the Circle decided to take a position on questions of linguistic norm. For this purpose, it organized the above-mentioned lecture series, publishing the lectures in a volume titled *Standard Czech and Language Culture* (Havránek and Weingart 1932).

Besides giving the Circle an established enemy, the controversy gave the Circle an opportunity to present itself as a coherent group to the domestic audience. Such an opportunity is not always easily available to a scholarly group; it requires a topic that is of immediate general interest. The question of linguistic correctness was exactly such a topic. The echoes of the lecture series were overwhelming.[16] In addition, the lecture series was immediately recognized as something unusual as far as public behavior of scholarly groups is concerned. Otokar Fischer (1932: 269) noted that "what characterizes the method of the members of the Prague Linguistic Circle is their collective way of acting, the collective character of their tactics, of their fight."

In addition, the discussion was a slap in the face of established Slavic scholarship. Mathesius stated that such scholarship had little relevance to questions of standard language and stressed the fact that among the authors of *Standard Czech and Language Culture* there was not a single specialist in Czech "but instead an Anglicist, two Slavic comparatists, a Russist, and an aesthetician" (1934b : 345). He may have exaggerated a little bit (Havránek, Jakobson, and Weingart *were* Slavists), but he was essentially right in pointing out that Bohemists (i.e., specialists in Czech philology) played no role in forming the Prague doctrine of language culture.

The impact of the aforementioned debate on a number of younger authors is perhaps best summarized by Olbracht's statement that, for a writer, language is merely an instrument. This statement shows that among the young generation of authors the attitude toward language had changed greatly. The counterposition, represented by the older generation, was that language was a national heritage, a sacred treasure that had to be kept pure. Such opinions were openly voiced until the 1930s in *Naše úřední čeština* [*Our Administrative Czech*], a journal whose name may have well been invented by the good soldier Švejk.

Many other writers, along with much of the general public, were impressed by the expertise, the scholarship, and the assertiveness of the Prague Circle linguists. The Purism Debate thus reinforced the position of specialists, who were now seen as more than mere advisors—and some of whom now thought of themselves as social planners.

One of the reasons why the Circle was reaching the avant-garde artistic audience with such ease is that it had assimilated itself to avant-garde standards by its conscious emphasis on collectivism and its bellicose public appearance. Much of this attitude remained visible throughout the 1930s. The Russian pattern of a merger between scholars and the avant-garde was effective in Prague as well. The affinity was deep. The magic of a common language was accompanied by the magic of a common behavior.

9

The Rhetoric of Modernity: More on Ideals of Scholarship and Society

The 1930s—the period in which the Prague Circle flourished—was a period vastly different from the 1920s. Young intellectuals were more and more preoccupied with social and cultural projects in which planning, order, and cooperation were assuming value in and of themselves. Of course such sentiments had been present in European ideological discourses for a considerable period of time, especially among thinkers unsympathetic to capitalism and its nineteenth-century ideology, liberalism; however, in the 1930s there was a particularly strong desire for grand visions—a penchant for monumental clarity that was, perhaps, nowhere so transparent as in the cold merger of Classicism and Gothic that occurred in architecture and design. That desire had a certain impact on Czech social and cultural thought, and thus on the Prague Circle. In this chapter I will survey the specific language and the specific figures of thought that were involved. In particular, I will document the discourse on anarchy and order via Roman Jakobson's writings, touching upon the emergence of a major theme in the Circle: dialectic, which was thought to provide the key to a modern synthesis. I will also discuss Josef Ludvík Fischer, a Czech social philosopher whose language shows a striking affinity with Jakobson's. Finally, I will analyze one of the Circle's late programmatic statements, the introduction to the first volume of the Circle's journal *Slovo a slovesnost,* pointing to the image of medieval society and its role in intellectual work.[1]

9.1 Jakobson's Ideological Lexicon

Jakobson's bibliography between 1915 and 1939—essentially the period covered here—lists more than 200 publications, including books, scholarly articles, and newspaper glosses. Many of these items are strictly technical, but many others are essayistic and topical. Regarding all these texts with a philological eye, one soon recognizes a unique universe of words that is characterized by a specific rhetoric and a very consistent set of topoi. In the following I will concentrate on topoi extracted from texts that have been regarded as marginal, such as obituaries, salutations, and congress reports. The selection revolves around Jakobson's evaluation of the second part of the nineteenth century, and around the alternative—a cultural synthesis of the twentieth century.[2]

Discourse on the Past and the Future

An instructive case is Jakobson's use of the term "mechanical." This term, which occurs early in his discourse (see Flejšman 1977: 127), is quite frequent toward the end of the 1920s—consider the final pages of the *Remarques*:

Mechanical accumulation resulting from a fortuitous coincidence or heterogenous factors—such is the favorite image of European ideology ruling in the second half of the nineteenth century. Contemporary ideology . . . highlights . . . a functional system instead of a mechanical addition. . . . (Jakobson 1929a: 100)

In the same passage, Jakobson contrasts Einstein's conception of the universe with the old conception, describing the latter as a "mechanic sum." Also, the association psychology of the nineteenth century is characterized as taking recourse to "a mechanical concatenation of associations." (Association psychology remains "mechanical" to Jakobson throughout the 1930s; see Jakobson 1936g: 81.)

The 1930s provide further instances of this usage, always with a negative connotation: the Czech literary scholar V. Jirát applies psychoanalysis "mechanically" (Jakobson 1931e: 452); it is a dangerous mistake to make "mechanical and simplistic distinction between poetic and practical language" (Jakobson 1932a: 114); the naturalist approach of the nineteenth century merely recognizes "relations of quantity and mechanic causality" (Jakobson 1933a: 639); causality is a category of a mechanical worldview (Jakobson 1939a: 68); the Neogrammarians stayed "in the drag of a mechanistic approach," their insistence on the infallibility of sound laws proving "too mechanistic" (Jakobson 1935d: 1214). Finally, language is given a new definition in structuralism, one that is incompatible with that of the Neogrammarians: "Language is not an accidental, mechanical conglomerate, but a whole; individual linguistic components can only be understood through its relation to the whole." (Jakobson 1935d: 1214)

"Mechanical" is not the only anathema applied to the era of Positivism—there is a whole cluster of passages in which Jakobson uses "atom" and "atomistic" in exposing misguided methodology:

In opposition to atomistic study of individual verse components . . . a conception of verse is growing which views parts as inseparably determined by the whole, and the whole determined by its parts. (Jakobson 1936b: 214)

To a naturalistically oriented researcher the sound-inventory of language turned into a mass of oscillating motoric and acoustic atoms. (Jakobson 1939c: 280)

Further tokens of "atomism" document this approach: Naturalism "reduces reality to atomic dust" (Jakobson 1933a: 639); European science is fighting for the "overcoming of atomistic methods" (Jakobson 1935e); individual scholars are praised for rejecting atomism (Jakobson 1932b) or for successfully overcoming it (Jakobson 1937a, 1938d). Atomism even befriends anarchy, and the fight against anarchy is a prime feature of modern scholarship:

Hand in hand with the fight of European scholarship against the atomism of the West there go the efforts to overcome the anarchy of scholarly creativity and the extreme individualism inherited from the recent past. (Jakobson 1935e)

"Fragmentation" is a closely related key word from the negative list. Reporting on the Second International Congress of Linguists in Geneva, Jakobson asserts:

It seems to me that the spirit of this congress can be most concisely and appropriately described by stating that this was a fight of a systematic, constructive scholarly worldview against the spirit of anarchy and fragmentation. (Jakobson 1931i)

Less conspicuous but quite characteristic of Jakobson's style is "episodic." Only once do we find it used positively: Porzeziński's influence on Polish linguistics was "fortunately only episodic" (Jakobson 1929d). Obviously, that Polish linguist does not receive a kind treatment here, and no wonder—he was just a Neogrammarian follower.

Elsewhere we read that Meillet knew how to avoid episodic work ("Slavic issues were not a mere episode in Meillet's biography" (Jakobson 1937a: 24)), that the contact between the West and the USSR is still "too casual, episodic, private, unorganized" (Jakobson 1935e), and that the nineteenth century produced paintings characterized by "episodism":

Let us compare discontinuity and episodism of a naturalist painting to a composition by Cézanne, an integral system of relations of volumes. (Jakobson 1929a: 100)[3]

Jakobson's negative vocabulary also includes "(the second half of the) nineteenth century," "individualism,"and "causality." His positive vocabulary is perhaps less striking, since it includes elements we may not necessarily understand as ideological today—"plan," "planning," "coordination," "organization." But the value of these elements to Jakobson is clear. Meillet's complaint that "scholarship . . . is badly organized, actually not organized at all" (Jakobson 1937a: 240) ranks the French linguist among scholars with contemporary concerns. Mathesius, and his spiritual father Masaryk, and the Czechs in general, remain the classic examples of an organized approach to scholarship:

As a researcher and organizer Mathesius proceeds strictly systematically. One can entertain high expectations as far as the realization of the plan is concerned. (Jakobson 1932b)

I think that Masaryks' grandiose organizational vision is a concentrated expression of Czech mentality, as documented in various periods of Czech cultural history. (Jakobson 1930: 414)

Significantly, the ideal of organization is not constrained by political boundaries; for Jakobson, Soviet scholarship is a great example:

The grandiose Russian attempts to *plan* scholarship are especially instructive for Western scholarship. . . . (Jakobson 1935e)

Grand contours matter, rather than details:

. . . it is not so much the details that are so instructive about the new Soviet scholarship but the overall unbroken tendency to overcome the fragmentation of knowledge and to replace the membra disjecta of the individual disciplines through a unified interlocked system of a coordinate science. (Jakobson 1935e)

This brief survey is intended to show that we are dealing with a set of expressions, used very consistently over a span of many years, that elevate structuralism to a worldview. The subsequent discussion will elaborate on this claim and give further details.

Discourse on Dialectical Synthesis

Dialectic in History and in Language

Whereas a radically critical stance vis-à-vis the second part of nineteenth century and a vision of meaningfully planned research began to emerge early in Jakobson's reasoning, another major ingredient of the new synthesis—dialectic—made a forceful appearance only in the 1930s. References to dialectic are relatively rare in Jakobson's writings from the 1920s (e.g., Jakobson 1927b: 7). However, in the mid 1930s the term begins to appear significantly more frequently, often as an antonym to "mechanical":

Formalism was developing toward dialectical method, but was still considerably marked by mechanistic heritage. (Jakobson 1935c: 192)

The relation of literature to social structure is changeable, and must be understood dialectically, not mechanically. . . . (Jakobson 1935c: 192)

[In the study of metrics] the question of evolutionary tendencies is now asked; the idea of mechanical replacements of forms gradually gives way to questions about internal dialectic of the evolution of rhythm. (Jakobson 1936b: 214)

The use of "dialectic" in these passages is especially significant in view of what the antonyms of "mechanical" had been before: "teleological,"[4] "functional,"[5] and "structural,"[6] among others. All these now recede and a single notion, "dialectical," appears in their place.

Jakobson takes recourse to a dialectical perspective not only in linguistic contexts but also in the context of a progression toward synthesis in culture and scholarship. The latter context might well be called that of a "Romantic-Positivist Synthesis," since the alternative he was seeking was neither a return to Romantism nor a return to Positivism but, rather, a dialectically structured synthesis incorporating

both Romantism and Positivism. An early example of this approach is
Jakobson's evaluation of positivistic dialectology. Recall that Jakobson
did not reject the positivistic legacy in this discipline, but stressed that
its results should be incorporated into current research.[7] However, by
the middle of the 1930s a dialectical gesture raises the synthesis to a
very general level:

> European Romantic science represented an attempt at establishing a *global*
> conception of the Universe. The antithesis of this epoch, Positivistic science,
> sacrified the idea of totality for the price of a maximally exhaustive accumu-
> lation of facts, for a price of discovering a vast repertory of *partial truths*. The
> present time seeks a *synthesis;* it does not wish to lose the general meaning
> and the lawful structure of the dynamics of reality [Geschehen] out of sight.
> And, at the same time, it draws upon the inventory of facts accumulated by
> the preceding epoch. (Jakobson 1935e)

That the study of language should not be exempted from the application of a dialectical perspective is logical from this point of view,
since language was understood as a set of social values and the laws
of dialectic ruled the evolution of social systems in general. A number of passages could be given in which dialectic now victoriously
marches into linguistics to drive out the spirit of the second part of
the nineteenth century. Some of these passages mention the name
of the French linguist Victor Henri, who had introduced an antinom-
ical point of view into study of language. Hegel, however, is the ultimate point of reference:

> Baudouin de Courtenay, Saussure and his predecessor V. Henry uncovered
> sharp linguistic antinomies "speech-language," "synchrony-diachrony," etc.,
> but it only became possible to surmount these antinomies when linguistics,
> turning back to Hegelian tradition, made recourse to the principle of a
> "unity of oppositions" (Prague School, advances in the dialectic of language
> in new Russian scholarship, W. v. Wartburg). (Jakobson 1935d: 1215)

Likewise, the concept of Selbstbewegung indicates the influx of German idealism:

> ... dialectical method underscores the concept of self-movement [Selbstbe-
> wegung] of the linguistic system and raises to a new level [hebt auf] a num-
> ber of fundamental antinomies which were not solvable under any other
> approach. (Jakobson 1936g: 82)

But whatever historical sources may exist for this, the main idea is to have an instrument that describes "tension solving," a notion that appears often in this context:

> One must not forget about the possibility of dialectical tension among specific planes of reality. These contradictions represent substantial levers that move cultural history. (Jakobson 1935 [1971: 392f.])

Thus, the laws of dialectics appear to be the principal movers of history, finally contributing to the overcoming of the stiff Saussurean world of antinomies.

Some Dialectical Parallels
Clearly the upsurge of dialectic is embedded in a more general frame. Essentially, there there is the broader context of Russian Hegelianism and the narrower one of Marxism, each of which left an imprint on the intellectual climate of the 1930s.[8]

The popularity of Hegelianism in Russia is well established (see Holenstein 1984); so are its typically Russian metamorphoses, such as the merger of Husserl's phenomenology with dialectic. Turning to the Prague Linguistic Circle, we find an important advocate of the dialectical approach in Dmytro Čyževśkyj, whose Prague years were sketched in chapter 6. Čyževśkyj was a philosopher with an intensive interest in Hegel and in Slavic Hegelianism; when Jakobson pointed to advances of dialectic in Russian scholarship, he may have actually been referring to Čyževśkyj rather than to the Marxists. Čyževśkyj commented critically on the development of Marxist dialectic in the Soviet Union, noting that in most cases this line of thought consisted of abuse of "dialectically sounding words" (Čyževśkyj 1928), but he regarded this as only an instance of vulgarization. Hegelian dialectic and dialectical linguistics were matters of fact for him:

> Less and less can one ignore the conclusion that language is a unity of *"dialectical nature,"* i.e., that linguistic unity is a synthesis of contradictions, "coincidentia oppositorum." (Čyževśkyj 1936: 250)

In his 1934 monograph on Hegel, he also announced a study entitled "Dialectics of Language," to be jointly written with Jakobson (Čyževśkyj 1934: 250).

This dialectical point of view gained some popularity among the members of the Prague Circle, particularly the Russian ones. Even Trubetzkoy absorbed this language to some degree in his essay "O rasizme" ["On Racism"]:

The dialectic of the historical process requires not only confirmation, but also negation; no movement forward is possible without undermining the authorities, without destroying received traditional convictions. (Jakobson 1975: 473)

With the sole exception of Mukařovský, in whose writings "dialectical" began to appear in 1933[9] and soon became overpowering, the Czechs were not taken with this new point of view. I know of no reference to dialectic by Mathesius, Trnka, or Vachek, although all of them accepted the use of "mechanical" in reference to older linguistic theories. Havránek (1940) was happy with a simple concept of a hierarchically layered system. Defining the notion "structure," he used "sums," "wholes," and "hierarchies" but not "dialectical." (This changed dramatically, however, in the 1950s and the 1960s.)

Aside from the traditional Hegelian context, the penchant for dialectic was certainly enhanced by Marxist critiques of structuralism in literary theory. With the popularity of structuralist theories of literature growing, the Prague Circle became a target of various Marxist critics. Kurt Konrád, a Communist activist and one of the early executors of the Marxist cultural doctrine in Czechoslovakia, was the most prominent.[10] In 1934, Konrád used the occasion of a Czech edition of Šklovskij's *Theory of Prose* to comment extensively on Russian Formalism and Czech Structuralism. While Šklovskij's aphoristic style was a relatively easy prey, the actual target of Konrád's criticism was the author of the afterword, Jan Mukařovský, and with him Roman Jakobson. Konrád's verdict was scathing: although Mukařovský (and Jakobson) had accepted social factors in literary analyses by this point, they remained idealists of the usual sort. "Structuralism," said Konrád (1934a [1980: 70]), "responded to dialectical materialism primarily in a negative way." Among the particularly bad points was the structuralists' subscription to Engliš's teleology—"a newer kind of pure idealism." Konrád thought there was some promise in the Circle's penchant for Gestalt psychology (a discipline he happened to regard as dialectical), but the sociology followed by the structuralists was "idealistic," "mechanistic," based on falsches Bewußtsein, and "non-dialectical" (ibid.: 71).[11] Commenting on *What Is Poetry?* (Jakobson 1934d), Konrád (1934b) targeted structuralism anew, repeatedly raising objections to the absence of dialectic: "Jakobson's analyses certainly cannot be regarded as a step toward materialist dialectic."

Jakobson and Mukařovský were apparently interested in this critique. Some of the Marxist commentators—including Záviš Kalandra, a Surrealist and a radical leftist—were even invited to the Circle's meetings in 1934.[12]

The First Congress of Soviet Writers (Moscow 1934), which produced the doctrine of Socialist Realism, prompted numerous discussions and publications and may well have affected the fate of dialectic in the Circle. Most of the occurrences of the term "dialectical" in the writings of Circle members are from 1934 and thereafter, i.e., from the period of the first major confrontation with Marxism. As a result, the scholars of the Circle actually found themselves in the good graces of their former critics. In 1936, Konrád referred to Jakobson's "Poetry of the Hussite Times" (Jakobson 1935d) as "brilliant" (Konrád 1936 [1980: 140]) and attested to Jakobson's deep understanding of the Hussite revolutionary ideology.

Clearly, the present task is not to establish whether the nature of evolution and the nature of language are properly explained by recourse to dialectic—in all likelihood, they are not. A more interesting question is: Why was the line of dialectical reasoning attractive at all? Although it is certainly possible that Marxism in some sense contributed to the spread of dialectic, it would be somewhat superficial to assign it a key role (or to conclude that Jakobson's study on the Hussite period was a Marxist study). Far more important was the possibility of approaching a particular historical period in a holistic and dynamic way. For this enterprise, dialectic seemed to provide an excellent instrument—one that seemed to appeal to laws while remaining free of causal vocabulary. In pre-structuralist terms, causality acted in evolution blindly and without goal; but the dialectical approach presented historical dynamics in a lawlike appearance, with no reference to causality, and with ample space to build in dynamic solutions of evolutionary goals. Dialectic seemed to offer a perspective that was philosophically better established than such alternatives as teleology, finalism, and functionalism, especially in the Russian tradition, and that seemed particularly suited for historical analyses.

A Postscript on Dialectical Poems
An interesting postscript to the preceding subsection concerns the spread of the language of dialectic in the avant-garde. In view of the ties between the avant-garde and the Prague Circle (represented primarily by Jakobson and Mukařovský), this development is not trivial. Nezval, in the 1930s a surrealist poet, illustrates the fashionable side of the trend—his appeal to dialectic is so inflatory that it strikes the observer immediately. After Nezval published a text on dialectic by Marx in his journal *Zvěrokruh* [*Zodiac*] in December 1929, "dialectical" became one of the most frequent predicates in his theoretical writings. A few examples suffice to illustrate this curious usage:

We Surrealists, aware of the dialectical nature of all processes, know that consciousness is permanently in movement. . . . Only an anti-dialectician can view consciousness and unconsciousness as something imovable, absolute, detached, metaphysical. (Nezval 1934a [1974: 146])

In his Surrealist manifesto of 1934, virtually any piece of surrealist knowledge and activity, including poetry, is termed "dialectical." The Surrealists claim:

5. to understand the [poetic] expression in the dialectical sense of the word . . . ,
6. not to distinguish anti-dialectically the noetic side of the [poetic] expression form its emotional side . . .
7. to understand our [poetic] expression as a result of a dialectical conjunction activity and passivity. . . . (Nezval 1934b [1974: 76])

Dialectical figures also began to appear in Nezval's poetry (Nezval 1933: 157):

Mít vše co měli klasikové	To have everything the Classics had
A přece je to všecko nové	And yet is all this new
Malherbe má čapku pilota	Malherbe wears a pilot-cap
Fotograf zlepšil Corota	Photographer improves on Corot

Not all Western poets were able to find such an ingeniously easy-sounding approach—as is obvious from a comparison with Louis Aragon's "Front Rouge" (1931), in which the French poet also sings of dialectic (the following is quoted from Breton 1932 [1992: 37]):

Il faut que l'univers entende
une voix hurler la gloire de la dialectique matérialiste
qui marche sur ses pieds sur ses millions de pieds
chaussés de bottes militaires
sur ses pieds magnifiques comme la violence
tendant sa multitude de bras armés
vers l'image du Communisme vainqueur
Gloire à la dialectique matérialiste
et gloire à son incarnation
l'armée
Rouge

9.2   Other Synthetic Visionaries

Josef Ludvík Fischer and Bedřich Václavek—neither of them a linguist or a structural theorist of literature—became members of the Prague Linguistic Circle in the mid 1930s. The language of these men, who had once been independent of the Circle, reveals "Jakobsonian" topoi.

Bedřich Václavek
In his 1929 essay-manifesto "The New Man and the New Culture," Bedřich Václavek,[13] a critic and literary scholar today known primarily as a theoretician of Marxist aesthetics in interwar Czechoslovakia, outlined the characteristics of the New Man and the type of society which he creates. Václavek's New Man is agile, inventive, uncomplicated, optimistic, precise, mobile, unsentimental, and naturally curious. He adjusts to new goals. His values are clear. He works methodically rather than relying on ingenuity. He does not indulge in individualistic diversity; he loves integration into the whole. His characteristics are "fundamentally human and socially desirable." All this is congruous with the new type of society:

In personal life—just like in the life of society—plan, order, and law now advance to the foreground. They can fully dominate the life of an individual only in a new society, one liberated from anarchy and "individualism."

Unhealthy *finesse* of the downgraded race of intellectuals and the loneliness of creators is disappearing and will disappear completely. Subordination under artificial dead ideologies will likewise vanish. *Cultural will* of the new growing world is *focusing on the creation of a cultural unity* which had been lacking in Europe since the disintegration of the medieval society. Desire for a higher order cultural unit, for cultural solidarity of classless society, *for an organized and planned cultural production,* is growing on all sides. (Václavek 1929: 1)

It would be somewhat superficial to see this passage as merely an exercise in Czech proto-Communism (or proto-Fascism). The term "classless society" appears only once; the emphases are on an all-European "cultural will" and on "organized and planned cultural production." But these expressions are also crucial to an understanding of the Prague Circle's cultural aspirations. In fact, only a year earlier Vilém Mathesius had written the following, in an essay entitled "The Will for Culture":

A truly cultural life demands a considerable degree of inner discipline from those who actively participate in it. When a thoughtful critic asserts that culture is order in the first place, or when a leading technical practitioner says that culture is primarily the ability to organize work, they ultimately claim the same. The key point is that we subordinate ourselves in a necessary degree to something that is outside of us, or—if you wish—above us, that we subtract something from our subjective Narcissism and sovereignty. (Mathesius 1928b [1982: 346])

No doubt there are considerable differences between Mathesius and Václavek, and specialists in Czech intellectual history may even view the whole comparison as far-fetched. Nebulous attraction by a new order was more typical of the younger generation, and Mathesius continued to refer to cultural prototypes that he thought were already available (such as discipline—a trait of the gentleman-intellectual [džentlmenský typ vzdělance; ibid.] and an ideal instantiated in England). But a basic convergence of cultural ideals cannot be dismissed. The idea of synthesis had an encompassing character that cut across political camps.

Josef Ludvík Fischer

In Josef Ludvík Fischer[14] we also find a Czech intellectual engaged in a systematic (and vociferous) elaboration of an encompassing socio-cultural vision. In developing his conception of society, Fischer stressed the idea that European culture was dominated philosophically and culturally by mechanistic-scientistic concepts and politico-economically by capitalism. The alternative he was developing was a new cultural prototype: a "synthetic society" [skladebná společnost] that would liberate the West from the legacy of mechanism and capitalism. In Fischer's view, steps in the right direction had already been taken in a variety of disciplines:

> The concepts of the whole and Gestalt are now replacing the old mechanistic understanding of atomistic and summative nature of organic and psychic objects, deposing the idea of unique causal determination and meaning-free nature of relationships such objects enter. These concept establish organic and psychic domains in a non-mechanical and meaningful way. (Fischer 1929: 48)

To Fischer, Einstein's theory of relativity and Planck's quantum theory were reactions against the materialistic and mechanistic spirit of the nineteenth century. The latter, in particular, represented a true revolution, because it forcefully devaluated the idea of causal laws. Naturally, the collapse of the Enlightenment and of the spirit of mechanism (including Darwinism) figure in Fischer's argument. In a mechanically conceived science, reality appears senseless [sinnfrei], while meaningful phenomena are regarded as having originated by chance. In contradistinction, new approaches deal with sense.

Much of Fischer's program is formulated in a language that shows striking proximity to the structuralist discourse of the 1930s—Jakobson's in particular. In fact, in "On Two Orders" (1930) Fischer embarked upon foundations of what he literally called a philosophical structuralism. This programmatic statement appeared in the form of a list of theses (naming the old "cultural prototype") and antitheses (developing a new "structural orientation" the fundamental traits of which are synthetism and the resulting interdependence of individual parts and social wholes). This kind of "scientific and philosophical structuralism" includes the idea that "the process of reality is shaped in such a way that its individual constituents are determined by the perspective of totality, i.e., they are incorporated into hierarchically layered wholes as more or less independent constituents" (Fischer 1930: 350).

Fischer also exploited the concept of function, linking it with other key notions of his system: synthesis, hierarchy, hierarchy of functions, and order. He explicated the concept of order as follows in an essay dedicated to the critic and homme des lettres F. X. Šalda:

The epoch we are entering—and one cannot emphasize this enough—is an epoch of order. In sharp contradiction to cultural and social disconnectedness, even anarchy, of the preceding period . . . there emerges a period of cultural and social order, a synthetic period, which embarks upon materializing what the present time so desperately lacks: a unity of the cultural universe—in philosophy, in science, in society, in short, everywhere where the order-creating effort of human spirit can reach. (Fischer 1933: 41)

Fischer's cultural and social philosophy were, in certain respects, quite typical of the sort of Czech philosophy that was (partially under Masaryk's impact) strongly preoccupied with the development of socially effective cultural conceptions and which thus often tended toward social or socio-cultural activism. Needless to say in view of the political reality of the period, writings such as these drew mixed reactions. Critics pointed out the nebulous character of Fischer's concepts, and some also suggested that Fischer had been inspired by slogans familiar from Syndicalism, Italian Fascism, and the ideology of the Soviets, all gravitating toward a critique of capitalist liberalism.[15] Such reactions aside, Fischer, although certainly not a core member of the Prague Circle, is interesting as an advocate of a variant of cultural activism—and dissent—that was couched in a language that was especially appreciated by Roman Jakobson. Indeed, in a survey of the Circle, Jakobson singled out Fischer's *Foundations of Knowledge* (1931) as an example of tendencies that, despite certain differences, were close to the Circle's work:

Factors which bring J. L. Fischer's book into the proximity of the Linguistic Circle include efforts to work out a consequent structuralism and a resistance against scientific currents which atomize reality and apply causally-quantitative categories in social analysis. (Jakobson 1934a: 8)

In an article written a year before for the Italian journal *La Cultura,* Jakobson had simply classified Fischer as a strutturalista.[16]

9.3 A Gothic Note

The main purpose of these sections—and of a large part of this book, for that matter—is to document the vision of a cultural synthesis, and to show that this vision was effective in the Circle and involved a specific language and a specific rhetoric. An important example is the editorial statement in the first issue of *Slovo a slovesnost,* a journal which the Prague Circle began to publish in 1935.[17] This introduction, the Circle's last collective statement, begins with a few historical references to the Prague linguistic tradition of the nineteenth century, naming Masaryk and Marty among the predecessors of structural linguistics. The main part, however, motivates a new Prague vision, arguing for active and planned intervention by linguists into language. Preoccupation with language in general, and linguistics in particular, is now defined (in contradistinction to the nineteenth century) as part of language culture—a domain which can be shaped, and in which planning and intentional action have their places. The topic of language shaping is said to have practical components and to be applicable to a number of areas (education, journalism, translation) however, the integrating point of view is that of a fundamental language criticism:

Be it philosophical literature of the Husserl School, or new Russian journalism and linguistics, or Čapek's inspired essay on cliches,[18] we everywhere encounter the same, intensified efforts at a strict control of linguistic signs. The question whether linguistic signs are adequate and can carry the appropriate load, is permanently asked. In short, the relation between the sign and its referent is being checked. (Circle 1935: 3)

In line with this, the statement talks about "regulation of language" (ibid.: 4), "planned approach in linguistic economy" (ibid.: 2), "linguistic responsibility" (ibid.: 3), and so on.

These key words, of course, only summarize a tendency that had been articulated in the preceding years. By appealing to the social nature of language, the Circle had been merging cultural ideology and scholarship for quite a while. It had also been encouraging linguists not to remain mere onlookers. In characterizing the contemporary society as one striving toward rationality and scientific order, Mukařovský clearly implied in 1933 that linguists should be involved in controlling the signs:

Contemporary cultural life is all characterized by a more and more intensive intervention of science in matters of organization of diverse social values. Independently of political persuasions and in a broad variety of social fields, an increasingly strong tendency towards a shift from economic anarchy to a more rationalized and planned production is being encountered. The necessity to organize the language culture is becoming increasingly pressing. . . . Yes, we want linguistic regulation, just like we want the overdue architectural regulation of cities, but we want a regulation which is determined by the goals of today, not by archaic or "archaizing" considerations. (Mukařovský 1933: 2)

The parallel between the regulation of the economy and the regulation of language is particularly interesting.[19]

In line with the theme of scholars serving the society, the aforementioned statement in *Slovo a slovesnost* says that "Czech linguistics must once and for all overcome the conflict with the cultural values of the present epoch and must make itself available for service in a direct manner. . . . the urgency of this task requests a collective, organized union of scholarly forces" (Circle 1935: 3f.). The journal is thus conceived as a grand enterprise in which the Circle's collective asserted its aspirations to sociocultural activism.[20]

Not only does the new vision attempt to integrate linguistics into a system of meaningful social needs; it also has recourse to the Gothic[21] period and its constitutive elements:

The epoch of Gothic thought in dimensions of centuries. Ignát Herrman[22] was right when he contrasted the far-sighted imperial construction of Prague by Charles the Fourth with Prague's narrow horizon fifty years ago, when, as he put it, whatever was undertaken "was tailored just according to the measure of the day." We cannot—and do not want to—return back to Gothic culture, but its grandiose, self-conscious and goal-oriented construction provides a more contemporary and inspiring example than the poverty of yesterday, heroic and full of sacrifices as it might have been. (Circle 1935: 7)

This allusion to the Middle Ages captures certain sentiments of the 1930s very well in its expression of admiration for an epoch of order, monumentality, and the individual's subjugation to higher goals. Medieval, or Gothic, society inspired a number of intellectuals—among them, not surprisingly, Josef L. Fischer, who saw this epoch as speaking to the present "in a familiar language . . . of beauty and desire for the unity of order" (Fischer 1932: 101).[23]

Medieval society had a special mystique for other members of the Circle, too. Mukařovský, in his book *Aesthetic Function, Norm and Aesthetic Value* (1936), assigns the Gothic society a special status. For Jakobson the preoccupation with the Middle Ages was important not only within the context of literary history—"Considerations About the Poetry of the Hussite Period" (Jakobson 1936d) is more than an exercise in dialectical reasoning:

The Gothic order did not know the strict division of spheres of interest—religion, art, science, socio-economical, national, erotic spheres—that became characteristic in modern times. Each phenomenon had several levels and each event belonged necessarily to several levels at the same time. This is the essence of Gothic symbolism—only the Renaissance began to introduce autonomy of individual areas. (Jakobson 1936d: 2)

This emergence of the Gothic theme in the Prague Circle during the interwar period was a late occurrence of an ideal that had been present in a variety of social analyses and visions for quite a while and which was cultivated by artists who, in workshops and in craftsmen's guilds, dreamt of joint work on a Cathedral of the Future.[24] For Trubetzkoy, the image of the cathedral merged with the vision of the New Jerusalem, as is witnessed by his ex libris.[25]

Much of this imagery had been disseminated through turn-of-the-century Symbolism and through German Expressionism. Both the Prague German poet Rainer Maria Rilke and the Bauhaus organizer Walter Gropius used the image of cathedral builders. (The name originally contemplated for the Bauhaus was Bauhütte, which had strong medieval connotations.) The Prague Linguistic Circle was certainly not a medieval guild, but the reference to the Middle Ages still had meaning—especially in a period of a looming crisis. It pointed to a future society in which everything would fall into place, including language and its students.

10

Russian Images of the Whole: Trubetzkoy, Sprachbund, and Eurasia

. . . they all deeply scorn our half-Asiatic country.
Trubetzkoy 1921a: xiv

. . . evolutionary science, the idea of progress and all these concoctions of Romano-Germanic egocentrism . . .
Trubetzkoy to Jakobson, March 7, 1921

. . . I only like to "philosophize" a little . . .
Trubeztkoy to Jakobson, July 28, 1921

So far, not much has been said about Prince Nikolai Sergeevič Trubetzkoy, one of the best-known members of the Prague Linguistic Circle. Although Trubetzkoy only visited his Prague colleagues from Vienna, he had a great impact on their work, and his research—in particular his phonology—was fully integrated into the work of the Circle. For the broader community of scholars, it was his phonology rather than Mathesius's or Jakobson's that became the hallmark of the Circle.

An analysis of Trubetzkoy's linguistics would easily fill a monograph. This chapter will focus on a well-defined complex of questions revolving around Sprachbund (language union), a notion he originated. Taking this occasion to outline Trubetzkoy's beginnings and his early writings, I will also examine how Eurasianism (a political and cultural movement among Russian émigrés) affected the emergence of Sprachbund studies. Sprachbund—the proposition that historically unrelated languages may follow a pattern of mutual assimilation within a given geographic area—leads to a discussion of the scientific imagination and of scholars' commitment to frames of reference that are external to the technical dimension of scholarship. In other words, the embedding of linguistics into a wider cultural and ideological context is particularly visible in the topic selected here.[1]

10.1 Trubetzkoy's Beginnings

[Rosenberg and Nikolaj in a hotel; Rosenberg writes poems.]

[Nikolaj:]   What about?

[Rosenberg:]   About the free mountain man.

[Nikolaj:]   Really? Aren't you sick and tired of him yet?

[Rosenberg:]   Not at all. I am ready to live in the Caucasus all my life. . . The mountain man—oh, he is a free spirit, an eagle hovering in the skies. The mountain man is not afraid of bullets or daggers, or the Russians, or the Cherkessians—he is afraid of no one![2]

Formative Years

It has become a commonplace among Trubetzkoy's biographers to call the young prince a wunderkind. Born into an old and prominent aristocratic family in which scholarship was held in high esteem, Trubetzkoy started his academic work very early. According to his own testimony, he was working on folklore and ethnography at the age of 13 (Trubetzkoy 1958a: 273).

In an unpublished survey of his earliest work and plans—henceforth referred to as the Intellectual Autobiography[3] —Trubetzkoy lists a score of essays and projects, mostly on the Finnic themes that preoccupied him during his school years. As early as 1904 he analyzed a number of motifs in the Kalevala (a Karelian epic) and projected an encyclopedic "Religion of Finnic Peoples." Although most of these projects were beyond his capabilities, he succeeded in completing a few. At the age of 15 he published his first article in the journal of Moscow Ethnological Society (Trubetzkoy 1905), and further articles (e.g. Trubetzkoy 1906, 1908a) followed before he entered Moscow University in 1908.

The young Trubetzkoy had private tutors and was treated exceptionally in many other respects. His was a family in which many of the males were well-known scholars and intellectuals; his father, Sergej Nikolaevič, was a well-known philosopher and a major advocate of university autonomy.[4] Young Nikolai Sergeevič must have received some intellectual support from his father (in the Intellectual Autobiography he mentions having written an essay on the cult of the bear in the Kalevala "after a conversation with papa"), but the father died too early to have a lasting effect on his son's later education. The son eventually became much more conservative than the father. That N. S. Trubetzkoy should develop into a promising ethnologist was due in part to the tutelage of Vsevolod Fedorovič Miller, a prominent specialist in Russian epic folklore and Caucasian ethnology. Miller soon recognized Trubetzkoy's unusual scholarly gifts and invited him to spend the summers of 1911 and 1912 at his residence in the foothills of the Caucasus, pursuing ethnological work.[5] Another influential mentor was S. K. Kuznetsov, a specialist in Finno-Ugric folklore, under whose guidance Trubetzkoy, in 1907, became interested in Paleo-Siberian languages. At roughly the same time, the languages of the Caucasus also began to attract him. In tracing his early Caucasian inclinations, Trubetzkoy (1958a: 274) referred to a lecture by V. S. Miller on the importance of linguistic data in the historical study of Caucasian ethnology. Notebooks from his school days[6] reveal that he worked on a historical comparative phonology of Caucasian languages, perhaps as early as 1907.

Unique as the seriousness of his endeavors is, Trubetzkoy's preoccupation with ethnology reflects the spirit of a period in which studies of the non-Slavic peoples of the Russian Empire were beginning to flourish. The Empire had ceased to view its ethnic structure from an exclusively military and administrative point of view and had begun to take a deeper interest in the ethnic mosaic it encompassed. The combination of ethnography and language study certainly left a lasting trace on Trubetzkoy's intellectual development. As he later emphasized, he approached language as a phenomenon deeply embedded in culture, viewing it as closely linked with religion, with folklore, and with culture in general (Trubetzkoy 1958a).

In 1908, Trubetzkoy entered the Philosophico-Psychological Division of the Historico-Philological School of Moscow University. He intended to study "mainly national psychology, philosophy of history and problems of methodology" (ibid.: 274), but after two semesters he switched to linguistics (more precise, historical comparative philology). The curriculum in this discipline also disappointed him; nonetheless, he had reasons for staying faithful to it:

Firstly, I concluded already then that linguistics was the only branch of humanities that had a real scientific method, and that all the other branches of sciences of the man (ethnography, history of religion, cultural history) could move from an "alchemistic" stage of development only if they followed the example of linguistics as far as methodology is concerned. Secondly, I knew that Indo-European studies were the only really well worked out branch of linguistics and that one could learn the proper linguistic method precisely there. (ibid.: 275)

One of Trubetzkoy's teachers at the university was Wiktor Porzeziński, a Polish-born disciple of Filipp Fëdorovič Fortunatov. (Interestingly, Hjelmslev (1939: 56) saw some similarities between Porzeziński's and Trubetzkoy's theories.) In 1916, Trubetzkoy was authorized to lecture and began to teach Sanskrit, one of Porzeziński's courses. A cluster of articles on Slavic linguistic history from the early 1920s—the earliest documented studies by Trubetzkoy devoted to linguistics (including Trubetzkoy 1922 and 1925a)—show him as a practitioner of historical linguistics. Historical linguistics also seems to have preoccupied him during his stay in Leipzig in 1913–14, during which he studied with Karl Brugmann, August Leskien, Ernst Wilhelm Windisch, and Bruno Lindner. These men, like Trubetzkoy's Moscow teachers, were all historically oriented—in fact, they were among the most prominent senior representatives of a historical approach to language.[7]

Early Methodology

Trubetzkoy's first published article, "The Finnish Song 'Kulto neito' as an Instance of Survival of a Pagan Custom" (1905), deals with Finno-Ugric folklore. Trubetzkoy claims that the episode in the Kalevala in which the blacksmith Ilmarinen makes a golden statuette and treats it as a living substitute for his deceased wife cannot be understood without a historical reconstruction of the original context. He therefore undertakes a comparison with the myths of other Finno-Ugric tribes and establishes that many of those tribes entertained the belief that the dead still participated in the life of earthly relatives by watching from the netherworld. It was customary to show concern for the dead by making models, marionettes, and the like and treating them as if they were living. Ilmarinen's story turns out to be a distorted remnant of this custom.

The study thus falls within the domain of cultural survival, a popular ethnological topic then. The early students of this phenomenon, such as the British anthropologist Edward B. Tylor, were historically oriented, and this approach is also dominating in Trubetzkoy's analysis. His historicism is particularly apparent in his conclusion that the Ilmarinen story is a reflex of a pagan belief. This conclusion is reminiscent of Tylor's tendency to determine the original meaning of a specific instance of survival and to deduce from it what sort of religion was practiced by the society.

While the range of themes in which Trubetzkoy was interested can easily be described, only one passage in his articles from before the First World War explicitly touches upon questions of methodology. This passage is found in Trubetzkoy's recollections of S. K. Kuznetsov:

When describing some fact or phenomenon in the life of a nation, ethnographers tend in the overwhelming majority to lose sight of the fact that these phenomena and facts are not objects with an existence of their own; they are not more than an abstraction of the familiar kind. For instance, analyzing the image of a deity of a particular nation, ethnographers speak about it as if this image were an entity. . . . But this in fact is not so. The image of a deity exists in reality . . . only under certain conditions—during the process of prayer and during listening to, remembering of, or staging of a myth, i.e., of a narrative in which the deity appears an actor. Outside this context, the image of a deity does not exist in reality.

The conditions of praying or narrating a myth are determined by other phenomena in the life of the given nation: for instance, a prayer of supplication is connected with those needs that agricultural life emphasizes etc. We could continue this endless chain of these phenomena which mutually condition each other also in other parts of ethnography. On the whole, particular facts in the life of a nation have only non-independent existence. (Trubetzkoy 1913: 326–328)

This complex cluster of ideas might be read as a psychologistic critique of certain ideas entertained by the French sociologist Emile Durkheim. In Durkheim's sociological theory, "social facts," including customs, appear in a reified form by virtue of the fact that they are observable and exist, according to Durkheim, independent of their particular manifestations, they are on a par with other types of documents of social life—they are just like things. Evidently, Trubetzkoy was not comfortable with this type of approach. The passage above shows, among other things, that he was trying to establish a more realistic mode of description by including psychological criteria. But he also stressed what might be termed a strict contextualism—the phenomena he discussed were relational; they existed only within certain contexts, and these were not always understood in causal terms. In line with this approach, Trubetzkoy explicitly asserted the idea of system. The passage quoted above leads to the statement that social facts are "inseparably interwoven with each other into one complex whole, a system" (ibid.: 328).[8]

Structural or "proto-structural" as all this sounds, one should be very cautious about assuming automatic endorsement of specific doctrines. Trubetzkoy's path toward modernistic currents such as Russian Formalism was still long. Indeed, as late as 1923 he was very negative about the Formal School. He wrote to his friend Petrovskij from Sofia that "to see everything as a device [priëm]—even in Tolstoy's letters to his wife— ... is a kind of degenerative defect in perception, some kind of Daltonism" (August 3, 1922; quoted from Toman 1994). Trubetzkoy mellowed later, even writing in a Formalist vein (Trubetzkoy 1927c).[9] Rigid as he may have been in many ways, here he showed versatility and a readiness to change opinion under the force of arguments.

10.2 Relativism and Cultural Autonomy

The Heart of the Matter—"The Wild Face of the Asiatic Barbarian"

Leaving Moscow for the North Caucasian spa of Kislovodsk in the fall of 1917 in order to restore his health, Trubetzkoy may not have realized that he would never again see his home. Clearly the Bolshevik Revolution and the subsequent civil war did not make Moscow a safe environment for an aristocrat whose father was, moreover, strongly disliked by Lenin. After two years of peregrinations through Russian provinces, he found himself an émigré in Constantinople in early 1920. From there he soon moved to Bulgaria, where he taught at the University of Sofia in 1920–1922.[10] The change of environment was shockingly painful:

As far as scholarship goes, the Balkans are rather bad. I am trying as much as I can to move somewhere else, but am afraid that such an intensive intellectual life that I was living in Moscow . . . is not to be found anywhere. Solitary work is of course difficult. How dearly would I pay in order to be able to participate in the meetings of Moscow's learned societies! (to F. A. Petrovskij; undated [1922]; quoted from Toman 1994)

But Trubetzkoy did not stop working. In Sofia only a few months after leaving Russia, he published a brochure, entitled *Europe and Mankind,* which introduced a long series of his essays on cultural and political themes. Most of them were published in the 1920s, a few more in the 1930s. Trubetzkoy spent much of the 1930s on *True Ideocracy as a Solely Desirable and Viable Form of Rule* (see Jakobson 1982: 312), intending it as a synthesis of the reflections he had begun with *Europe and Mankind.* The apparently complete manuscript was seized by the Gestapo in Vienna in 1938 and must be regarded as lost.[11]

Trubetzkoy's state of mind in the days just after his emigration is revealed by his preface to H. G. Wells' *Russia in the Shadows,* issued by an émigré publisher in Russian translation in Sofia in 1921. Printing Wells' account of a trip to post-revolutionary Russia—an account in which criticism of Western policy toward Russia merges with an apparently sympathetic depiction of the Bolshevik regime—was a rather odd enterprise for an émigré, but prefacing it with Trubetzkoy's devastating remarks is perhaps even more curious.[12] In order to understand this, one must realize that H. G. Wells ranked among the most influential political essayists of the period. Ironically, certain elements of his social thinking—in particular, his preference for rule by an intellectual elite rather than for democratically elected representation—were essentially compatible with Trubetzkoy's political philosophy. However, Wells had a long history of association with various persuasions of socialism and was an advocate of a World State in which racial and regional differences would play no role. This, as we shall shortly see, must have been enough to make him quite unacceptable to Trubetzkoy. At any rate, the book provided Trubetzkoy with ample space to treat Wells with a great amount of sarcasm. He portrayed him as a prototypical naive Westerner, insensitive to Russia and to what had happened to her recently. But Trubetzkoy quickly raised his charges to a more general level, citing the book as a source of insight into the psychology of a typical representative of "Romano-Germanic culture." For Trubetzkoy, Wells' observations and proposals were hardly worth taking seriously—not only because of Wells' political naiveté but also, and in the first place, because of the inability of a Westerner to understand Russia and her spiritual needs: "It is sufficiently clear that Mr. Wells grasped neither the substance of Bolshevism nor—and that is the main point—that of Russia" (Trubetzkoy 1921a: xii). In Trubetzkoy's view, this was an attitude representative of the Western politicians and intellectuals who "deeply scorn our half-Asiatic country." Certain passages, though, witnessed Wells' artistic intuition. He was, Trubetzkoy noted, able to sense "a strange and wild face behind the mask of Bolshevism—the face of an Asiatic or semi-Asiatic 'barbarian.' " "But," Trubetzkoy continued, "the insurmountable arrogance with which he views all non-Europeans prevents him from taking this very face seriously. Yet this face—that is precisely the heart of the matter. . . . In its essence, national 'Bolshevism' in Russia and Asia is not a revolt of the poor against the rich, but of the disregarded against the disregarding. Its edge is mainly aiming against those arrogant Europeans who regard the entire non-European mankind only as source of ethnographic material, as slaves, good enough only for supplying Europe with raw materials and buying European goods." (Trubetzkoy 1921a: xv–xvi)

Clearly, Trubetzkoy's remarks reveal a great deal of hatred for the West. Their intensity may reflect his immediate political bitterness and disappointment, but on the whole his later statements (including private ones) leave little doubt about a fundamental attitude.[13] For example, in a letter to Jakobson describing a visit to France, Trubetzkoy complained about French Slavists: ". . . in the depth of their hearts [they] scorn everything Slavic, Central-European and Russian and consider it barbaric. Slavic scholars are good enough as collectors of material, but when they begin to reason their *manque de culture* and their *âme slave* shows through. . . . " (Jakobson 1975: 301) The presence of the Slovak phonologist, Ludovít Novák, a man "who smells of slivovitz and peppers" (ibid.), was greatly appreciated by Trubetzkoy during social encounters with French Slavists.

Thus, on the whole, the feeling of displacement was strong in Trubetzkoy during his years in exile. As early as 1921 he wrote: "Isn't it all the same where we go once Russia is out of reach?" (ibid.: 5). His attitude did not change much over the years.

Europe and Mankind

When Trubetzkoy was writing the preface to H. G. Wells' book, he had already worked out some of the aforementioned themes. This is abundantly clear from *Europe and Mankind* (Trubetzkoy 1920), not only his first publication as an émigré but also the source of many ideas associated with the "Eurasian movement."[14] In Trubetzkoy's own words, the origins of *Europe and Mankind* lay far back in prewar times.[15]

At first glance *Europe and Mankind* may seem to address the traditional question of Russia's relation to the West, discussions of which characterize long stretches of Russian intellectual history, especially throughout the nineteenth century. The Slavophiles were particularly prominent in these discussions, and aside from some crucial differences there is a relatively clear link between their ideas and Trubetzkoy's book. The title *Europe and Mankind* seems to allude to *Russia and Europe,* in which the Slavophile thinker Nikolai Jakovlevič Danilevskij takes up questions of European (or Western) hegemony and cultural domination as it was felt in Russia, not recognizing anything like a universal human civilization, a universal idea of progress, or Universal History but instead advocating autonomous "historic-cultural types."[16] However, Trubetzkoy's differences with Danilevskij are more important. The two men embedded the idea that Russia is not a part of the West in different frameworks. There is little in Danilevskij's thought about Asia, and nothing about the Asiatic roots of Russian civilization with which Trubetzkoy was so much preoccupied. Trubetzkoy's regard for non-Slavic cultures thus asserts a shift to a perspective quite different from the standard Slavo-centric considerations that dominated Russian thinking in the middle of the nineteenth century. In historical terms, the absence of the "aboriginal" perspective in Slavophile literature is not surprising, since the Slavophiles were strongly preoccupied with Russia's European role—particularly with regard to the Southern (Orthodox) Slavs. Danilevskij's aim was to present arguments for a new world power, a Slavic Union under the "natural" leadership of Orthodox Russia. His vision of establishing Constantinople as a new center of the Slavs is symbolic of this orientation.

Trubetzkoy's insistence on the "wild face" of a semi-Asiatic barbarian may well have been shocking and iconoclastic to his Slavophile Orthodox contemporaries, yet it also clearly pointed to the growth of scholarship dealing with non-Indo-European nationalities in the Russian Empire. Knowledge about the roles of Finnic and Oriental peoples in Russian history was becoming a commonplace in scholarship in the late nineteenth century (see Riasanovsky 1967: 64ff.) and was making its way to general readers.

Another important difference between Danilevskij and Trubetzkoy is that in Trubetzkoy's *Europe and Mankind* the words "Russia" and "Asia" do not appear at all. Rather, he presents abstract prolegomena to formal social psychology, the applications of which were to be explored in subsequent studies. This very circumstance makes a simplistic alignment with traditional questions about Russia's identity somewhat misleading. The contrast Trubetzkoy was asserting was that between Europe and the rest of the world, not that between Europe and Russia. Rejection of the West and emancipation of non-European cultures were the general causes—Russia's emancipation was a special case. The fact that the book was soon translated into Japanese, the language of a culture that dramatically tried to assert itself vis-à-vis the West, must have been a great vindication of this general scheme and of Trubetzkoy's hope that the book would bring about a revolution in the thinking of non-European intellectuals in general (see Jakobson 1975: 16; March 7, 1921).[17]

The Main Thesis: Cultural Relativism

Right from the beginning, Trubetzkoy's *Europe and Mankind* focuses on showing that the European (or "Romano-Germanic") cosmopolitanism is nothing but a brand of brute chauvinism. Europeans have raised themselves to a universal measure of things, thus manifesting their egocentrism:

The psychological foundation of cosmopolitanism is the same as that of chauvinism. They both are variants of a subconscious prejudice, a particular psychology, which is best termed *egocentrism*. A person with an articulate egocentric psychology sees himself subconsciously as the center of the universe, the coronation of creation, the best and most perfect being. (Trubetzkoy 1920: 6)

Although the general direction of the argument is obviously polemic, it would be incorrect to see only the "pamphlet quality" of *Europe and Mankind*. Long sections of the book are couched in the style of a sociological or ethnological treatise. This is visible, among other places, in Trubetzkoy's treatment of whether it is possible to prove objectively that Romano-Germanic culture is superior (chapter 1) and whether an ethnic group can accept the culture of another group without an "anthropological merger" (chapter 2). The answer to the first question—which takes up almost one-third of the book—constitutes a clear formulation of cultural relativism; the answer to the second can be viewed as a discussion of diffusionism (a major ethnological doctrine of the late nineteenth century—also discussed by the French sociologist Gabriel Tarde, one of the few scholars Trubetzkoy quotes). Both of these points underscore the scholarly aspirations of the work.

As far as cultural relativism is concerned, Trubetzkoy argues at length that cultural ranking—the idea of an evolutionary ladder, a scale of evolution—is untenable. Such a perspective is based entirely on the egocentrism of those who set up the scale—the "Romano-Germanic" peoples:

Regarding matters objectively, we only find in individual cultures features of greater or lesser similarity. On the basis of these features we can group all cultures of the Earth so that the most similar cultures appear one next to another, while cultures with little similarity, consequently, appear in a greater distance. This is all we can do while maintaining objectivity. (Trubetzkoy 1920: 17f.)

The argumentation aims at a valuation-free ethnology in which the principle of progress along an evolutionary scale is emphatically denied:

Instead of a scale we obtain a horizontal plane. Instead of the principle of ranking of nations and cultures according to the degree of perfection, we postulate a new principle of equal value and qualitative incommensurability of all cultures and nations of the globe. The element of valuation must once for all be purged from ethnology and history of culture, and in general from all evolutionary sciences, because value judgment is always based on egocentrism. There is no higher or lower. There is only similar and dissimilar. Declaring similar for higher and dissimilar for lower is arbitrary, unscientific, naive, and, ultimately, simply dumb. (Trubetzkoy 1920: 42)

Trubetzkoy's resolute insistence on cultural relativism is succinctly condensed in his belief that the essence of the revolution in consciousness consists in a full abandonment of egocentrism and excentrism—"a transition from absolutism to relativism" (Jakobson 1975: 13; March 7, 1921). The relativistic approach—which is called by its name here—also represents a critique of evolutionist ethnography. This critical attitude toward evolutionism was also instrumental in Trubetzkoy's critique of linguistic ranking.

Relativism vs. Ranking in Linguistics

The relativistic perspective that Trubetzkoy so passionately embraced is certainly not unique in modern Western intellectual history. Historians of European Humanism had already opened this avenue. Many German Romantic thinkers loudly opposed the (French) Enlightenment doctrines of universalism and progress. However, in the nineteenth century universalistic ideas of progress were reestablished. This was quite visible in ethnography, where evolutionary doctrines became intimately linked with the ideology of Western superiority. In Trubetzkoy's days, however, a reaction to evolutionism was occurring in ethnology and in other social sciences. Cultural relativism in anthropology was emerging in Franz Boas's work of the 1890s, and a statement by the American anthropologist Alfred L. Kroeber might also be adduced here for comparison:

The so-called savage is no transition between the animal and the scientifically educated man.—All men are totally civilized. . . . There is no higher and no lower in civilization for the historian. The ranking of the portions of civilization in any sequence, save the actual one of time, place and connection, is normally misleading and always valueless. (Kroeber 1915: 286) [18]

Trubetzkoy was not quite correct when he claimed that there was not a single Westerner who would regard "wild" cultures as on a par with Romano-Germanic culture (Trubetzkoy 1920: 8f.); however, the idea of cultural ranking was still very common, and it was a long a time before the existence of a counterposition was even acknowledged.

Various evolutionist ideas—including that of language ranking—were very much alive in the linguistics of Trubetzkoy's time. The degree of perfection of non-Indo-European languages was a frequent topic in semi-popular magazines for the educated. Some such "ranking sentiments" certainly carried over to Jespersen, as is evident from his open Anglocentrism. Also, the work of August Schleicher, who was the very image of naturalistic evolutionism in linguistics, has a very strong evaluative component. In his survey *The Languages of Europe,* Schleicher (1850: 9) clearly adhered to the idea of ranking languages according to linguistic type: "Languages with inflection are . . . at the top of the scale of languages. In them the organism of the word has finally become truly articulated—the word represents a unity in the diversity of its parts, just as in animal organism, of which this also holds." The scale referred to is one leading from monosyllabic languages to agglutinative languages and then to languages with inflection. (Remarkably, Schleicher parallels this scale with a scale projected from crystals to plants to animals.)

Why the notion of the high grade of perfection of flective languages (such as Latin) and the corresponding imperfection of agglutinative languages (Turkish) was so persistent with Schleicher seems obvious—the former was the type of language that Indo-European comparative linguistics was about: "The great majority of European languages belongs to that language stem in which the essence of language, as shown above, reveals itself in its most perfect state, namely the Indo-European." (Schleicher 1850: 123) Before embarking upon the languages of Europe, Schleicher treats a wide array of non-Indo-European languages and language groups, including Chinese, Mongolian, the Caucasian and the Turkic groups, and Finno-Ugric. By this token, the number of languages (and cultures) over which he passed judgment is vast and offensive. Throughout the book one encounters words such as "corruption" and "decay." This extends to the Indo-European core, in fact. The West-East Slavic trajectory from Czech through Moravian dialects to Slovak is for Schleicher (1850: 217) "a gradual decrease in language corruption." This judgment is not only odd; it also has interesting theoretical implications. In particular, the idea of relegating language mixing to a phenomenon of corruption and decay prevented Schleicher—but not so much Trubetzkoy—from seeing convergence as a force in linguistic history.

10.3 Language and Eurasia

Eurasianism—Tartars, Turks, and Other Wild Men

A year after his arrival in Sofia, Trubetzkoy had became a leading advocate of Eurasianism, probably the most important movement in Russian interwar emigration. The doctrine not only stressed Russia's uniqueness and her distinct position between Europe and Asia; it also insisted on her roots in the semi-Asiatic culture of the steppe.

Certain elements of Eurasianism can be placed into the context of the literary sentiment of the turn of the century. The concern with Russia's Asiatic background was strong among some Russian poets rooted in the Symbolist tradition—particularly, Trubetzkoy's contemporary Aleksander Blok. As has often been acknowledged by students of modern Russian literature, a prominent expression of Blok's sentiment toward the culture of the steppe, and a prominent literary assertion of Russia's non-Western identity, is his poem "The Scythians" (1918 [1960: 360]), which contains these famous lines:

Yes—we are Scythians,
yes, Asians, a slant-eyed, greedy brood.

Trubetzkoy was interested in Blok. In 1920 he wrote a commentary on Blok's essay "Russia and Intelligentsia," but P. B. Struve, the editor of *Russkaja mysl'*, a Russian journal in Sofia, rejected it (Jakobson 1975: 17); since the manuscript does not seem to exist any longer, there is no way of reconstructing Trubetzkoy's argument.

The Eurasians' allegiance to Blok was also expressed symbolically in *Exodus to the East,* the first published collection by the Eurasians. The cover, designed by the Russian avant-garde artist Pavel F. Čeličev (then also in Sofia) [19] shows a galloping mare. This is an allusion [20] to Blok's 1908 poem "On the Field of Kulikovo" (Blok 1960: 249), which contains the following lines:

The mare of the steppe flies on and on,
    and tramples the feather-grass

But this is an image that Trubetzkoy also used. In a 1921 letter to Jakobson, he compared Russia to a horse that must liberate itself from the West:

The horse without a rider will fall into the hands of horse thieves—the Romano-Germanic West. Let it break out, let it run away; what does it matter when there is no real rider! (Jakobson 1975: 25; July 28, 1921)

Eurasianism, however, developed far beyond a literary worship of the wild. Within a few years it was a prominent intellectual and political current among the Russian émigrés. Although the term "Eurasian" does not appear in *Europe and Mankind,* the brochure became immediately associated with it and subsequently played a catalytic role.[21]

The Eurasians formed in Sofia in 1920 and 1921.[22] In July 1921, Trubetzkoy wrote from Sofia to Roman Jakobson, announcing the appearance of *Exodus to the East,* a collection of articles by P. Suvčinskij, G. V. Florovskij, P. N. Savickij, and himself:

We united on the basis of certain common attitudes and "Weltanschauung," although each of us has his own approach and convictions. Suvčinskij is closest to me, Florovskij much farther, in particular because of the abstractness of his thinking (he is a philosopher, I only like to "philosophize" a little); Savickij, one can say, has not found his way yet; mainly, he has not yet liberated himself from his old nature (he is a disciple Struve's), but he is on the way of casting off all this. (Jakobson 1975: 21; July 28, 1921)

With the exception of G. V. Florovskij,[23] these men played crucial roles in the emerging Eurasian movement. Petr Nikolaevič Savickij, who Trubetzkoy characterizes with a certain distance[24] in the above lines but for whom he later developed great admiration, became one of the leading organizers of the movement. Petr Suvčinskij became one of the organizers of the Paris chapter of the Eurasians. The internal development in this group eventually led to the pro-Moscow course that made Trubetzkoy dissociate himself from the Parisians in early 1929 (see Trubetzkoy 1929c[25]).

The Eurasian doctrine highlights the idea that Russia is an entity of its own between Europe and Asia. While this proposition was also cultivated in earlier East-West discussions in Russia—and Eurasians indeed claimed intellectual ancestors reaching as far back as the early-nineteenth-century Russian thinker P. J. Čaadaev—the goal of the movement was to elaborate an integrated political, economic, and socio-cultural doctrine based on geographic, ethnographic, *Völker*-psychologic, linguistic, historical, and (last but not least) religious considerations. The element of integration (or, to continue the topic of the previous chapter, synthesis) is quite prominent in the doctrine. Eurasia was projected to be not simply a complex entity, but an entity with a natural, law-determined structure manifesting harmony and natural connectedness. The social dimension was expounded less technically than in Western images of synthesis (such as J. L. Fischer's). This is especially striking in Savickij's conception of Eurasia, which is based on a spatially defined image of symbiosis within a region. In political terms, the Eurasians rejected Marxism and Bolshevism[26] but realized the need for radical changes in Russian society, ultimately accepting the overthrowing of the tsar as an inevitable historical fact. One of the contributions that Trubetzkoy tried to make was to develop an ideology that could serve as a competitor to the Bolshevik doctrine. His proposals revolved around the notion of "ideocracy," a form of rule that would supersede monarchy and democracy and would be compatible with the nation's

ethnic and Völker-psychological nature. Trubetzkoy defined ideocracy as a form of rule based on a high degree of identification of a
ruling group with an ideology. According to him, ideocracies tended
to establish close ideological unity through a "prestigious leader"
and a "disciplined organization":

... in an ideocratic state the ruling body consist of a firmly amalgamated
and internally highly disciplined organization of "one and only party"; ... if
one of its leaders, members of the council, has a greater prestige and influence in comparison with the others, he effectively functions as the head of
the government. (Trubetzkoy 1927b: 9)

The desire for a strong hand is visible in Trubetzkoy's political
writings, among other places in his anonymously published brochure
The Legacy of Genghis Khan (Trubetzkoy 1925b). Clearly, all the aforementioned ideas are to be seen against the background of an extensive discussion about the crisis of democracy and the failing values of
traditional liberalism.[27] For Trubetzkoy, in any case, the Soviet system and Italian Fascism were typological approximations to ideocracy. However, as he repeatedly emphasized, these two were false
ideocracies. A true ideocracy of the future, a challenge to the Eurasians, was yet to be worked out. The fact that *True Ideocracy*, Trubetzkoy's ideological magnum opus, disappeared in the archives of the
Gestapo was only one of the ironies of an era of ideologies.

First Steps to Eurasian Linguistics—"Highs and Lows of Russian Culture"

Leafing through *Europe and Mankind*, the reader will find nothing at
all about language. This is somewhat surprising in view of Trubetzkoy's background and in view of the fact that the only Western
scholar he acknowledged, the French sociologist Gabriel Tarde, paid
some attention to language, among other things by recognizing the
phenomenon of language mixing.[28] Evidently, Trubetzkoy pulled
the booklet out of his "ethnographic drawer," which had been closed
a long time ago. Trubetzkoy soon began to fill the gap, however.
Essays subsequent to *Europe and Mankind* became more concrete and
more specific, also in linguistic respects.

One of these essays, "Highs and the Lows of Russian Culture" (Trubetzkoy 1921c), forecasts the emerging Sprachbund idea. Here Trubetzkoy, reviewing Russia's linguistic descent, is in fact searching for evidence divorcing Russia from the Indo-European West. He argues that Proto-Slavic was much closer in pronunciation to Indo-Iranian than to Western Indo-European dialects, and (most important) that the Proto-Slavic religious lexicon had borrowed from Indo-Iranian. There are of course connections between Proto-Slavic and the Western Indo-European dialects, but Trubetzkoy is very cautious in asserting their value; in any case, he regards them as being of quite a different nature. Specifically, he relegates them to the area of the lexicon, arguing that the vocabulary shared with the Western Indo-Europeans includes mainly technical terms and terms of physical culture. Thus, he suggests, the Proto-Slavs tended with their "body" and technology toward the Western Indo-Europeans, but with their "soul" toward the East—i.e., the Indo-Iranians. Trubetzkoy acknowledges that the geographical position of the Slavs already invited Eastern and Western influences at a very early point in history, but he underscores that the later development of the Eastern Slavs was characterized by a link with Byzantium. This was a lucky event, since "everything that was received from Byzantium was taken over organically and served as a creative model" (Trubetzkoy 1921c: 26). On the other hand,

Nothing we received from the "West" was accommodated organically and inspired popular creativity. Western goods were brought in, bought, but were not produced. Masters were appointed, not to teach Russian people, but to fulfill commissions. . . . In general, everything Byzantine was undoubtedly accommodated in Russia more easily and organically than anything from the West. . . . An instinctive feeling of repulsion against the Romano-Germanic spirit was visible in this, a recognition of one's inability to create in this spirit. And in this respect, the eastern Slavs proved to be true descendants of their pre-historic ancestors, those speakers of the Proto-Slavic dialect of the Indo-European proto-language, who, as lexical investigations show, did not feel any spiritual proximity to Western Indo-Europeans and who were spiritually oriented toward the East. (Trubetzkoy 1921c: 27)

Gradually something autonomous and whole evolved. According to Trubetzkoy, this development is more manifest in the domain of "low" culture than in the "high" culture of Russia's modern pro-Western rulers:

> The culture . . . which has always characterized the life of the Russian people, represents from the ethnographical point of view a quite singular entity which cannot be completely subsumed under some broader cultural group or cultural zone. In general, this culture represents a particular "zone" of its own, which, besides the Russians, also includes Finno-Ugric "aborigines" and the Turkic tribes of the Volga basin. (Trubetzkoy 1921c: 28)

This is a very clear articulation of an areal image in which genetically unrelated peoples coexist. This specific whole borders on, and has common traits with, the culture of the steppe in the East, and through it is connected, in Trubetzkoy's view, with Central Asian cultures. Again, this bond is stronger than that with the Western Slavs. A certain affinity with the Slavs of the South is acknowledged, yet, remarkably, this relationship is due less to the fact that they are Slavs than to the fact that they, like the Russians, were influenced by the Turks. The substantiation of all these claims is based on ethnographic data. Trubetzkoy examines music, dances, ornaments, and oral folklore and finds parallels everywhere. Finally, Russians turn out to be also physically and psychically closer to "those Asiatics" than to other Slavs. Thus, Trubetzkoy collects arguments at many levels, and often in a somewhat sketchy manner, to assimilate Russia to Turkic Central Asia. This is a tour de force, needless to say—the Finns and the Siberian tribes fade into the background without further commentary.

"The Tower of Babel and the Confusion of Languages"

1923 Trubetzkoy contributed to *The Eurasian Contemporary* an essay entitled "The Tower of Babel and the Confusion of Languages"—essentially a theological treatise in which he demonstrates his interest in religion not only as a scholar but also as a practitioner of Eastern Orthodoxy.[29] He discusses the Old Testament story of the Tower of Babel and attempts to interpret the confusion of languages as a divine and hence necessarily meaningful act, explicating its deeper sense as follows: The confusion of races and languages (itself a manifestation of the "Law of National and Cultural Fragmentation") negated the state of a universal, homogeneous mankind that was technologically unified and thus able to erect the tower.

Trubetzkoy discusses in great detail the character of the pre-Babel mankind, a society representing a complete nonentity: a universal [obščečelovečeskij] culture. The parallel with his earlier criticism of European cosmopolitanism is visible here, and is also made explicit. European civilization essentially aims at restoring the pre-Babel state of affairs, but "the 'Brotherhood of Nations,' obtained for the price of spiritual de-personalization of all nations, is a disgusting hoax" (Trubetzkoy 1923: 114).

A major task for a Christian, and for Trubetzkoy, is then to show that, despite the divine necessity of the Law of National Fragmentation, the universal mission of Christianity is not made ineffective— there is no religious relativism when Christian matters are addressed. The larger part of the essay is devoted to this argument. Trubetzkoy essentially tries to say that Christianity does not spread; rather, it "enfolds," and hence it is not subject to considerations associated with the borrowing of cultural values. This is the theological context in which the Sprachbund question was originally posed.

Linguistic diversity is a consequence of the Law of Cultural and National Fragmentation. This diversity, Trubetzkoy recognizes, can be explained by genealogical considerations, i.e., by viewing related languages as developing from a common proto-language. This, however, is not the only way of looking at linguistic diversity:

... besides such genetic grouping, languages which are geographical neighbors also often group independently of their origin. It happens that several languages in a region defined in terms of geography and cultural history acquire features of a particular congruence, irrespective of whether this congruence is determined by common origin or only by an prolonged proximity in time and parallel development. We propose the term language union [jazykovyj sojuz] for such groups which are not based on the genetic principle. (Trubetzkoy 1923: 116)

In a footnote to this passage Trubetzkoy points to the Balkan languages—Bulgarian, Romanian, Albanian, and Modern Greek—as a striking example of language union in Europe. Although they belong to entirely different branches of the Indo-European family,

these languages nevertheless agree in a number of general characteristics and share certain minute details of grammatical structure.

Despite this clear proposal of a convergence model, Trubetzkoy
does not abandon the idea of a genealogically defined relationship,
i.e., a family. In fact, in the subsequent discussion he proposes the
universal notion of a "union of families" (exemplified by the languages of the Mediterranean region). This approach implies a combination of the genetic and non-genetic perspectives such that "all
languages of the globe represent an uninterrupted network of members merging into one another, a kind of rainbow pattern" (Trubetzkoy 1923: 117). Nonetheless, the overall impression is that the
relevance of the family relationship is deemphasized. The image of
a tree is replaced by that of a chain or a net. (These are, incidentally,
two major images with which pre-Darwinian zoology and biology
worked in establishing relations among species.)

Trubetzkoy also interprets this situation in terms of an overall harmony, thus clearly underscoring an almost mystical image of a whole:

> . . . particularly because of the non-discreteness of this linguistic rainbow-
> net and because the transitions from one segment to another are gradual,
> the entire system of the languages of the globe still represents a definite,
> although only intellectually perceivable whole, all the diversity notwith-
> standing. In such a way, the existence of the Law of Fragmentation in the
> domain of language does not lead to an anarchic dispersion, but to a harmo-
> nious system in which each part, however tiny, preserves its genuinely unre-
> peatable individuality, and the unity of the whole is achieved not through
> de-individualization [*obezličenie*] but through the non-discreteness of the
> rainbow network of languages itself. (ibid.)

This statement clearly connects with Trubetzkoy's general dislike of
hierarchies, scales, ladders, and the evolutionary perspective, an attitude which is abundantly documented in *Europe and Mankind*. Although one might well argue that no particular ranking or hierarchy
must be involved in the divergence model, it is more important to
note that Trubetzkoy's ideological commitment was simply incompatible with hierarchical concepts—recall his reasoning about the
representation of diversity on a plane. Here is a crucial link between
Trubetzkoy's linguistics of convergence and his overall cultural relativism. In addition, "rainbow" and "harmony" more or less clearly

point to religious imagery; other notions, such as the theologically motivated Law of Fragmentation, are cast in quasi-sociological language. The ensuing Sprachbund concept is thus rooted in a number of traditions and perspectives, the religious being obvious.

Love of Symmetry

Trubetzkoy's scholarly and cultural commitment was in all likelihood also effective elsewhere in the field in which he became most famous: phonology.[30]

Consider the following passage:

A Turk loves symmetry, clarity and a stable equilibrium; [the worldview he accepts must be characterized by] clarity and simplicity, and, what matters most, it must provide a convenient scheme by which everything can be ordered, all the world in its entire concreteness. (Trubetzkoy 1925c [1927: 42])

Curiously enough, among the evidence for this quality of the Turkish (i. e., Turanian; i.e., Eurasian) mind was the finding that Turkish—a language that has "no 'exceptions' "—followed simple and logically clear schemata. Trubetzkoy concluded that "this linguistic type is characterized by schematic regularity and a consequent realization of a small number of simple and clear principles which mold the language into one single whole" (ibid.: 38). Thus, when in 1928 he reported to Jakobson that phonological systems are organized by laws of symmetry and simplicity, he might have been thinking about the Turkic mind. Turkish phonology provided Trubetzkoy with an example of a simple and strikingly symmetrical vocalic system, thus leading to the above generalization. Specifically, Trubetzkoy reported that all vocalic systems are reducible to a very small number of basic types and "can always be represented by symmetrical schemata (such as triangles, parallel rows, etc.)" (Jakobson 1975: 117; October 19, 1928). The idea was formally developed in a separate article (Trubetzkoy 1929a).

By formulating the idea of a universal symmetry of vocalic systems, Trubetzkoy was exploiting not only the generic Eurasian mind but also his own visual imagery. The copybooks from his student years contain numerous drawings and scribblings, both figurative and ornamental.[31] Various calligraphic sketches can also be found. Trubetzkoy's striking sense of symmetry is especially evident in a sketch that represents his analysis of a structure of a fairy tale.[32] Another sketch shows a design for the title page of a Zeitschrift für vergleichende Märchenkunde [Journal of Comparative Fairy-Tale Studies], a dream project of the young Trubetzkoy.[33] On a conservative reading, the latter sketch merely indicates how to center the lines on the title page. However, in conjunction with the sketch of a symmetrical structure of the fairy tale and with symmetric sketches of vocalic systems, this is more than an accidental document of Trubetzkoy's penchant for symmetry—as if the Turanian mind was (also) located in Trubetzkoy's brain.

"The Indo-European Problem" and Freedom of Scholarship

Only toward the end of the 1920s did Trubetzkoy present his ideas about the Sprachbund theory to a wider professional audience. At the First International Congress of Linguists, held in the Hague in 1928, he defined the notion Sprachgruppe and went to distinguish its two manifestations: Sprachbund and Sprachfamilie (Trubetzkoy 1929b). His proposals were discussed and accepted, but the Dutch ethnographer and linguist J. Schrijnen noted that the idea was not really new and pointed to work by the classical scholar Eduard Schwyzer, no doubt referring to Schwyzer's "Genealogical and Cultural Cosanguinity of Languages" (1914).

Nonetheless, Trubetzkoy's presentation in the Hague had more impact than "The Tower of Babel." Back from the Congress, the Prague linguists set to work on the issue immediately, as is evident from the Theses (which contain a long section on linguistic geography) and from a number of individual studies. Jakobson embarked on a longer monograph (1931a) and also wrote some shorter articles (i.a., 1938a). Younger members of the Circle also became attracted by the topic in the 1930s; Skalička (1935)[34] and Isačenko (1934) deserve mention. Paradoxically, Trubetzkoy himself made only relatively brief contributions to the topic in the next years, although the problem continued to preoccupy him (Trubetzkoy 1931a,b; 1935b).

Not until 1936 did he lecture on this matter before the Prague Linguistic Circle.[35] Trubetzkoy's approach to what was traditionally viewed as a common Indo-European proto-language was soon bound to become a provocation to traditional Indo-European scholarship.

The aforementioned lecture stands in close proximity to Trubetzkoy's review of a collection entitled *Die Indogermanen und Germanenfrage—Neue Wege zu ihrer Lösung* (Koppers 1937), which appeared in Vienna and contained mainly archaeological and ethnological studies. In the review, "New Book on the Indo-European Homeland" (Trubetzkoy 1937a), Trubetzkoy is in sympathy with Koppers's rejection of the theory of the Nordic homeland of the Indo-Europeans, a theory that located the original Indo-Europeans in the area of contemporary Germany and thus viewed the Germans as their more or less direct descendants. He uses the occasion to denounce the Nordic Homeland thesis as an instance of Blut und Boden ideology and to express resentment toward its authority within the field:

> This theory is backed by acknowledged authorities and certain circles sympathize with it, which in some sense rules out the existence of any other competing theory about the origin of Indo-European nations. But scholarly research does not tolerate prohibitions even if they were carried by "public opinion." The connection between the success of the theory of the "Nordic homeland" and extra-scholarly factors is too obvious in order not to meet with resistance among all those to whom the freedom of scholarship is still dear. (Trubetzkoy 1937a: 105f.)

Trubetzkoy viewed Koppers's book as a healthy and necessary reaction to Nazi-tainted scholarship and was happy to see that free research was possible—outside Germany, at least. However, he sharply criticized the methodology that underlay the book. In his view the question of the homeland could not be solved by ethnological investigations.

In the article "Thoughts about the Indo-European Problem,"[36] Trubetzkoy rejects ethnological, archaeological, and similar approaches to the problem, arguing that questions of the original habitat, race, and culture had no place in an investigation of Indo-European linguistic proto-history. Not only is it impossible to verify the existence of the original Indo-European nation, but it is an incorrect question in and of itself; accepting this concept, this "romantic phantom of a proto-nation" (Trubetzkoy 1987b: 49), obscures the fact that the Indo-European question is exclusively a linguistic problem—more specific, a problem of language mixing. Trubetzkoy's major thesis—that there was no single homogeneous Indo-European proto-language in the first place—was based on the idea that the predecessors of languages in the Indo-European family were originally dissimilar and that they significantly assimilated one to another only in the course of time (via permanent contact, mutual influences, and borrowing) without merging completely.

As in his "Tower of Babel" article, Trubetzkoy does not reject divergence as a possible mechanism of language change. He merely asserts that convergence and divergence are both effective. But he degrades the usefulness of this distinction when he says that at times: "it is even difficult to draw a sharp line between these two modes of evolution" (Trubetzkoy 1987b: 46). He then goes through several European linguistic families, even challenging an account in terms of a simple divergence in the development of the Romance languages from Latin by drawing attention to the status of "semi-Romance" languages such as Albanian. He also cites the Slavic linguistic family as an example of a family with a net, rather than branching, structure. In short: "a language family can be a product of a purely divergent or a purely convergent development, or, ultimately, a product of the conjunction of both in different proportions" (Trubetzkoy 1987b: 47).

The specific core of Trubetzkoy's proposal is the claim that there is a cluster of properties that characterize the Indo-European languages and only those languages:

• a lack of vowel harmony

• a specific relation between consonantal clustering in the word onset and coda (the onset is not more restricted than the inlaut and coda)

• no condition requiring that words begin only with the root

• the presence of apophony (ablaut)

• the presence of consonantal alternations in morphology

• a nominative-accusative, rather than ergative, case system.

Each of these traits can be encountered in languages outside of the Indo-European family; however, all six of them, Trubetzkoy suggests, occur in this family only. The moment an arbitrary language acquires these six features, it becomes an Indo-European language. And, similarly, when one of these features is lost, an Indo-European language ceases to be Indo-European. A language that borrowed most of its lexical stock from Indo-European but did not have these features could not be termed Indo-European. Identity of substance, such as shared lexical stock, is of subordinate importance in any case.

It is interesting to see that Trubetzkoy continues to visualize linguistic diversity and language contact in terms of certain metaphors he had used earlier. The basic image, that of the chain (cep'),[37] remains. A family located between two other families can be interpreted as a link between the two if it shares some structural features with its neighbors. The Indo-European family is in fact nothing but an element in a chain: on the one end there is the Uralo-Altaic family, with which Indo-European shares the nominative-accusative characteristics, and on the other end there is the Caucasian-Mediterranean complex, with which it shares the first four of the above characteristics. But this gives only a very elementary approximation as far as geographical location is concerned; the link is always viewed primarily as a chain between linguistic types, not territories: "The Indo-European linguistic structure represents a connecting link between the Uralo-Altaic structure, on the one hand, and the Mediterranean, on the other hand" (Trubetzkoy 1987b: 54).

A characteristic trait of Trubetzkoy's style and argumentation is his assessment of the Indo-European linguistic type against ideals of linguistic evolution. In particular, Trubetzkoy argues that Indo-European languages had departed from the highly valued flective stage and moved toward the Uralo-Altaic agglutinative type. This latter type, however, is not inferior at all:

> ... if linguists have up to now considered agglutinative languages as more primitive than flective languages, they have only been driven by their egocentric prejudices, being obviously representatives of various Indo-European and, in particular, flective languages. Throwing away these prejudices, one must admit, that purely agglutinative languages of the Altaic type ... represent a technically more advanced instrument than languages with inflection. (Trubetzkoy 1987b: 58)

Thus, in the end, Romano-Germanic egocentrism is denounced again. But ironically, in adopting considerations of economy and efficiency, Trubetzkoy is close to making a value judgment: the Altaic type is at least "technically" more advanced. Clearly, the wild is ultimately more perfect than the civilized—die Umwertung der Werte is complete, and the Turanian spirit wins.

Whether or not Trubetzkoy's "Thoughts about the Indo-European Problem" provides the proper account of the basic questions of the Indo-European linguistic reconstruction, what is important and interesting is the radicality with which traditional scholarship is attacked and the homogeneity of thinking that links the article with the idea of relativism. Furthermore, in view of the remarks about Nazi scholarship that Trubetzkoy made around the same time, "Thoughts" is also a remarkable assertion of scholarly heroism, comparable to "On Racism" (Trubetzkoy 1935a).[38] With the Nazis making inroads in Austria, Trubetzkoy was asserting a non-evolutionistic approach over against the idea of cultural and racial supremacy.

10.4   Other Ideas on Language Contact and Convergence

Although Trubetzkoy was among the most visible students of linguistic convergence, he was by no means the first scholar to address the issue (see Birnbaum 1985). Language contact, language mixture, and convergence had long been familiar phenomena at an observational level. The Slovenian linguist Jernej Kopitar had observed similarities between the languages of the Balkans, and as early as 1826 he had stated that in the territory of the Balkans "there reigns only one language-form, visible in three different language-substances" (quoted from Asenova 1979: 5). The features Kopitar listed in common among these languages were the post-positive article and the loss of the infinitive.

The phenomenon of convergence became of theoretical interest only when it became the explicit competitor of what is now known as the standard Schleicherian tree of language descendence. The very presence of Schleicher's model of linguistic divergence prompted a number of alternative proposals that purported to account for language change by focusing on language contact, the spread of linguistic innovations across genetic boundaries, and so on. Johannes Schmidt (1872) denied the existence of a European proto-language [Grundsprache] in the sense of the tree theory and postulated a simple continuum of Indo-European dialects reaching from Asia to Western Europe. Trubetzkoy's intellectual debt to him is obvious. Although Schmidt's treatment was largely anchored in linguistic considerations, he used "chain" (of languages, dialects), "wave" (of innovations), and other such imagery. The whole theory became better known under the label Wellentheorie [wave theory]. It clearly embodies certain diffussionistic and non-evolutionistic images, thus representing an early reaction to the guiding image of divergence.

Around the same time, another influential reaction to Schleicher's tree image emerged in the work of Hugo Schuchardt. An early example of his ideas is found in a lecture, read at the University of Leipzig in 1870,[39] in which Schuchardt set out to discuss the classification of the Romance languages, eventually coming to the conclusion that there was no point in pursuing Schleicher's perspective: "The image of a tree of descent simply cannot stand on its feet." (Schuchardt 1900: 5) The tree-icon was particularly ill suited to representing language convergence: "We connect the branches and twigs of the tree of descent with innumerable horizontal lines—and the tree ceases to be a tree of descent." (ibid.: 11) Schuchardt proposed the mechanism of Sprachkreuzung in order to overcome the inadequacy of genealogical classification, which he associated with Darwin.

Another early statement from the Leipzig ambience is August Leskien's preface to his study of declination in Germanic and Slavic (1876). Leskien's conclusion that there is no fundamental difference between Schleicher's Stammbaum and Johannes Schmidt's wave model is interesting in view of the fact that also Trubetzkoy made statements in which he attempted to downplay the contrast between the two perspectives. Trubetzkoy had studied with Leskien in Leipzig on the eve of the First World War, and it seems almost unthinkable that he would not have been familiar with Leskien's book, a veritable classic in Slavic comparative linguistics.

Curiously, in the autumn of 1900—the same year in which Schuchardt decided to dust off his Leipzig lecture—Baudouin de Courtenay, in St. Petersburg, opened his course on "Comparative

Grammar of Slavic Languages in Connection with Other Ario-European Languages" with a lecture which was subsequently published under the title "About the Mixed Character of All Languages" (Baudouin 1901). Baudouin flatly rejected the idea of a pure language and proceeded to enumerate various kinds of language mixing. He pointed out that languages mix not only in space but also in time: all languages are mixed with themselves, i.e., with their earlier stages. Particularly interesting are Baudouin's observations about what happens when languages of different types mix. He stated that under the influence of incoming foreign elements a language may lose inflection and develop analytic (periphrastic) forms where there had been synthetic ones. Shifting stress may become stabilized, and "irrational" paradigmatic irregularities may be leveled. Baudouin thus not only asserted the role of language contact as a force in language history; he also attempted to analyze the grammatical mechanism of contact.[40]

If this survey were to be continued,[41] a number of Russian linguists would certainly deserve mention—among them V. A. Bogorodickij, a disciple of Baudouin who devoted a brief chapter to mixed languages in his introductory book on linguistics (Bogorodickij 1910: 26), and N. J. Marr, who emphatically asserted that a single Indo-European proto-language was "a scientific fiction which has ceased to serve its function" (Marr 1924 [1933: 185]). But it may be more interesting to return to Baudouin and note that he addressed the question of the mechanism of language contact when he discussed (in principle, at least) what specifically happens in language contact—a point about which Trubetzkoy's "Thoughts" was silent. In a way, Trubetzkoy's silence on this issue is surprising. Gabriel Tarde, the only author Trubetzkoy mentions explicitly in *Europe and Mankind,* did some work on invention and imitation of cultural values across cultures. (It is expounded in *Le lois de l'imitation* (Tarde 1890) and in *La logique sociale* (Tarde 1895).) Tarde thought of inventions as spreading from a particular center in waves, their progress being modified by the properties of environment. One crucial aspect of the spread of inventions is the compatibility of the potential recipient with the innovation: if the innovation is compatible with the environment that it reaches, then the conditions for its spread are met.

Tarde elaborates a number of specific configurations in this process, introducing such concepts as *duel logique* (a situation of conflict arising in the process of spread). Trubetzkoy accepts Tarde's categories and utilizes them in order to present a final and resolute rejection of the idea that a particular culture might fully accommodate another culture without annihilating itself. All this should ultimately yield a notion of "possible borrowing," a notion certainly transposable to linguistics of contact as well. But there is no such notion in Trubetzkoy's Sprachbund studies. Was Trubetzkoy about to work out this question, or was he really implying that his set of defining criteria for the Eurasian Sprachbund was as accidental as the ethnic composition of the Eurasians?

By contrast, Roman Jakobson, who explicitly acknowledged divergence and convergence as mechanisms of diachronic change (1929a: 12) and later devoted much energy to the Sprachbund idea (1931a, c; 1932c; 1938a), touched in his *Remarques* on the notion "possible borrowing."[42] Aside from this, however, there is an immense difference between Jakobson and Trubetzkoy as far as the overall frame of reference (i. e., the kind of thematic commitment) is concerned. An instructive piece is "On the Characterization of the Eurasian Language Union," written in Prague in the summer of 1930 and published as a brochure in Paris (Jakobson 1931a). Here, as elsewhere, Jakobson accepted certain elements of Trubetzkoy's rhetoric. Commenting on Father Wilhelm Schmidt, the influential author whose book *Die Sprachfamilien und Sprachkreise der Erde* (1926) included a great deal of material on cultural and linguistic convergence, Jakobson found that the author was not free of "European egocentrism" (Jakobson 1931a [1962: 155]). He particularly objected to the fact that Father Schmidt appealed to an evolutionary perspective formulated in such terms as Urkultur, fortgeschrittene Kultur, weiter fortgeschrittene Kultur, and Hochkultur. More important, however, for Jakobson, the idea of linguistic convergence, and the Eurasian approach, primarily represented a conceptual revolution in science—a revolution that indicated a decisive rupture with mechanistic methods. Quite characteristically, he supported the concept of convergence by reference to the work done in the natural sciences, primarily by the Russian naturalists Lev Berg and Petr Savickij. Berg, a biologist and a geographer, had studied convergence phenomena, including mimicry, within closed ecological systems (Berg 1922; see Toman 1981); Savickij, a geographer, had postulated Eurasia as an integral geographical zone. No doubt there was a patriotic component in Jakobson's choice of references, the obvious idea being that progress on the path of abandoning the nineteenth century was particularly manifest in the work of Russian intellectuals. But on the whole the genesis of his Eurasian studies was quite different from that of Trubetzkoy's, and political Eurasianism was of little interest to him.

11

The Linguist Remains a Futurist: Roman Jakobson and the Czech Avant-Garde between the Two Wars

Roman Jakobson's years in Czechoslovakia provide additional data on the embedding of scholarship in culture, one of the central concerns of this book. This chapter surveys the motives that underlay the interaction of scholars and artists.[1]

The Czech avant-garde considered Jakobson a scholarly ally and referred to certain aspects of his linguistics in order to assert its position. This alliance continued throughout the 1930s, but its focus was changing. Jakobson gradually began to participate in public defenses of the avant-garde, even becoming its political ally. One of the major issues was the self-defense of the avant-garde against political pressures, mainly from the pro-Moscow Left. In these polemics Jakobson argued for free, uncensored work, both in art and in scholarship. Despite contradictions, this engagement is noteworthy for its interpretation of intellectual work as free of political utilitarianism.

11.1 First Contacts—Radical Journals of the 1920s

As we have seen, the early 1920s—a time that appears to have been quiet from the point of view of linguistics—was a period in which a rather "hot" line of commitment emerged in Roman Jakobson's activity. He not only published in the outlets of Masaryk's Realists; he also contributed to the journals of the Left, such as *Den* [*The Day*], *Kmen* [*The Stem*], and *Červen* [*June*]. These publications represented a direct continuation of his Russian years.

Den, in which the first contact between Jakobson and the artists of the Czech avant-garde was established, was a short-lived journal published by a wealthy enthusiast. Originally intended as a cultural daily, it became a weekly before ceasing publication altogether. For about three months during its initial phase, *Den* was imbued with a distinct anarcho-Communist spirit. One of its more important ventures was a double issue on modern Russian art (December 27, 1920) that carried articles on Archipenko, Blok, Gončarova, Larionov, Stravinsky, and others. Publishing an issue on modern Russian art at that time of year might appear odd; however, there was political and social unrest in Czechoslovakia in the winter of 1920, including violent clashes between demonstrators and the police during the so-called December Strike. Under these circumstances the "Russian issue" was an overt expression of political sympathy with the young Bolshevik state, and it was in this issue that Jakobson's (1920d) translation of a brief excerpt from Xlebnikov's "Sisters-Lightnings" was published:[2]

Kol úlu ulice	Around the beehive of the street
husté jak včely	dense as bees
poletují kule.	bullets fly around.
Chvějí se stoly	The tables tremble,
bledne i smělý.	even a brave man pales.
V ulici dlouhé	In the street, long
jak kule let	as the flight of a bullet,
znovu kulomet	again the machine gun
kosí, mete	scythes, sweeps
jak smeták listy	as a broom sweeps leaves
kulemi drtí	with bullets crushes
kapitalisty.	capitalists.

But the translator's name was given only as "R. A." (standing for "Roman Aljagrov," Jakobson's pseudonym). Thus, Jakobson's participation in this Russian issue remained virtually unknown. Indeed, Zdeněk Kalista—in 1920 a young radical poet and the driving force behind *Den*—believed as late as the time of his memoirs (Kalista 1969) that the translation was by his collaborator, the young Communist Jiří Weil. Kalista recalled the provocative value of publishing Majakovskij and Xlebnikov and the fact that at the time it was seen as "a sign of unbroken self-confidence, a sign of forward-looking hope, an impetus to those minds were losing power under the burden of a temporary disappointment" (Kalista 1969: 135).[3] Jakobson's translation was undoubtedly expected to keep the flame alive; and, indeed, it is hard to imagine that the choice of the passage and even the translation itself could have been dispassionate. Where Xlebnikov merely speaks about bullets crushing "shepherds of money" [pastuxi deneg], Jakobson's machine gun unequivocally "crushes capitalists."

Kmen and *Červen* were major outlets of the budding interwar Left. *Kmen* was a literary weekly. As regards *Červen*, much can be concluded from the fact that in 1921, when Jakobson published in it, it was subtitled "Proletkult—Communism—Literature—New Art." The two journals look almost identical, which is not surprising as they were both edited by the poet Stanislav K. Neumann. With Neumann, Jakobson was definitely in the hands of an ardent supporter of the young generation. Although his poetry was beginning to be parodied (brilliantly, by Jiří Hausmann), Neumann's prestige among the postwar generation was immense. And some of his editorial ventures of the early 1920s were unorthodox. For instance, *Kmen* published Milena Jesenská's translations of the Prague author Franz Kafka in 1920, while Kafka was still living, and in June 1921 *Červen* devoted a special issue to the introduction of the avant-garde group Devětsil.

11.2 The Avant-Garde and Functionalism

First Conflicts—Debates about the Non-Utilitarian Nature of Art

Devětsil[4] soon attracted Roman Jakobson's attention. Established in November 1920, this group developed a movement, called Poetism, that uniquely combined Constructivism with naive lyricism and hedonism. Among its members were poets and artists, some of whom were to become Jakobson's close friends: the poets Konstantin Biebl, Vítězslav Nezval, and Jaroslav Seifert, the author Vladislav Vančura, the essayist and advocate of modern art Karel Teige, the painter Josef Šíma. Writing in 1950, Jakobson remembered this group very well:

I came to Prague in 1920 and made the acquaintance of Seifert in 1921. A little later, but still in the early twenties began my friendship with Biebl and especially with Nezval. I brought to Czechoslovakia the first information about Xlebnikov and Majakovskij. Even their names were completely unknown in Prague before I came. Often I spoke with the Devětsil people about the above-mentioned Russian poets and about the current problems of Russian poetry of that time. Some of these slogans influenced the "poeticism" [Poetism] in birth, but the influence of modern Russian poetry as such was rather weak, much weaker than that of the French. The lack of knowledge of the Russian language was at that time general and the whole preceding development of Czech poetry favored much more the influence of Western trends. But Nezval with his extreme capacity of grasping new poetic values succeeded by listening to my readings and word for word translations of some of Xlebnikov's and Majakovskij's poems to catch their poetic individuality. (Jakobson 1950: 26, n. 2)[5]

The playful nature of Poetism eventually led to a conflict with S. K. Neumann. In 1925 Neumann's journals were superseded, under the auspices of the Communist Party, by *Reflektor*, a propagandistic popular fortnightly intended to counterbalance the influence of bourgeois picture magazines. *Reflektor* featured large photographs of Soviet children, new Soviet airports and power plants, and, again and again, Soviet politicians and functionaries. Replies to letters from readers were published in a special section. In one telling case, a reader had proposed that *Reflektor* start a new section devoted to riddles. Neumann did not take this suggestion very seriously, thus proving that there was not much fun in the kind of edification he was committed to; nevertheless, he indicated in his reply that he would accept a riddles corner provided really good riddles were submitted. "Of course," he added, "it will also be necessary to make the riddles useful to our readers by designing solutions which will represent truths needed by the proletariat." (Neumann 1925a).

Neumann was already a dogmatic cultural bureaucrat, completely submissive to the policy of the Communist Party. Devětsil, on the other hand, was drifting toward the international avant-garde, which encompassed Purism, Bauhaus, Constructivism, abstract art, and other comparable movements that Neumann considered not to be very useful to the workers. In fact, on the same page on which he demanded riddles with ideologically adequate solutions, Neumann also voiced his negative opinion of the prose of Vladislav Vančura. The task of the contemporary writer, he noted, was to escape the bourgeois class, put off his bourgeois artistry, and "see his only goal in being understood by the working masses" (Neumann 1925b); Vančura qualified on none of these points.

Jakobson reacted to Neumann's ideas about art in an article entitled "The End of the UMPRUM-Designership and Small Undertakings in Poetry"[6] (Jakobson 1925a). It appeared in *Pásmo*, the journal of the Brno chapter of Devětsil. Even the design of this issue of *Pásmo* indicates the depth of the rift between Neumann's utilitarian propaganda and the aspirations of the postwar avant-garde. The journal changed the color of the paper for each issue—this one was blue. The front page, on which Jakobson's article appeared, featured photos of Charlie Chaplin, Harold Lloyd, and Douglas Fairbanks, who had all just been awarded honorary membership in Devětsil.[7] Jakobson calls Neumann's guidelines concerning proletarian riddles "sweet" [milé], refers to their author as "venerable S. K. Neumann" [velebný S. K. Neumann], and depicts the former anarchist as a person completely submerged in a petty-bourgeois way of life:

It's just like him to contemplate imprinting a puzzle with the motto about the proletarians of all countries. . . . He puts a proletarian crossword puzzle together, transforms Doležal's article into a tender lyric poem, contentedly sips coffee with rum from a cup with a flower design and happily naps on a cushion embroidered by a careful hand—not with the words "Fifteen minutes only" (that would be petty-bourgeois), but with the words "Honor work!" (Jakobson 1925a: 1)

As might be expected, Neumann reacted in a very unfriendly manner. His answer appeared in the section of *Reflektor* in which he ordinarily responded to questions from workers. It went as follows:

To Roman Jakobson. Dear Roman, although I don't know why you are using this tone in a polemic against me, a tone I am familiar with from your émigrés who talk to our people somewhat arrogantly and superciliously when one meets them on the train—as if they were proselytizing us. I do however understand that given your partyless and "classless" attitude you sympathize with this circus of *Pásmo* whose major daring consists in frivolously mixing Marxism and communism with the latest convulsions of bourgeois art. Your (and your Russian) philological toys fit into this environment very well. I can give you only one piece of advice in our "Answers to Letters" section: not to talk about such things as riddles in workers' magazines. . . . For arrogant intellectuals of your kind, this is all Chinese. (Neumann 1925c)

Objects Corresponding to Their Purpose—A Note on the Strict Division of Functions

Although the *Reflektor* controversy is of some historical interest because of the prominence of persons involved (Stanislav Neumann was stylized by later historiography as a prophet of the proletarian culture), its political dimension was not really new. Similar conflicts had arisen from the uneasy symbiosis between Social Democrats and naturalist authors, the avant-garde of the late nineteenth century (see Toman 1985a). But Jakobson's reply is important in the present context because it is based on a functional point of view:

> . . . communicative language with its orientation towards the object of the utterance and poetic language with its orientation towards the expression itself represent two different, in many respects opposed, language systems (these two do not, of course, by any means exhaust the multitude of language functions). And because it is constructive things we want, things corresponding to their purpose, we are appalled by lampshades imitating flowers or by false windows you cannot see through. It is for this reason that we haven't the slightest desire to express the truths useful for the proletariat in the form of riddles or rhymes. The communication of "useful truths" requires completely different modes of expression: clarity, brevity, precision, absence of ambiguity, etc. When a worker is called to a rally, it is not suggested that he walk from one suburb of Prague to another in fox-trot steps. If a useful truth is to be passed on to the worker, elementary integrity prohibits the use of rhymes, poetic metaphors or other such imaginative gear.
>
> This is not to deny the social role of poetry but merely to protest against making poetry into a contraband smuggled in under the pretext of truths useful for the proletariat. (Jakobson 1925a: 1)

Owing to this functional unequivocality, or monofunctionalism (a position that was rapidly gaining influence, not only as a scholarly doctrine but also as an expression of a whole lifestyle,[8]) Jakobson's reply is an important document of the state of linguistics shortly before the emergence of the Prague Circle and of the close link between functional linguistics and the functionalist currents in avant-garde art.

A general tendency toward rational, or functional, design was quite important in the West—e.g., in *De Stijl* (from 1917 on) and *L'Esprit Nouveau* (from 1920 on)—and in Czechoslovakia Devětsil also adhered to it. In 1922, the architect Jaromír Krejcar—member of Devětsil, advocate of modern architectural currents, and editor of *Život*—proclaimed the introduction of Purism as a major goal:[9]

> The collection programatically introduces purist aesthetics and approaches to us, which are in our opinion especially healthy for architecture. Purism . . . is a logical phenomenon of our time. Its presuppositions are given by the modern civilization and its character by the demands of modern life. (*Život II*, 208; signed Redakce [editors])

A major component of this "logical phenomenon of our time" was rational design, and indeed the aforementioned issue of *Život* includes, besides modern film and primitivist "poetical" painting, a large number of motifs typical of *L'Esprit Nouveau*. There are sections on modern naval architecture and on skyscrapers, and there are substantial translations of Le Corbusieur and Ozenfant. Equally important is a translation from Ilja Èrenburg's *But It Does Turn* (1922), a breviary of Constructivism perceptibly influenced by *L'Esprit Nouveau*. All this is relevant here because one of the main constructive tenets of the purist *Esprit Nouveau* was the idea of a clear definition and exposure of functions associated with objects, tools, etc.: "Today, only precisely executed products that conform to a specific purpose can be justified."[10] (Ozenfant and Jeanneret 1922: 10) On this reading, functionalism is based on an explicit dissociation of functions. That idea, which became very popular among architects and designers, was of course contingent on a mixture of contemporary ideas of expedience, efficiency, and social purpose. Krejcar's *Život* included a good example of this attitude, a text by the Czech painter Josef Šíma:

ADVERTISEMENT cannot be approached from the point of view of painting: a product painted according to the rules of artistic beauty is bad from the point of view of advertising. The purpose of an ad does not consist in showing the qualities of modern painting or sculpture or photography. All these artistic posters, these terrible products of schools for industrial art (what does industrial art mean ?) are bad from the point of view of advertisement. A poster must always be an ad and not a painting or decoration. The only point the two have in common is that the poster is a patch of color just as a painting is. The beauty of an ad lies only in perfectly achieving its purpose. (Šíma 1922: 102)

The basic affinity between this mini-manifesto of monofunctionalism and Jakobson's essay seems obvious. Both stress the idea of a "thing corresponding to its purpose"—Šíma by showing what is not the purpose of advertising and stressing the idea of perfect achievement of the purpose, Jakobson by asserting that "it is constructive things we want, things corresponding to their purpose."

Jakobson's essay, in addition, has quite a strong affinity with Èrenburg's *But It Does Turn*. For Èrenburg, handcraft was a manner of production that deserved contempt; functional unequivocality, on the other hand, gave "a clear insight into tasks: narrative narratives, poetical poetry, theatrical theater etc." (Èrenburg 1922: 96). In close parallel, Jakobson's *Pásmo* article expresses contempt for small handcrafts even in its title and takes up a clear division of tasks as one of its major themes.[11]

And the controversy in which Jakobson and Neumann were engaged went beyond questions of efficiency and functional unequivocality; it also had an ethical dimension. In Jakobson's words, it is not only a matter of being "appalled by lampshades imitating flowers or by false windows you cannot see through"; it is a matter of "elementary integrity" which "prohibits the use of rhymes, poetic metaphors or other such imaginative gear" (Jakobson 1925a: 2). Here we encounter a moral argument for functionalism. This is probably Jakobson's first moral judgment in this connection.[12]

Words, Words, Words—Teige's Reception of Jakobson's Theories

Jaroslav Seifert, one of the leading poets of the Devětsil generation, later recalled "the ingenious Roman Jakobson" as a mediator of the new Russian poetry:

He made us familiar with all the remarkable Soviet poets, whose books were not accessible at that time: with Xlebnikov, Esenin, Axmatova, Aseev, and Majakovskij. In this way we not only became familiar with their poems but also with their passionate fights for the new poetry. (Seifert 1966)

And Vítězslav Nezval later recalled Jakobson as a scholarly ally of modern Czech poets:

In Roman Jakobson I found a friend for many years with whom I shared a deep understanding in matters of poetry. He was a friend of Majakovskij's, Pasternak's and of Russian futurists, and his experience was interesting for us. He defended us against the artistically narrow-minded and often did so with a well aimed blow—in polemics, he was not to be surpassed by anyone. (Nezval 1959: 138f.)

To consider this alliance between poetry and scholarship in more detail, it is instructive to turn to Karel Teige, another important member of the Devětsil group.

Karel Teige (1900–1951), a legendary theorist of the avant-garde whose light and dark sides have by now preoccupied generations of historians of the Czech avant-garde, was an extremely prolific author who took stances on a number of aspects of modern art, including painting, film, architecture, and literature. Although his political position with respect to the Soviet Union ranged at various times from total adoration to radical rejection, his interest in the Soviet avant-garde and his emotional attachment to the Soviet Union were considerable.[13] From about 1922 on he was a fervent advocate of Constructivism, the emergence of which he regarded as nothing less than the beginning of a new epoch in culture and civilization. In this new era, art did not have a future; Modern Beauty, however, which was best exemplified by properly functioning machines, did. The point was to take the lesson of machines seriously. Machines were constructed by engineers for particular purposes, and they represented the functional application of constructive means—and the same was true of the new Constructivist aesthetics. Constructivists did not think about art. Rather, they concentrated on fulfilling a specific task perfectly—the result was beauty:

... whenever a concrete task or problem will have a perfect fulfillment or solution, as exact and complete as possible, the purest modern beauty will be achieved, without any aesthetic ulterior motives. ... The moment we achieve all-round purposeful perfection, we automatically achieve beauty. (Teige 1925: 8)

Thus, the abolition of art, which was inherent in this interpretation of Constructivism, did not really imply the abolition of beauty. And one may infer that there were some hopes for artists—if only they would adopt an engineer-like approach: "All the confusion of contemporary artists originates in their uncertainty about the goal and purpose and about the sense of their work." (ibid.)

Many artists of the avant-garde believed in the production of Modern Beauty in laboratories under the care of specialists, and many formulations similar to Teige's can be documented. Teige's ideas were modern but not original. Bearing this in mind, let us now turn to Teige's 1927 essay "Words, Words, Words."

As the title indicates, "Words, Words, Words" is devoted mainly to the question of language. In particular, it deals with modern attitudes

toward language and with the changing conditions for its use in literature, journalism, and the new media. Teige was in complete
agreement with Jakobson regarding the idea that poetic language is
an autonomous system with its own rules and its own purpose:

> Roman Jakobson correctly notes that a general notion of language is a mere
> fiction. Language is nothing but a system of conventional values, words, just
> like a pack of cards. Just as there are no laws of a universal card game valid
> for old maid as well as for poker or for building houses of cards, language
> laws can be established only for a system determined by some specific task.
> (Teige 1927 [1972: 338f.])

Although this is more or less directly copied from Jakobson's article
in *Pásmo,* concluding that Teige was a mere copyist is not particularly
helpful. For one thing, neither Le Corbusier nor the Soviet Constructivists had attempted to discuss language. Thus, the fact that a
theoretician of the avant-garde was also covering this topic deserves
attention.

In fact, Teige tried to integrate poetry into the general framework
of Constructivism. He suggested in a passage devoted to modern Russian poetry that zaum' was in fact nothing but Constructivism in the
domain of the word, and that zaum' poets developed their poetry in
scientific, engineer-like procedure, referring to modern linguistics:

> Their effort is assisted by modern Russian linguistics and philological criti-
> cism; Jakobson, Šklovskij, Brik, Kušner, Arvatov, are undertaking a labora-
> tory experiment of immense importance. They determine experimentally
> the semantic meaning of word and speech. They study properties of word-
> masses, the nature of their relations, the way they differ from a natural ob-
> ject. Zaum' poets Xlebnikov, Kručenyx, Aljagrov, Zdanevič (Iliazd), Tretja-
> kov, Tereskovič, Terentev realize poetry of pure form, a poetry which has
> no naturalistic meaning, a poetry which sings in order to sing, a poetry of
> ringing words. The linguistic-poetic theories of these philologists and the
> practice of these poets—a kind of a marvelous chemical laboratory which
> explores basic elements of poetry, revives the word, brings discipline into
> the rhythm—make truly abstract and objectless poetry possible. This is the
> birth of a new aesthetics supported by the research of exact science. It is
> only here that word-art gains pure and genuine elements. (Teige 1927
> [1972: 338f.])

The important thing for Teige was that this approach was making
headway in the Czech avant-garde. Czech poets, he believed, were

also becoming aware of the engineering approach to poetry, thus following the overall tendency toward Constructivism:

This revitalizing work on language has not remained without influence on modern Czech poets: analogous efforts can be traced in some of Biebl's and Seifert's poems. The cooperation of modern Czech poets with Roman Jakobson's scholarly research (cf. his book *Foundations of the Czech Verse*) will hopefully bring about an enrichment of Czech poetic language. . . . (Teige 1927 [1972: 338f.])

The idea of scholarly guidance was, of course, quite clear in Jakobson's *Pásmo* article, which was explicit about how Czech poetry could be "modernized." Naturally, the underlying impetus of Jakobson's modernization precepts was the Russian Formalist point of view. And, not surprisingly, the final paragraph of Jakobson's *Pásmo* article is written in a manner of a manifesto, the vehemence of which resembles his "Tasks of Propaganda in Art":

Let us do away with unorganized work in poetry, with poetical hucksterly. The science of poetic form must go hand in hand with poetry. Let us do away with priestly mysteries, Delphic oracles. The course of the poet must be conscious, while at the same time his poetic intuition can only profit if it takes hold on the iron and concrete foundation provided by scientific analysis. And conversely, science is fructified by its contact with new art. It is an unnatural state of affairs, brought about in the 19th century, for science to pay attention to a literary movement only when it has turned into an archeological fossil. In Russia, the new literature and the young science of literature (the OPOJAZ group) more often than not advance side by side. (Jakobson 1925a: 2)

Clearly, "prophetic mysteries, Delphic oracles" is a shot at the Symbolist understanding of imagination. "Unorganized work" castigates the old era as well. At the same time, the encouragement resembles later encouragements to leave behind the era of discussions and proceed with a radical reformulation of linguistics and literary studies.

In 1925, Jakobson's study of Czech verse (1923a) was available only in Russian, and evidently few Czech poets had read it. A year later, however, a Czech translation appeared, and it soon became a subject of reviews, discussions, and polemics.[14] The Czech edition (Jakobson 1926a) included statements by Czech poets and actors about the prosodic problems of Czech verse. Jakobson elicited some of these answers; thus, we seem to be dealing here with a kind of field work, reminiscent of Jakobson's earlier dialectological field work. Jakobson's close relationship to the artists of the avant-garde is further evident from the fact that the Czech edition appeared in the series Edice Odeon, which included poetry and prose by Vančura, Apollinaire, Cendrars, Nezval, and Souppault. Quite in line with the Zeitgeist, the series was directed by J. Fromek, a Communist publisher.

11.3 Poets, Writers, Scholars

By the late 1920s, Devětsil and its doctrine of joyful life amidst Modern Beauty were no longer in existence. Many of the artists who had once been associated with Devětsil were now drifting toward Surrealism, some of them trying to marry Surrealism with dialectical materialism. Their basic attitude toward the Prague Linguistic Circle remained unchanged, however. Roman Jakobson and Jan Mukařovský kept in close contact with their old friends and continued to be regarded the avant-garde's scientific allies.

Jakobson's friendship with Vladislav Vančura is not documented particularly well, yet it was substantial.[15] Vančura admired Jakobson's attempts to reevaluate Czech medieval poetry; in turn, Jakobson's interest in Vančura's unique style is evident in his brief essay on Vančura's *Markéta Lazarová* (Jakobson 1931g). The language of *Markéta Lazarová* (a story inspired by the life of the medieval robber knights) was a highly stylized Czech, full of artificial archaisms. Jakobson appreciated this style and felt, correctly, that *Markéta Lazarová* was a major work of art:

It is quite curious to see how its basic motifs, primitive expressivity, an almost irrational semantic load and its exciting unacceptability to "journalists" bring Vančura's prose in the proximity of Velimir Xlebnikov, one of the greatest new Russian poets, who remained almost unknown to Vančura and the Czechs on the whole. Another visible example of a convergent development. (Jakobson 1931g)

The evaluation is curious—this major author turned out to be akin to Jakobson's Russian enigma Xlebnikov. Given Jakobson's authority, one might well take this comparison seriously—and one might find sound reasons for it. At the same time, one cannot dismiss the possibility that most of the poetics rooted in Poetism, and then transformed to Czech Surrealism, were probably not very close to a thinker who grew on Russian Futurism. In the *Pásmo* essay, Jakobson praised Jaroslav Seifert's use of sound repetition—a feature that Jakobson himself advocated in his zaum' experiments. But Seifert, in a 1984 interview (Seifert 1984), essentially denied that the theories of the Prague Circle had influenced his poetry, his warm friendship with Jakobson notwithstanding; he stressed the impact of French poets such as Apollinaire, Verlaine, and Tzara—poets rarely, if ever, mentioned by Jakobson. In the long run, the common denominator between the Prague Circle and the avant-garde poets was, perhaps paradoxically, not stylistic; rather, it seems to have been an overall attitude of iconoclasm, formal innovation, and poetry rooted in language.

A very different angle on the link between the Circle and the avant-garde poets can be found in the poetry of Vítězslav Nezval, whose works of the 1930s include poems dedicated to Jakobson and to Biebl, Honzl, Teige, Štyrský, Toyen, and other artists of the avant-garde and whose 1932 collection *Five Fingers* begins with a letter addressed to the structuralist aesthetician Mukařovský. Nezval incorporated everyday events into his texts, writing about his avant-garde friends and their bohemian life. For instance, Nezval's 1932 collection *A Havelock of Glas* contains a lengthy poem, entitled "Vyzvání přátelům" ["An Address to Friends"], in which the poet's friends pass by in a loose associative pageant[16]:

hle jindřich štyrský	look, jindřich štyrský
doprovází mne na nádraží	accompanies me to the station
hovoří o zvláštní úloze kterou	he speaks of the special role which
hrají v jeho životě konvalinky	lilies-of-the-valley play in his life
bude ilustrovati mou báseň	he will illustrate my poem
nádražní restaurace mění svůj smysl	the station restaurant changes its meaning

pak sedáme všichni den co den v baru	then we sit day after day in a bar
mluví se o vladislavu vančurovi	we speak of vladislav vančura
jenž přijížděl velmi zřídka	who calls on us very rarely
roman jakobson nám mává z vyslanectví	roman jakobson waves to us from the embassy
popěvky z bajadery a	songs from bayadère and
z madame pompadoure	from madame pompadour
shimmy je vrchol estetiky	shimmy is the peak of aesthetics
zpívá se sborem	it is sung in the choir
pijeme graves	we drink Graves
seifert usíná o desáté hodině	seifert falls asleep at ten
a o půlnoci se znovu probouzí	and wakes again at midnight

The following poem, from the same collection, is about the "deep understanding in the matters of poetry" which Jakobson and Nezval shared:

Roman Jakobson

Bez jediné ze svých proslulých vad	If of his famous failings there was just one less
byl by ničím	he would be nothing
Skála již trpělivě cvičím	The scale I patiently practise
nemá předepsaný prstoklad	has no prescribed fingering
Ty ze všech nejvíc Romane	You of all, Roman,
odpovídáš mým skrytým pákám	correspond to my secret levers
Vyluzuji zpěv i kdákám	I produce song and I cackle
jak se mi namanc	just as I please
A když se občas jedlík postí	And when occasionally the eater fasts
není to pokrytecká askeze	it is not hypocritical asceticism
Blesk doletí a želva doleze	The lightning will fly, the tortoise crawl to destination
Na zdraví poesie v její celistvosti	A toast to poetry in its entirety!
(Nezval 1932: 109) [17]	

Another poem from these years that relates to Roman Jakobson can be found in Nezval's *Return Ticket* (1933). "Dopis Romanu Jakobsonovi" ["A Letter to Roman Jakobson"] contains a reflection on Jakobson's role in Nezval's poetry. Nezval first expresses dissatisfac-

tion with his style of life and with the style of his poetry; he then
unfolds a vision of a new type of poetic creation:

Básníku odstraň psací stůl	Poet, remove your desk
Procítám jako somnanbul	I awake like a somnanbulist
Změnils svět v rým jak boháč	You have turned the world into rhyme
v rentu	as a rich man turns it into interest
Chci tvořit básně z dokumentů	I want to create poems out of documents
Co je jich v tomto obchodě	As many as you see in this shop
Cele se vzdáti náhodě	To fully submit to chance
Brát jenom to co spadne samo	To take only things that come of themselves
Váš rozhovor je báseň dámo	Your conversation is a poem, madam
Dnes vyzpovídám jeptišku	Today I'll hear the confession of a nun
Směs z novinových výstřižků	A mixture of newspaper clippings
Chansony promíchané s daty	Chansons intermixed with dates
Podivuhodné inseráty	Marvelous small ads
Zapiš co volal kamelot	Write down what the newspaper-man was shouting
Tři čtyři řádky jarních mod	Three or four lines of summer fashions
Popis mně dodá vlastivěda	The description will be supplied by the encyclopaedia
Fabule necht' se sama hledá	The plot should look for itself
Jídelní lístek Jízdní řád	Menu, timetable
Lži prodavaček marmelád	Lies of jam-sellers
Novinky Gaumontova týdne	The news of the Gaumont news-reel
Mé sny zas potom budou klidné	My dreams will be quiet again
Nůžky a malou tubu klihu	Scissors and a little tube of glue
Dnes básník montuje svou knihu	Today the poet assembles his book
Změnil se vskutku na děcko?	Can he really have become a child?
Romane díky za všecko!	Roman, thanks for everything!
(Nezval 1933: 158f.)	

The thanks expressed in the last line are, of course, not intended to
imply that Jakobson invented the collage. Nezval is really describing
the making of a chance poem, something he certainly did not owe
to Jakobson. Yet there seem to be allusions to some intriguing facts
which we may not be able to appreciate in full. Noting that Jakobson
liked literary collages and produced some collage-like texts himself
(e.g. Jakobson 1934c) may thus be helpful at this point.

While the previous poems were indicative of Nezval's surrealist commitment to the stream-of-consciusness method and his love of rhyme, a long poem from the 1936 collection *Prague with the Fingers of Rain* adds an element of intertextuality in that it varies a theme familiar from Guillaume Apollinaire:

Poříč
Romanu Jakobsonovi

Dnes se podobá Praha vylisované květině
A všem městům
Všem městům která jsi navštívil všem městům která chceš
    navštívit
Připadáš si tu jak cizinec jenž právě přijel a hledá hotel
Hledá hotel na Poříči kde jsou zbytky šantánu
Vyjeven sedíš v pivnici jako bys nerozuměl česky
O čem asi hovoří tito dva pijáci bez věku
Hovoří o tobě
Z které země přišel
Hovoří
Jakobys tu poznával zajímavý dosti zvláštní národ
Poznáváš po slepu jeho mrav
Podivný cestovatel jenž touží po cizokrajné ženě
Po této poněkud bez vkusu oblečené paní nebo dělnici
Nostalgicky dotčen vůní neznámé uzeniny
Podivný cestovatel jenž přerušuje cestu nevěda kde a proč
Podivný cestovatel jenž nemá nikdy nazbyt
A kterého jak se zdá neděsí vůbec čas
Jenž přijel odnikud a odjíždí náhle s deštěm
(Nezval 1936: 50f.)

Poříč
For Roman Jakobson

Prague is like a pressed flower today
And like all towns
All towns you have visited all towns you wish to visit
You feel like a stranger here who has just arrived and looks for a hotel
Looks for a hotel in Poříč where cabaret survives
In consternation you sit in a beer-hall as though you didn't understand
    Czech
What might these two ageless drinkers be talking about
They are talking about you
From which country did he come

They say
As if you studied here an interesting and rather strange nation
You recognize blindfold its customs
Strange traveler who longs for an exotic woman
For this lady, or for a working woman, dressed without much taste
Nostalgically touched by the scent of unknown smoked goods
Strange traveler who breaks his journey without knowing where and why
Strange traveler who never has money to spare
And whom, so it seems, time does not terrify at all
Who came from nowhere and suddenly leaves with the rain

Here Nezval reached for something that was not quite literary history for his generation, exploiting Apollinaire's short story "L'intransigeant de Prague" (in itself a reflection of the French poet's visit to the Czech capital in 1902).[18] Apollinaire located his story at Poříč, also the scene of Nezval's poem on Jakobson. At the turn of the century this was an area of cabarets, beer gardens, and all sorts of popular amusements. Here, the narrator of Apollinaire's story meets Ahasverus, the intransigeant de Prague, who guides him through the city. Clearly, Nezval was playing, in his typical manner, with the melancholy and enigma of the Ahasverus myth, and with the cult of Apollinaire that was so dear to Devětsil poets; yet his mood is somewhat more grave than Apollinaire's. If blunt biographism is permitted, and if the address "you" in the poem refers to Jakobson (a possibility strongly suggested by the poem), we might attribute this change of mood to the fact that in the Czechoslovakia of 1936 the idea of "suddenly leaving with the rain" was no longer merely a poetical one; for many, leaving was becoming a practical problem.

11.4 Final Conflicts: The Apparatchiks on the Eve of the Second World War

In Czechoslovakia the transition from the 1920s to the early 1930s and that from the early 1930s to the late 1930s were marked by sharp changes in the political and cultural climate.[19] Whereas the 1920s had been a fairly uncomplicated and optimistic period in the newly established Czechoslovak state, the 1930s were becoming more complicated and depressed. Immediately after a devastating depression, Hitler gained power in Germany in 1933, a fact deeply felt in

Czechoslovakia not only because Germany was a geographic neighbor but also because a large part of Czechoslovakia's population was German; indeed, the German minority in Czechoslovakia mimicked the political developments in Germany during the 1930s, eventually contributing to the doom of the Czechoslovak republic.

Czechoslovakia's avant-garde, with its emotional attachment to the Soviet Union, was facing events which it felt were more than disconcerting. One was the fate of the left in Nazi Germany. Another was the aftermath of the Spanish Civil War—not only Franco's victory but also the uncomfortable questions raised by the involvement of the Soviet Union. André Gide's "defection" from the left after his visit to the Soviet Union in 1935 was further undermining the self-confidence of the leftist intelligentsia. Finally, a deep rift was caused by the Moscow Trials.

One particularly depressing aspect of the late 1930s, often hard to understand on the left, was the fact that Nazi Germany and the Soviet Union could now be spoken of in the same vocabulary. Visitors to the 1937 World Exhibition in Paris noted with shock that the German and Soviet pavilions, which faced each other, were embarrassingly similar. Some authors eventually addressed this convergence. In 1938, Karel Teige, who had taken a rather dogmatic pro-Soviet course for most of the 1930s, published *Surrealism against the Current*, a passionate pamphlet against the Soviet Union's cultural policy and, consequently, against its executors in Czechoslovakia. (The cover illustration depicted a hand with a pen breaking through a brick wall.) It was at this time, shortly before Munich and the Nazi invasion of March 15, 1939, that the polemics about the cultural and political orientation of the avant-garde reached their dramatic peak.

Several years before, Roman Jakobson had also started to participate in discussions that had obvious political implications. In general, his tack was to criticize the view of Czech cultural history as the history of a culture that merely copied its neighbor, Germany. (He also intended to revise the history of Czech Jews along similar lines.) Jakobson's efforts can be seen particularly clearly in his criticism of the work of Konrad Bittner, a scholar specializing in the history of Slavo-Germanic contacts and claiming cultural superiority for the Germans (Bittner 1936; Jakobson 1936f). These discussions, although scholarly in nature, had a wide public echo. Jakobson's writings on Czech history were reported on and popularized by journalists and essayists such as A. Mágr, P. Eisner, and G. Winter.

As the polarity was building up, there was more and more talk of rapprochement with the Soviet Union (see Krofta 1935, Ripka 1935, and Jakobson 1935e in this context). On the avant-garde scene, a part of which followed a pro-Moscow course, demands for a cultural Popular Front were then quite common. Not surprisingly, pro-Moscow intellectuals such as S. K. Neumann and B. Václavek took the idea of a cultural Popular Front as a welcome opportunity to impose censorship within the leftist intelligentsia and to make the official cultural policy of the Soviet Union appear tolerable—in short, to silence criticism of the Soviet Union. Much to the disappointment of these intellectuals, Jakobson did not follow this course. For instance, on the occasion of a new staging of Pushkin in the theater D 37, he stressed the right to interpret the cultural heritage freely. In particular, he spoke out against the view of Pushkin as a precursor of socialist realism—a view that was being used in the Soviet Union to make that doctrine appear legitimate (Jakobson 1937c).

Also in 1937, Jakobson wrote the following in a contribution to a volume in honor of Jiří Voskovec and Jan Werich, two famous Prague actors whose Liberated Theater was celebrating its tenth anniversary:

True, I like your social satire and multifaceted literary parody, but [your] greatest novelty, most original and timely contribution is, I insist, your "objectless, pure comic . . . which is able to introduce the viewer into the magical world of absurdity." (Jakobson 1937b: 27) [20]

There is a remarkable correspondence between this statement and the above-mentioned critique of Neumann's utilitarianism. Although the political contexts differed, on both occasions Jakobson asserted the autonomy of art and the freedom of the artist to choose themes and forms.

Slowly but distinctly, *cenzorský dnešek* [the censorial present] and *usměrnění* (the Czech equivalent of German Gleichschaltung, meaning, in the usage of the day, elimination of the plurality of opinions) became the central notions in Jakobson's essays of the late 1930s. There are three recorded instances of Jakobson's involvement in the fight against Gleichschaltung, all of them crucially connected with the fate of the Czech avant-garde: In January 1938, he published an article in *Lidové noviny* that resulted in a bitter polemic with S. K. Neumann (Jakobson 1938b).[21] In March of the same year, he participated in a discussion in *U Blok* (Jakobson 1938c). And, also in 1932, he delivered an address at the opening of an exhibition of the surrealist painters Štyrský and Toyen in Brno. On each of these occasions he stressed the principles of free speech and uncensored exchange of opinions. The point was vital, since the Czechoslovak left was groping with the idea, and the practice, of self-censorship—and with early Stalinism. The heated debate in *U Blok* about the intellectual Popular Front and the uncensored exchange of opinion is an instructive example.

One shocking piece of news that arrived from the Soviet Union in late 1937 was that Vsevolod Meyerhold's theatre had been ordered closed—a measure that eventually culminated in the arrest and death of this famous avant-garde director, who only a year earlier had been enthusiastically received in Czechoslovakia (see Honzl 1937). The Communist-associated press hailed the closing (see, e.g., Nejedlý 1938). S. K. Neumann, at this point the editor-in-chief of the journal *Lidová kultura* [*Popular Culture*], in which the Soviet cultural policy was propagated, promptly commented on the closing in a manner that anticipated the language of journalism soon to come:

The historical fight between the decadent remains of bourgeois culture and the cultural ideals of the socially conscious working class is beginning everywhere in the cultural world. In the Soviet Union, it is the victorious working class that is carrying out this fight together with its state, and in capitalist states, voices are freeing themselves which were hitherto terrorized by bourgeois avantgardists. It is therefore a duty of sincere socialists, especially in the Marxist-Leninist avant-garde, to support the fight against decadent cultural forms in a principled and energetic manner. Each unprincipled wavering is a betrayal of the proletariat. The dissolution of Meyerhold's theatre in Moscow is merely a tiny episode in this fight. It is necessary to agree with it clearly and unconditionally. (Neumann 1938a)

Shortly after Neumann's comments appeared, *U Blok* (a quarterly that paralleled the cultural efforts of *Lidová kultura*) circulated among the intellectuals a questionnaire in which one of the questions concerned the cooperation among the various factions of intelligentsia in the face of the Nazi threat and the usefulness of free discussion and criticism in circumstances that might call for a monolithic position. Whatever the intentions behind this questionnaire may have been, the discussion immediately got out of hand. Out of about 30 responses, only six were published (in the March 1938 issue)—among them, the replies of Roman Jakobson and his friend Jiří Kroha, a functionalist architect. The discussion was then discontinued by the editors—that is, suppressed by the Communist Party.

Jakobson took the occasion of the questionnaire to react to Neumann's approval of the measures taken against Meyerhold. After quoting Soviet commentaries on cultural dirigisme in Italy, he continued:

One of the elementary truths that unfortunately tend to be forgotten in these days is that all intrusions from above into scholarly and artistic creation which have the character of censorship and persecution are absolutely impermissible. Persecution of artists because of their scientific or artistic attitude is a crime against cultural progress. The sovereign right of art and scholarship to search and discover implies also the right of artists and scholars to "untimely" ideas and statements, and the right to make "errors" and "deviations." (Jakobson 1938b: 86)

Jakobson may well have been embarking on a strategy that he thought would be authoritative in the eyes of the leftist readership of *U Blok* when he cited a Soviet source in his criticism of leftist *usměrnění* in Czechoslovakia: apparently, the Moscow daily *Izvestija* had published an article criticizing dirigiste tendencies on the day before the closing of Meyerhold's theatre. Clearly, this strategy was bound to fail.

Several weeks after the *U Blok* discussion, two prominent representatives of the Czech avant-garde, Jindrich Štyrský and Toyen,[22] opened an exhibition of their surrealist paintings in Brno. The art they represented had been attacked intensely both from the left and from the right, the respective accusations of "perverse formalism" and "degenerate art" sounding remarkably similar.[23] The content of Jakobson's speech at the opening is known only indirectly, via a report in the Brno newspaper *Ranní noviny:*

Roman Jakobson shaped his brief speech into a sharp polemic against the *Gleichschaltung* tendencies that "funnel" creation which is uncomfortable to reactionary ideology. Basing his arguments on quotations from Majakovskij, he defended the work of the avant-garde and surrealist activity against attacks which recently abounded in [the Communist] *Tvorba* and [the Communist] *Rudé právo*. . . . (B. 1938)

Again Jakobson appealed to the authority of a Soviet source, Majakovskij, thus both reasserting the depth of commitment to his late friend and to the authority of the Russian (and Soviet) avant-garde.

The months thereafter are hard to reconstruct in detail, but the major political events—the Munich Treaty of September 1938 and the occupation of Czechoslovakia in March 1939—are well known.[24] Roman Jakobson himself was fleeing Czechoslovakia in April 1939. Boarding the train, he ran into Jaroslav Seifert. The unexpected encounter was very emotional. More than 40 years later, Jakobson recalled it distinctly,[25] remembering Seifert's wish that Jakobson might take with him the message of the golden era of Czech culture which he had helped shape in Prague and Brno between the wars. Seifert recalled the moment in his memoirs, too:

I think that we were both happy about this unexpected encounter. It was a short, quick good-bye, rather sad.

"I was glad to live in this country and I was happy here too," Jakobson said. "And if it gives you comfort, I can tell you that I feel myself a Czech and am depressed." (Seifert 1981: 323)

Not surprisingly, each man remembered the encounter from his own perspective—yet there is no contradiction.

11.5 . . . and the Deeper Meaning

Can a unifying perspective be formulated from the episodes recounted above? There seems to be a distinct message in the destiny of the avant-garde—a message of which Roman Jakobson was one of the most prominent bearers. What emerges in his interwar work is nothing less than an articulate commitment to the idea of free, non-utilitarian creation, both in art and in science. This is particularly visible in the conflicts that arose from this commitment, but the conflicts by themselves do not make it quite apparent that this commitment had always been a cornerstone of avant-garde thinking.

The driving forces behind the formation of the European avant-garde have been often described in terms of an apparently adequate language of formal analysis, and arguments have been given purporting to show that the stylistic evolution was determined intrinsically. Although much is correct in this approach, it is important to realize that in many instances the artists insisted on a close link between formal innovation and a "Utopian vision." For instance, much of the original impetus behind Kandinsky's, Kupka's, or Mondrian's elementarism consisted in the belief that elementary visual forms appeal to everyone in a universal and direct manner, thus providing the very basis for a genuinely free spiritual creation—for the New Man. Particularly important in the present context is the fact that this new universalism was seen as ultimately independent of political links and constraints. The ways to achieve this freedom were diverse, but, as is worth stressing in the context of the Eastern European avant-garde, they were neither a logical outcome of the proletarian revolution nor its historical product. The following statements document this line of thought:

Constructivism is neither proletarian nor capitalist. Constructivism is primordial, without class and without an ancestor. It expresses the pure form of nature, the direct color, the spatial element not distorted by utilitarian motifs. . . . [Constructivism] is the socialism of vision—the common property of all men. (L. Moholy-Nagy 1922 [1970: 185f.])

The idea was also current in the Russian avant-garde, perhaps most visibly in Kasimir Malevič's denial of any utilitarian integration of the new art into the service of a political system: "The element of Suprematism, in painting as well as in architecture, is free of any social or other materialistic tendencies." (Malevič 1927: 98) In other Russian sources, references to elementary qualities of visual categories not only reveal a belief in their universal validity but also explicitly contrast them with the temporary nature of human institutions, those of politics included:

We say:
   Space and Time are now born to us.
   Space and Time are the only forms on which life is founded and art must consequently be constructed on them.
   States fall into pieces, political and economical systems die, ideas crumble under the strain of epochs, but life is strong and time goes on in its actual reality.
   Who will show us forms more real than these?
   Who is the great one to give us foundations firmer than these?
   (Gabo and Pevsner 1920) [26]

This fundamental aspect of elementarism in avant-garde art and literature before and after the First World War [27] was permanently obliterated in a number of ways. This was to be expected, in view of the generality of this idea and its utopian character. One of the critical points was the clash between individualism and collectivism. Sympathies with the latter were strong and influential—particularly after the war (which, it should be recalled, was often interpreted as a logical result of the perverted individualism of the preceding epoch). Even Mondrian briefly believed that the spirit of universal creativity, although directed toward the liberation of individual creativity, could best be realized in a collective.

   As is fairly evident (and as was also obvious to some contemporary critics), the political commitment of the Czech avant-garde was more than dubious at times. But there were always some individuals who attempted to keep the utopia free of utilitarian goals and constraints. This engagement did not disappear even in the late 1930s. It is telling that the fight against Gleichschaltung brought Jakobson close to Štyrský and Toyen—two artists who, despite their overt leftist commitments, had always vehemently opposed political art.

   But Jakobson's case provides a chance to elevate the issue beyond the question of the autonomy of art. Recall that in his answer to *U Blok* Jakobson did not separate art from scholarship—both artists and scholars, he insisted, had the right to "untimely" ideas and "deviations." Scholars were the allies of poets, and they too were attracted by the vision of an avant-garde thinker, never at rest and always open to new ideas. Just like the avant-garde poet, the scholar listened to "the winds blowing from the future" (to paraphrase Xlebnikov).

Also, the linguist was a Futurist. Recall the young Jakobson's obituary for Šaxmatov:

> ... Šaxmatov loved only his future works. His past merits did not interest him, he did not know them. . . . He never rested, he was never satisfied with a "definitive" solution. When he was once shown that the conclusions he made in 1912 did not agree with those he made in 1915, he simply answered: "That's why I published a new book,—to nullify old conclusions." (Jakobson 1920c)

Some twenty years later, this was still a guiding image.

12

Epilogues

Tragic as Jakobson's departure in 1939 was, the idea of scholarship that the Prague Circle represented was now on its way to the West with him. I review selected aspects of Jakobson's activity in the United States in the first section of this chapter, primarily in order to document Jakobson's defense of the spirit of the Circle. In the second section I survey the fate of the Circle in Czechoslovakia after the seizure of power by the Communists in 1948. My survey of the disintegration of the Circle under the Communist regime is brief, leaving ample space for contemporaries with firsthand knowledge of the period to complete the account.[1]

12.1 The Impact of the Second World War

The work of the Prague Circle went on with considerable intensity for a while after Hitler's troops invaded Czechoslovakia (on March 15, 1939). Vilém Mathesius responded to the occupation with a massive collection involving more than fifty authors and bearing a proud patriotic title *What Our Lands Gave to Europe and Mankind* (Mathesius 1940). For a brief while the Circle actually held more lectures—perhaps owing to the fact that in 1940 the universities in the so-called Protektorat Böhmen und Mähren were closed and so the scholars were on their own.[2] But clearly it would be misguided to look at the Protectorate period as anything close to a golden time. Already in Mathesius's collection, and then in *Slovo a slovesnost*, some authors felt compelled to publish under pseudonyms. In 1940, all the members of the Circle were required by the Protectorate authorities to swear they were not Jewish.[3] In 1942, despite the imposition of martial law, the Circle was still meeting and succeeded in publishing an important collection: *Readings on Language and Poetry* (Havránek and Mukařovský 1942). However, *Slovo a slovesnost* did not appear after 1942, and a festschrift for Mathesius could not be published either.

Most important, however, the Circle's membership underwent profound changes as a result of the war. The German members ceased to participate, Jakobson and Bogatyrev left the country, and the remaining Russian and Ukrainian émigrés became much less visible. And the Circle lost a number of members and close friends to death. N. S. Trubetzkoy, Otokar Fischer, and Arne Novák died on the eve of the war, and Vilém Mathesius in April 1945. Vladislav Vančura and the Slavist Jan Frček were executed. The Brno musicologist Vladimír Helfert did not return from Theresienstadt. Věra Lišková, a promising young literary scholar, was a casualty of an air raid. The Russian émigré scholar Bém has remained unaccounted for since Soviet security men arrested him in Prague in May 1945; another émigré, Petr N. Savickij, was forcibly deported by the Soviets.

Whatever changes were occurring, though, it would be wrong to claim—as is occasionally done—that with the occupation of Czechoslovakia in 1939 the Prague Linguistic Circle ceased to exist. Although the Circle's linguistic program was affected strongly, very productive work on aesthetics and literary criticism was done during the Protectorate period. Mukařovský alone held ten lectures in the early 1940s, most of them based on formal manuscripts that were published later. Significant work in aesthetics was also conducted by Jaroslav Průšek and Jiří Veltruský, and Felix Vodička began to formulate his theories of literary history (highly valued today in the context of "reception theory").

12.2 An Epilogue with a Crack—Jakobson in New York

In contrast with Bogatyrev, Jakobson did not return to the Soviet Union after March 15, 1939. After several weeks of hiding in occupied Prague, he left Czechoslovakia for Denmark on April 23, 1939, on the invitation of the University of Copenhagen. He then moved to Norway, where he lectured at the University of Oslo in the autumn of 1939. After Germany invaded Norway, he escaped to Sweden, where he arrived on April 23, 1940, and where he stayed mostly at

Uppsala and Stockholm. He eventually left Europe for New York, on a Swedish freighter, on May 23, 1941.[4] This brief sequence of dates reads rather simply, and so does Jakobson's bibliography for these years—one might almost think that nothing very extraordinary had happened in March 1939. There are lectures, articles, and a book. However, a postwar letter by Svatava Pírková-Jakobson, his second wife, gives a somewhat more vivid picture of the peregrinage:

And how about us? Temporary apartments, clothes in suitcases, boxes in storages, losses during transportation from one country to another, looking for new apartments, visas, places on boats and trains, switching from one language to another, from one environment to another, and people, people, people of all countries, characters, professions, destinies; greeting and parting, lifting of anchors barely laid, the escape from Norway on foot with the Germans on our heels, arrested and killed friends there, tension in Sweden, which functioned as a safe haven for thousands, again a whole year of visits to consulates and embassies, acrobatic attempts to leave, sunk boats, besieged transatlantic agencies, a German search on the Atlantic, and finally an unbelievable feeling of freedom and peace with mines just in reach, and then America, constantly surprising in all respects. Roman—all this time with an attaché case under his arm and long hair, waging an everyday fight for positions for linguistics and himself, lecturing in many languages ex cathedra, working through nights—but his terribly depleted energy was always coming back mysteriously. (to Zdena Havránková, November 6, 1945)[5]

Arriving in New York in June 1941, Jakobson was just one of many in a vast migration of European academics. That some of them could continue their previous work was due in large part to the existence of the New School. Originally established in New York in 1919 and later named The New School for Social Research, this institution began to host a German university in exile.

In 1942, when French academic émigrés formed their university, the New School stepped in again and accommodated the Ecole Libre des Hautes Etudes, a French institution officially authorized by Charles de Gaulle's government in London. Many of its activities are represented in the three volumes of *Renaissance* (1944–1945), a journal whose name alluded to the exodus of Greek scholars from Constantinople in 1453 and their contribution to Europe's Renaissance.[6] In 1943, the Czechoslovak exile government in London concluded an agreement with the French government allowing the old

Sorbonne chair of Czechoslovak studies to be transferred to the Ecole Libre. The Ecole Libre already had an active Slavic section, and the Sorbonne chair of Czech studies fitted well into this environment. It was assigned to Roman Jakobson, who had been teaching linguistics at the Ecole Libre since the summer of 1942.[7] As a result, the Ecole Libre became a highly visible center of Slavic—and Czech—studies. There Jakobson launched a number of projects, such as the interdisciplinary meetings on the enigmatic Russian epic *The Lay of Prince Igor'*, that resembled the collective projects of the Prague Circle. Another lecture series was dedicated to the "Czech Contribution to World Culture" (the title alluded to Mathesius's collection, mentioned above). Great Moravia and some Eurasian themes (e.g., "The Slavs and the Peoples of the Steppe") were also pursued. The Circle was entering the United States through the Ecole Libre. The methods of work were changing, but there was still much willingness to pursue the idea of international collaboration and the spirit of collective work. The metamorphosis that the Circle experienced in New York was in no way negative—in fact, a new circle was founded in 1942: the Linguistic Circle of New York.

Just as in Prague, the émigré academics in New York had their avant-garde counterparts. A community of Czech artists gathered in New York during the war. A cartoon by the Czech caricaturist Antonín Pelc in the exile review *Obzor* [*Horizon*] shows twelve Czech artists and intellectuals celebrating New Year's Eve 1942 in New York. Among them are the actors Jiří Voskovec and Jan Werich, the composer Jaroslav Ježek, the composer Bohuslav Martinů, the young novelist Egon Hostovský, the caricaturist and journalist Adolf Hoffmeister, the music critic Jan Loewenbach, and the actor Hugo Haas. Roman Jakobson was, of course, among them—he can be seen next to Pelc.[8]

To appreciate the vibrance of the Czechoslovak-émigré cultural community in New York during the war, and to further trace Roman Jakobson's role in this ambience, let us consider in some detail the case of one of the characters in Pelc's cartoon: Egon Hostovský. Hostovský (1908–1973) had developed a literary style very different from that of the generation that created Devětsil. Among the prominent themes in his novels are existentially extreme situations. Critics compared him to Dostoevskij and later to Kafka, pointing to his spiritual-ism, mysticism, and lack of interest in social reality. Hostovský's novel *Seven Times the Leading Man* (1942), published while the author was an émigré in New York, soon became a literary scandal within the community.

Hostovský 's novel was situated in the Czechoslovakia of the 1930s; however, it did not present a commonly accepted portrait of Czech life in that period. The hero, Josef Kavalský, a professor of Russian origin and a novelist of European reputation, is fascinated by the dark side of life and is contemplating collaboration with the secret Brotherhood of the New Order, an instrument of Hitler's intellectual subversion. His attitude is not politically calculated, however; it is instead dictated by his decadent outlook, by an interest in "the beauty of horror" and a feeling of ennui. Kavalský is an intellectual leader of a small circle of friends, some of whom share his attitude. Life in the circle revolves around alcohol abuse, sexual orgies, and Kavalský's monologues on the upcoming doomsday. The narrator, Jaroslav Ondřej, is a student of modern Russian poetry and a member of Kavalský's circle.

The character of Kavalský and the descriptions of other intellectuals in his circle immediately struck some émigré critics as offensive to the Czech intelligentsia (Budín 1943). The names of Karel Čapek (a Czech author whose death in 1938 was seen to symbolize the end of democratic Czechoslovakia) were invoked. Others—among them Josef Hromádka, a well-known Czech Protestant theologian then at Princeton—acknowledged the novel's intellectual and literary value.

Roman Jakobson took a stance on Hostovský's book in a lecture given on February 25, 1943, at the Astor Branch of the New York Public Library, which had a Czech section and which therefore was a cultural center for Czechs in Manhattan. Jakobson was well aware of certain problems involved in criticizing Hostovský's novel. The idea of equating an author and a narrator was certainly alien to him. But although Hostovský was exempted as a person, the way Jakobson approached the novel was basically not different from a critique treating fiction as an account of fact:

I belong to the Prague school of linguistics and literary history. When we look at a work of literature, we are only considering the literary work, what it conveys to us, what is actually included in it, and not the background of its origin and private motives of the author; we are neither detectives nor do we seek to penetrate the mysteries of the author's soul; we are not interested in the individual psychology of the novelist, but in his novel as an objective social fact, in its socio-cultural functions, i.e., the role or, better, roles, a given work of literature fulfills in a given society, in a given collective.

We are thus asking an objective, socially based question of what the author Egon Hostovský said in his novel "Seven Times the Leading Man" and leave the deeply subjective question as to what he really wanted to say with his new book, and what actually made him write it, to detective agencies and lovers of all kinds of gossip and rumor. (RJP, box 32, folder 46)

Jakobson argued passionately that virtually nothing described in the novel could have been encountered in prewar Czechoslovakia. Furthermore, "there was no Czech genius, no great poet, no famous writer, who would have a single thing in common with this despicable, whining, poor Fifth-Columnist [Kavalský]. . . . Everyone who had some standing in Czech literature of the 1930s, everyone who was talented, important, promising, threw himself into the deadly fight against Nazi Germany. . . ." The novel, although it refers to life in Czechoslovakia, has "nothing in common with Czech reality and cannot be a source of knowledge about it." Most important, Hostovský's perspective is totally misguided—there are other things to focus upon:

I do not think that there are any doubts about the nature of the intellectual legacy with which the Czechoslovak resistance has to identify itself today and tomorrow. Above all, it is the legacy of the avant-garde, in fact revolutionary, cultural development of the first twenty years of the Czechoslovak Republic. Telling me goodbye, a great Czech poet [Jaroslav Seifert] said most beautifully in Prague of April 1939: "There is only one thing you must not forget— these twenty years were immensely beautiful. Remind everyone of how much work we managed to do." (ibid.)

Jakobson then recalled the Prague Linguistic Circle as one of the products of this unique environment and stressed that "the intellectual élite did not betray, it did not lose its convictions, there was not, and is not, any split between the intellectuals and the people." In asserting this, he also recalled the fight against the manipulation of the avant-garde on the eve of the war.

Jakobson's commitment to the spirit of the Circle and the Republic could not have been more emphatic and explicit than in this lecture. But given precisely this intellectual tradition, how could one subject Hostovský's novel to this kind of criticism—how could one read it at face value as a source of knowledge and information? Jakobson was aware of this question:

I completely endorse freedom of literature and freedom of criticism. But a critic is allowed to say: there are exceptional times in which not only telegrams but also works of art must be clear and unambiguous. We are certainly for independence of works of literature, but I admit the fight for the independence of Czechoslovakia is today dearer and more pressing to us than artistic independence. (ibid.)

We saw in the previous chapter that Jakobson was a prominent fighter for that line of thought which insisted on freedom of art and scholarship and did not accept their use or evaluation for the sake of political goals. We also saw that this was a position that had much backing in the avant-garde spirit of a creation not subjugated to political utilitarianism. Jakobson's words about the right to non-conformist ideas, or "untimely errors," will be recalled. Was not much of this sentiment now nullified? Didn't Hostovský have a right to bold ideas and "untimely errors"? Is it correct to say that he was treated in a manner resembling political censorship—something to which Jakobson strongly objected in the case of Majakovskij's critics, for instance? With the benefit of hindsight one must say Yes—the edifice of the avant-garde had begun to crumble, and perhaps not for the first time.[9]

But just with the benefit of hindsight—isn't this a somewhat frosty judgment? Clearly, this was self-defense in a time of crisis, a reaction to something that put into doubt what Jakobson had himself helped construct. He felt that if Hostovský's novel were to be accepted as even vaguely expressive of Prague's intellectual atmosphere then his efforts and those of his generation would have been in vain. Had he not responded, Seifert's message would have lost all its meaning. However, some doubts about the fairness of such a response must have remained; although he could have easily published his speech, Jakobson never did so. Drafted on some 70 small sheets, in careful handwriting at the beginning and in increasingly rapid strokes toward the end, the speech survived only among his papers, a witness of the combative spirit of the Circle as well as of Trubetzkoy's pragmatic recognition that in matters of culture and politics value judgment cannot be done without.

12.3   An Epilogue with More Cracks—The End

After 1945—Patterns of Hope

The year 1945 brought the end of the World War II and hopes that the liberated Czechoslovak state would continue its prewar course. The editors of *Slovo a slovesnost* resumed the publication in 1947, remarking that no special statement was necessary as they could "also now refer with pride to every single letter of the journal's program as printed in the first volume in 1935" (*Slovo a slovesnost* 10, 1947: 64).

Enthusiasm appeared to abound, at least in the letters that Roman Jakobson began to send to Prague. Besides proudly reporting his accomplishments, he issued urgent calls for cooperation in new projects. In 1945 he wrote to his old friend Mukařovský:

I do not have to tell you how I am missing you and the others, how often I am thinking about you, Jan, and how I emphasize your name and your ideas to the students. You indeed have devoted admirers among the scholars here. I am dreaming about the restoration of our old cooperation. Write me (Columbia University, Dept. of Comparative Linguistics) about yourself, your family, the friends. We have successfully founded the Linguistic Circle of New York and have been publishing the journal "Word" (in English and French). We are anxiously waiting for contributions from you and from friends. . . . How few of us, scholars in the field of Czech culture, survived— it is necessary to keep together. I recall how you were rigorously outlining to me once fifteen years ago during a walk in Smíchov what you, Božek [Havránek] and myself have to study and write about. The task has not been fulfilled yet. (to Mukařovský; undated draft; RJP, box 44, folder 4)

There were warm responses from Prague. Havránek many times expressed hopes that Jakobson would return to Brno and resume teaching at the university.

In some sense, Czechoslovakia seemed to echo the spirit of the prewar years. The Linguistic Circle's lectures continued, and new members were joining. Old colleagues, such as Louis Hjelmslev, and new followers, such as the Polish literary scholar Renata Mayenowa, came to visit Prague. And the news about developments in Soviet linguistics seemed initially positive. Havránek visited the Soviet Union in the summer of 1946 and got a rather optimistic picture of the state of linguistics there. Reporting to Jakobson on a meeting of Soviet Slavists in Leningrad, he noted strong interest in phonology and in the Prague School—particularly in Leningrad, where the tradition of Baudouin and Ščerba, and also of Šaxmatov, seemed to be alive. Many new studies were in preparation or nearing completion there. And:

The most important thing according to all of my informers: Marr's school is in a complete retreat. Only Deržavin and Moscow caucasiology (contrary to caucasiology in Tbilisi) stick to it. The Institute of Russian Language (where academic Slavistics currently also is) is free of it. (Havránek to Jakobson, August 13, 1946; RJP, box 42, folder 20)

But prewar Czechoslovakia and the prewar Linguistic Circle were not to return. As early as November 1945, Stanislav Mágr noted in a letter to Jakobson that the "Circle no longer is the old circle from your and Mathesius's days" (RJP, box 44, folder 7). Tensions had arisen, and political perspectives were uncertain. Furthermore, although his chair in Brno was explicitly reconfirmed by the university, Jakobson's security in Czechoslovakia could not be guaranteed. Letters by Mukařovský and Havránek allude to a small but incalculable risk and mention a crucial piece of information to be obtained from Ilja Èrenburg. We can only speculate what that piece of information was, but it is well known that hundreds of Russian and Ukrainian émigrés—including the two members of the Circle, Bém and Savickij—were arrested when the Red Army entered Czechoslovakia.

Before 1948—Patterns of Anticipation

That the Circle no longer was the old one, as Mágr had put it, was of course a simple consequence of the fact that the whole prewar epoch had come irreversibly to an end. There was a widespread feeling that the liberated republic, in its democratic form, might well be only temporary.

A number of intellectuals began to open a pro-Soviet "escape hatch." Between 1945 and 1948 Jan Mukařovský was clearly moving from positions that might be described as leftist-progressive to positions of strict adherence to the Communist line. After the Communists seized power, in 1948, he immediately became a highly visible political dignitary, portrayed as a scholar who, though not a Communist before the war, understood the logic of history and had joined the forces of progress.[10] One would err, however, if one were looking for political opportunism only. Although Mukařovský's assimilation to Party standards was grotesque (he eventually denounced all of his pre-1948 scholarship), in retrospect certain elements of his thinking—especially those relating to prewar discussions about the nature of modern society and the role of the intelligentsia in it—make his conversion less than surprising.

A recurring theme in Mukařovsky's writing from 1945–1948 is the role of art and intelligentsia in society. For example, in an essay written on the occasion of the tenth anniversary of F. X. Šalda's death, Mukařovský (1947) ostensibly highlighted collectivism, utilitarian aspects of literature, "populism" [lidovost], the impact of literary criticism on social thought, and so forth. He managed to argue that F. X. Šalda's individualism was consonant with societal needs and with the idea of collectivism. He even documented Šalda's positive relationship to workers. His assertion that this man of letters "arrived to socialist persuasion and to the conclusion that art is fundamentally 'serving' " (Mukařovský 1947 [1948a: 327]) was of course in deep consonance with the changes that were about to materialize.

Although much of Mukařovský's reasoning was couched in a deliberative language of a theoretician, he was not incapable of straight language—especially when writing for the popular media. In January 1946, he discussed the role of the intelligentsia in society in *Rudé právo*, the daily of the Czechoslovak Communist Party. While certain phrases recall the prewar constructive mood and the concern for a meaningful social order, there are also statements that, except on the dogmatic left, would have been unthinkable before the war because of their propagandistic flavor. Mukařovský states that the function of the intelligentsia is "to think for the whole and to its advantage; to feel unity with the people; to understand that the intelligentsia must stand on the side of social and cultural progress against the powers of reaction if it is to fulfill its political task in these days" (1946: 1). Here the image of a clear-cut "for" and "against," the question "on whose side," and the opposition of "progress" vs. "powers of reaction" represented a visible assimilation to the black-and-white language of the Communist political propaganda. Mukařovský also made other propagandistic statements around that time, including one about the lasting and beneficial impact of the Bolshevik Revolution on Europe.

After February 1948, Mukařovský's language simply collapsed. In "Intelligentsia in Socialism," an appeal to the intellectuals on the eve of the first elections in the Communist state, the values of the bourgeois society were done away with through simple prefixation with "so-called": "so-called freedom of opinion," "so-called individual freedom of a creative researcher," "so-called objectivity of scholarship," etc. (Mukařovský 1948b, passim). There was also such political kitsch as this:

Realize [thou, intelligentsia,] that you should not only march along with the people, but that you should become the people itself, that you should use your abilities and means with the same impersonal humility with which the worker works. Only in this way will an artist and a scholar again find the power that was taken away from him by the decaying capitalist society. . . . Walking home from your office, from your factory, you can see happy people, a quiet joy of everyday life. And you can feel that you also have contributed with your daily part to this, to a state in which everything is as sound as it is. Capitalism was not able to reward its intelligentsia with this feeling of joy. . . . (Mukařovský 1948b) [11]

Though it is clear that the winning over of influential scholars—intellectuals who "recognized the logic of history"—represented a major inroad for the Communists, the ultimate motives of Mukařovský's subordination to Party guidelines, his extensive propagandistic writing, and his complete renunciation of structuralism (Mukařovský 1951) will probably never be explicated in detail. Subtle personal factors, such as the experience of the occupation and the execution of Vladislav Vančura by the Nazis, may have contributed to his political decisions. The news of Vančura's death was among the earliest pieces of information that the Mukařovskýs communicated to Jakobson after the war, and Vančura was the topic of the first postwar meeting of the Circle. The death of a close friend and a leading representative of the interwar Left was obviously deeply traumatic for Mukařovský. But while there might be a great deal of subtlety involved, the overriding line of commitment was one rooted in the prewar discussions about the deficiencies of a liberal capitalist society. The case is thus an important reminder that Stalinism in Czechoslovakia began in the late 1930s rather than in 1948.

After 1948—Patterns of Defense and Adaptation

Several months before the Communist seizure of power, the architect Jaromír Krejcar, editor of the remarkable collection *Život* (1922), used the occasion of a trip abroad to write to Jakobson that "a time would come when [Krejcar] would be glad to stay out of the country for a while." He inquired about job possibilities and continued:

Our lines—I mean of your and my generation—have gotten very thin. The time is not yet favorable to intellectual life.

I occasionally see Teige, but the regular contact among all of us, as we had it before the war, does not exist any longer. There is no café where you would always find someone. People see one another more often in political meetings or mostly gather at home. All these are considerable changes, and it is hard to say where this will lead—elections are scheduled in the early summer, or in the spring, and they are bound to be stormy. (to Jakobson, January 8, 1948; RJP, box 42, folder 50)

Krejcar managed to escape to the West, and in his first letter to Roman Jakobson he reported from Paris on June 18, 1948, that "the atmosphere in Czechoslovak Republic was bleaker than in 1939" (ibid.).

The new regime aspired to reshape of all aspects of public and private life. Shortly after the takeover, it launched a number of campaigns aimed at a large-scale assimilation of Czechoslovak social standards to those of the Soviet society. The policy was concisely expressed in the political slogan Sovětský svaz—náš vzor [The Soviet Union—Our Example]. The generic nature of the slogan is instructive: the Soviet Union did not provide examples in particular areas;

its example was total. The Czechoslovaks were now discovering, to their considerable surprise, that all segments of political, economic, and cultural life were much more advanced in the Soviet Union than anywhere else in the world. An important element in this development, which was designed to strengthen the power of the Communist party, was a complete assimilation of Czechoslovak scholarship to Soviet scholarship.

In linguistics, assimilation to Soviet norms meant assimilation to Marrism, the officially endorsed linguistic doctrine in the Soviet Union. Marr's theory made reference to such basic Marxist notions as base, superstructure, and the class nature of society. Its introduction to Czechoslovakia clearly caught the local linguists by surprise.[12] It took almost two years after February 1948 for the first accounts of Marrism to appear in Czech and Slovak, and even then Marrism was represented only by translations and surveys. Obviously, Czech linguists did not have much to contribute creatively. In November 1949 the first anthology of Marrist writings finally appeared, with the colophon stating that the collection was translated "by the student collective of the Department of Slavic Philology . . . as a present to the Ninth Congress of the Communist Party of Czechoslovakia" (Bosák et al. 1949: 163). Ironically enough, the colophon also includes the information that the font used was called Ideal News and that the cover was designed by one J. Smutný, literally J. Depressed. While a Švejk might still have been joking, the more important thing was that the student collective was supervised by a group that also included prominent members of the Prague Circle: Havránek, Horálek, and Skalička.[13]

Alexander Isačenko, another member of the Circle and an important linguist who was not only Trubetzkoy's direct disciple but also his son-in-law, followed in December 1949. His "Foundations of Materialist Linguistics" (Isačenko 1949) was the first substantial apology of the new current.

Thus, by late 1949 the leading structuralists saw that if they wanted to retain their positions they would have to take Marr seriously—and take him seriously they did. Further apologies began to pour in quickly: "The Creator of New Soviet Linguistics" (Havránek 1950a), and "Academician Marr and His Approach to Linguistics"

(Trávníček 1950a). Skalička lectured on Marr to the Circle on April 24, 1950. All these apologies agreed on Marr's central place in the Marxist theory of language.

The intellectual devastation caused by Marrism derived not only from the content of this doctrine but also from the burlesque character of the entire episode. By the time Marrism reached Czechoslovakia (in part, through officially orchestrated lectures by the leading Soviet Marrist I. I. Meščaninov (1950)), certain of its aspects had already become subjects of discussion in Soviet publications (as the above quotation from Havránek's letter to Jakobson suggests). In May and June of 1950, a full-fledged dispute over Marr began to fill the pages of *Pravda.* But this dispute, which seemed to involve the free exchange of opinions, was in fact carefully staged by Stalin, who decided to dismantle Marrism to strengthen his own political authority.[14]

Stalin acted in June 1950, only a few months after the above-mentioned Czechoslovak linguists managed to declare their adherence to Marr's teachings. Naturally, most of the them were taken by surprise again—but with Stalin's authority coming down, their reorientation was very fast. An unhesitating display of loyalty was vital, especially for those who had already proclaimed their Marrist sympathies. The content of the display didn't even matter; all that mattered was that one declare loyalty to the Party line. Stalin's first critique of Marrism is dated June 20, 1950; in Prague, the first organized discussion in response to it took place on June 29. The keynote address was delivered not by a linguist but by the deputy secretary of the Communist Party, Gustav Bareš (see Bareš 1950). This fact alone reveals the intensity of the intimidation and the purely political nature of the whole event. Serious linguistics was by now forgotten. Several articles prepared by the leading members of the Circle promptly appeared in *Tvorba,* a weekly functioning as a major instrument of Communist propaganda (Havránek 1950b; Skalička 1950; Trávníček 1950b). This first wave of apologetics also included articles by a variety of political functionaries and professional propagandists, among them the ill-famed Jan Štern (see Štern 1950). Havránek, Skalička, and Trávníček were the most vociferous members of the Circle in the following period. Between 1950 and 1952, Havránek published more than a dozen items on Stalin's importance for linguistics, including a small monograph (Havránek 1951). Trávníček[15] wrote a number of articles of the same nature and also published a monograph denouncing Czechoslovak structuralism and praising Stalinist linguistics (Trávníček 1951).[16] Isačenko was the fastest to come up with a volume of translations covering the Stalin debate (Isačenko 1950); he distanced himself from Marrism in other publications, too, as did Havránek and Trávníček later the same year.

Among the techniques that were used to forge loyalty and ease the imposition of the new doctrine were Soviet-style public discussions in the universities, with young radical activists playing prominent roles and effectively intimidating the rest. "Stalinian discussions" (discussions about Stalin's linguistic ideas) started with the academic year 1950–51 at Charles University in Prague. (Similar colloquia followed at universities in Brno and Olomouc.) The atmosphere can be gleaned from the language, which has been vividly preserved in contemporary reports. For example, a certain Jaroslav Krejčí praised Petr Sgall, a young Prague linguist, for critically analyzing structuralism. Krejčí valued Sgall's denouncements of the work of the "anti-Soviet émigré R. Jakobson," especially as regards the idea of the immanent development of language system and the elevation of phonology as a model of research. Krejčí was not entirely satisfied, but on the whole he felt Czechoslovak linguistics was on the right track: "Although the rotten nature of the cosmopolite ideas of structuralism had not yet been unveiled with sufficient force, Sgall's account was a step forward." (Krejčí 1951: 142) Structuralism in literary theory was also dealt with—it had "fouled our scholarship with the reactionary ideas of cosmopolitanism and formalism and provided a refuge from which Trotskyiates and anti-Soviet émigrés of Jakobson's and Kalandra's sort recruited themselves" (ibid.: 143).

Despite savage attacks, the Structuralists developed some defensive strategies in an attempt to ease the impact of Marrism and Stalin's linguistics. Havránek, in one of the first pro-Soviet reactions from among the Circle's members, suggested that structuralism and Marr's New Teaching were in fact much closer than it would appear; he listed the emphasis on linguistic convergence as one of the common denominators (Havránek 1948: 266). Skalička (1950) suggested that, although certain aspects of structuralism (including phonology) were problematic, the theory was still open to discussion and amenable to correction. Skalička also stressed that the creators of structuralism had embraced a fundamentally leftist worldview from the very beginning, and that they had played a progressive role in the bourgeois state.[17]

Another frequently used defensive strategy consisted in dividing the Circle into a healthy core and a foreign, imported overlay. Under this strategy, the Circle consisted of a group of sincere, mostly leftist, but otherwise somewhat confused Czech and Slovak scholars who had been ideologically misguided. Skalička, for instance, took pains to stress that the most problematic advancement of the Circle, structural phonology, was not really a Czech innovation; it had been mainly worked out by the Russian émigré members of the Circle, Jakobson and Trubetzkoy. Although the Czech members had contributed numerous studies, these were only applications to new data. The latter, Skalička wrote (1951: 1011), did not diminish their responsibility.

The young linguist Petr Sgall emphasized the elements of deceit and seduction: Czech scholars, decent characters of healthy substance, had been deceived by an evil monster:

the Prague Linguistic Circle was . . . penetrated by a foreign element, above all by the anti-soviet émigré, cosmopolite and hidden Trotzkyite, a veritable monster of our linguistics, Roman Jakobson, who was deceiving a number of our excellent linguists and leading them astray. . . . The role of Roman Jakobson as a main pillar of structuralism clearly proves that by its nature structuralism in linguistics represented one of these "modernisms" which under the cloak of progressive ideology served as a sophisticated ideological weapon of disorientation among outstanding representatives of the leftist intelligentsia. . . . (Sgall 1951a: 674)

Like Skalička, Sgall claimed that the Circle had never been a unified group; unlike Skalička, he suggested that the split was a matter of "contrary class positions":

It is by no means possible to view the Prague Circle as a unified whole: the hidden enemy Jakobson has wound up on the rubbish heap of history, while honest representatives of our linguistics, Professors Havránek, Trávníček and Skalička have put their great scholarly energy to the service of the fight for socialism and a bright future of mankind. This fundamental difference is by no means an accident. It was present during the entire time of existence of the Prague Linguistic Circle, expressing two contrary class positions. (Sgall 1951a: 676)

Sgall's style exploited the standard derogatory common places of the period. Odd as it may sound, the quotations also allow for a certain amount of "textual criticism." Comparing the first of the above passages on Jakobson (from Sgall 1951a) with a variant of the same article that appeared in *Slovo a slovesnost* (Sgall 1951b), one finds that the phrase "the veritable monster of our linguistics" is missing. Clearly, *Tvorba,* a mass-circulation magazine, called for a more aggressive tone; perhaps the editors thought that Sgall's discourse needed some additional pepper and felt free to add it.

Discourse of this type transcended the limits of defense and adaptation to which the older members of the Circle were accustomed. While they were essentially trying to preserve their work (and positions), the younger members radicalized the issue, making it a part of current political affairs. Sgall's classification of Jakobson as a Trotskyite complied with the intention of the political leadership to invent a Czechoslovak Trotskyism and present it as a conspiratorial force exerting considerable influence on current political events.[18] Trubetzkoy was dead and Jakobson thousands of miles away, but some individuals were put at risk by this politicization. Young activists depicted Karel Teige as a Trotskyite, a cosmopolite, and even a theoretician of pornography (Grygar 1951: 1060)—the last on account of Teige's interest in Freud. Teige, who remained in Prague, died in the midst of a fierce defamatory campaign on October 1, 1951.[19]

In the course of these events, the Prague Circle lost its cohesion and ceased to function as it had before and during the war. Administrative measures sealed the result.[20] The process was gradual, but relatively straightforward. The record of lectures shows no clearly politicized lectures immediately after February 1948, with the exception of Mukařovský's "On Structuralism and Dialectical Materialism in the Theory of Art" (December 1, 1948). Only eleven persons attended that lecture, but things started to change soon. The turning point seems to have come on June 20, 1949, when Havránek conducted a "Conversation about the Development of the Prague

Linguistic Circle" and Skalička gave a lecture on "New Paths of the Prague Linguistic Circle." The audience for this politically laden lecture numbered 81. After Stalin's intervention, the rupture was even more dramatic. Skalička's lecture on Marr (April 24, 1950) and Ctirad Bosák's on "Soviet Linguistics after Marr" (May 30, 1950) may still have been open to Marrism; however, Stalin's June intervention must have devastated the Circle completely. By the end of 1950 the Circle was barely visible. *Slovo a slovesnost* continued to appear, but the metamorphoses of its subtitle tell a history: *Slovo a slovesnost* was the Journal of the Prague Linguistic Circle in 1948 and 1949; it was changed to the Journal of the Institute for Czech Language and the Prague Linguistic Circle in 1950—and in 1951 the name Prague Linguistic Circle disappeared from the title entirely.

12.4 No Grand Finale—Just Linguists in Society

The demise of the Prague Linguistic Circle raises many questions— above all, the question of the participation of the Circle's members in this process. One wonders, for instance, how it was possible for a prominent member of the Circle to say:

Structuralism is undoubtedly a child of the First Czechoslovak Republic, a period in which bourgeois scholarship, serving the ruling class, was drifting toward obscurantism and self-contained frivolity. (Skalička 1951: 1011)

Answering the question of why and how this was possible, we enter the realm of political history. For one thing, the imposition of Soviet doctrines largely occurred in a situation of overall social collapse. The very tense political atmosphere that emerged in Czechoslovakia in late 1950 and prevailed through 1951 played an important role. These were years marked by political purges, culminating with the Slánský trial in late 1951. Jakobson's friend Vladimír Clementis was sentenced to death and executed. Under these circumstances, one of the most striking aspects that emerges after 1948—the almost grotesque malleability of the Circle's leading members—is perhaps not so surprising.

Significantly, malleability could be found virtually anywhere in those days—in scholarship, art, religion, politics, economics. Thus, an overall profile of the society is at issue, not a development in a particular discipline. In this sense, there is no grand finale. Just as the Prague Circle was intimately embedded in the culture and society of the Czechoslovak Republic before 1948, it was an integral part of this society's breakdown after 1948. Its fate was just one of the many cases illustrating the force with which the New Order was installing itself.

Appendix

The By-Laws

Among the most important archival documents from the "heroic period" of the Prague Linguistic Circle are its by-laws, drafted in connection with the official registration of the Circle as a society and approved in a formal business meeting of the Circle on December 1, 1930.

The following translation is based on a four-page typescript kindly provided by Jiří Nosek; further copies are extant in APLK.

The list of members' names that appears in the by-laws is a subset of the persons who had lectured before the Circle. Persons who lectured but whose names do not appear in the list are I. Brun, D. Čyževśkyj, B. Ilek, S. Karcevskij, P. Savickij, and J. V. Sedlák. Some of them probably no longer lived in Prague (Karcevskij and, perhaps, Brun); some ceased to be members (Sedlák) or lost interest in the Circle (Ilek).

By-Laws of the Society "Prague Linguistic Circle"
(Cercle Linguistique de Prague.
Prager sprachwissenschaftliche Vereinigung.)

§1 The purpose of the society "Prague Linguistic Circle" is to work on the basis of functional-structural method toward progress in linguistic research.

§2 The means to achieve this goal are:

1. regular membership meetings with lectures and debates;

2. business meetings;

3. public meetings the purpose of which is promotion of interest in questions of general linguistics;

4. establishing commissions for the collective work on scholarly problems;

5. publishing of scholarly literature;

6. Establishing and maintaining of specialized archives and library.

§3 The society will obtain means necessary for the materialization of these goals through:

a/ annual contributions from regular and corresponding members,

b/ income from the sale of the society's publications,

c/ support awarded to scholarly corporations,

d/ donations and inheritance.

§4 The society "Prague Linguistic Circle" is composed of:

1. regular members,

2. corresponding members.

§5 The first regular members are the founders of the Prague Linguistic Circle, whose names are given below. Membership will be granted to every further scholar who was invited by the Circle to give a lecture as a guest, was recommended by the executive committee and accepted as a regular member by a two-thirds majority of members present in the business meeting the agenda of which explicitly included the proposal.

The status of corresponding member can be granted to any scholar whose work is in consonance with the purpose of the Circle but who cannot participate in membership meetings, provided the proposal is accepted by a two-thirds majority of members present at a business meeting. A regular member who cannot for serious reasons attend the society's meetings can also become a corresponding member.

§6 Rights of regular members:

1. to participate in scholarly discussion and business meetings,

2. to obtain one free copy of each publication published by the society,

3. to elect the executive committee (the chairman, deputy-chairman, treasurer, and secretary), two comptrollers and members of committees for the collective work on scholarly problems,

4. to introduce guests to lecture meetings and recommend scholars as regular or corresponding members to the executive committee.

§7 Duties of regular members:

1. to participate in scholarly, discussion and business meetings, and in the entire activity of the society,

2. to pay member's fees the amount of which will be determined annually by the business meeting.

§8 The rights and duties of corresponding members are identical with the rights and duties of regular members except for the duty to participate in the meetings (aside from executive committee's meetings) and the right to elect officers of the society and be elected as officers of the society.

§9 A member loses his membership 1) by notifying the executive committee in writing that he is leaving the society; 2) if he does not fulfill any of the member's duties for one year without an appropriate excuse; 3) if he is excluded from the society. Each member of the Circle has the right to propose to the committee that a member whose activity is at variance with the purpose of the society be excluded. Decision on such a proposal is taken in the business meeting in the same way as in the admission procedure.

§10 The seat of the society is Prague.

§11 The executive committee of the Society Prague Linguistic Circle steers a four-member committee, also called the Presidium, that meets at least once per month and can make decisions when three of its members are present. Decisions are accepted by simple majority of votes; in case of a tie vote the proposal supported by the president's voice is accepted. The committee is entitled to invite into its meetings reviewers and chairmen of commissions for the collective work on scholarly problems in order to report on the results of the commission. The invited members of the Circle have an advisory vote.

§12 The executive committee is elected at a general assembly that meets every third year in January, or at an extraordinary general meeting that is convened by the Presidium or upon request of a two-thirds majority of regular members of the Circle. Besides the executive committee, the general assembly also elects two comptrollers, whose tenure is also three years. See §§ 14, 16, a 17.
The general assembly is convened by a simple letter or notification sent to members at least ten days in advance.
Except for restrictions given in §§ 16 a 17, the general assembly is capable of decision by simple majority of members, provided at least one half of regular members is present. If a sufficient number of members is not present, a new general assembly is reconvened half an hour later; it is capable of decision with whatever number of members is present.

§13 Business meetings are held at least twice in a year. They deal with internal matters of the society. See § 5, § 6 sect. 3, § 7 sect. 2, § 9. Except for instances of admission and exclusion, business meetings as well as meetings of elected research commissions decide matters within their competence by simple majority and with any presence of membership.

§14 Disagreements resulting from membership in the society are settled by a simple majority by a three-member arbitration commission elected in the general meeting.

§15 The society is represented by the chairman, in his absence by the deputy chairman or the managing director. All the written documents are signed by the chairman (or the deputy chairman or the managing director, respectively). Financial matters are also signed by the treasurer. The society's statements are communicated to members in writing.

§16 The society ceases to exist when it decides so by a two-thirds majority of a general assembly specifically convened after a proposal by the committee. The property of the society will be transferred to the Public and University Library in Prague.

§17 Any changes in the statutes are decided in the general assembly by a two-thirds majority of membership present.

	B. Trnka		V. Mathesius	
P. Bogatyrev	O. Hujer	J. Mukařovský	J. Rypka
Vl. Buben	R. Jakobson	F. Oberpfalzer	Fr. Slotty
O. Fischer	L. Kopeckij	E. Rippl	M. Weingart
B. Havránek	V. Machek	G. Ružičić	

Appendix

Mathesius's Letter of Recommendation for Roman Jakobson

In the early months of 1939, Roman Jakobson was looking intensively for ways to leave Czechoslovakia. One concrete possibility consisted in applying for a grant from the Society for the Protection of Science and Learning (the former Academic Assistance Council) in London. The letter below is a recommendation that Mathesius wrote for Jakobson on this occasion. I reproduce the text, with a few emendations, from a typescript (probably a copy of the original) preserved in RJP, box 1, folder 7; for a philologically accurate edition see Toman 1994.

Prof. Vilém Mathesius
19 Maiselova
Praha V. (Prague)
Czechoslovakia.

To all whom it may concern.

Mr. Roman Jakobson called on me very soon after his arrival at Prague in 1920 and I have been in a close contact with him ever since, so that in my judgment of his character and abilities I can rely on my personal experience of nearly 20 years. Mr. Jakobson came to Prague equipped with the excellent scientific schooling which the old Moscow University could give him and endowed with the insatiable thirst of knowledge so characteristic of the best Russian scientists. He at once plunged into the study of the problems offered by the inaccountable excellence of the old Czech poetry and nowadays it may be safely said that he is one of the very few really good specialists in that field. His interest in Czech poetry was, of course, not limited to the old periods. Accustomed as he was from Russia to take part in the struggle for modern poetry he was attracted by the actual literary problems of the youngest generations of Czech poets. Before long, he traced the whole development of Czech poetry in a series of painful metrical analyses, and Czech literature and language, as the other chief pillar of his work. Form these centers he approached the other Slavonic literatures and languages, so that at the end there has not been left a single important field in that vast area untouched by him.

Rich and important as is his work in the history of literature, still better and wider he is known as an eminent linguist. From the very beginning he has been one of the leading members of the group of linguists who in 1926 founded the Cercle Linguistique de Prague. In that group he combined influences of the Czech, Russian and Geneva schools of linguistics [which (?)] led to the formulation of the programme of the new linguistics based on functional and structural points of view and Mr. Jakobson has become together with the most regretted Prince Trubetzkoy, Jagic's successor in the University of Vienna, one of the chief pioneers of the most prominent part of it,—structural phonology or, as the Americans call it, phonemics. In that field all the splendid gifts of Mr. Jakobson have appeared in the best light, his wonderful mastery of vast and varied linguistic materials, his ability of clear and abstract thinking and devoted passion for scientific work. I must frankly say that I have come to think highly of Mr. Jakobson's abilities and achievements and that I regard the chair of Russian language and literature which was offered to him by the Masaryk University of Brno, Czechoslovakia, as a due acknowledgment of what he has done. If he should be given the opportunity of spending a year or so in Great Britain, I am sure that it would not only considerably widen his horizon and make him acquainted with linguistic facts and methods which have been lying outside his sphere of investigation until now, but also enable him to communicate the chief results of his linguistic and literary research work with the leading British specialists.

Prague, March 3rd, 1939.

Vilém Mathesius
Head of the English Department of the
Charles University in Prague, President
of the Cercle Linguistique de Prague
and Member of the Comité International
Permanent des Linguistes.

Notes

Chapter 1

1. Unpublished lecture from 1943; RJP, box 32, folder 46.

Chapter 2

1. Studies dealing with Jakobson's formative years, especially his avant-garde engagement, include Parnis 1987, Ivanov 1987, Rudy 1978, 1987, and Winner 1977. Jangfeldt 1992 is an important recent source. General surveys of Jakobson's biography include Halle 1979 and Rudy 1986. Rudy 1990 is Jakobson's most comprehensive bibliography so far.

2. The "Retrospect" of 1966 (Jakobson 1966), the lectures for Swiss Radio (Jakobson 1974), and the interviews with László Dezö (Jakobson 1973), Krystyna Pomorska (Jakobson 1988), and Tzvetan Todorov and Jean José Marchand (Jakobson 1984b) are particularly rich in details. Bengt Jangfeldt's conversations with Jakobson are now available in Jangfeldt 1992. They focus on the avant-garde ambience in particular.

3. For a historical sketch of the Lazarev Institute see Bazijanc 1973.

4. The contemporary encyclopedic dictionary *Granat* (vol. 26: 374) says: "The gymnasium classes [of the Lazarev Institute] offer a standard classical Russian curriculum with the addition of instruction in the Armenian language and Armeno-Gregorian religion for Armenians, who constitute more than one half of the overall number of students."

5. As for Bogdanov: "Il était professeur de langue russe, mais il était avant tout un éthnographe et un folkloriste connu, il était le rédacteur de la revue de la Société éthnographique de Russie. Il a eu une grande influence sur moi. . . ." (Jakobson 1984b: 4)

6. The following entry can be found in Moscow University's list of students for the year 1914 (*Alfavitnyj spisok* 1915: 477): Якобсон Роман-Иоселъ Берович. Фил. Iуд.

с. инж.-мех. 1896 г. Москва. Лазар. Инст. № 1478-914 г. 14 I read this as follows: "Jakobson, Roman-Iosel' Berovič, School of Philology, Judaic religion, son of an engineer-mechanic, born 1896, birthplace (or domicile) Moscow, graduate of the Lazarev Institute, diploma number 1478-914, year of admission to the university 1914."

7. On Šaxmatov's scholarly mores see chapter 3 below; on Jakobson's obituary for Šaxmatov see chapter 11.

8. The paper was read before the Commission for Oral Folklore in early 1915 and was published as Jakobson 1966b.

9. Cf. *ÈO* 1916, no. 107–108, p. 146.

10. Recorded as a lecture in Ušakov and Golanov 1927 (p. 8). A precise date of his presentation is not given in this source, but the period 1916–1918 is plausible.

11. Recall Osthoff and Brugmann's (1878: vii) well-known dictum: "Also von der Ursprache ab und der Gegenwart zuwenden muss der vergleichende Sprachforscher den Blick, wenn er zu einer richtigen Vorstellung von der Art der Fortentwicklung der Sprache gelangen will."

12. The lecture on Xlebnikov was presented in May. The futurism article was published in August 1919.

13. For a few remarks on Tasteven see Markov 1968: 147ff. Very little is known about him; Felix Tastevin (1858–1911), author of French-language guides to Russia and owner of *Librairie F. Tastevin* in Moscow, is a possible relative.

14. For translation see Jakobson 1988: 444.

15. The source is a manuscript in pre-1917 orthography, most likely a copy of the original; see also Jangfeldt 1992.

16. I am grateful to Michael Makin for kindly providing this near- literal translation.

17. Kručenyx's *Piglets* (in Compton 1977), a tiny brochure from 1913 with lithographs by Malevič, names as a co-author Zena V., a 10-year-old girl. Whether this co-authorship is a matter of fact is a subordinate question; selecting a child was the main point.

18. The letter (Jakobson 1985b) gives important insights into the atmosphere of the prewar discussions about new art and the nature of Jakobson's participation in it. Also interesting is Jakobson's 1915 letter to Matjušin. Most of the early letters are now collected in Jangfeldt 1992.

19. The source is a typescript in post-1917 orthography, most likely a copy of the original; see also Jangfeldt 1992: 116f.

20. Translated by Michael Makin.

21. Hofmannsthal's short prose work "Ein Brief" (usually referred to as "A Letter by Lord Chandos") appeared in 1902; the first book edition dates to 1905. I have no

information as to the existence of a contemporary Russian translation; nontheless, it should be noted that Jakobson read German fluently even then.

22. A drawing by Larionov appears in the lower part of the page. Of the two following poems the second is not in "hard" *zaum*'. As in other books by Kručenyx, the poem is in handwriting. Although it might be argued that the first word of the poem actually spells *dir*, it is generally transcribed as *dyr*. This keeps in with the intuition of a "Turkic" flavor of some parts of the text. Word breaks in the second line are uncertain; for instance, Šklovskij (1916) transcribes the second line as a single word. Kručenyx may have had difficulties to produce a mirror-image text because of the lithographic reproduction technique; however, in view of the "positive philosophy" of errors and typos that was a part of Futurist book-making, this could hardly have bothered him very seriously.

23. He says "Pook" instead of "Book."

24. For a microfiche reproduction of this book see Compton 1977.

25. Aljagrov was Jakobson's Futurist pseudonym. Some of his Futurist articles, such as the brief essay "Tasks of the Art Propaganda" (Jakobson 1919b), are also signed with this name. For interesting observations on the name see Vallier 1987.

26. Quite correctly, yet somewhat ironically, the title is in pre-1917 orthography.

27. As for the last two words, Dora Vallier reports that Jakobson explained to her that *evreec* is a portmanteau word based on *evrej* "Jew" and *evropeec* "European"— something like "Jewroepan"—and that the combination *evreec černil'nica*, literally "Jewropean [is an] ink pot," is a pun on a contemporay "witticism" *evrej černil'nica* ("All a Jew can do is scribble"; see Vallier 1987: 297 and 303). Curiously, Jakobson omitted these last two words without comment when he reprinted the text in his study on Aljagrov (i.e., himself) in V. Erlich's festschrift (Jakobson 1985b).

28. Rudy (1987) and Vallier (1987) give a list. Vallier also relays Jakobson's information that *kitajanki* "Chinese women" is actually a misprint; Jakobson had originally written *kitajaki*, a nonexistent word; see Vallier 1987: 299f. and 303.

29. The first five lines develop permutations on the sound theme *a, n, k;* lines 6–8 introduce the theme *t, k, n;* lines 9–12 focus on *m, j, a,* among other things. The last three lines introduce *p*'s and *v*'s, entirely missing so far, and repeat the prefix *pere-* "over-" three times. They also stand out for not having italicized letters which are otherwise used throughout the poem to mark stress.

30. Hugo Ball, a German Dadaist from the Zürich Cabaret Voltaire who became famous for his sound poems, also acknowledged his preoccupation with the glossolalia of German medieval mystics. However, it seems that Ball asserted this interest only in retrospect when he was experiencing a period of deep religiosity and began to view his conversion to Catholicism as a peak of his biography. At this point he edited his diary heavily, making its earlier parts fit his path to Catholicism. Whether religious mysticism was actually effective in his Dada years must therefore remain an open question. Nevertheless, his statement makes sense typologically. Note that V. I. Nejštadt, a member of the Moscow Linguistic Circle, reporting on his recitation of Majakovskij's poetry in Jakobson's Old Church Slavonic translation in 1919, used the wording "I shamanized in Slavic [*ja i zašamanil po-slavjanski*]" (from Katanjan 1985:

146). Nejštadt refers to a Majakovskij evening in the Moscow cabaret Café Pittoresk in 1919.

31. In a well-defined sense, there is no sharp boundary between the historical avant-garde and many of its contemporaries and immediate successors, either. On *zaum'* outside avant-garde poetry, see Ronen 1991.

32. Jakobson returned to the spell of pure sounds as late as 1979—see the last chapter of Jakobson and Waugh 1979. It is not easy, however, to discern his theoretical position in this account.

33. In a lecture from 1922: "If, on the one hand, suprematism is a result of a whole culture of painting, on the other hand, the intensity of its colours and its observation of life are deeply-rooted in the Russian village." (Lissitzky 1922 [1968: 335])

34. Other kinds of poetical experiments that Jakobson was engaging in around 1914 are also worth noting. Reacting to Xlebnikov's complaint that a traditional alphabet, such as the Russian one, is a dead tool for modern poetry, Jakobson reported an invention that employed standard characters and thus in fact made it possible to use letters: "I have now arrived at a curious innovation, the reason of my writing to you. The innovation consists of clusters of letters, a sort of analogy to musical chords. This is a way of achieving simultaneity of two or more letters, and, moreover, of a diversity of graphic combinations, that defines various relations of letters. This all enriches verses and opens new paths." (quoted from Xardžiev 1940: 385) In order to be able to interpret this statement one would have to know precisely what kind of visual effects were actually involved. Direct or indirect inspiration by Futurist experiments in typography is plausible at this point.

35. This was a survey in a series of reports on modern art that Jakobson wrote for IZO Narkomprosa [Otdel *izo*brazitel'nyx iskusstv pri *Na*rodnom *kom*issariate *pros*veščenija, i.e., Division of Visual Arts at the People's Commissariat for Education]. Other articles covered German Expressionism (Jakobson 1920a) and Dadaism (Jakobson 1921d).

36. As Jakobson noted, the same law had been formulated in psychology by Carl Stumpf, the German student of perception to whom Husserl dedicated his *Philosophical Investigations*.

37. Rudy's translation from Jakobson 1987b: 30f.

38. Rudy's translation from Jakobson 1987b: 35.

39. From the late 1920s on, Jakobson often employed the term "egocentrism" in relativistic connections, obviously following N. S. Trubetzkoy (see chapter 10 below).

40. The dictionary remained unpublished during Polivanov's life. An exact dating of the entry is not possible; entries were added until 1935.

41. Henry (Gustav) Lanz (1886–1945) was one of the early Russian commentators on Husserl's antipsychologism; see Lanz 1909.

42. There is, however, a curiously anarchic remark in Čyževśkyj's recollections. Reminiscing about his first encounters with Jakobson in Prague, Čyževśkyj wrote: "But which Jakobson? Some Jakobson from Moscow had visited me already in Kiev. He

was a small red-haired man, who kept dreaming about Potebnja and, to be frank, created very little sympathies. This was not necessarily the Jakobson I would have liked to meet abroad," (Čyževśkyj 1976: 18) The reference to a Jakobson fascinated by Potebnja is one to a psychologistically oriented beginner—something clearly negative from Čyževśkyj's point of view.

43. Holenstein 1975 and Holenstein 1977 are the first extensive discussions of Jakobson's Husserlianism. See also Toman 1979.

44. Among the members of the Circle Karel Hais, Stanislav Lyer, Vladimír Skalička, and Alexandr Isačenko have the letters L and S in their names. (Notably, the German philosophers Wilhelm Landgrebe and Emil Utitz do not qualify on this count.) If the report was by a member of the Circle—definitely not a necessary premise—I tend to opt for Isačenko, since his interventions in other philosophical discussions are documented, among other places in Carnap's lecture (see chapter 6). (He may be the author of the summary of Carnap's lecture in the *Prager Presse* as well; see the acronym -ss- in "Sources and References" below.)

45. Kandinsky was criticized for the same reasons by Ivan Puni (1923), a constructivist painter whom Jakobson knew.

46. The translation exploits that by S. Rudy in Jakobson 1987b.

47. The sporadic references to Husserl from the 1920s and the 1930s (Jakobson 1927b: 8; 1936a) are not analytically relevant in the contexts given, I believe.

48. References to the "pre-Gestalt" psychologist Vittorio Benussi in Jakobson 1923a have a similar character.

49. The passage incorporates an allusion to Alexander Pushkin's 1830 poem "The Hero," in which one of the protagonists—a poet—declares "Deception that elevates us is dearer to me than a multitude of low truths."

50. The materials are being prepared for publication.

51. A 1920 report by Bohumír Šmeral (1880–1941), one of the founders of the Czechoslovak Communist Party and later a functionary of the Komintern, turns out to be of some interest here. Šmeral traveled to the Soviet Union in 1920 and was processed by the mission in Tallinn in late March of that year. In *The Truth about Soviet Russia* (Šmeral 1920) he described the atmosphere at the mission, highlighting its communal character. Although Jakobson's name does not appear in his report, the account is a useful reminder of the mission's importance.

52. Account based on Gornung (ca. 1970).

53. Petr Zenkl (1884–1975) was a leading representative of the National Socialists (not connected with the German National Socialist Workers' Party), an influential political party in interwar Czechoslovakia. He held various governmental positions, including the mayoralty of Prague, in the late 1930s and after 1945. In 1948 he emigrated to the United States.

54. Although the details are not known, the main point is clear: Jakobson asked Zenkl, a leading Czech émigré politician and an outspoken anti-Communist, to write a clearance for him. This may have been necessary because of the ongoing search

for Communists in the United States, or because of Jakobson's application for U.S. citizenship, or both. Zenkl, together with Hubert Ripka, another prominent Czechoslovak politician who had emigrated and a friend of Jakobson's from the prewar period, complied with this wish, but Zenkl cautiously requested that Jakobson explaing the details of his Russian years. Jakobson's letter was an answer to these questions.

55. CGALI, Coll. 336 (Majakovskij), inventory list 5, item 119, autograph in red ink. The account is exaggerated. The newspaper article Jakobson refers to (Papoušková-Melniková 1921) is harsh, but the expression "son of a bitch" does not appear in it.

56. Jakobson's Jewish identity also seems to have been subordinated to the Russian, and occasionally even the Czech, point of view.

57. See the appendix for the full text.

Chapter 3

1. There is a rich interpretive literature on Russian Formalism. Newer documentations and historiographical accounts include Kasatkin 1990, Šapir 1991, and Šapir's commentaries in Vinokur 1990.

2. One of the prominent advocates of university autonomy was Sergei N. Trubetzkoy, the father of Nikolaj S. Trubetzkoy (see chapter 10).

3. Stepanskij (1987) makes a similar observation.

4. The Academy, in any case, had to cope with its "German image" well into the twentiethth century, while the societies, largely because of their university connections, typically appealed to domestic intellectuals.

5. The 1914 report of a Geographical and Anthropological Circle of Students of Moscow University is a good example. It contains minutes from nine meetings, including summaries of lectures, a financial report, a list of members, and the by-laws of the Circle. See *Geografičeskij i Antropologičeskij Kružok* 1914.

6. The Commission recruited its members in part from the Circle for Research in the History and Dialectology of the Russian Language [Kružok dlja izučenija istorii i dialektologii russkogo jazyka], established in 1901.

7. On the final years of the Moscow Commission for Dialectology and Marr's role in its dissolution, see Bernštejn 1973: 84.

8. The membership is given as 14 in 1904, as 44 in 1922 (Ušakov 1922: 287), and as 46 in 1924. There is not much information about the decision-making mechanism within the group, but the general outline of the Commission's orientation can be easily reconstructed from publications and from lists of lectures read before the Commission (Ušakov and Sokolov 1914, Ušakov 1922, Golanov 1925, Ušakov and Golanov 1927). These sources also give a fairly detailed account of expeditions organized by the Commission.

9. For personal accounts of these trips see Jakobson 1966 and Bogatyrev 1930.

10. The circle apparently had no name of its own. Golanov 1925, one of the lists of lectures presented before the Commission, lists three lectures by Jakobson without mentioning the Circle at all. Quite characteristically, the existence of the Circle in Golanov's report is only documented in a footnote that Jakobson appended to this report himself (Jakobson 1925c). Nontheless, there was a feeling of independence and continuity among the members of the Moscow Linguistic Circle. In 1920, for instance, the Circle celebrated five years of its existence.

11. Relatively little is known about the internal process effective within the newly founded group. Apart from Jakobson's own later description (1966, 1981, 1984b) and a brief discussion in Cejtlin 1965, only few studies exist in which primary sources are directly evaluated. This lacuna is partially compensated for by Boris Vladimirovič Gornung's lecture dealing with the history of the Moscow Linguistic Circle (Gornung ca. 1970). Gornung (1899–1976) was a member of the Circle from 1918 on. (A recording of his lecture made by R. Kasatkina is in the archives of the Institute of Russian Language of the Soviet Academy of Sciences, in Moscow; I am indebted to her for pointing out this source.)

12. On Bogatyrev see chapter 6. N. F. Jakovlev, a Caucasiologist, worked on the development of new alphabets for non-Russian nationalities of the Soviet Union. His work, especially Jakovlev 1923, was carefully followed by Jakobson and Trubetzkoy in the 1920s and was instrumental in the development of phonology.

13. A relative of the renowned philologist F. I. Buslaev (1818–1897), A. A. Buslaev also took part in Futurist bohemian life. When Majakovskij held a reading on May 1, 1918, in Moscow's Café Pittoresk, Buslaev read an English translation of his poetry. Other members of the Circle read their translations, too: Jakobson translated Majakovskij into French and Old Church Slavonic, Vladimir Il'ič Nejštadt (1898–959) into German. See Majakovskij 1961: 155 and 365; a facsimile of the program follows p. 156.

14. Morris Halle, personal communication; see also Ragozin's letters in RJP.

15. Cf. Jakobson to Ragozin, December 4, 1956 (RJP, box 45, folder 4).

16. Vinokur's "first phase" corresponds to my second phase, i.e., the period between the fall of 1918 and spring of 1919.

17. This is the abbreviation for Obščestvo izučenija poetičeskogo jazyka [Society for the Study of Poetic Language].

18. Cf. Eagle 1988, Erlich 1955, Hansen-Löve 1978, Steiner 1984, and Striedter 1989.

19. From Šklovskij's curriculum vitae written in 1920: "In 1915 I retuned to Peterburg and, having organized a circle of philologists, edited the first *Collection on the Theory of Poetic Language.*" (quoted in Toddes et al. 1977: 504)

20. This interest extended beyond academic deliberations. Jakubinskij wrote some poetry, none of which was published during his lifetime. A poem entitled "Lenin," written in the 1930s, is dedicated to the memory of Majakovskij, with whom he was on friendly terms; excerpts can be found in Leont'ev 1983: 56.

21. For a survey of Polivanov's poetology see Leont'ev 1983.

22. Two important literary scholars, B. Èjxenbaum and J. Tynjanov, will not be discussed here. The former appears to have embraced the OPOJAZ line in 1918 (Čudakova and Toddes 1987: 16); the latter's association with OPOJAZ came later. I shall not trace the subsequent development within OPOJAZ here either; I will merely note that a number of lesser-known scholars were associated with OPOJAZ in its later phases, i. e., from 1919 on. The St. Petersburg journal *Žizn' isskustva* [*Life of Arts*], no. 273, Oct. 21, 1919, lists besides the above-named persons S. I. Bernštejn, A. Vechsler, B. A. Larin, V. A. Pjast, E. G. Polonskaja, A. I. Piotrovskij, and M. A. Slonimskij (cf. Toddes et al. 1977: 505). It will be noted that Tynjanov's name was not included at this point. Toddes et al. also list S. M. Bondi, M. K. Kleman, L. N. Lunc, and A. L. Slonimskij.

23. Roman Jakobson, personal communication, 1970s.

24. Some reminiscences by Šklovskij can also be found in Čudakov 1990. See also Jangfeldt 1986 and Šklovskij 1940.

25. Several years before work from the Moscow Circle began to appear in print, two volumes of original analytic studies had been available in St. Petersburg. They are the *Collections on the Theory of Poetic Language* [*Sborniki po teorii poetičeskogo jazyka*], published in 1916 and 1917, respectively. The first volume contains Šklovskij 1916, Jakubinskij 1916, Polivanov 1916b, and Kušner 1916. It also includes excerpts from Grammont 1916 and Nyrop 1916, both translated from the French by Viktor Šklovskij's brother Vladimir. The second volume contains the same Russian authors and also an article by Brik. It lists Viktor Šklovskij 1917, Jakubinskij 1917a, b, Brik 1917, Kušner 1917, and Vladimir Šklovskij 1917. A third collection, entitled *Poètika*, appeared in 1919. It is a selection from articles published earlier in *Sborniki* 1916 and 1917 to which Šklovskij 1919a, b, Jakubinskij 1919, and Èjxenbaum 1919 are added.

26. Recall that Jakobson was attending Šaxmatov's courses when visiting St. Petersburg in 1917.

27. Polívka (1921: 236) gives a similarly worded assessment.

28. On Baudouin's social activism see Rothstein 1975 and Toman 1991.

29. For accounts see Janecek 1981 and Šklovskij 1926. A facsimile of the program can be found in Michelis 1973. There were two papers (Benedikt Livšic: "The Relationships between the Italian and Russian Futurism"; Artur V. Lur'e: "Italian Futurist Music") and a discussion in which the following participated: N. D. Burljuk, A. E. Kručenyx, M. V. Matjušin, V. A. Pjast, N. A. Roslavev, Viktor Xlebnikov, and V. B. Šklovskij. Many visitors were appalled. Boris Èjxenbaum, at that time not yet associated with OPOJAZ, wrote to a friend: "Some kind of ghosts appeared on the stage, real monsters, with coarse and loud voices, just like predatory birds, and then there was just shouting, name-calling, offenses—and lying, lying, without end." (quoted in Čudakova and Toddes 1987: 11f.)

30. The interest in the poetry of the avant-garde was also shared by Baudouin's wife, Romualda Baudouin de Courtenay, apparently an outspoken feminist.

31. In his *Third Factory* Šklovskij described his encounter with Baudouin as follows: "I took my booklet of 32 pages in Cicero (*The Resurrection of the Word*) and set off to

Baudouin. He is a quarrelsome great old man. . . . Baudouin—a king of Jerusalem, as he once put it on his *Privat-Dozent* card in Kazan. Badouin, or Baudouen, is no doubt a descendent of the first king of Jerusalem. He listened to me and, in any case, got me together with Jakubinskij." (Šklovskij 1926: 51f.) Among other things, Šklovskij alludes here to Baudouin's aristocratic background; Baudouin believed that his pedigree reached as far back as to Baldwin, the medieval Christian king of Jerusalem.

32. Baudouin's political associations included the Russian liberals—he was close to the Kadets (Constitutional Democrats) in the time around the Revolution of 1905—and Polish Free Thinkers in the 1920s.

33. See L. V. Ščerba, also quoted in Rothstein 1975.

34. A. S. Vengerov, the founder of a Pushkin seminar at the University of St. Petersburg (1908), is also of some interest in connection with the style of teaching. Some of the members of OPOJAZ with a primary interest in literary studies (Tynjanov, Èjxenbaum, Šklovskij) went through this seminar. Vengerov, originally a traditional literary historian, initially had reservations about the work of OPOJAZ, but then let himself be carried along by the enthusiasm of its members (Erlich 1955: 65). Šklovskij recalled the early days of his studies with Vengerov in Šklovskij 1983.

35. The two groups probably held joint sessions throughout the entire period of existence of the Moscow Linguistic Circle.

36. Dated in Gornung (ca. 1970).

37. Minutes are available; CGALI, coll. 1525 (Nejštadt), inventory list 1, item 418, leaf 1–2.

38. Some of these lectures are available in printed form: (4) appeared as Bogatyrev 1923b, (6) as Jakobson 1921a, and (10) in Flejšman 1977 (where minutes from this meeting are also published and dated).

39. This group's activities seem to have been somewhat irregular. In 1918 there were only five lectures, in 1919 none. Then again, in the winter of 1920–21 the philosopher Gustav Špet lectured on theoretical aspects of "ethnic psychology," his variant of Völkerpsychologie. These lectures were later integrated into the second half of his *Introduction to Ethnic Psychology* (Špet 1927: 5).

40. In addition to the seven founding members, the following 22 members were confirmed on March 1, 1919, by the Scholarly Division of Narkompros: L. I. Bazilevič, S. P. Bobrov, S. M. Bondi, O. M. Brik, G. G. Dinges, V. I. Kamenev, I. L. Kan, S. O. Karcevskij, B. O. Kušner, V. V. Majakovskij, V. I. Nejštadt, M. N. Peterson, Ju. M. Sokolov, B. V. Tomaševskij, B. V. Šergin, E. M. Šilling, Vladimir B. Šklovskij, Viktor B. Šklovskij (Buslaev et al. 1956).

41. Jakobson's parents left the country in 1919, leaving a bourgeois-size apartment behind. Jakobson converted two of its rooms into the Circle's offices, obviously saving the apartment from the authorities.

42. A few unpublished minutes are deposited in CGALI, mostly in collection Vinokur (2164).

43. CGALI collection 2164 (Vinokur), inventory list 1, item 1, leaf 19–20.

44. I believe this distance is visible throughout Gornung's (ca. 1970) entire account. The fact that he seems to have an agenda pointing to the Art Form Group ultimately turns out to be positive since he is neither apologetic about the Circle (as Jakobson later was) nor hagiographic about Jakobson (as many, including Jakobson, later were).

45. Sergej Pavlovičk Bobrov (b. 1889), a poet interested in the theory of verse.

46. Majakovskij, the reader will recall, lived in the building. His participation in the lecture by [Gurvic-]Gurskij on May 2, 1919, probably the first analysis of the post-Revolutionary avalanche of abbreviations and acronyms, is documented. A brief question of Majakovskij's is recorded in the minutes (CGALI coll. 1525 (Nejštadt), inventory list 1, item 418, leaf 1-2).

47. Jangfeldt 1976 is a detailed source on Komfut.

48. Even during the years of persecution he was among those scholars in the Soviet Union who were in contact with the Prague Circle, as is evidenced by his review of Jakobson's *Remarques* of 1929 (Polivanov 1932).

Chapter 4

1. Previous literature on Mathesius includes Fried 1985, Vachek 1982, Vočadlo 1948–49, and Wellek 1976. Macek 1982a is a complete bibliography.

2. Roman Jakobson recalled this factor distinctly in our conversations and attributed much in Mathesius's work to it.

3. He was known well enough to appear in one of Jaroslav Hašek's short stories from the time before the World War I. It need not be stressed that Hašek, the author of *The Good Soldier Švejk* and a master of sarcasm and anarchy, saw Dušek's role in Kolín somewhat less piously than Mathesius did.

4. One of the few exceptions was Olaf Broch, a Norwegian Slavist who came to Prague to study Czech phonetics in the summer of 1905 and to whom Mathesius was assigned as a local assistant. Mathesius recalled him warmly, and his example may have fostered Mathesius's early interest in phonetics.

5. I translate filosofická fakulta, literally philosophical faculty, as School of Arts throughout.

6. For a detailed description of the Manuscript controversy in English see Otáhal 1986.

7. The harshness of this judgment is echoed in a later assessment by Jakobson, who, although he could not have known Gebauer personally, compared him with Šaxmatov and deplored the lack of "the fireworks of ingeniously seductive hypotheses" that characterized Šaxmatov's work (Jakobson 1934a: 6f.).

8. For similar judgments see Havránek 1931.

9. Pedagogical concerns among linguists in the late nineteenth century are represented, among others, by the German linguist Wilhelm Viëtor, the Dutch movement taal-en-letteren (cf. van Essen 1983) and, last but not least, Otto Jespersen.

10. In a later formulation Mathesius says "common sense dictates [to Henry Sweet and Otto Jespersen] that language is an instrument whose value can be measured in its appropriateness for particular use" (Mathesius 1933).

11. Vachek (1966: 17) points out that Mathesius followed the work of Vossler and the Idealists with interest.

12. It is interesting to note that D. Čyževśkyj actually regarded Mathesius as a precursor of literary formalism (Čyževśkyj 1976: 28).

13. Several translations of Mathesius's essay into English are available, e.g., Vachek 1964: 1–32. Mathesius himself considered the essay important and referred to it on a number of occasions. An interesting document is a letter, dated May 12, 1913, in which Mathesius explains to the French linguist Antoine Meillet that their thoughts on historical and general linguistics converge (Swiggers 1990: 201).

14. Trnka's impression was obviously lasting: "From the philosophical viewpoint the lack of interest in abstract thinking and abstract theories might be regretted, but we, his students, were fully satisfied by his firm belief and his statement that the most important demand to be made of every linguistic theory will always remain that it must fit the actual entities specific to linguistics as a science concerned with the observation of speech and the analysis of its systematic organization." (Trnka 1983: 250)

15. Masaryk's book appeared first in Czech in 1885; I quote from a slightly expanded German version published in 1887. The notion "concrete logic" essentially corresponds to German Methodenlehre, and is a historical predecessor of modern philosophy of science. It proceeds by classifying major scientific disciplines and establishing their scopes and relations, a common approach in those days.

16. For an analysis of Masaryk's social doctrines see Szporluk 1981.

Chapter 5

1. The letter is published in Toman 1994.

2. Mácha impressed Jakobson so much that later, in Prague, he tried to convince the Russian poet Xodasevič to translate his May into Russian. Xodasevič remained lukewarm, however (Berberova 1983: 242).

3. Nette, a Latvian Communist who also appears in one of Majakovskij's poems, served in the function of a diplomatic courier; he was later murdered on one of his missions. For more on him and the early days in Prague see Jakobson 1984c.

4. Olivová (1957: 278) quotes from a police report preserved in the Archives of the President of the Czechoslovak Republic: "The official mission of the Russian Red Cross arrived on July 10. Head of the mission: Gillerson; members: Viškovskij, Jacobson [sic], Levin, Nette and Kuzmin. Ten sealed boxes accompanying." The mission was replaced by a higher-level trade representation in the summer of 1921. However, a full-fledged Soviet embassy did not open until 1934, when Czechoslovakia acknowledged the USSR *de jure*.

5. Eduard Beneš, the Czechoslovak Minister of Foreign Affairs, stated, in a rare admission of the anti-Semitic sentiment prevalent in those days, that the fact that the mission was staffed entirely by Jews made its work in Prague impossible (internal communication, January 21, 1921; see *Dokumenty a materiály*, 425).

6. In an unpublished (?) gloss from the mid-1920s entitled "A Response to L. D. Trotskij" [Otvet L'vu Davidoviču Trockomu], Šklovskij wrote: "Jakobson arrived with Šaxmatov's letter to Prague as an employee of the Soviet mission. The letter, worded in glowing terms, astounded Czech scholars, but there were people who claimed that the real Jakobson, a talented philologist indeed, was killed by the Bolsheviks and the Soviet Jakobson was a fake." (CGALI, coll. 562 (Šklovskij), inventory list 1, item 72)

7. I. Gillerson, the head of the mission, was beginning to attract of leftist politicians in Prague, so the Czech authorities wished to get rid of him. He left in 1921 when the mission's status changed. Ironically, he later emigrated from the USSR and died in Paris.

8. In a Soviet diplomatic report from January 21, 1928, Jakobson is referred to as an "attaché of the Plenipotentiary Representation" (*Dokumenty i materialy. . .*, 331).

9. As political atmosphere was changing in the 1930s, attacks also came from the pro-Moscow left. It was the poet S. K. Neumann who in 1938 publicly denounced Jakobson—this time as a defector from the USSR. This accusation had to be recalled under court order.

10. Jakobson 1920c. I quoted from this obituary in chapter 3.

11. Jaroslav Papoušek (1890–1945), a Czech historian and an officer in the Czechoslovak Ministry of Foreign Affairs.

12. Vladimir A. Antonov-Ovseenko (1884–1939), head of the Soviet diplomatic representation in Czechoslovakia from 1924 to 1928.

13. Jakobson insisted on the influence of Sechehaye as late as 1939 (Jakobson 1939b: 124f.).

14. There is a similarity between this definition and that in Polivanov 1916a (also quoted in chapter 3 above).

15. The founding of the Masaryk University in Brno is particularly noteworthy, because this university gradually attracted a number of young scholars and became the most important counterweight to Prague within the Republic. Thus, some of the founding members of the Prague Circle began their academic careers in Brno: Bohumil Havránek went there as a professor in 1929, and Roman Jakobson took up duties there as a lecturer in 1933 (he was promoted to full professor in 1938). In the

1930s, Brno Slavistics became a stronghold of structuralism in Czechoslovakia. Other scholars whose ideas were in many respects influential in the development of the Prague School's doctrine were also on the faculty at Brno. One of them was Josef Ludvík Fischer, a structurally oriented philosopher (see chapter 9). The sociology department, headed by Inocenc A. Bláha (1879–1960), also subscribed to structuralist approaches. The Gestalt psychologists Mihajlo Rostohar (1878–1966) and Ferdinand Kratina (1885–1944) and the structuralist musicologist Vladimír Helfert (1886–1945) are also worthy of mention in the context of prewar Brno structuralism. The economist Karel Engliš (1880–1961), the principal representative of the so-called Brno legal economic school, had a certain degree of influence in structuralist circles, too, although he himself was not a structuralist.

16. The roots of Mathesius' s attraction to England were discussd in the preceding chapter. He published a number of analyses in which he drew parallels between English and Czech history and tried to show that England managed to cope with social crises by falling back on common sense. He saw this as an example for the resolution of Czech or Czechoslovak social problems: "The way consists in sober judgment and concreteness of goals." (Mathesius 1914: 528) Admiration for England was shared by a number of Mathesius's contemporaries, including Otakar Vočadlo. The whole trend was connected with a conscious attempt at abandoning German cultural ideals. (On Mathesius and English culture, see Fried 1985.)

17. Roman Jakobson referred to it in one of his surveys (Jakobson 1934a) and later emphasized it in conversations with me.

18. That Mathesius published in German was occasionally deemed unpatriotic. Recall also that he attended lectures at the German University.

19. Mathesius's critical attitude toward malfunctioning cultural and scholarly institutions remained strong throughout the interwar period. See Mathesius 1934b.

Chapter 6

1. To my knowledge there has not been a systematic survey of the East European emigration to Czechoslovakia so far. A documentation from the period is Postinkov 1927; reminscences include Novikov 1952, 1957, Puškarev 1983 and some more. Also Czechoslovak newspapers from the interwar period chronicled this area attentively. Raeff 1990 is a general recent survey, but many of the references to the Prague Linguistic Circle are imprecise. See also Makin and Toman 1990.
   The reasons for this lacuna are of course clear. Both Soviet and Czechoslovak historiography of the past decades criminalized this emigration and attempted to disinform the readership as much as possible. Mejsner 1966 is an instructive example of the latter approach.

2. Other sources put the number of students at more than 5000 (hbl 1925; Puškarev 1983).

3. See Morkovin 1971: 169 for the quotation.

4. Another philosophical society, the Philosophical-Pedagogical Skovoroda-Society, was active at the Ukrainian Dragomanov Institute.

5. On the Dostoevsky Society see Morkovin 1971.

6. For a brief but informative biography of Karcevskij see Soloviev 1959.

7. I am grateful to the administration of the University of Geneva for kindly providing a transcript of the courses in which Sergej Karcevskij was officially enrolled.

8. However, he delivered on two lectures before the Circle: "On the Question of Ethnological Geography" (May 11, 1928) and "On Problems of Structural Ethnography" (June 25, 1935).

9. On the pages of the 1949 volume of *Soviet Ethnography* we read: "P. G. Bogatyrev's so-called 'functional-structural method' was subjected to sharp criticism in the Ethnological Institute in a discussion last year; all the participants agreed that this was an anti-marxist formalist method, converging with reactionary conceptions of Malinowski-Smeets functional school. The formalist method infallibly leads to cosmopolitism—but one cannot be a patriot and a cosmopolite at the same time." (Potexin 1949: 25)

10. The literature on Bogatyrev includes Beneš 1968, Jakobson 1976b, and Veltruský 1987.

11. Data collecting was also the focus of the field trips he and Jakobson undertook in their student years. Bogatyrev later reflected on these trips, recalling that he was regarded as a German spy by the peasants in the Archangelsk area in 1916, and that on a trip with Jakobson and N. Jakovlev the peasants were about to lynch them, thinking they were sent by the Germans to poison the wells in the villages (Bogatyrev 1930: 333). These reminiscenses had more than anecdotal value for Bogatyrev, as they prompted reflections on the relationship between the ethnographer and his informant.

12. Other authors from this circle include V. Kochol and R. Mrlian.

13. Čyževśkyj's name occurs in a number of spelling variants, including the Czech Dmitrij Čiževský and the German Dmitrij Tschižewskij. I will use the Ukrainian form Dmytro Čyževśkyj throughout.

14. Jakobson was deeply loyal to Durnovo and drew attention to his activities in Czechoslovakia, where he was largely unknown (Jakobson 1926b).

15. A reproduction of this photograph can be found in this volume.

16. For a bibliography see Durnovo 1969. On his imprisonment see Robinson and Petrovskij 1992.

17. Obviously, there was a certain tension between the two scholars. Karcevskij viewed Durnovo as a "formalist" and a follower of Fortunatov.

18. Savickij wrote prolifically under his own name and a number of pseudonyms, including Vostokov and Lubenskij. His writings, scattered over interwar Slavic journals and Eurasian publications, are perhaps most easily accessible in Savickij 1933, a collection he prepared in Czech. It is here that he also introduces the Czech

term *vývojiště* for Russian *mestorazvitie*. Savickij's contributions to the Circle's publications include Savickij 1929; see also the Theses (Circle 1929). For an obituary of Savickij, see Vernadsky 1968. A brief list of his works can be found in Kudělka and Šimeček 1972. For correspondence between Savickij and Jakobson see Toman 1994.

19. For a selected bibliography of Bem's published works see Kudělka and Šimeček 1972. A large collection of his papers can be found in the PNP in Prague.

20. On February 24, 1932 ("Written Language") and on December 18, 1933 ("Phonology and Writing"). See also Artymovič 1932 .

21. On May 14, 1934; subsequently published as Artymovič 1935.

22. He lectured on the "Inflection of Ukrainian Adjectives" (May 14, 1931).

23. He began to attend the Circle's meetings in October 1928. He lectured on "Application of Phonology in School Instruction" (November 4, 1930) and "Recent Linguistic Discussion in the USSR" (December 14, 1931).

24. The head of the department, Franz Spina (1868–1938), received his *habilitation* from the Prague German University in 1909 and worked on Czech medieval literature among other things. See Jakobson 1938e.

25. Becking is registered as a full member of the Circle in the *Decennial Report* of 1936. The following lectures are recorded: "Sound-Analysis" (June 22, 1930), "Musicology and Phonology" (November 30, 1932), and "Musical Artwork as Sign" (January 1935). On Becking see also Stangl 1949/51.

26. In addition, there are several German-speaking scholars whose participation in the Circle was either brief or cannot be reliably documented. Ferdinand Liehwehr, assistant and later docent at the Slavic Department of German University, was briefly active in 1930. He lead a critical discussion of the Theses on January 30, 1930, but his name no longer appears in records after this date. Eugen Seidl gave a lecture on Heinrich Heine on October 15, 1934. The *Decennial Report* lists him as a member and gives České Budějovice as his domicile. Ernst Otto lectured twice (May 7, 1934: "Basic Questions of Linguistics"; June 23, 1936: "Grammar and Stylistics from an Educational Point of View") but is not listed in the *Decennial Report*.

27. Cf. Jakobson 1932c; see also his letters to Otokar Fischer in Toman 1994.

28. The thesis is listed among doctoral dissertations submitted at the German University in the academic year 1929–30: "Roman Jakobsen [sic], 28. 9. 1896, Moskva. 'Zur vergleichenden Forschung über die slawischen Zehnsilber.' Gesemann - Spina. [*Disertace...* 1965, p. 75, entry no. 1.]" The date of birth is in the Old Style. Gesemann and Spina were the reviewers. It is not clear whether the text itself is extant, but Jakobson's article entitled "Zur vergleichenden Forschung über die slawischen Zehnsilber," which appeared in the festschrift for F. Spina in 1929 (Jakobson 1929b), is close to the thesis topic.

29. The newer literature on Marty includes Raynaud 1982 and Mulligan 1990.

30. Carnap's authorship is attributed; summaries in *Slovo a slovesnost* were not signed.

31. I have not succeeded in deciphering this acronym—A. Isačenko, in the German spelling Issatschenko, is a possibility. Another candidate is S. Hessen.

32. Commenting on a draft of this section, Jiří Veltruský wrote to me (in Czech) on October 21, 1990: "Carnap was an antagonist and his invitation to the Circle had a purpose of confrontation. The Circle actively participated in the encounter between phenomenology and logicism that occurred at the international philosophical congress in Prague in 1934, naturally on Husserl's side."

33. Slovak structuralists of the 1940s differed fundamentally from the Prague mainstream in their attitude toward Carnap. On Hrušovský see Chvatík 1981a.

34. Landgrebe lectured on "Concepts of Lexical Fields in Linguistics and Language Philosophy" (May 18, 1936).

35. Utitz lectured on "Language as Culture" (May 6, 1935).

36. Gojko Ružičić, who taught Serbo-Croatian at the German University, was an active member after January 1929.

37. Savickij taught Ukrainian at German University after 1935.

38. Oskar Kraus lectured on "Reistic Language Philosophy and Its Relation to Logism and Penomenology."

39. See *Slovo a slovesnost* 2, 127f., for a summary of the discussion.

40. Gustav Becking, in a letter of resignation dated December 12, 1938, said that he was unable to follow the Circle's activity since most of the lectures were in Czech. Eugen Rippl resigned in a letter in Czech from December 9, 1938, giving no reasons for his decision. See Toman 1994.

41. The information is based on a letter by Klára Mágrová, the wife of Stanislav Mágr, to Roman Jakobson, dated November 10, 1946 (RJP, box 44, folder 7). The letter is a sad document of Czech attitudes toward Germans after 1945.

42. Trnka notes that Jespersen does not distinguish between synchrony and diachrony clearly. Saussure, on the other hand, "exposes the fundamental importance of a precise and consequent separation of the two methods" (Trnka 1924: 33). This lack of methodological reflection appears curious to Trnka because it was precisely Jespersen who had presented a synchronic analysis of four historically distinct stages of English in his *New English Grammar,* thus departing from methods accepted in historical grammars.

43. For a bibliography covering a major part of Trnka's career see Nosek 1965.

44. This first Czech reaction to Saussure's *Cours* says: "A general introduction to the science of language was compiled by Ch. Bally and A. Sechehaye from the papers of F. Saussure (*Cours de linguistique générale,* in Lausanne and Paris 1916). It briefly treats the history of comparative linguistics, its tasks and methods, the word, etc." (Novotný 1920: 253) Novotný was a classical philologist. An earlier mention of Saussure in Czech journals, a brief obituary (Hujer 1913), obviously could not have dealt with Saussure's *Cours* .

45. For other early references to Saussure see Havránek 1924a: 349 and Havránek 1925.

46. For a recent bibliography of Havránek's writings see Tylová 1990.

47. Studies in English include Steiner 1978, Veltruský 1980/81, Vodicka 1972, and treatments in Doležel 1990, Galan 1985, and Striedter 1989.

48. For a bibliography of Mukařovský's published works see Macek 1982b.

49. For a selected bibliography of Weingart's works see Kudělka and Šimeček 1972.

50. The other lecture, which he gave on October 25, 1935, bears the rather vague title "My Impressions from a Trip to Iran and USSR."

51. Some of his translations were done together with major Czech poets, including V. Nezval, J. Seifert, V. Holan, and S. Kadlec.

Chapter 7

1. Aiming to study the socio-cultural frame of the Prague Circle rather than its linguistic doctrines, I will not review the existing literature on Prague linguistics here. For a comprehensive recent monograph see Raynaud 1990 and the newer literature quoted therein. In contradistinction to standard approaches, Raynaud complements a doctrinal exposition of Prague School linguistics with a sketch of the Circle's cultural background, thus coming very close to my concerns.

2. Becker lived in Leipzig, where he studied with Eduard Sievers, Wilhelm Streitberg, and Gustav Weigand. His curriculum vitae can be found on the last unnumbered page of his book *Der Sprachbund* (Becker 1948).

3. Figures based on attendance lists preserved in APLK.

4. Trnka (1929: 172) refers to "regular meetings of a more intimate character."

5. These materials are preserved, some of them fragmentarily, in APLK. I hope to publish a selection from these documents.

6. Some passages in the minutes from 1929 suggest that there may have been "proto-statutes" before December 1930.

7. Information about lectures given before the Circle is, in general, easy to access. From 1926 through 1935 lists of lectures, occasionally with summaries, were compiled by B. Trnka (and in one case by Vachek) and published in *Časopis pro moderní filologii* (Trnka 1928–36; Vachek 1933). From 1935 on, abstracts of lectures were regularly included in the Chronicle section of *Slovo a slovesnost*. All lectures until 1936 are also listed in the *Decennial Report* (Circle 1936a). For a list with titles translated into English see Kochis 1976.

8. Of the 23 lectures given between October 1926 and November 1928, only four dealt with questions of literary theory. Of these, three were read by Mukařovský and

one by Tomaševskij (the first of the Russian (or, Soviet) scholars to lecture as a guest of the Circle. The proportion between linguistics and literary theory—not mentioning topics such as ethnology—began to change only in the 1930s.

9. These appear to have included B. Ilek's "Language Culture in Recent Russian Publications" (December 2, 1926), B. Trnka's "Semasiology and its Meaning for Linguistics" (February 3, 1927), and F. Oberpfalcer's "Bally's *Langue et la vie*" (March 3, 1927) and "Psychoanalysis and Linguistics" (December 2, 1927).

10. On March 3, 1927, at the sixth meeting of the Circle, František Oberpfalcer reported on Bally's *Langage et la vie* , seemingly valuing the chapter on expressivity most of all. On May 12, 1927, Karcevskij reported on *Sur les rapports entre le langage et la pensée*. This was a topic strongly influenced by Bally. See also Trnka's lengthy survey of the Geneva School, later published as Trnka 1928.

11. The *Decennial Report* of 1936 (Circle 1936a) lists 159 lectures, 41 of them related to poetics and literary theory. The same source shows that, of all the lectures given up to that point, 114 were delivered in Czech or Slovak, 32 in German, 11 in French, and 2 in Russian.

12. De Groot 1928 (p. 433) contains very similar wording in a report from the Congress in the Hague. The Dutch linguist became an important ally of the Circle during the Congress.

13. Mathesius's term "characterology," rather than "typology," may well go back to the German philosopher Ludwig Klages.

14. Information based on minutes preserved in APLK. There are unfortunately no minutes from F. Oberpfalcer's "Psychoanalysis and Linguistics" (December 2, 1927).

15. The term "activistic" is often used by Mathesius in this very context—e.g.,"Modern linguistics with its activistic approach to language . . ." (Mathesius 1927: 203).

16. Priority of acoustic perception was underscored: "It is not the motor but the auditive image which, as the speakers' task, is a social fact." (Jakobson 1928b: 184) Jakobson retained this idea for well over five decades, as its reverberations in *Preliminaries to Speech Analysis* (Jakobson, Fant, and Halle 1952) show.

17. Nerlich (1990) shows that the question of will in language change was important to Whitney, Bréal, and Wegener in the 1880s.

18. Consider again A. W. de Groot's report from the Congress in the Hague (de Groot 1928), especially this: "We no longer see behind sound-changes only blind forces, but also the needs and intentions of the speaker and the speech-community. The new readiness to recognize goal-orientation, teleology—manifest either in a consciously articulated plan or in adaptation to circumstances—is certainly a sign of the times." (p. 438)

19. See Halle 1977, 1983, 1987, 1988a; Krámský 1974; Viel 1984

20. Stumpf's (1907: 61f.) definition of the structural law is very important in this connection: "The so-called descriptive sciences are essentially sciences of structural laws. . . . Mineralogy, systematic botany and zoology do not deal about individual

objects, but about nomothetic coexistence [*gesetzliche Koexistenz*] of certain perceptual properties of such objects. " Note Stumpf's recourse to "coexistence," a notion that crucially avoids a causal or evolutionary point of view; see Toman 1979 for discussion. Elmar Holenstein (personal communication) reports that Jakobson was originally not familiar with Stumpf's notion of *Strukturgesetz,* but embraced it fully in their conversations.

21. In some sense Karcevskij's statements bear similarity to Gustav Špet's discussion of the notion structure in his *Esthetic Fragments* (Špet 1923, especially pp. 11–13; see Steiner 1988 for discussion). Špet not only asserts that structure cannot be equated with a simple aggregation of elements, but underscores that it consists of further self-contained substructures. Thus a hierarchy within structure is clearly implied. However, although he is concerned with permanent properties of structure, e.g., as manifest in the fact that under certain circumstances parts can be eliminated from the structure without causing a change in its essence, his discussion does not strongly focus on the implicational nature of structure. The discussion is clearly Husserlian, nonetheless, inasmuch the notion *edios* is explicitly invoked.

22. Among the forms that characterized the articulation of the new ideal were introductory surveys of a synthetic nature. The number of introductions to linguistics, (most of them French or German), especially in the period after 1900, is astonishing—see Oertel 1902, Ginneken 1907, Bally 1909, Dauzat 1910, Jespersen 1904a,b, Porzeziński 1910 (originally published in Russian in 1907), Bloomfield 1914, Sandfeld-Jensen 1915, and—naturally—Saussure 1916. In Russia, a number of introductory linguistic works also appeared before the First World War: Kudrjavskij 1912, Ušakov 1913, Bogorodickij 1913. Baudouin de Courtenay gave the material a pedagogic orientation in a linguistic exercise book (Baudouin 1912).

23. For all practical purposes, the Czech text of the Theses was not available until 1970, when it was republished in its entirety (Vachek 1970). By that time the original leaflets from the congress of Slavists were a bibliophile rarity. However, the Theses were well known in their canonical form from the first volume of *Travaux du Circle linguistique de Prague,* where they appeared in the French translation by Louis Brun. There are two English translations: John Burbank's (in Steiner 1982) and Josef Vachek's (in Vachek 1983).

24. There are following theses: no. 1, Methodological Problems Resulting from the Conception of Language as a System . . . ; no. 2, Tasks of the Study of a Language System, the Slavic in Particular; no. 3, Problems of Research on Different Functions of Language, Particularly Slavic Languages; no. 4, Current Problems of Old Church Slavonic; no. 5, Problems of Phonetic and Phonological Transcription in Slavic Languages; no. 6, Principles of Linguistic Geography, their Application, and their Relation to Ethnographic Geography in Slavic Regions; no. 7, Problems of a Pan-Slavic Linguistic Atlas, a Lexicological Atlas in Particular; no. 8, Methodological Problems of Slavic Lexicography; no. 9, Importance of Functional Linguistics for the Cultivation and Critique of Slavic Languages; no. 10, Application of New Linguistic Trends in Secondary Schools.

Chapter 8

1. The present chapter expands Toman 1986, providing among other things a contrast between the Prague Circle's and the Neogrammarians' attitudes toward

collective work. Group- dynamic analyses are rare in the historiography of linguistics, although they are by no means unusual in literary studies (see Prosenc 1967).

2. The entire wording is an amusingly Czech variant of the topos of modesty: "The Prague Linguistic Circle *arose from small beginnings, but grew steadily* and organically because it was no product of chance." (Mathesius 1936b: 137; emphasis added)

3. In my opinion this is clear as far as the Russian linguists are concerned. Note that they advanced their own initiative in the Hague (Jakobson et al. 1928a), and that Jakobson called the Circle "Mathesius's circle," rather than "our circle" as might perhaps be expected (in a letter to Durnovo, February 4, 1927; see Toman 1994).

4. Milada Součková (1898–1943), a versatile femme des lettres who was on friendly terms with the members of the Circle and participated in some of its meetings. According to Jakobson (personal communication), she helped the Circle by providing a generous sum for the publication of the first volume of its *Travaux*. Her account obviously relates to the 1930s.

5. In a personal communication, Jiří Veltruský disagreed with this observation, stating that the Czech spoken in the Circle was quite normal. I have no way to resolve this contradiction except by suggesting that the phenomenon observed by Součková might have been characteristic of an early phase of the Circle.

6. See the appendix to this volume for the full text.

7. There exist at least three further letters in the Archives of the Circle in which new members asserted their conformity with the Statutes: Pavel Trost (June 16, 1935), František Trávníček (June 25, 1935), Louis Hjelmslev (February 20, 1939).

8. Consider Weingart's 1932 assessment of the intellectual position of the Circle: "Contemporary influences can also be found in the Circle's theories. Thus the theses about synchrony show not only an apparent connection with Masaryk's Realism, but also with the departure from Historism, something that figures among the most characteristic features of European intellectual life after the war; structural approach resembles to me technical thinking and other comparable phenomena in sciences and arts (Constructivism). This approach as well as functional perspective are also apparent echoes of the influence of sociology on linguistics, visible earlier in the linguistic school of Paris. Finally, the fact that the post-war collectivism, so much stressed in today's Russia, but not only there, has also influenced this conception of language cannot be denied either." (Weingart 1932: 77)

9. The academically subdued language of Weingart's analysis suggests that the evaluation was worked out in connection with Mukařovský's nomination for the position of a full professor of aesthetics at Charles University in 1934. Weingart, a member of the nominating commission, strongly but unsuccessfully opposed Mukařovský's candidacy.

10. The emotions ran high even after decades. In one of our conversations in 1976, Roman Jakobson almost declined to continue when asked about Weingart. He merely glossed him as *ten státotvorný nacionalista,* something close to "that loyal nationalist."

11. The quotation is a translation from a Czech source that renders Einstein's text. I have not been able to identify the original.

12. This is the editorial statement in the first issue of *Slovo a slovesnost* (Circle 1935). I ignore minor statements by the editors, most of which are signed rd (for *redakce*, i.e. editorial board).

13. Drafts for, or larger portions of, individual theses can be attributed as follows: thesis no. 1 was written jointly by Jakobson and Mathesius (see Jakobson 1969a); no. 2a by Jakobson (see Jakobson 1969a); no. 2b by Mathesius (see Macek 1982a: 493); no. 3a is claimed by Jakobson (1969) but also by Havránek (see Horálek and Tyl 1954: 533); no. 3b is by Havránek (see Horálek and Tyl 1954: 533); no. 3c by Jakobson and Mukařovský (cf. Jakobson 1969a); no. 4 by Durnovo (see Jakobson 1969a; Vachek 1970: 74); no. 5 by Trnka (see Vachek 1970: 74); no. 6 by Savickij (see Vachek 1970: 74); no. 7 by Trubetzkoy (see Jakobson 1969a); no. 8 is ascribed to Trubetzkoy by Jakobson (1969a) but to L. Kopeckij by Vachek (1970: 74); no. 9 cannot be attributed; no. 10a is by Havránek (see Horálek and Tyl 1954: 533); no. 10b cannot be attributed either.

14. On Nezval's importance and his relation to Roman Jakobson see chapter 11 below.

15. Otokar Fischer (1883–1938) began to attend meetings of the Circle in January 1929. He was a well-known literary scholar specializing in German literature, a poet, a dramatist, and a co-director of the National Theater. He lectured several times before the Circle, although he was not a structuralist. In fact, he is to be counted as an early advocate of psychological and psychonalatic approaches in literary studies.

16. I have registered some 50 references for the period between 1931 and 1934, mostly in cultural journals. A survey of newspapers would certainly add some more. Among the literary authors who voiced their opinion was also S. K. Neumann. The reader will not be surprised to hear that he took the part of Haller.

Chapter 9

1. With the exception of Holenstein (1984), few have studied the impact of guiding cultural images on the Circle in sufficient detail. Holý (1990) provides an interesting background with his study of the Czech author V. Vančura.

2. The following sections are based on Toman 1984.

3. Note the remarkable consistency of usage: in the Futurism essay the set toward nature (as in Naturalism) was claimed to create connections between elements that are essentially disconnected (see chapter 2).

4. For instance, the abandonment of the Neogrammarian conception consists in "the replacement of the mechanical conception by a teleological one" (Jakobson 1928b: 184).

5. ". . . a functional system instead of a mechanical addition" (Jakobson 1929a: 100).

6. Ibid.

7. A similar example: "[Peškovskij's] conception is a fortunate synthesis of the Romantic tradition and the Fortunatovs' analytic approach." (Jakobson 1933b).

8. Jakobson did not, however, want to see the introduction of dialectics into the Circle as a Russian import. Structural laws were dialectical, no matter who asserted this first: "Little matters from where the works of the Circle received the Hegelian conception of the structure of systems and its dialectics." (Jakobson 1933a: 637f.) Compare a similar statement from 1934: "As if it were not the same whether the Hegelian concept of structure has come into the Circle from Russian science, where Hegelian tradition is uninterrupted and has been fully alive, or whether the decisive point was the Saussurean tradition, which absorbed Hegels teaching on dichotomies mediated through *Linguistic Antinomies* of the Hegelian Victor Henry." (Jakobson 1934a: 8)

9. Compare this: ". . . there is no way of understanding the dialectical nature of any process without attempting to grasp its 'selfmovement,' to use a Hegelian term" (Mukařovský 1933: 4).

10. Kurt Konrád (pseudonym for Kurt Beer) was active for a relatively short period between 1930 and1938. His early death in Nazi captivity places him among the Communist victims of Nazism, such as Bedřich Václavek and Julius Fučík. In post-1948 Czechoslovakia he was elevated to an official classic of the early Czech Marxist theory of culture.

11. For details of Konrád's critique of Mukařovský see Galan 1985: 60f.

12. Záviš Kalandra participated in the discussion of Mukařovský's work in December 1934 (*Slovo a slovesnost* 1, 1935: 190; Galan 1985: 61).

13. Václavek lectured before the Circle on "Czech Songs Incorporated into Folklore" (February 22, 1936) and is listed as a member in the *Decennial Report*.

14. J. L. Fischer lectured before the Circle on "The System of Meanings" on April 28, 1934, and is listed as a member in the *Decennial Report*.

15. Chvatík 1981b, a survey of some of J. L. Fischer's ideas, does not deal with this important issue, thus greatly simplifying the roots of the so-called "dialectical structurology," which he and other Czech scholars (e.g. Robert Kalivoda) were trying to work out in the late 1950s and the early 1960s.

16. "The spirit of the book by the Structuralist Fischer aims at showing the fallacy of the philosophical conception of naturalism that turns reality into a dust of atoms and can only see relations of quantity and mechanical causality." (Jakobson 1933a: 639)

17. Whereas *slovo* is straightforwardly rendered as *word* in English, *slovesnost,* literally "word-ity," has no direct eqivalent. My understanding is that the term refers to literature in the broadest sense of the word, oral literature included.

18. See Toman 1992a,b.

19. The language of the Circle was remarkably consistent with respect to this parallel: "In the same degree as social reconstruction acquires an ever more planned and goal-oriented character, as an ever greater number of social value-systems enters the domain of planned economy, so is the production anarchy in the life of language system naturally condemned to retreat step by step in the face of plan and regulation." (Jakobson 1934b: 325)

20. Not everyone in the Circle was convinced of the appropriateness of such orientation. In a letter dated January 25, 1935, Trubetzkoy reprimanded Jakobson for involving himself in "journalism" and other kinds of nonsense [*pročaja erunda*; Jakobson 1975: 313]. Two months later he was able to take the fist issue of the new journal under his scrutiny. Not unexpectedly, he praised Jakobson's contributions and the article by Mukařovský—but the rest was bland, little original, good for printing in an arbitrary journal for high school teachers. A journal addressed to a wide audience was inevitably bound to lower the standards: "The Czech reader may be saluted, but the Circle not." (Jakobson 1975: 327)

21. "Gothic" is a synonym of "medieval" in this context.

22. Ignát Hermann (1854–1935), a Czech prose writer.

23. J. L. Fischer even contemplated "Gothic society" as a name for what he later called "synthetic society."

24. Also recall Václavek's appreciation of the Middle Ages in his "New Man," quoted above.

25. The artist and the exact date are not known. I am indebted to Elmar Holenstein for discussions on the meaning of this image.

Chapter 10

1. The literature on N. S. Trubetzkoy has recently been growing. See Liberman 1991, Seriot (to appear), Stolz and Toman 1993, Toman 1987 and Toporov 1990/91, and . Toman 1992c is an excerpt in Russian from the present chapter.

2. From "Nikolaj and Rosenberg," an unpublished fragment of story by N. S. Trubetzkoy; CGALI, coll. 1337 (Diverse diaries and memoirs), inventory list 2, item 52, thick black copybook, pp. 15f. The fragment was probably written in 1902, when Trubetzkoy was 12 years old.

3. CGALI, coll. 1337 (Diverse diaries and memoirs), inventory list 2, item 52, thin copybook, pp. 155–158 (text entered *a tergo*).

4. In the days after the revolt of 1905 it was he who was selected to address the tsar on behalf of the group of liberal constitutionalists and to ask him to endorse fundamental changes in Russia's political system. For a biography see Bohachevsky-Chomiak 1976.

5. Three letters by Trubetzkoy to Miller from 1912 and 1913 are included in Toman 1994.

6. Trubetzkoy Papers, BLOR; see also Superfin 1967.

7. Lindner was an Indologist, this is of some interest in view of Trubetzkoy's later publications on Indian religions.

8. There is one brief indication from before World War I that Trubetzkoy entertained concepts which have a certain proto-structuralist flavor in matters relating to language. He criticized a comparative historical analysis because its author merely compared inflection of separate grammatical forms rather than comparing grammars of the languages involved (Trubetzkoy 1908b: 147).

9. See also Titunik 1977.

10. On Trubetzkoy's academic activity in Bulgaria see Simeonov 1976, 1977.

11. Trubetzkoy's views can be reconstructed to some degree from articles such as Trubetzkoy 1927b.

12. Trubetzkoy regarded the effect of Wells' book as harmful but thought that its availability would harm the reputation of the English among the Russians (Jakobson 1975: 24).

13. In our conversations Petr Suvčinskij also recalled Trubetzkoy's strong dislike of Vienna and the emigration in general. In this respect, Trubetzkoy had many sarcastic anecdotes and jokes in his repertoire.

14. For a discussion of *Europe and Mankind* see also Burbank 1986.

15. It seems that some readers of *Europe and Mankind* have tried to grasp the book in terms of its immediate political context, i.e., as a result of revolution and civil war (Polívka 1922). Jakobson (1975: 12) seems to have reacted along these lines. However, Trubetzkoy did not wish to see so simple a motivation and stressed the fact that the project extended far back into the prewar time. As he wrote to Jakobson, in 1909–10, when he was 20, he intended to write a study which would provide scientific foundations for the understanding of nationalism. The project. to be entitled *A Justification of Nationalism* [*Opravdanie nacionalizma*], was envisioned to have three parts. One part actually appeared as *Europe and Mankind*, the remaining two were published as comparatively brief essays: "About the True and False Nationalism" (Trubetzkoy 1921b) and "The Highs and the Lows in Russian Culture" (Trubetzkoy 1921c).

16. Similarities between Danilevskij and Trubetzkoy were also observed by other scholars. See Riasanovsky 1967: 60.

17. Despite its almost didactic clarity, the book was far from simplistic. Trubetzkoy himself had little doubt that this was an important study, and was evidently satisfied to see an edition in German (in addition to the Japanese translation). As is apparent from the correspondence with Roman Jakobson's brother Sergej (Pomorska 1977), who translated the book into German, he originally planned to have the German translation prefaced by Oswald Spengler, thinking that *Europe and Mankind* and Spengler's *Untergang des Abendlandes* had certain ideas in common. This is understandable in view of Trubetzkoy's negative ideas about "Romano-Germanic" civilization—a civilization Spengler saw declining and giving way to fresh and authentic vigor of the East.

18. Kroeber also commented on comparisons of aborigines with children; interestingly, Trubetzkoy too spent some space on the value of this comparison.

19. This artist later moved to the United States, where he was known as Tchelitchew.

20. The meaning of the emblem was explained to me by Petr Suvčinskij. The cult of the horse was popular among the Eurasians.

21. The term "Eurasia" originated in natural sciences. Its usage in geographical works by Eduard Suess (1892) is usually taken to be decisive for its acceptance. It was in Savickij's review of *Europe and Mankind* (Savickij 1921) that the term seems to have been used for the first time in the context of the new movement.

22. There is an extensive literature on Eurasianism from the interwar period. However, after the Second World War only few historians proceeded to offer an analytic account. They include Otto Böss, whose dissertation (Böss 1961), isolated in its time, stands out, and Nicholas Riasanovsky, who also studied Eurasianism and Trubetzkoy's role in it in detail (Riasanovsky 1964, 1967).

23. Georgij Vasilevič Florovskij (1893–1968), a Russian Orthodox priest, soon distanced himself from the Eurasians. He later moved to the United States, where he eventually became a professor of Orthodox theology at Princeton.

24. It is likely that Trubetzkoy's reservations were in part motivated by Savickij's somewhat negative review of "Europe and Mankind" (Savickij 1921). Although Savickij agreed with Trubetzkoy on certain very general principles, he occasionally was quite polemic, if not sarcastic. Savickij's review is the earliest familiar to me; the text is dated January 8, 1921.

25. A reference to this open letter is missing in Havránek and Jakobson 1939.

26. Trubetzkoy made it abundantly clear that Marxism and Communism were among the emanations of the Romano-Germanic spirit. Already the fact that they were Western products made them incongruous with Russia.

27. Trubetzkoy (1927b: 6) was convinced that these forms were dead: "The so-called crisis of parlamentarism and the crisis of democracy are facts not to be doubted about; not even the veterans of liberalism can overlook them."

28. In the opening section of a chapter devoted to language in his *Les lois de l'imitation,* Tarde describes linguistic changes accompanying the merger of families into tribes and the resulting linguistic mixture. It is interesting to note that he consciously took a non-evaluative point of view by stressing that *syncretisme philologique* of the type he was describing was not a phenomenon of decadence. In fact, he acknowledged the agency involved in language mixture as something primeval and basic (Tarde 1890: 278f.).

29. Trubetzkoy remained a religious person throughout his life (P. Suvčinskij, personal communication, 1979).

30. On Eurasian influences on the development of Trubetzkoy's phonology see Gasparov 1987, Toman 1987b, and Viel 1984.

31. Erotic and obscene drawings are rare, but not lacking.

32. Trubetzkoy Papers, BLOR; copybook no. 24, pp. 18a–19a.

33. CGALI, Coll. 1337 (Miscel. diaries), inventory list 2, item 52.

34. As far as the members of the Prague Circle are concerned, their approaches to convergence underwent some development. Henrik Becker's lecture of 1926 and Jan Rypka's lecture of October 6, 1926, revolved around culturally driven convergence, apparently stressing questions of lexical borrowing. This cultural approach gave slowly way to a more technical, mainly phonological perspective, in Jakobson's, Skalička's and Trubetzkoy's work.

Becker's later work shows a continuation of his early approach and that sections of his monograph *Der Sprachbund* (Becker 1948), which were written according to the foreword in 1931-33, deal with the question of how "languge unions form and dissolve" (p. [5]). Among other things, Becker introduces a distinction between a "Meistersprache" and a language (or languages) leaning onto master-languages. Clearly, alone this terminology would hardly have found Trubetzkoy's approval because of the ranking connotations it implies.

Another member of the Circle, the Slovak phonologist L'udovít Novák, was also attracted by the *Sprachbund* idea in the technical sense. He might have wanted to "Eurasianize" Slovak under Trubetzkoy's influence when he wrote that in contradistinction to Czech, Slovak can appears as "relatively simple and regular" (Novák 1933/34: 143).

35. The printed version of this lecture (Trubetzkoy 1939b) became the most frequently quoted contribution to the linguistics of convergence. The lecture, given on December 14, 1936, is summarized in Trubetzkoy 1937b. Trubetzkoy never saw his study in print. His bibliographers in *Travaux* vol. 8 gloss it as appearing in *Evrazijskaja Chronika* vol. 13 under the Russian title "Mysli ob indoevropejskoj probleme" [Thoughts about the Indo-European Problem], but this publication did not materialize. The Russian text finally appeared in *Voprosy jazykoznanija* in 1958 (Trubetzkoy 1958b). The study, however, had become known well before 1958 through its German version, first published by Jakobson in Denmark (Trubetzkoy 1939b). This version is approximately forty per cent shorter than the Russian original, excludes footnotes, illustrative examples and a longer passage in the first third of the text where Trubetzkoy's imagery of chains, nets, and "brick-layering pattern" is particularly evident.

It is curious to note that an editorial comment to the 1958 Russian publication indicates that the manuscript also contains a section critical of Marr. This section was never published and is also missing in the newest Russian reprint of the article in a Soviet Trubetzkoy's anthology (Trubetzkoy 1987a), which, moreover, lacks any reference to the existence of the section on Marr. In short, the complete text of Trubetzkoy's study has never been published.

36. I refer to the Russian version (Trubetzkoy 1987b) throughout.

37. This is also the image used by Johannes Schmidt (1872).

38. The article was among the major reasons why Trubetzkoy was subjected to a search and interrogation by the Gestapo in 1938, which aggravated his condition. It is ironic, however, to find that Trubetzkoy's relation towards Jewry was not always as

liberal as generally assumed. Reviewing some of his private letters to Petr Suvčinskij from the early 1920s, one is actually justified to speculate that like many Russian intellectuals shaped by Orthodoxy, Trubetzkoy was close to a cultural anti-Semite. In one of his letters to Suvčinskij (July 11, 1923) he reports that he introduced himself to Count Keyserling as an "anti-Semite," motivating this attitude by what he believed was a purely negative role Jews played in contemporary Russian culture. The passage can be related to a very sharp judgment that he passed on Ilja Èrenburg's *But It Does Turn* (Èrenburg 1922) in an earlier letter to Suvčinskij (August 9, 1922). One may reason that Jews were for Trubetzkoy representatives of a total Europeanization and could be integrated neither in Orthodox Russia nor in his vision of a Eurasian state. A mention of these private communications is certainly in order, let alone for the development which lies between them and the article "On Racism," where Trubetzkoy denounced anti-semitism based on racial considerations. (I am grateful to the late Petr Suvčinskij for having shown me selected parts of his correspondence with Trubetzkoy in 1979.)

39. The lecture was published as Schuchardt 1900. It can only be speculated whether the 1870 text underwent changes when being prepared for publication.

40. Although the lecture appears relatively late in Baudouin's work, the topic was among Baudouin's permanent interests; cf. entries "smešannyj jazyk" [mixed language] and "smešenie jazykov" [language mixing] in the subject index in Baudouin 1963. Baudouin was also familiar with Schuchardt, to whom he gives credits, although without acknowledging any particular title. Schuchardt (1884) had published in Russian journals on the topic of language mixing.

41. Comparable discussions are well documented in francophone linguistics. Much of these discussions was also embedded in the cultural context of the epoch, this time in the perspective of "Europeanization." Bally (1909) explicitly underscored that Europeanization extends to languages such as Finnish and Hungarian, i. e., to genetically unrelated languages.

Classical philologists were concerned with language contact, in particular when dealing with the linguistic situation in the Roman empire. An interesting example is Schwyzer 1914, in which the notion "Europeanization" also appears. Schwyzer's concern was not only convergence in the area of vocabulary, but, primarily, in the area of "spiritual influences," i.e., culture. He explicitly restricted this kind of convergence to the area of literary language, idioms of scholars, and professional specialization. Again, the basis was cultural affinity, and the main carrier of this affinity were higher classes; Europeanization was a matter of "obere Sprachschicht" (Schwyzer 1914: 144). Some of these themes might be reflected in Trubetzkoy 1921c.

Kristian Sandfeld's influential *Linguistique balkanique* (1930) represents extensive work reaching back to his habilitation from 1900.

42. Jakobson studied the question of innovation spread across dialects, particularly focusing on *akanje*, a familiar dialectal phenomenon of Russian. Among other things, he suggested that spread of lexical borrowing with *akanje*-vocalism into dialects with okanje vocalism should be expected, but not the other way round. This was so because options for accommodation of akanje forms in okanje dialects are available given the structure of the phonological system of okanje dialects, while they are absent in the other direction. Hence, the spread and adoption of akanje can be entirely accounted for by "internal linguistic reasons" (Jakobson 1929a: 94).

Chapter 11

1. This chapter is a revised and abbreviated version of Toman 1987a. For earlier studies of the subject see Effenberger 1983, Linhartová 1977, and, in a way, Štoll 1966.

2. All the poems in this chapter are given in literal translation only. Some of the originals are based on rhyme associations, which are lost in this literal translation. The original text of the lines from "Sisters-Lightnings" goes as follows: Из улицЬ улся / Пули как пчелы. / Шатаются стулья / Бледнеет веселый / По улицам длинным, как пули полет, / ОпятЬ пулемет, / косит, метет / пулями лиственный веник, / Гнетет / Пастухов денег. (Xlebnikov 1933: 162)

3. Zdeněk Kalista, poet and historian, recalled the circumstances under which Den was edited in his reminiscences about Jiří Weil (in Kalista 1969) and in extensive commentaries to his correspondence with the Czech poet Jiří Wolker (Kalista 1978, esp. pp. 58–82).

4. A useful source on Devětsil in English is Švácha 1990. Devětsil is a name of a plant; the literal meaning of this compound is "nine powers." It is not particularly clear why and how this name was selected.

5. From Jakobson's letter in English to the Italian Slavist A. M. Ripellino.

6. This is a rough translation of "Konec básnického umprumáctví a živnostnictví." UMPRUM is the abbreviation for the name of the academy of industrial design in Prague (Umělecko-průmyslová škola).

7. The front page is reproduced in Švácha 1990.

8. A great number of relevant documents are presented and discussed in Holenstein 1979/1981. Holenstein's term is "monofunctionalism."

9. The volume usually referred to is the second volume of an art journal called *Život*, published between 1921 and 1948. Krejcar would, in modern terms, be called a guest editor of this particular volume. The remaining volumes have little to do with Krejcar's.

10. The idea is echoed by constructivist formulations from the Soviet Union. Speaking about the modern architect, Moisej Ginzburg said in 1924: ". . . his goals entail neither an unhampered search for self-contained forms nor the ambiguities produced by inspired hands, *but the clear recognition of his problems and the means and methods for their solution*." (Ginzburg 1982: 88; emphasis in original)

11. On the whole, monofounctional tendencies, especially in the wave of post-revolutionary utilitarianism, is well documented in Russian art. Ivan Puni wrote in 1919: "The fire-ladder possesses a different kind of beauty which is inherent in its construction, its optimal usability, its portability, its manipulability—that is what modern production means. The construction of an object is completely dependent on the purpose for which it is intended; seen from this point of view, what the artist can add is only a triviality" (Puni 1919 [1975], n.p.; only a German translation of the original was available). Jakobson knew Puni. In Šklovskij's diary in letters *Zoo—Or Letters not*

about Love we find a reminiscence of Šklovskij's visit to Ivan Puni together with and R. Jakobson, P. Bogatyrev and C. Einstein (Šklovskij 1923b: 61).

12. De Zurko 1957 and Watkin 1977 are useful in the present context. De Zurko, who traces functionalist ideas prior to the twentieth century, regards moral considerations as one of the sources of architectural functionalism. Ligo (1984: 11) is correct, however, in pointing out that it is often diffucult to identify this aspect explicitly. Jakobson's text provides an explicit instance of this type of argument.

13. Teige's final days were tragic. The Communist mass media of the early 1950s depicted him as a vicious intellectual terrorist whose main aim was to desecrate everything that was pure in the new socialist culture. A lengthy defamation in which Teige is accused of criminal activities and of collaboration with "the Trotzkyite R. Jakobson" (Grygar 1951: 1036) stands out. The cause of Teige's death, which occurred at the onset of this campaign, remains veiled.

14. I am familiar with some twenty Czech reviews of Jakobson 1923a and Jakobson 1926a.

15. In the early 1930s Jakobson and Vančura embarked on a movie project together. The film was an adaptation of the Czech variant of the Baron Münchhausen story. Eventually Jakobson brought in Nezval to rework the script, but new producers requested further changes. When the film eventually opened, on December 1, 1933, under the title *On the Sunny Side,* it was no success. Owing to extensive editing, the text of the script has little value from the point of view of Jakobson's authorship. Excerpts can be found in Blahynka 1978. Blahynka attempts to portray Vančura as an innocent victim of a foreign manipulator who had to pay for his association with "the leading representative of the structuralist conception of art" and agree on a film full of unusual shots, peculiar metaphors and other unorthodox ideas while "burrying its important social theme" (ibid.). As was discussed in the preceding chapter, Vančura saw a genuine liberation in the removal of ideology from art.

16. When Nezval began to edit his *Collected Works,* in the 1950s, he left out all references to friends who now were in disgrace or emigrated. The omissions were so obvious that he had to comment upon them. He chose to say that he undertook them for artistic reasons (Nezval 1958: 381).

17. This and the following poem were also included in a small festschrift dedicated to Jakobson by his students when he was leaving Brno in 1939 (*Romanu Jakobsonovi...* 1939).

18. Originally in *La Revue Blanche,* June 1, 1902; later incorporated into his collection *Heresiarque et Cie,* 1910.

19. Especially in literature and art, the years 1926 and 1927 represent a first dividing point. In order to avoid terms such as "post-mid-1920s," I will take the liberty of using the term "1930s" throughout.

20. I have not been able to identify the quotation in this paragraph—Nezval might be the source.

21. Neumann's response to this article prompted a court action, as a result of which Neumann had to withdraw his statements. See Neumann 1938b.

22. "Toyen" was a pseudonym.

23. Some of Jakobson's Soviet friends participated in these campaigns. Ilja Èrenburg published an article describing French surrealists as "perverse monsters" whose program consisted in "onanism, pederasty, and, ultimately, in intercourse with animals" (Èrenburg 1933). The attacks on the surrealists only contributed to their popularity (see Toman 1985b).

24. Among the other events that dramatically marked the cultural left was the dissolution of the Surrealist group by Nezval in March 1938. In the days leading up to this singlehanded coup, it became obvious that only he took seriously a breakdown in the militant attitude of the avant-garde under external pressures; thus, Nezval is reported to have called the Prague Circle a suspicious group "backed by something international and Jewish" (Teige 1938: 34; see also Ripellino 1950: 38). But he later changed his mind (again).

25. He also recalled it in his last conversation with me, in September 1981.

26. Quoted from the facsimile of the "Realistic Manifesto" (1920), reproduced and translated into English in Gabo 1957. I have altered the translation in places.

27. This line of thought was also represented in the West. Jaffé (1965: 142) quotes the Dutch artist and critic Theo van Doesburg as having said: "Art, as we demand, is neither proletarian nor burgeois. Art itself is strong enough to determine the entire culture."

Chapter 12

1. There is no study addressing Jakobson's activities during the war years in their entirety; however, fragments can be gleaned from Baecklund 1977. Halle 1988b is an interesting document of Jakobson's American 1940s. The institutional background of European academic emigration is covered to some extent by Rutkoff and Scott 1983; see also Sprondel 1981 and the references cited therein. On the demise of the Prague Linguistic Circle in post-1948 Czechoslovakia, see Novák 1990.

2. Eleven lectures were delivered in the academic year 1938–39; 21 in 1940–41; seven in 1941–42; 13 in 1942–43 ; eight in 1943–44; four in 1944–45.

3. A bundle of forms mimeographed for this purpose is preserved in APLK.

4. This summarizes Jakobson's own account from 1945 (RJP, box 1, folder 15). Note the recurrence of the number 23 in the dates.

5. This letter was kindly made available by Marie Havránková. The details of the passage from Sweden to the United States are also recorded in the memoirs of Toni Cassirer (1981), the wife of Ernst Cassirer.

6. I am grateful to Sylvain Bromberger for this information.

7. Some of Jakobson's lectures from this period are now available in *Six leçons sur le son et le sens* (Jakobson 1976a) and "La théorie Saussurienne en rétrospection" (Ja-

kobson 1984a). The following is a list of his courses as entered in the catalogues of the *Ecole Libre:*

Spring 1942: *Le son et le sens des mots* (6 leçons, cours public [March 1942]); *Linguistique générale* (Conférences de licence; 15 leçons, cours fermé)

Academic year 1942–43: *Les changements de la langue* (4 leçons, cours public [beginning January 15, 1943]); *Phonologie* (15 leçons, cours fermé [Fall and Spring terms]); *L'affinité et la parenté des langues* (4 leçons, cours public); *La poésie tchèque du IXe au XVe siècle* (5 leçons)

Academic year 1943/44: *La langue russe, miroir et véhicule de culture* (4 leçons, cours fermé [January 1943]); *Linguistique générale* (14 leçons, cours fermé [beginning Oct. 1943]); *Les grandes figures de la littérature tchécoslovaque. Lecture et interprétation de poèmes tchèques et polonais.* [With Julian Tuwim.]

Academic year 1944–45: *Les troubles du langage* (cours public, 5 leçons [January–February 1945]); *La révolution russe vue par un linguiste* (Cours public, 5 leçons [May–June 1945]); *La structure grammaticale du russe comparée avec celle du français et de l'anglais* (conférences de license, 30 leçons [Octobre 1944–May 1945]); *Lecture et interprétation de poèmes polonais, tchèques et slovaques* [with Julian Tuwim]

For the academic year 1945–46, Jakobson announced, among other topics, a class with Claude Levi-Strauss (*Structure des institutions populaires-Langue, moeurs, folklore).* This course was not held, however.

8. There are also two seated men, described as Adler and Kopf, about whom I could not find any information.

9. It is possible that personal animosity between Jakobson and Hostovský was involved, but Jakobson's statements cannot really be trivialized by recourse to personal feelings—the identification with the spirit of the interwar time is straightforward and does not call for any backstage information.

10. A collection of corresponding common places is the festschrift on the occasion of Mukařovský's sixticth birthday (Havránek and Černý 1952).

11. This may have been written by a journalist, in which case Mukařovský's signature would be his only contribution.

12. For a useful survey of the years 1948 and 1949 see Kopál 1949.

13. The full title is *Soviet Linguistics—Translations of Selected Studies* (Bosák et al. 1949). The volume contained articles by N. Ja. Marr, I. I. Meščaninov, S. D. Kacnel'son, A. P. Riftin, A. V. Desnickaja, and F. P. Filin. The editorial group consisted of C. Bosák, K. Hausenblas, B. Havránek, K. Horálek, J. Sedláček, and V. Skalička.

14. There is general agreement that Stalin's linguistic remarks represented primarily a political rather than an academic intervention. In all likelihood, Stalin intervened in an attempt to strengthen his centralized system by an appeal to the leading role of Russian people and its national continuity, expressed among other things in its linguistic history. A critical account of Marrism provided a welcome opportunity in this respect, since there was one obvious flaw in Marr's Marxist theory of language: it had no particular provison for the concept of nation, something Stalin was always

concerned with. Clearly, traditional concepts of linguistic history were much more useful for him than Marr's radically nationless doctrines. Stalin asserted the traditional view of the history of Indo-European languages and deemphasized the idea of linguistic convergence, which entered Marrism in the form of "linguistic hybridization." For a recent study of Marrism see Alpatov 1991.

15. František Trávníček (1888–1961), a specialist in Czech, became a member of the Circle in 1935, but distanced himself from it soon after 1948.

16. A telling illustration of the intensity with which Stalinism was introduced is the establishment in 1950 of the Czechoslovak-Soviet Institute, whose main purpose was not to propagate Marxism as such, but Soviet scholarship. An important instrument toward achieving this objective was the bimonthly *Soviet Science,* a translation digest which appeared in not less than nine fields, including mathematics, physics, chemistry, and medicine. Among these mutations, *Soviet Science—Linguistics [Sovětská věda - Jazykověda]* remains a valuable document of the process of subordination of Czechoslovak linguistics to Soviet norms.

17. Skalička's statement is worthy of note because its author had previously repudiated some early Soviet critiques of the Prague School. Soviet attacks against structuralism appeared early and continued in the 1940s. Čikobava 1944 is generally regarded as the earliest denouncement of the Prague school, although it is not clear in detail what impact this article exactly had because it only appeared in Georgian. Čemodanov 1947 attracted more attention. Čemodanov, who had some knowledge of Prague publications, targeted Saussurean linguistics—"an idealist bourgeois current." Skalička reviewed and refuted Čemodanov in late 1947 (Skalička 1948), but he followed the official doctrine in subsequent years. Of his numerous apologies I list only Skalička 1950, 1951, and 1953.

18. Attempts to construct Trotskyism as a vital political force have their roots in the 1930s, as do many other aspects of Czechoslovak Stalinism. V. Kopecký, the minister of information after 1948, was active along these lines; see Kopecký 1937.

19. In 1956, a time of liberalization, Sgall, in contrast to many other writers who had been active in the early 1950s, retracted his critique of the Circle (Sgall 1956). Clearly, the Stalinist episode continued to haunt him for a long time. Addressing an international linguistic meeting in Prague in 1983, he conceded: "I am fully aware that it is questionable whether I have the right to address this audience in the present context, since thirty years ago I helped those who mistreated the Praguian linguistic tradition and attempted to restrict its further influence. I can only hope that my development during these years has been convincing in this respect." (Sgall 1983: 277) Sgall's attempts to preserve the Prague tradition were indeed extensive. Ironically, this was detrimental to his career in the post-1968 period of "normalization."

20. For some administrative aspects of this process see Míšková (to appear). Although for all practical purposes the Circle had ceased to exist, it was neither dismantled nor formally banned. This apparent administrative mistake made it possible for the Circle to resume its activity in 1991 without asking for new registration.

Sources and References

Main Archival Sources

APLK: Archiv Pražského lingvistického kroužku [Archives of the Prague Linguistic Circle], Archives of the Academy of Sciences of the Czech Republic, Prague

BLOR: Gosudarstvennaja biblioteka SSSR imeni V. I. Lenina—Otdel rukopisej [Lenin State Library—Manuscript Division], Moscow

CGALI: Central'nyj gosudarstvennyj arxiv literatury i iskustva [Central State Archives of Literature and Arts], Moscow

LAPNP: Literární archiv, Památník národního písemnictví [Literary Archives, Museum of National Literature], Prague

RJP: Roman Jakobson Papers, Archives and Special Collections, Massachusetts Institute of Technology

SK: Slovanská knihovna [Slavic Library], Prague

Abbreviations of Series and Titles

Actes. . .: Actes du premier congrès international de linguistes à La Haye, du 10–15 avril 1928. Leiden: A. W. Sijthoff.

ČMF: Časopis pro moderní filologii (Prague)

ÈO: Ètnografičeskoe obozrenie (Moscow)

LF: Listy filologické (Prague)

NŘ: Naše řeč (Prague)

PrPr: Prager Presse

SaS: Slovo a slovesnost (Prague)

Sborniki: Sborniki po teorii poètičeskogo jazyka. Petrograd: Tipografija Z. Sokolinskogo.

SRund: Slavische Rundschau

SW: The Selected Writings of Roman Jakobson. The Hague, 1962.

TCLP: Travaux du Cercle linguistique de Prague

Principal Reference Manuals

Bulaxov, Mixail Gapeevič. *Vostočnoslovjanskie jazykovedy.* Biobibliografičeskij slovar' [East Slavic Linguists—Bio-bibliographical Dictionary]. Minsk: Izdatel'stvo BGU. Vol. 1, 1976; vol. 2, 1977; vol. 3, 1978.

Kudělka, Milan and Zdeněk Šimeček. 1972. *Československé práce o jazyce, dějinách a kultuře slovanských národů od r. 1760.* Biograficko-bibliografický slovník. Praha: SPN.

Kudělka, Milan and Zdeněk Šimeček, Vladislav Šťastný, Radoslav Večerka. 1977. *Československá slavistika v letech 1918-1939* [Czechoslovak Slavistics in the Years 1918-1939]. Praha: Academia.

Rudy, Stephen. 1990. *Roman Jakobson 1869–1 Čemodanov 982. A Complete Bibliography of His Writings.* Berlin: Mouton de Gruyter.

References

Alfavitnyj spisok studentov i postoronnyx slušatelej Imperatorskogo Moskovskogo Universiteta za 1914–1915 akademičeskij god [The Alphabetical List of Students and Auditors of the Imperial Moscow University for the Academic Year 1914–1915]. Moskva: Tipografija Vil'de, 1915.

Alpatov, Vladimir Mixailovič. 1991. *Istorija odnogo mifa: Marr i Marrism* [History of a Myth: Marr and Marrism]. Moskva: Nauka.

Armstrong D. and C. H. van Schooneveld, eds. 1977. *Roman Jakobson: Echoes of his Scholarship.* Lisse: de Ridder.

Artymovič, Agenor. 1932. "Fremdwort und Schrift." In *Charisteria...* , 114–117.

———. 1935. "O potenciálnosti jazyka" [About the Potentiality of Language]. *SaS* 1, 148–151. [In English in Vachek 1964: 75–80.]

Asenova, Petja. 1979. "Aperçu historique des études dans le domaine de la linguistique balkanique." *Linguistique balkanique* 22, 1, 5–42.

Association Internationale pour les études phonologiques [. . .] *Bulletin d'information* no. 1, 1932: *ČMF* 19, 1932/33, 59–64; no. 2, 1935: *ČMF* 22, 1935/36, following p. 112.

Avanesov, R. I. 1973. "Dmitrij Nikolaevič Ušakov (K stoletiju so dnja roždenija)" [D. N. Ušakov—On the Occasion of his 100th Anniversary]. *Izvestija Akademii nauk SSSR—Serija literatury i jazyka* 32, 201–204.

B. 1938. "Výstava Štyrský a Toyen v Brně" [Exhibition Štyrský and Toyen in Brno]. *Ranní noviny* (Brno) April 15, 1938.

Baecklund-Ehler, Astrid. 1977. "Roman Jakobson's Cooperation with Scandinavian Linguists." In Armstrong and Schooneveld, 21–27.

Bally, Charles. 1909. *Traité de stylistique française.* Hedielberg: C. Winter. 2 vols. [Quoted from 3rd ed., Genève, 1951.]

————. 1921. "Langage naturel et langage artificiel." *Journal de psychologie* 18, 625–643.

———— et al. 1928. Theses in the panel *"Quelles sont les méthodes. . ."* In *Actes. . .*, 85–86.

Bareš, Gustav. 1950. "Stalin ukazuje cestu" [Stalin Shows the Way]. *Tvorba* 19, 659–661.

Baudouin de Courtenay, Jan Ignacy Niecisław. 1901[1963]. "O smešannom xaraktere vsex jazykov" [On the Mixed Character of All Languages]. *Žurnal Ministerstva narodnogo prosveščenija* no. 337, 12–24. [Quoted from Baudouin de Courtenay 1963, 1, 362–376.]

————. 1912. *Sbornik zadač po "Vvedeniju v jazykoznanie," po preimuščestvu primenitel'no k russkomu jazyku* [A Collection of Homeworks Accompanying 'The Introduction to Linguistics'—with special reference to Russian]. S.-Peterburg. Izdanie Studenčeskogo Izadatel'skogo Komiteta pri Istoriko-Filologičeskom Fakul'tete S.-Peterburskogo Universiteta.

————. 1914a. "Slovo i 'slovo'" [Word and 'Word']. [Quoted from Baudouin de Courtenay 1963, 2, 240–242.]

————. 1914b. "K teorii 'slova kak takovogo' i 'bukvy kak takovoj'" [On the Theory of 'the Word as Such' and 'the Letter As Such']. [Quoted from Baudouin de Courtenay 1963, 2, 243–245.]

————. 1963. *Izbrannye trudy po obščemu jazykoznaniju* [Selected Works on General Linguistics]. Ed. by V. P. Grigor'ev and A. A. Leont'ev. 2 vols. Moskva: Izd. Akademii nauk SSSR.

Bazijanc, A. P. 1973. *Lazarevskij institut v istorii otečestvennogo vostokovedenija* [The Lazarev Institute in the History of Oriental Studies in Russia]. Moskva: Nauka.

Becker, Henrik. 1948. *Der Sprachbund.* Leipzig and Berlin: Die Humboldt-Bücherei Gerhard Mindt. (Erkenntnisse aus allen Gebieten der Geistes- und Naturwissenschaften. Sprachwissenschaften, 1.)

Sources and References

Becking, Gustav Wilhelm. 1932. "Der musikalische Bau des Montenegrischen Volks-epos." *Proceedings of the International Congress of Phonetic Sciences*, 53–62. Amsterdam.

Bem, Al'fred Ljudvigovič. 1935. "Methodologické poznámky ke studii Jana Mukařov-ského *Polákova vznešenost přírody*" [Methodological Remarks on Mukařovský's 'Polák's *Grandeur of Nature*']. *ČMF* 21, 1934/35, 330–334.

Beneš, Bohuslav. 1968. "P. Bogatyrjov a strukturalismus" [P. Bogatyrev and Structur-alism]. *Český lid* 55, 193–206.

Berberova, Nina Nikolaevna. 1983. *Kursiv moj*. Avtobiografija [The Italics Are Mine—Autobiography]. 2nd ed. New York: Russica. 2 vols.

Berg, Lev Semenovič. 1922. *Nomogenez - ili èvoljucija na osnove zakonomernostej*. Petro-grad. [In Engl. as *Nomogenesis, or Evolution Determined by Law*, London: Constable, 1926.]

Bernštejn, Sergej Ignatevič. 1973. "Dmitrij Nikolaevič Ušakov (stranicy vospomi-nanij)" [Recollections of D. N. Ušakov]. *Vestnik Moskovskogo universiteta - Serija filolo-gija* 1973, no. 1, 78–85.

Birnbaum, Henrik. 1985. "Divergence and Convergence in Linguistic Evolution." *Papers from the 6th International Conference on Historical Linguistics*, ed. by J. Fisiak, 1–24. Amsterdam: Benjamins.

Bittner, Konrad. 1936. *Deutsche und Tschechen*. Zur Geistesgeschichte des böhmischen Raumes, I, Von den Anfängen zur hussitischen Kirchenerneuerung. Brünn: Rohrer.

Blahynka, Milan. 1978. *Vladislav Vančura*. Praha: Melantrich.

Blok, Aleksandr Aleksandrovič. 1908. "Poèzija zagovorov i zaklinanij" [The Poetry of Incantations and Magic Spells]. In *Istorija russkoj literatury do XIX v.*, ed. by E. V. Aničkov et al., vol. 2, 81–106. Moskva: Tov. I. D. Sytina [. . .].

———. 1960. *Sobranie sočinenij* [Selected Works], vol. 3. Moskva: Gos. izd. xudožest-vennoj literatury.

Bloomfield, Leonard. 1914. *An Introduction to the Study of Language*. New York: Henry Holt.

Böss, Otto. 1961. *Die Lehre der Eurasier*. Ein Beitrag zur russischen Ideengeschichte des 20. Jahrhunderts. Wiesbaden: Harrasowitz. (Veröffentlichungen des Osteuropa-Institutes München, 15.)

Bogatyrev, Petr Grigor'evič. 1916. Review V. F. Čiž *Psixologija derevenskoj častuski;* etc. *Russkij filologičeskij vestnik*, no. 76, 339–341.

———. 1923. *Češskij kukol'nyj i russkij narodnyj teatr*. [Czech Puppet Theatre and Rus-sian Folk Theatre.] Berlin and Peterburg: Izdatel'stvo OPOJAZ. (Sborniki po teorii poètičeskogo jazyka, 6.)

——— and R. Jakobson. 1923. "Programma po sobiraniju svedenij o narodnom tea-tre" [A Program for Collecting Data about Popular Theatre]. In Bogatyrev 1923: 91–121.

————. 1926. "Les apparitions and et les êtres surnaturels dans les croyances populaires de la Russie Subcarpathique." *Le Monde Slave* 3, no. 7, 34–55.

————. 1929. *Actes magiques, rites et croyances en Russie Subcarpathique.* Paris: Champion. (Travaux publiés par l'Institut d'études slaves, 11.)

————. 1930. "Erfahrungen eines Feldethnographen in Rußland und KarpathorußScience of Language]. Kazan': Tipogr. Imperatorskogo Universiteta. 3rd edition.

Bogorodickij, V. A. 1910. *Očerki po jazykovedeniju i russkomu jazyku.* Posobie pri izučenii nauki o jazyke. [Sketches on Linguistics and Russian Language. Introduction to the Science of Language]. Kazan': Tipogr. Imperatorskogo Universiteta. 3rd edition.

Bohachevsky-Chomiak, Martha. 1976. *Sergei N. Trubetskoi:* An Intellectual Among the Intelligentsia in Prerevolutionary Russia. Belmont, Mass.: Nordland.

Bosák, Ctirad et al. 1949. *Sovětská jazykověda.* Překlady vybraných studií [Russian Linguistics: Translations of Selected Studies]. Praha: Orbis.

Bowlt, John E., ed. 1976. *Russian Art of the Avant-Garde:* Theory and Criticism 1902–1934. Edited and translated by John E. Bowlt. New York: Viking.

Breton, André. 1932. *Misère de la poésie: "L'Affaire Aragon" devant l'opinion publique.* Paris: Ed. du Seuil. [Quoted from his *Œuvres complètes,* vol. 2, Paris: Gallimard, 1992.]

Brik, Ossip M. 1917 "Zvukovye povtory. (Analiz zvukovoj struktury stixa.)" [Sound Repetitions (An Analysis of the Sound Structure of the Verse)]. *Sborniki po teorii poètičeskogo jazyka* 2, 24–62. [Also in *Poètika* 58–98.]

————. 1923. "T. n. 'formal'nyj metod'" [The So-called 'Formal Method']. *Lef* 1, 213–215.

————. 1936. "Majakovskij—redaktor i organizator" [Majakovskij—Journal Editor and Organizer]. *Literaturnyj kritik* 4, 112–146.

Budín, Stanislav. 1943. "Román o zradě českých vzdělanců" [A Novel About the Treason of Czech Intellectuals]. *(Nedělní) New-Yorské Listy* vol. 53, no. 6. (Jan. 24, 1943.)

Bühler, Karl. 1909. Review Anton Marty, *Untersuchungen zur Grundlegung der allgemeinen Grammatik und Sprachphilosophie;* 1908. *Göttingische gelehrte Anzeigen* 171, 947–979.

Burbank, Jane. 1986. *Intelligentsia and Revolution:* Russian Views of Bolshevism, 1917–1922. Oxford University Press.

Burljuk, Nikolai and David. 1914[1988]. "Poetic Principles." In Lawton 1988, 82–84. [Originally 1914 under the title "Poètičeskie načala."]

Buslaev, A. A., B. V. Gornung, V. I. Nejštadt. 1956. "Materialy po istorii Moskovskogo lingvističeskogo kružka" [Materials on the History of the Moscow Linguistic Circle]. Typescript; RJP, box 28, folder 71.

Carnap, Rudolf. 1928. *Der logische Aufbau der Welt.* Scheinprobleme in der Philosophie. Berlin: Weltkreis

[———— et al.] 1929. *Wissenschaftliche Weltanschauung—Der Wiener Kreis.* Hrsg. vom Verein Ernst Mach. Wien: A. Wolf.

————. 1935. "O logické syntaxi" [On Logical Syntax]. *SaS* 1, 256. [Summary of a lecture; authorship attributed.]

Cassirer, Ernst. 1910. *Substanzbegriff und Funktionsbegriff.* Untersuchungen über die Grundfragen der Erkenntniskritik. Berlin: Bruno Cassirer.

Cassirer, Toni. 1981. *Mein Leben mit Ernst Cassirer.* Hildesheim: Gerstenberg Verlag.

Cejtlin, R. M. 1965. *Grigorij Osipovič Vinokur. 1896–1947.* Moskva: Izd. Moskovskogo universiteta.

Čemodanov, N. S. 1947. "Strukturalizm i sovetskoe jazykoznanie" [Structuralism and Soviet Linguistics]. *Izvestija Akademii nauk SSSR—Otdelenie literatury i jazyka* 6, 2, 115–124.

Červinka, Vincenc. 1921. Review Jakobson 1920/21. *Národní listy (Literární příloha)* Sept. 11, 1921. [Signed: V. Č.]

Charisteria Gvilelmo Mathesio quinqvagenario [...] oblata. Pragae, svmptibus Pražský lingvistický kroužek. 1932.

Chomsky, Noam. 1983. Untitled contribution in [no editor] *A Tribute to Roman Jakobson 1986–1982,* 81–83. Berlin: Mouton.

Chvatík, Květoslav. 1981a. *Tschechoslowakischer Strukturalismus.* Theorie und Geschichte. München: Fink.

————. 1981b. "J. L. Fischer—The Founder of Dialectical Structurology in Czech Philosophy." *Semiotics and Dialectics: Ideology and Text,* ed. by Peter Zima, 223–241. Amsterdam: Benjamins. (Linguistics and Literary Studies in Eastern Europe, 5.)

Čikobava, A. S. 1944. [In Georgian] "Structuralism as a School of Contemporary Linguistics in the West." *Trudy Tbilisskogo Gos. Universiteta,* vol. 26b, 231–244. [Title not consulted by the author.]

[Circle.] 1929. "Thèses." *TCLP* 1, 5–29. [Originally in Czech as "These k diskusi"; distributed at the First Congress of Slavic Philologists, Prague, 1929.]

[————. 1930] *Stanovy spolku "Pražský linguistický kroužek"* [Statutes of the Society 'Prague Linguistic Circle']. Typescript, 4 pp., no date [= 1930].

[————.] 1931a. "Projet de terminologie phonologique standardisée." *TCLP* 4, 309–323.

[————.] 1931b. "Principes de transcription phonologique. (Propositions du Cercle linguistique de Prague.)" *TCLP* 4, 323–326.

[————.] 1932. "Obecné zásady pro kulturu jazyka" [General Principles of Language Culture]. In Havránek and Weingart, 245–259.

[———.] 1933. "Odpověd' výboru Pražského linguistického kroužku na Hallerovy posudky [. . .]" [A Reply by the Presidium of the Prague Linguistic Circle to Haller's Reviews [. . .]]. *NŘ* 17, 204–209.

[———.] 1935. "Úvodem" [By Way of Introduction]. *SaS* 1, 1–7. [Signed by B. Havránek, R. Jakobson, V. Mathesius, J. Mukařovský, B. Trnka.]

[———.] 1936a. *Zpráva o činnosti Pražského linguistického kroužku za první desítiletí jeho trvání 1926–1936* [Report on the Activity of the Prague Linguistic Circle during the First Ten Years of Its Existence, 1926–1936]. Nákladem Pražského linguistického kroužku. [Printed in Brno.]

[———.] 1936b. "Diskuse o kritických a badatelských metodách prof. M. Weingarta" [A Discussion of Prof. M. Weingart's Critical and Scholarly Methods]. *SaS* 2, 59–61.

Č. J. 1935. Untitled gloss on Ilja Èrenburg. *Lidové noviny* Dec. 15, 1935, p. 12.

Compton, Susan, ed. 1977. *Russian Futurism 1910–1916: Poetry and Manifestos.* 54 titles on colour and monochrome microfiche. Cambridge: Chadwyck-Healy.

Čudakov, Aleksandr Pavlovič. 1990. "Sprašivaju Šklovskogo" [Asking Šklovskij Questions]. *Literaturnoe obozrenie* 1990, no. 6, 93–103.

Čudakova, M. O. 1988. *Žizneopisanie Mixaila Bulgakova* [A Biography of M. Bulgakov]. Moskva: Kniga.

——— and E. A. Toddes. 1987. "Nasledie i put' Èjxenbauma" [Èjxenbaum's Legacy and Path]. In *O Literature* by Boris Èjxenbaum, 3–32. Moskva: Sovetskij pisatel'.

Čyževs'kyj, Dmytro [Dmitrij]. 1924. *L'ogika. Konspekt lekcij* [. . .]. Praga: Vidavniče t-vo SIJaČ. [Mimeographed.]

———. 1927. "Filosofická společnost při Ruské národní universitě v Praze" [Russian Philosophical Society at the Russian National University in Prague]. *Ruch filosofický* 7, 1927/28, 63–64.

———. 1928. "Rudá filosofie" [Red Philosophy]. *Ruch filosofický* 7, 1927/28, 129–135.

———. 1930. "Krizis sovetskoj filosofii" [Crisis of Soviet Philosophy]. *Sovremennye zapiski* (Paris) 43, 471–488.

———. 1931. "Phonologie und Psychologie." *TCLP* 4, 3–22.

———. 1932. "Zur Geschichte der russischen Sprachphilosophie. Konstantin Aksakov." In *Charisteria. . .* , 18–20.

— (ed.). 1934. *Hegel bei den Slaven.* Reichenberg. Veröffentlichungen der Slavistischen Arbeitsgemeinschaft an der deutschen Universität in Prag, Heft 9. (Reprinted by Wiss. Buchgesellschaft, Darmstadt, 1961.)

———. 1936. "K problému filosofického jazyka a jazykové filosofie" [On the Problem of Philosophical Language and Language Philosophy]. *SaS* 2, 248–250.

————. 1939. "Knjaz Nikolaj Sergeevič Trubeckoj." *Sovremennye zapiski* (Paris) 68, 464–468.

————. 1976. "Prager Erinnerungen: Herkunft des Prager linguistischen Zirkels und seine Leistungen." In Matejka 1976, 15–28.

Danilevskij, Nikolai Jakovlevič. 1871. *Rossija i Evropa.* Vzgljad na kul'turnye i političeskie otnošenija Slavjanskogo mira k Germano-Romanskomu. [Russia and Europe—A View on Cultural and Political Relations Between the Slavic and Germano-Romanic World]. [Quoted from the 5th ed., St. Petersburg 1895.]

Darwin, Charles. 1983. *Autobiographies: Charles Darwin and Thomas H. Huxley,* ed. by Gavain de Beer. Oxford University Press.

Dauzat, Albert. 1910. *La vie du langage.* Paris: Armand Colin.

Decennial Report. See Circle 1936a.

de Groot, A. W. 1928. "Het eerste wereldcongres van linguisten" [The First World Congress of Linguists]. *Vragen des tijds* 1928, 432–431.

de Zurko, Edward Robert. 1957. *Origins of Functionalist Theory.* Columbia University Press.

Disertace pražské university. 1882–1945. [vol.] 2, *Německá universita* [Dissertations of the Prague University, 1882–1945, vol. 2, German University]. Praha: Universita Karlova 1965.

Dokumenty a materiály k dějinám československo-sovětských vztahů [Documents and Materials on the History of Czechoslovak-Soviet Relations]. Vol. 1, 1975. Praha: Academia.

Dokumenty i materialy po istorii sovetsko-čexoslovackix otnošenij [Documents and Materials on the History of Soviet Czechoslovak Relations]. Vol. 2, 1977. Moskva: Nauka.

Doležel, Lubomír. 1990. "Structuralism and the Prague School." (To appear in *Cambridge History of Literary Criticism.*)

Douglass, Charlotte. 1980. "Views from the New World. A. Kruchenykh and K. Malevich: Theory and Painting." In *Russian Futurism,* ed. by Ellendea and Carl R. Proffer, 353–370. Ann Arbor: Ardis.

Durnovo, N. N., N. N. Sokolov and D. N. Ušakov. 1915. *Opyt dialektologičeskoj karty russkogo jazyka v Evrope s priloženiem očerka russkoj dialektologii* [A Dialectological Map of the Russian Language in Europe Accompanied by a Sketch of Russian Dialectology]. Moskva. (Trudy Moskovskoj Dialektologičeskoj Komissii, 5.)

Durnovo, Nikolaj Nikolaevič. 1917. *Dialektologičeskie razyskanija v oblasti velikorusskix govorov.* Čast I, Južnovelikorusskoe narečie. Moskva. Trudy Moskovskoj Dialektologičeskoj Komissii, 6.

Sources and References

————. 1924. *Očerk istorii russkogo jazyka* [A Sketch of the History of Russian Language]. Moskva-Leningrad: Gos. izd.

————. 1927. *Vvedenie v istoriju russkogo jazyka*. Čast' I, Istočniki. [An Introduction to the History of Russian Language; Part One: Sources.] Brno: Filosofická fakulta.

————. 1931. Review of Karcevskij 1927. *Slavia* 10, 140–165.

————. 1969. *Vvedenie v istoriju russkogo jazyka* [An Introduction to the History of Russian Language]. Moskva: Nauka.

Eagle, Herbert. 1990. "Afterword." In Lawton 1990, 281–304.

Effenberger, Vratislav. 1983. "Roman Jakobson and the Czech Avant-Garde between the Wars." *American Journal of Semiotics* vol. 2, no. 3, 13–21.

Einstein, Albert. 1930. "Alber Einstein o kolektivismu" [Albert Einstein on Collectivism]. *Plán* 1, 1929/30, 316. [Translation from Russian of a letter in *Literaturnaja gazeta*, Moscow.]

———— and Michele Besso. 1972. *Correspondence, 1903–1955.* Ed. by Pierre Speziali. Paris: Hermann.

Èjxenbaum, B. M. 1919. "Kak sdelana 'Šinel' Gogolja" [How Gogol's Šinel is Done]. *Poètika* 151–165.

Èrenburg, Ilja. 1922. *A vse-taki ona vertitsja* [But It Does Turn]. Berlin-Moskva: Gelikon. [Excerpts in Czech in *Život* 2, 29–34.]

————. 1933. "Surrealisté" [Surrealists]. *Tvorba* 8, 645–646. (Oct. 12, 1933.) [Translated from Russian, originally in *Pravda* (?).]

Erlich, Victor. 1955. *Russian Formalism: History, Doctrine.* The Hague: Mouton.

Essen, Arthur Joseph van. 1983. *E. Kruisinga:* A Chapter in the History of Linguistics in the Netherlands. Leiden: Nijhoff.

Fischer, Josef Ludvík. 1929. *Über die Zukunft der europäischen Kultur.* München: Drei Masken Verlag.

————. 1930. "O dvojím řádu" [On Two Orders]. *Česká mysl* 26, 347–353.

————. 1931. *Základy poznání;* 1: Soustava skladebné filosofie na podkladě zkušenosti. [Foundations of Knowledge, Book 1: The System of Synthetic Philosophy on the Basis of Experience]. Praha: Melantrich. (Výhledy, 8.)

————. 1932. *Zrcadlo doby*—Abeceda skoro filosofická [Mirror of the Time—A Breviary Almost Philosophical]. Praha: Orbis. (Perspektivy, 2.)

————. 1933. "Potřeba kulturní revise" [Necessity of a Cultural Revision]. *Listy pro umění a kritiku* 1, 34–41.

Fischer, Otokar. 1932. "Nástup linguistů" [Linguists' Offensive]. *Čin* 4, 1932/33, 267–273.

Flejšman, Lazar, ed. 1977. "Tomaševskij i Moskovskij lingvističeskij kružok" [Tomaševskij and the Moscow Linguistic Circle]. *Trudy po znakovym sistemam* 9, 113–132. [Author's name missing.]

Fried, Vilém. 1985. "Vilém Mathesius—Begründer der tschechischen Anglistik. Englische Literatur und englische Kultur im tschechischen Kontext." *Literatur im Kontext—Festschrift für Helmut Schrey* [. . .], ed. by R. Haas and C. Klein-Braley, 95–112. Sankt Augustin: H. Richarz.

Frinta, Antonín. 1931. "Německá společnost pro slavistické badání v Praze" [German Society for Slavic Research in Prague]. *Slovanský přehled* 23, 474–475.

Gabo, Naum. 1957. *Gabo:* Constructions, Sculpture, Paintings, Drawings, Engravings, with introductory essays by Herbert Read and Leslie Martin. Harvard University Press.

Galan, František W. 1985. *Historic Structures*. The Prage School Project, 1928–1946. University of Texas Press. (University of Texas Press Slavic Series, 7.)

Gasparov, Boris. 19264. "The Ideological Principles of Prague School Phonology." In Pomorska et al., eds., 49–78.

Gebauerová, M. 1926. *Rodinné vzpomínky na Jana Gebauera*. [Family Recollections of Jan Gebauer]. Vol. 2, [The Years] *1886–1888*. Kladno: J. Šnajdr.

Geografičeskij i Antropologičeskij kružok studentov Moskovskogo Universiteta [The Geographical and Anthropological Student Circle at the Moscow University]. Moskva: Tipogr. Kušnerev, 1914.

Ginneken, Jacobus van. 1907. *Principes de linguistique psychologique*. Essai de synthèse. Paris: M. Rivière.

Ginzburg, Moisei. 1982[1924]. *Style and Epoch*. Introduction and translation by A. Senkevich, Jr. MIT Press. [Originally 1924.]

Golanov, I. 1925. "Moskovskaja Dialektologičeskaja Komissija (1904–1924)" [Moscow Commission for Dialectology 1904–1924]. *Slavia* 3, 1924/1925, 749–757.

Gornung, Boris Vladimirovič. Ca. 1970. Recording of an untitled lecture on the Moscow Linguistic Circle. Deposited in the Institute of Russian Language, Russian Academy of Sciences, Moscow, Phono-archives A-790.

Grammont, Maurice. 1916. "Zvuk, kak sredstvo vyraziteľnosti reči" [Sound as a Means of Linguistic Expressivity]. *Sborniki. . .* 1, 51–60. [Vladimir B. Šklovskij's translation from Maurice Grammont *Le vers francais*, 195–207, Paris: Champion, 1913.]

Grygar, Mojmír. 1951. "Teigovština—trockistická agentura v naší kultuře" [Teigeism—A Vehicle of Trotskyism in Our Culture]. *Tvorba* 20, 1008–1010; 1036–1038; 1060–1062.

Halle, Morris. 1977. "Roman Jakobson's Contribution to the Modern Study of Speech Sounds." In Armstrong and Schooneveld, 79–100.

———. 1979. "Roman Jakobson." *International Encyclopedia of the Social Sciences* 18, Biographical Suppl. 335–341. New York: Macmillan.

———. 1983. "On the Origin of Distinctive Features." In *Roman Jakobson: What He Taught Us*, ed. by Morris Halle. *International Journal of Slavic Linguistics and Poetics*, vol. 27, 77–86; Supplement.

———. 1987. "Remarks on the Scientific Revolution in Linguistics 1926–1929." In Pomorska et al., 95–112.

———. 1988a. "N. S. Troubetzkoy et les origines de la phonologie moderne." *Cahiers Ferdinand de Saussure* 42, 5–22.

———. 1988b. "The Bloomfield-Jakobson Correspondence, 1944–1946." *Language* 64, 737–760.

Haller, Jiří. 1930. Review V. Nezval *Kronika z konce tisíciletí. NŘ* 14, 153–163.

———. 1931a. "Služba jazyku" [In Service of Language]. *Přítomnost* 8, 204–205 .

———. 1931b. Review O. Fischer *Duše a slovo. NŘ* 15, 44–62.

Hansen-Löve, Aage. 1978. *Der russische Formalismus: Methodologische Rekonstruktion seiner Entwicklung aus dem Prinzip der Verfremdung.* Wien. (Sitzungsber. d. Österr. Akad. d. Wiss., Phil.-hist. Klasse, 336.)

———. 1937. *A. St. Mágrovi k padesátým narozeninám* [For A. S. M. On the Occasion of His 50th Birthday]. Praha. [Published privately.]

Havránek, Bohumil 1919. Review *Encyklopedia polska. , Język polski. LF* 46, 231–250.

———. 1922. Review J. Reisser *Česko-německý poštovní a telegrafní slovník;* 1919/21. *NŘ* 6, 212–216.

———. 1923. Review A. Mazon *Grammaire de la langue Tchèque. NŘ* 7, 298–306.

———. 1924a. "K české dialektologii" [On Czech Dialectology]. *LF* 51, 263–271; 337–358.

———. 1924b. Review M. Weingart (1924). *Južnoslovenski filolog* 4, 216–219.

———. 1925. "Přehled vědecké činnosti Josefa Zubatého" [A Survey of J. Zubatý's Scholarly Work]. *ČMF* 11, 1924/25, 193–205.

———. 1928. *Genera verbi v slovanských jazycích* [Verbal Gender in Slavic Languages]. Praha. (*Rozpravy Královské české společnosti nauk;* tř. fil.-hist.-jazykozpytná, nová řada, 2.)

———. 1931. "Josef Zubatý." *The Slavonic Review* 10, 176–179.

————— and Miloš Weingart, eds. 1932. *Spisovná čeština a jazyková kultura* [Standard Czech and Language Culture]. Praha: Melantrich.

————— [& Roman Jakobson]. 1939. "Bibliographie des travaux de N. S. Trubetzkoy." *TCLP* 8, 335–342. [Jakobson's name not included in the list of authors.]

—————. 1940. "Strukturalismus." *Ottův slovník naučný nové doby — Dodatky* vol. 6, pt. 1, p. 452. Praha: Otto.

————— and Jan Mukařovský, eds. 1942. *Čtení o jazyce a poesii* [Readings on Language and Poetry]. Praha: Družstevní práce.

—————. 1948. "Naše pojetí slovanské filologie a její dnešní úkoly" [Our Conception of Slavic Philology and Its Present Tasks]. *Slavia* 18, 1947/48, 264–268.

—————. 1950a. "Tvůrce nové sovětské jazykovědy" [The Creator of New Soviet Linguistics]. *Slovanský přehled* 36, 33–34. [January 1950.]

—————. 1950b. "Stalinova stat' a česká linguistika" [Stalin's Article and Czech Linguistics]. *Tvorba* 19, 688–689.

—————. 1951. *Stalinovy práce o jazyce a jazyk literárního díla* [Stalin's Works on Language, and the Language of Literary Works]. Praha: Československý spisovatel. (Knihovnička Varu, 29.)

————— and František Černý, eds. 1952. *Janu Mukařovskému k šedesátce.* Praha: Československý spisovatel.

—————. 1979. "Retrospektivní pohled na jazykovou kulturu" [A Retrospective Look at Language Culture]. In *Aktuální otázky jazykové kultury v socialistické společnosti,* ed. by J. Kuchař, 9–11. Praha: Academia.

hbl. 1925. "Russische Studentenzeitschriften in Prag." *PrPr* January 31, 1925, p. 6.

Hjelmslev, Louis. 1939. "N. S. Trubetzkoy †." *Archiv für vergleichende Phonetik* 3, 55–60.

Hofmannsthal, Hugo von. 1902. "Ein Brief." [Quoted from his *Gesammelte Werke,* vol. 7, 461–472, Frankfurt/M.: Fischer Verlag.]

Holenstein, Elmar. 1975. *Roman Jakobsons phänomenologischer Strukturalismus.* Frankfurt/M.: Suhrkamp.

—————. 1977. "Jakobson's Contribution to Phenomenology." In Armstrong and Schooneveld, 145–162.

—————. 1979. "Von der Poesie und der Plurifunktionalität der Sprache." In Jakobson 1979, 7–60.

—————. 1981. "Monofunctionalism in Architecture between the Wars (Le Corbusieur and the Bauhaus)." *Oppositions: A Journal for Ideas and Criticism in Architecture* 24, 49–61.

————. 1984. "'Die russische ideologische Tradition' und die deutsche Romantik." *Das Erbe Hegels, II*, mit Beiträgen von R. Jakobson, H.-G. Gadamer und E. Holenstein, 21–142. Frankfurt/M.: Suhrkamp.

Holton, Gerald. 1973. *Thematic Origins of Scientific Thought: Kepler to Einstein*. Harvard University Press.

Holý, Jiří. 1990. *Práce a básnivost*. Estetický projekt světa Vladislava Vančury. [Work and Poetic Vison. Vladislav Vančura's Esthetic Project of the World.] Praha: Československý spisovatel.

Honzl, Jindřich. 1937. "Po návštěvě Vs. E. Meiercholda v Praze" [After V. E. Meierhold's Visit to Prague]. *Praha/Moskva* 1, 1936/37, 276–277.

Horálek, K., and Z. Tyl. 1954 "Soupis prací akad. Bohuslava Havránka" [Bibliography of Works by Academcian Bohuslav Havránek]. *Studie a práce linguistické*, I [Festschrift Havránek], 529–551. Praha: Nakl. Českosl. akademie věd.

Hostovský, Egon. 1942. *Sedmkrát v hlavní úloze* [Seven Times the Leading Man]. New Yorkský Denník. (Knihovna Zítřka, 1.)

Hujer, Oldřich. 1913. Obituary F. de Saussure. *LF* 40, 160.

————. 1922. "Češka filologija i lingvisitka od 1907–1921 god" [Czech Philology and Linguistics between 1907 and 1923]. *Južnoslovenski filolog* 3, 1922/23, 112–130.

Husserl, Edmund. 1909. *Logičeskie issledovanija*. Čast' pervaja: Prolegomeny k čistoj logike. [. . .] perevod È. A. Bernštejna, pod redakciej S. L. Franka. Sankt Peterburg: Obrazovanie.

————. 1911."Filosofija kak strogaja nauka" [Philosophy as a Rigorous Science]. *Logos* (Moscow) 1911, no. 1, 1–56.

————. 1936. "O fenomenologii jazyka" [Phenomenology of language]. *SaS* 2, 64. [summary of a lecture]

Isačenko, Alexander. 1934. "Der eurasische Sprachbund." *Orient und Occident* no. 17, 30–34.

————. 1949. "Základy materialistickej jazykovedy" [Foundations of Materialist Linguistics]. *Slovenská reč* 15, 1949/50, 65–74.

————. ed. 1950. *Za marxistickú jazykovedu*. Sborník prejavov v diskusii o sovietskej jazykovede. [For Marxist Linguistics. A Collection of Contributions to the Discussion About Soviet Linguistics.] Bratislava: Slovenská akadémia vied a umení.

Ivanov, Vjačeslav V. 1957. "Lingvističeskie vzgljady E. D. Polivanova" [E. D. Polivanov's Linguistic Outlooks]. *Voprosy jazykoznanija* 1957, no. 3, 54–76.

————. 1987. "Poètika Romana Jakobsona" [Roman Jakobson's Poetics]. In Jakobson 1987a, pp. 5–22.

Ivask, George. 1976. "Russian Modernist Poets and the Mystic Sectarians." *Russian Modernism: Culture and the Avant-Garde, 1900–1930*, ed. by George Gibian and H. W. Tjalsma, 65–106. Cornell University Press.

Jaffé, H. L. C. 1965. *De Stijl 1917–1931*. Der niederländische Beitrag zur modernen Kunst. Frankfurt/M.: Ullstein. (Originally in English, Amsterdam 1956.)

Jakobson, Roman. Ca. 1907/08. "Èkskursija po moej komnate" [An Excursion Through My Room]. [Quoted from Jangfeldt 1990: 121–123.]

———. 1915 [1966]. "O jazyke proizvedenij Tred'jakovskogo" [On the Language of Tred'jakovskij's Works]. (Printed as "Vlijanie narodnoj slovesnosti na Trediakovskogo" [Influence of Folk-poetry on Trediakovskij] in his *SW* 4, 613–633.)

———. 1916a. Review of Durnovo et al. 1915. *ÈO* 1916, no. 109–110, 102–107. [Signed: R. Ja.]

———. 1916b. Untitled report on a field trip. *ÈO* 1916, 1–2, 147.

———. [not after 1919.] "K voprosu o nacional'nom samoopredelenii" [On the Question of National Selfdetermination]. [Lecture in Moscow Linguistic Circle; not preserved, listed in Golanov 1925, 753.]

———. 1919a. "Futurizm." *Iskusstvo* Aug. 2, 1919. [Signed: R. Ja.; collected in his *SW* 3, 717–722.]

———. 1919b. "Zadači xudožestvennoj propagandy" [Tasks of Artistic Propaganda]. *Iskusstvo* no. 8, p. 1. (Sept. 5, 1919.) [Signed: Aljagrov; collected in Jakobson 1987a, 421, with last paragraph missing.]

———. 1920a. "Novoe iskusstvo Zapada" [New Art in the West]. *Xudožestvennaja žizn'* March–April 1920, pp. 18–20. [Signed: R. Ja.]

———. 1920b. "Stav kultury v Rusku" [The State of Culture in Russia]. *Lidové noviny* vol. 23, no. 356, p. 5. (July 21, 1920.) [Interview by N. Melniková-Papoušková.]

———. 1920c. "Prof. Šaxmatov." *Čas* vol. 30, no. 68, p. 2. (August 31, 1920.)

———. 1920d. "Velimir Xlebnikov: Z poematu Sestry blýskavice." *Den* vol. 1, no. 24, p. 19. (Dec. 27, 1920.) [Translation, signed: R. A. (= Roman Aljagrov).]

———. 1920/21. "Vliv revoluce na ruský jazyk. Poznámky ke knize André Mazona *Lexique de la guerre et de la revolution en Russie*" [The Influence of the Revolution on the Russian Language. Observations on André Mazon's Book . . .]. *Nové Atheneum* 2, 1920/21, 110–114, 200–212, 250–255, 310–318.

———. 1921a. *Novejšaja russkaja poèzija*. Nabrosok pervyj [The Latest Russian Poetry: A First Sketch]. Tipografija "Politika" v Prage. [Also in his SW 5, 299–354.]

———. 1921b. "Professor V. N. Ščepkin. (1863–1920)." *Čas* Feb. 3, 1921, p. 4 .

———. 1921c. "Ruský básník před soudem ruské literatury" [A Russian Poet in the Court of Russian Literature]. *Tribuna* vol. 3, no. 45, pp. 1–2. (February 23, 1921.)

————. 1921d. "Dada." *Vestnik teatra* no. 82, February 1921. [Signed: R. Ja.; collected in Jakobson 1987a, 430–434.]

————. 1921d. Excerpt from a letter to Majakovskij from Feb. 8, 1921. In *Poètičeskaja kul'tura Majakovskogo*, ed. by N. I. Xardžiev and V. V. Trenin, p. 148. Moskva: Iskusstvo 1970.

————. 1921e. "Vivisekce jako nejbližší úkol vědy o umění" [Vivisection as the Nearest Goal of the Science of Art]. *Kmen* 4, 1920/21, 545–546 [no. 46, Feb. 10, 1921]. [An excerpt in Czech from Jakobson 1921a.]

————. 1921f. "O realismu v umění" [About Realism in Art]. *Červen* 4, 300–304. (Oct. 13, 1921.)

————. 1922. "Brjusovskaja stixologija i nauka o stixe." *Naučnye izvestija—Akademičeskij centr Narkomprosa RSFSR*, vol. 2: *Filosofija, literatura, iskusstvo*, 222–240.

———— and Petr Bogatyrev. 1922/23. "Slavjanskaja filologija v Rossii za g. g. 1914–1921" [Slavic Philology in Russia during 1914–1921]. *Slavia* 1, 1922/23, 171–184; 457–469; 626–636. [Authors listed in this order.]

————. 1923a. *O češskom stixe preimuščestvenno v sopostavlenii s russkim* [On the Czech Verse, Primarily in Comparison with the Russian Verse]. OPOJAZ-MLK (Berlin). [Quoted from reprint Brown University Press 1969.]

————. 1923b. "Zametka o drevne-bolgarskom stixosloženii" [A Note on Old Bulgarian Verse]. *Izvestija Otdelenija russkogo jazyka i slovesnosti Rossijskoj Akademii Nauk 1919* g. 24, 2, 351–358. [Dated 1917.]

————. 1924. "Staročešskie stixotvorenija, složennye odnorifmennymi četverostišijami." *Slavia* 3, 1924/25, 272–315. [Also in his *SW* 6, 538–583.]

————. 1925a. "Konec básnického umprumáctví a živnostnictví" *Pásmo* no. 14/15, pp. 1–2. (May 1925.)

————. 1925b. "Ein neuer Beitrag zur slavischen Verslehre." *PrPr* no. 183, p. 6–7. (July 5, 1925.)

————. 1925c. "Dopolnenie" [footnote in Golanov 1925]. *Slavia* 3, 1924/25, 753.

————. 1926a. *Základy českého verše* [Foundations of the Czech Verse]. Praha: Odeon.

————. 1926b. "Nikolaj Durnovo." *PrPr* Nov. 4, 1926.

————. 1927a. *Fonetika odnogo severno-velikorusskogo govora s namečajuščejsja perexodnost'ju*. [Phonetics of a North-Russian Dialect with a Transitional Character.] Praha: Litografie Jarkovský. [Also in his *SW* 1, 571–613.]

————. 1927b. "Dvě staročeské skladby o smrti" [Two Old Czech Compositions on Death]. In his *Spor duše s tělem: O nebezpečném času smrti*, pp. 7–36. Praha: Kuncíř.

————, S. Karcevskij, and N. S. Trubetzkoy. 1928a. "Proposition 22: Toute description scientifique..." *Actes...*, 33–36.

―――. 1928b. "O hláskoslovném zákonu a teleologickém hláskosloví" [The Concept of the Sound Law and Teleological Sound Study]. *ČMF* 14, 183–184.

―――. 1928c. "Wandlungen in der Sprachwissenschaft: Vom I. Internationalen Linguistenkongreß im Haag." *PrPr* April 25, 1928, p. 7.

―――. 1929a. *Remarques sur l'évolution phonologique du russe comparée à celle des autres langues slaves.* Praha. (*TCLP* 2.) [Also in his *SW* 1, 7–116.]

―――. 1929b. "Zur vergleichenden Forschung über die slavischen Zehnsilbler." *Slavische Studien V - Franz Spina zum sechzigsten Geburtstag* 7–20. Reichenberg. [Also in his *SW* 4, 19–37.]

―――. 1929c. *Nejstarší české písně duchovní* [The Oldest Czech Spiritual Songs]. Praha: Kuncíř. (Národní knihovna, 6.)

―――. 1929d. "Dem Gedächtnis Jan Wiktor Porzezińskis." *PrPr* March 17, 1929.

―――. 1929e. "Über die heutigen Vorraussetzungen der russischen Slavistik" *SRund* 1, 629–646.

―――. 1929f. "Kus literární pavědy" [A Piece of Literary Pseudo-science]. *Plán* 1, 593–597.

―――. 1929g. "Romantické všeslovanství—nová slavistika" [Romantic Pan-Slavism— New Slavistics]. *Čin* 1, 1929/30, 10–12.

―――. 1930. "Jazykové problémy v Masarykově díle" [Language Questions in Masaryk's Work]. *Masarykův sborník* 5, 396–414.

――― and Friedrich Slotty. 1930. "Die Sprachwissenschaft auf dem ersten Slavistenkongress in Prag vom 6.–13. Oktober 1929." *Indogermanisches Jahrbuch* 14, 384–391.

―――. 1931a. *K xarakteristike evrazijskogo jazykogo sojuza* [On the Character of the Eurasian Linguistic Union]. Paris: Izdanie Evrazijcev. [Also in his *SW* vol. 1, 144–201.]

―――. 1931b. "O fonologičeskix jazykovyx sojuzax" [On Phonological Language Unions]. In *Evrazija v svete jazykoznanija,* ed. by R. Jakobson and N. S. Savickij, pp. 7–12. Paris. [Printed in Prague.]

―――. 1931c. "Über die phonologischen Sprachbünde." *TCLP* 4, 234–240. [German version of Jakobson 1931b.]

―――. 1931d. "O pokolenii, rastrivšix svoix poetov" [About the Generation that Lost Its Poets]. In *Smert' Vladimira Majakovskogo* [no editor], 7–45. Berlin: Petropolis. [Also in his *SW* 5, 355–381.]

―――. 1931e. "Neue tschechoslovakische Arbeiten über die poetische Form (1929–1930)." *SRund* 3, 450–454.

―――. 1931f. "Pamjati Vjačeslava Vjačeslavoviča Ganki" [In Memory of Václav Hanka]. *Central'naja Evropa* 4, 268–275. [Also in his *SW* 6, 696–703.]

————. 1931g. "Vladislav Vančura: Markéta Lazarová." *Literární noviny* May 9, 1931.

————. 1931h. "Der russische Frankreich-Mythus." *SRund* 3, 636–642.

————. 1931i. "Der Genfer Linguistenkongress." *PrPr* Sept. 13, 1931.

————. 1931j. "Prof. Friedrich Slotty." *PrPr* Sept. 18, 1931.

————. 1932a. O jednom typu literárních historiků" [About a Type of Literary Historians]. *Jarní Almanach Kmene* 112–116. Praha: Kmen.

————. 1932b. "Prof. Vilém Mathesius: Zu seinem 50. Geburtstag." *PrPr* Aug. 3, 1932.

————. 1932c. "Musikwissenschaft und Linguistik." *PrPr* Dec. 7, 1932. [Also in his *SW* 2, 551–553.]

————. 1932d. "Fonéma." *Ottův slovník naučný nové doby* — *Dodatky* vol. 2, 608. Praha: Otto. [Signed: R. J.; in English in his *SW* 1, 231–233.]

————. 1933a. "La Scuola Linguistica di Praga." *La Cultura* (Firenze) 12, 633–641. [Also in his *SW* 2, 539–546.]

————. 1933b. "Aleksandr Matveevič Peškovskij." *PrPr* April 11, 1933.

————. 1934a. "O předpokladech pražské linguistické školy" [On Preconditions of the Prague Linguistic School]. *Index* (Brno) 6, no. 1, 6–9.

————. 1934b. "Slavische Sprachfragen in der Sovjetunion." *SRund* 6, 324–343.

————. 1934c. "Perpetuum mobile kyvadla: Pokus o montáž" [Perpetuum mobile of the Pendulum: An Attempt at a Collage]. *Listy pro umění a kritiku* 2, 73–79. [Signed: R. J.]

————. 1934d. "Co je poesie?" [What Is Poetry?] *Volné směry* 30, 1933/34, 229–239.

————. 1935a. "Poznámky k dílu Erbenovu [Notes on Erben's Oeuvre]." *SaS* 1, 152–164; 218–229.

————. 1935b. "Obecná linguistika v SSSR" [General Linguistics in the USSR]. *SaS* 1, 187–188.

————. 1935c. "Diskuse o metodologických problémech v práci Mukařovského 'Polákova vznešenost přírody'" [Discussion about Methodological Problems in Mukařovský's 'Polák's *Grandeur of Nature*']. *SaS* 1, 192.

————. 1935d. "Linguistika" [Linguistics]. *Ottův slovník naučný nové doby* - Dodatky [. . .], Vol. 3, ii, 1214–1216. Praha: Otto.

————. 1935e. "Společná řeč kultury. Poznámky k otázkám vzájemných styků sovětské a západní vědy" [A Common Language of Culture: Remarks on Relations between Soviet and Western Science]. *Země sovětů* 4, 1935/36, 109–111.—In German as "Gemeinsame Kultursprache" *PrPr* June 6, 1935, p. 2.

318
Sources and References

————. 1935f. "Kontury Glejtu" [The Contours of *The Safe Conduct*]. In *Glejt*, by B. Pasternak, pp. 149–162. Praha: SVU Mánes. [Quoted from his *Studies in Verbal Art*, pp. 386–394. Ann Arbor: Michigan Slavic Publications. 1971.]

————. 1936a. "Beitrag zur allgemeinen Kasuslehre (Gesamtbedeutungen der russischen Kasus)." *TCLP* 6, 240–288. [Also in his *SW* 2, 23–71.]

————. 1936b. "Metrika" [Metrics]. *Ottův slovník naučný nové doby — Dodatky* vol. 4, 213–218. Praha: Otto. [Signed: R. J.: also in his *SW* 5, 281–286.]

————. 1936c. "O cestách k české poesii gotické" [Approaches to Czech Medieval Poetry]. *Život* 14, 57–63.

————. 1936d. "Úvahy o básnictví doby husitské" [Thoughts on the Poetry of the Hussite Period]. *SaS* 2, 1–21.

————. 1936e. "Památce Agenora Artymoviče" [In Memory of Agenor Artymovič]. *SaS* 2, 63–64.

————. 1936f. "Usměrněné názory na staročeskou kulturu" [Curtailed Opinions on Czech Culture]. *SaS* 2, 207–222.

————. 1936g. "Um den russischen Wortschatz." *SRund* 8, 80–90.

————. 1936h. "Památce G. I. Čelpanova" [G. I. Čelpanov in Memoriam]. *Psychologie* (Brno) 2, no. 2, 41–43.

————. 1937a. "Antoine Meillet zum Gedächtnis." *SRund* 9, 24–26.

————. 1937b. "Dopis Romana Jakobsona Jiřímu Voskovci a Janu Werichovi o noetice a semantice švandy" [A Letter by Roman Jakobson to J. Voskovec and J. Werich about Noetics and Semantics of Fun]. *Deset let Osvobozeného divadla*, 27–34. Praha: Borový.

————. 1937c. "Puškin v realistickém světle" [Pushkin in the Light of Realism]. *(Program) D 37* vol. 6, 136–137. (Jan. 23, 1937.)

————. 1938a. "Sur la théorie des affinités phonologiques." *Actes du IV Congrès International des Linguistes*, Copenhague 1936, pp. 48–58. Copenhagen: Munksgaard. [Also in his *SW* 1, 234–246.]

————. 1938b. "Ruské výpravy do budoucna" [Russian Expeditions into the Future]. *Lidové noviny* Jan. 1, 1938. [Sunday supplement.]

————. 1938c. "Rád odpovídám na dotaz [. . .]" [I gladly answer the questions. . .]. *U: Čtvrtletník skupiny Blok* 3, 86–87. (March 31, 1938)

————. 1938d. "Professor František Trávníček 50 Jahre." *PrPr* Aug. 17, 1938.

————. 1938e. "Franz Spina." *SRund* 10, no. 6, 1–5.

————. 1939a. "Nikolaj Sergeevič Trubetzkoy (16. April 1890—25. Juni 1938)." *Acta Linguistica* 1, 64–76.

————. 1939b. Review N. van Wijk *Phonologie;* 1939. *Acta Linguistca* 1, 123–129. [Also in his *SW* 1, 311–316.]

————. 1939c[1962]. "Zur Struktur de Phonems." In his *SW 1,* 280–310.

————. 1941. *Kindersprache, Aphasie und allgemeine Lautgesetze.* Uppsala: Almquist and Wiksell. *Språkvetenskapliga Sällskapets i Uppsala Förhandlingar,* 1940–42. [Also in his *SW* 1, 328–401.]

————. 1950. Letter to Angelo M. Ripellino. In Ripellino, p. 26.

————, Gunnar Fant, and Morris Halle. 1952. *Preliminaries to Speech Analysis.* Technical Report no. 13, MIT Acoustics Laboratory.

————. 1962. "Zur Struktur des Phonems." In his *SW* 1, 280–310. [Written in 1939.]

———— and Morris Halle. 1964. "The Term Canaan in Medieval Hebrew." In *For Max Weinreich* [. . .], pp. 147–172. The Hague: Mouton. [Also in his *SW* 6, 858–886.]

————. 1966. "Retrospect." In his *SW* 4, 635–704.

————. 1969a. "Deux lettres de Roman Jakobson" [à Jean-Pierre Faye]. *Change* (Paris) 3, 51.

————. 1969b[1988]. "Přípitek české zemi a lidu" [A Toast to the Czech Lands and Their People]. *Wiener Slavistisches Jahrbuch* 34, 1988, 177–182. [Also in *SaS* 52, 1–3.]

————. 1973. "Interview with Laszlo Dezö." Undated tape; in Russian. Jakobson Papers, box 122.

————. 1974. *Der Lebensweg eines Sprachforschers—Roman Jakobson erzählt.* Radio der deutschen und der rätoromanischen Schweiz.) Redigiert von Elmar Holenstein. Typescript.

————, ed. 1975. *N. S. Trubetzkoy's Letters and Notes.* Prepared for publication by Roman Jakobson with the assistance of H. Baran, O. Ronen, and Martha Taylor. The Hague: Mouton.

————. 1976a. *Six lessons sur le son et le sens.* Préface de Claude Lévi-Strauss. Paris: Editions de Minuit. [Also in his *SW* 8, 2, 317–390.]

————. 1976b. "Petr Bogatyrev (29.I.93–18.VIII.71): Expert in Transfiguration." In Matejka 1976, 293–304.

————. 1976c. "Roman Jakobson osmdesátiletý" [Roman Jakobson Eighty Years Old]. *Listy* (Rome) 6, 6, 25–29. [Interview by A. J. Liehm.]

———— and Linda Waugh. 1979. *The Sound Shape of Language.* Indiana University Press.

————. 1980. "Art and Poetry: The Cubo-Futurists. An Interview with Roman Jakobson by David Shapiro." *The Avant-Garde in Russia 1910–1930: New Perspectives,* ed. by

Stephanie Barron and Maurice Tuchman, p. 18. Los Angeles County Museum of Art [. . .].

―――. 1981. "To [sic] the History of the Moscow Linguistic Circle." *Logos Semantikos: Studia in Honorem Eugenio Coseriu* 1921–1981, ed. by Horst Geckeler et al., vol. 1, 285–288. [Also in his *SW* 7, 279–282.]

―――. 1982. "Po povodu knigi N. S. Trubetzkogo *Evropa i čelovečestvo.*" In his *SW* vol. 7, 305–313. [Originally as introduction to the Italian translation of Trubetzkoy 1920, Torino: Einaudi, 1982.]

―――. 1984a. "La théorie saussurienne en rétrospection." *Linguistics* 22, 161–196.

―――. 1984b. "Réponses" [Interview by Tzvetan Todorov and Jean José Marchand]. *Poétique* no. 57, 3–25.

―――. 1984c. "Iz kommentarij k stixam Majakovskogo 'Tovariščū Nette—paroxodu i čeloveku'" [From the Commentaries to Majakovskij's 'For Comrade Nette—Steamer and Man']. *Semiosis* [. . .] *In Honorem Georgi Lotman*, ed. by Morris Halle et al., 65–69. Ann Arbor: Michigan Slavic Publications.

―――. 1985a. *Izbrannye raboty* [Selected Works]. Ed. by V. A. Zvegincev. Moskva: Progress.

―――. 1985b. "From Alyagrov's Letters." In *Russian Formalism: A Retrospective Glance* [V. Erlich Festschrift], ed. by Robert S. Jackson and Stephen Rudy, pp. 1–5. Yale Center for International Studies.

―――. 1987a. *Raboty po poètike* [Works on Poetics]. Ed. by M. L. Gasparov. Moskva: Progress.

―――. 1987b. *Language in Literature.* Ed. by K. Pomorska and S. Rudy. Harvard University Press.

―――. 1988. *Besedy* [Conversations]. In his *SW* 8, pp. 437–582.

Jakovlev, Nikolaj Feofanovič. 1923. *Tablicy fonetiki kabardinskogo jazyka / Tables phonétiques de la langue Cabarde.* Moskva. (Trudy podrazrjada issledovanija severnokavkazskix jazykov pri Institute vostokovedenija v Moskve, 1.)

Jakovenko, Boris. 1929/30. "Ed. Husserl und die russische Philosophie." *Der russische Gedanke* 1, 1929/30, 210–212.

Jakubinskij, Lev P. 1916. "O zvukax stixotvornogo jazyka" [On the Sounds of Verse Language]. *Sborniki.* . . 1, 16–30. [Also in *Poètika* 37–49.]

―――. 1917a. "Skoplenie odinakovyx plavnyx v praktičeskom i poetičeskom jazykax" [Clusters of Identical Liquids in Practical and Poetic Language]. *Sborniki.* . . 2, 15–23. [Also in *Poètika* 50–57.]

―――. 1917b. "Osuščestvlenie zvukovogo edinoobrazija v tvorčestve Lermontova" [Formation of Sound Uniformity in Lermontov]. *Sborniki.* . . 2, 63–70.

————. 1919. "O poetičeskom glossemosočetanii" [On Glossematic Complexes in Poetic Language]. *Poètika* 7–12.

————. 1931. "F. de Sossjur o nevozmožnosti jazykovoj politiki" [F. de Saussure on the Impossibility of Language Policy]. *Jazykovedenije i materializm*, vol. 2., ed. by N. A. Marr, pp. 91–104. Moskva/Leningrad: Gos. social'no-ekonomičeskoe izd.

————. 1986. *Izbrannye raboty: Jazyk i ego funkcionirovanie.* Moskva: Nauka.

Janecek, Gerald. 1981. "Baudouin de Courtenay versus Kručenyx." *Russian Literature* 10, 17–30.

Jangfeldt, Bengt. 1976. *Majakovskij and Futurism 1917–1921.* Stockholm: Almqvist and Wiksell.

————. 1986. "Introduction." In *Love is the Heart of Everything*, by V. V. Mayakovsky, pp. 3–41. Edinburgh: Polygon.

————, ed. 1992. *Jakobson-budetljanin:* Sbornik materialov [Jakobson, the Futurist—A Collection of Materials]. Stockholm: Almqvist and Wiksell. (Stockholm Studies in Russian Literature, 26.)

Janko, Josef. 1908. "Philologie.—Rückblick auf das Vierteljahrhundert 1882–1907." *Čechische Revue* 2, 204–209; 273–283; 378–388.

————. 1911. "Na filosofické fakultě. (Prvá z volné řady kapitol.)." *Přehled* 9, 1910/11, 389–390, 414–415.

Jankovič, Milan. 1965. "K pojctí sémantického gesta" [On the Concept of Semantic Gesture]. *Česká literatura* 13, 319–326.

Jespersen, Otto. 1904a. *Lehrbuch der Phonetik.* Autorisierte Übersetzung [from Danish] von Hermann Davidsen. Leipzig and Berlin: Teubner.

————. 1904b. *Phonetische Grundfragen.* Leipzig and Berlin: Teubner.

Joravsky, David. 1989. *Russian Psychology.* A Critical Analysis. Oxford: Basil Blackwell.

Kalista, Zdeněk. 1969. *Tváře ve stínu.* Medailony. [Faces in the Shadow. Portraits.] České Budějovice: Růže.

————. 1978. *Přátelství a osud.* Vzájemná korespondence Jiřího Wolkera a Zdenka Kalisty [Friendship and Destiny: Mutual Correspondence of Jiří Wolker and Zdeněk Kalista]. Toronto: 68 Publishers.

Karcevskij, Sergej. 1923a. *Jazyk, vojna i revoljucija* [Language, War and Revolution]. Berlin: Russkoe universal'noe izdatel'stvo. (Vseobščaja biblioteka, 47.)

————. 1923b. "Etudes sur le système verbal du russe contemporain." *Slavia* 1, 1922/23, 242–268; 495–523.

————. 1923c. Review V. Gippius *Sintaksis sovremennogo russkogo jazyka*; 1923. *Russkaja škola za rubežom* no. 5/6, 191–194.

————. 1924. "O formal'no-grammatičeskom napravlenii" [On the Formal-Grammatical Doctrine]. *Russkaja škola za rubežom* no. 1, 47–65.

————. 1927. *Système du verbe russe.* Essai de linguistique synchronique. Prague: Plamja.

Kasatkin, Leonid L. 1977. "Russkaja dialektnaja istoričeskaja fonetika v rabotax R. O. Jakobsona" [Russian Historical Dialect Phonetics in R. O. Jakobson's Works]. In Armstrong and van Schooneveld, 201–217.

————. 1990. "Moskovskij lingvističeskij kružok" [The Moscow Linguistic Circle]. In *Lingvističeskij èncyklopedičeskij slovar'*, 318. Moskva: Sovetskaja èncyklopedija.

Katanjan, Vasilij Abgarovič. 1985. *Majakovskij.* Xronika žizni i dejatel'nosti. [Majakovskij: Chronicle of Life and Work]. Moskva: Sovetskij pisatel'. 5th edition.

Kaverin, Venjamin Aleksandrovič. 1928/1980. *Skandalist ili večera na Vasil'evskom ostrove.* In his *Sobranie sočinenij*, vol. 1, 401–588. Moskva: Xudožestvennaja literatura. [Revised text of a 1928 journal publication.]

————. 1985. "E. D. Polivanov." In his *Pis'mennyj stol':* Vospominanija i razmyšlenija. Moskva: Sovetskij pisatel, pp. 87–94. [Text dated 1967.]

Kochis, Bruce. 1976. "List of Lectures Given in The Prague Linguistic Circle (1926–1948)." In Matejka 1976, 607–622.

Kolár, Jiří. 1972. "Dopisy Petra Bogatyreva Jiřímu Polívkovi" [P. Bogatyrev's Letters to Jiří Polívka]. *Slavia* 41, 306–309.

Konrád, Kurt. 1934a. "Svár obsahu a formy.—Marxistické poznámky o novém formalismu" [Conflict between Content and Form—Marxist Notes about New Formalism]. *Středisko* 4, 2, 56–65. [Quoted from Konrád 1980.]

————. 1934b. "Ještě jednou svár obsahu a formy" [Once Again the Conflict between Content and Form]. *Středisko* 4, 3, 98–99. [Quoted from Konrád 1980.]

————. 1936. "O revoluční tradici české literatury" [On the Revolutionary Tradition of Czech Literature]. *Tvorba* 11, 430–431. [Quoted from Konrád 1980.]

————. 1980. *O revoluční tradici české literatury* [On the Revolutionary Tradition of Czech Literature]. Praha: Československý spisovatel.

Kopál, V. 1949. "L'état actuel des études linguistiques en Tchécoslovaquie." *Lingua* 2, 226–236.

Kopecký, Václav. 1937. "Něco o čsl. trockismu" [A Word About Czechoslovak Trotskyism]. *Tvorba* 12, 11–118.

Koppers, Wilhelm, ed. 1937. *Die Indogermanen und Germanenfrage: Neue Wege zu ihrer Lösung.* Wien. (Wiener Beiträge zur Kulturgeschichte und Linguistik, 4.)

Kramář, Karel. 1929. "Ve slovanském ústavu" [In the Slavic Institute]. *Národní listy* June 23, 1929.

Krámský, Jiří. 1974. *The Phoneme: Introduction to the History and Theories of a Concept.* München: Fink. (Internationale Bibliothek für allgemeine Linguistik, 28.)

Krejčí, Jaroslav. 1951. "Řada diskusí o Stalinových článcích na Filosofické fakultě v Praze" [A Series of Discussions on Stalin's Articles at the Faculty of Philosophy in Prague]. *Sovětská věda—Jazykověda* 1, 141–143.

Kroeber, Alfred Louis. 1915. "The Eighteen Professions." *American Anthropologist* 17, 203–289.

Krofta, Kamil. 1935. "Sblížení mezi SSSR a Československem" [Rapprochement between the USSR and Czechoslovakia]. *Země Sovětů* 4, 1935/36, 5–7.

Kručenyx, Aleksej E. 1913. *Pomada.* [Quoted from Compton 1977.]

———— and Aljagrov [Roman Jakobson]. 1916. *Zaumnaja gniga.* [Quoted from Compton 1977.]

Kubíčková, V. and Z. Veselá. 1969. "Rozhovor s akademikem Janem Rypkou" [A Conversation with Academician Rypka]. *Nový Orient* 24, 129–134.

Kudrjavskij 1913. *Vvedenie v jazykoznanie* [Introduction to Linguistics]. Jur'ev: Tipogr. K. Mattisena. [*Učenye zapiski Imperat. Jur'evskogo universiteta* 21, 6, 1–130.]

Kušner, Boris. 1916. "O zvukovoj storone poètičeskoj reči" [On the Sound Aspect of Poetic Language]. *Sborniki.* . . 1, 42–49.

————. 1917. "Sonirujuščic akkordy. (Ritmičeskoe obosnovanie i klassifikacija èlementarnyx akkordnyx grupp.)" *Sborniki.* . . 2, 71–86.

Lanz, G. 1909. "Edmund Gusserl' i psixologisty našix dnej" [Edmund Husserl and the Psychologists of Our Days] " *Voprosy psixologii i filosofii* 20, 393–443.

———— [Henry Lanz]. 1931. *The Physical Basis of Rime.* An Essay on the Aesthetics of Sound. Stanford University Press.

Lawton, Anna, ed. 1990. *Russian Futurism through its Manifestoes, 1912–1928.* Cornell University Press.

Leont'ev, Aleksej Alekseevič. 1983. *Evgenij Dmitrievič Polivanov i ego vklad v obščee jazykoznanie* [E. D. Polivanov and His Contribution to General Linguistics]. Moskva: Nauka.

————. 1986. "Žizn' i tvorčestvo L. P. Jakubinskogo" [Life and Work of L. P. Jakubinskij]. In Jakubinskij 1986, 4–12.

Leskien, August. 1876. *Die Declination im Slavisch-Litauischen und Germanischen.* Leipzig: S. Hirzel. (Preisschriften [. . .] der [. . .] Jablonowski'schen Gesellschaft, 19.)

Liberman, Anatoly. 1991. "N. S. Trubetzkoy and His Works on History and Politics." In Trubetzkoy 1991, 295–375.

Ligo, Larry L. 1984. *The Concept of Function in Twentieth-Century Architectural Criticism.* Ann Arbor: UMI Research Press.

Linhartová, Věra. 1977. "La place de Roman Jakobson dans la vie littéraire et artistique." In Armstrong and van Schooneveld, 219–235.

Lissitzky, El. 1922. "New Russian Art: A Lecture." In English translation in *El Lissitsky: Life, Letters, Texts,* ed. by Sophie Lissitsky-Küppers, pp. 330–340. London: Thames and Hudson, 1968.

Lodder, Christina. 1983. *Russian Constructivism.* Yale University Press.

L. S. [Aleksandr Isačenko?]. 1935. "Linguistik und Phänomenologie." *PrPr* Nov. 22, 1935.

Macek, Emanuel. 1982a. "Soupis díla Viléma Mathesia" [Bibliography of Vilém Mathesius]. In Mathesius 1982, 473–525.

———. 1982b. "Soupis díla Jana Mukařovského [Bibliography of Jan Mukařovský]." In Mukařovský 1982, 835–896.

Majakovskij, Vladimir. 1961. *Polnoe sobranie sočinenij,* vol. 13, *Pis'ma i drugie materialy.* Moskva: Gos. izd. xudožestvennoj literatury.

Makin, Michael. 1993. *Marina Tsvetaeva: Poetics of Appropriation.* Oxford University Press.

——— and Jindřich Toman. 1990. "Prague: City of Russians, Ukrainians and Eurasians." *Cross Currents* 9, 69–71.

Malewitsch [Malevič], Kasimir. 1927. *Die gegenstandslose Welt.* Bauhausbuch, 11. [Facsimile ed.: Mainz: Kupferberg. 1980. (Neue Bauhausbücher)]

Markov, Vladimir. 1968. *Russian Futurism: A History.* University of California Press.

Marr, N. Ja. 1924. "Indoevropejskie jazyki Sredizemnomor'ja" [Indo-European Languages of the Mediterranean]. In his *Izbrannye raboty,* vol. 1, pp. 185–186. Leningrad: Izd. GAIMK.

Masaryk, Tomáš G. 1885. *Základové konkretné logiky. Třídění a soustava věd.* [Foundations of Conrete Logic. Classification and System of Sciences.] Praha: Bursík and Kohout.

———. 1887. *Versuch einer concreten Logik.* Classification und Organisation der Wissenschaften. Wien: C. Konegen. [German version of Masaryk 1885.]

———. 1908. *Česká otázka* [The Czech Question]. 2nd ed. Praha: Pokrok. [Originally 1895.]

Matejka, Ladislav, ed. 1976. *Sound, Sign and Meaning.* Quinquagenary of the Prague Linguistic Circle. Ann Arbor: Michigan Slavic Contributions, 6.

————. 1987. "Sociological Concerns in the Moscow Linguistic Circle." In Pomorska et al., 307–312.

————. 1988. "Chlebnikov and Jakobson's *Novejšaja russkaja poèzija.*" In *Velimir Chlebnikov (1885–1922): Myth and Reality* [. . .], ed. by Willem G. Weststeijn, pp. 529–542. Amsterdam: Rodopi.

Mathesius, Vilém. 1906. Review O. Jespersen, *Growth and Structure of the English Language;* 1905." *Věstník České akademie* 15, 313–320.

————. 1907/08. "Tainova kritika Shakespeara. Příspěvky k dějinám pokusu o zvědečtení literární historie" [Taine's Critique of Shakespeare. Contributions to the History of Attempts at Rendering Scientific the Historiography of Literature]. *Věstník České akademie* 16, 1907, 339–354, 533–539; 17, 1908, 227–239.

————. 1907/1910. "Studie k dějinám anglického slovosledu" [Studies on the History of English Word Order]. *Věstník České akademie* 16, 1907, 261–275; 17, 1908, 195–216, 299–311; 18, 1909, 1–12; 19, 1910, 125–130.

————. 1908. "K methodě výkladů literárních" [On the Method of Interpreting Literature]. *Věstník českých professorů* (Praha) 16, 1908/09, 18–21.

————. 1909. "Literatura fonetická" [Literature on Phonetics]. *Věstník českých professorů* 16, 1908/09, 205–206.

————. 1911. "O potenciálnosti jevů jazykových" [On the Potentiality of Linguistic Phenomena]. *Věstník Královské české společnosti nauk* 1911/12; Třída filosoficko-historicko-jazykozpytná, no. 2, 1–24. [Quoted from Mathesius 1982, 9–28.]

————. 1914. "K některým hlubším příčinám dnešních našich poměrů" [On Some Deeper Causes of Our Present Circumstances]. *Přehled* 12 (1913/14, 527–528).

————. 1920. "Národní tradice vědecká" [National Tradition in Scholarship]. *Česká stráž* 3, no. 3, 5–6.

————. 1925a. *Kulturní aktivismus.* Anglické paralely k českému životu. [Cultural Activism. English Parallels to Czech Life.] Praha: G. Voleský.

————. 1925b. "Česká věda" [Czech Scholarship]. In Mathesius 1925a, 85–91.

————. 1926. "Osmadvacátý říjen" [October Twenty-Eighth]. *Přítomnost* 3, 673. (Nov. 4, 1926.)

————. 1927. "New Currents and Tendencies in Linguistic Research." *Mnéma- Sborník* [. . .] *na paměť Josefa Zubatého* 1885–1925, pp. 188–203. Praha: Jednota českých filologů.

————. 1928a. "On Linguistic Characterology with Illustration from Modern English." *Actes. . . .* , pp. 56–63.

————. 1928b. "Vůle ke kultuře" [The Will For Culture]. [Quoted from Mathesius 1982, 346–347.]

————. 1929. "Pražský linguistický kroužek" [The Prague Linguistic Circle]. *Bratislava* 3, 1130–1131.

————. 1931a. "Die Persönlicheit Josef Zubatý's." *Prager Rundschau* 1, 239–247.

————. 1931b. "Discours d'ouverture." In *Réunion phonologique internationale tenue à Prague (18–21/XII 1930)*, pp. 291–293. (*TCLP* 4.)

————. 1933. "Otto Jespersen in Prag." *PrPr* Sept. 9, 1933, p. 6.

————. 1934a. "Osobnost Čeňka Duška a cesta českého protestantismu" [Čeněk Dušek's Personality and the Path of the Czech Protestantism]. *Naše doba* 41, 1933/34, 545–546. [Quoted from Mathesius 1982, 423–426.]

————. 1934b. "Čechische Slavistik nach fünf Jahren." *SRund* 6, 343–348.

————. 1935. "Užitečnost konvence" [On the Usefulness of Conventions]. *Naše doba* 43, 1935/36, 140–145.

————. 1936a. "Z mých pamětí: Gymnásium" ["From My Life: The Gymnasium"]. *Naše doba* 43, 1935/36, 551–554. [Quoted from Mathesius 1982, 417–422.]

————. 1936b. "Deset let Pražského linguistického kroužku" [Ten Years of the Prague Linguistic Circle]. *SaS* 2, 137–145.

————. 1937. "Z mých pamětí: Pražská filosofická fakulta na počátku století" ["From My Life: Prague School of Arts at the Beginning of the Century"]. *Naše doba* 44, 1936/37, 530–535. [Quoted from Mathesius 1982, 417–422.]

————, ed. 1940. *Co daly naše země Evropě a lidstvu* [What Our Lands Gave to Europe and Mankind]. Praha: Sfinx.

————. [ca. 1942]. "Kořeny mého lingvistického myšlení" [Roots of My Linguistic Thought]. In Mathesius 1982, 435–438.

————. 1982. *Jazyk, kultura a slovesnost.* [Language, Culture, and Verbal Arts.] Praha: Odeon.

Meillet, Antoine. 1911. "Différentiation et unification dans les langues" *Scientia* 9, 402–419.

————. 1918. *Les langues dans l'Europe nouvelle.* Avec un appendice de L. Tesnière [. . .]. Paris: Payot.

Mejsner, Dmitrij. 1966. *Miraži i dejstvitel'nost'* [Phantasies and Reality]. Moskva: Agentstvo pečati Novosti.

Melnikova-Papoušková, Naděžda. 1921. "Futurism jako oficiální bolševická poesie." *Čas* vol. 31, no. 32, pp. 2–3. (Feb. 8, 1921.)

Meščaninov, I. I. 1950. *Pražské přednášky o jazyce* [Prague Lectures on Language]. Praha: Slovanské nakladatelství. (Malá slovanská knihovna, 1.)

Michailovskij, G. N. 1924. "Die russische Verlagsproduktion im Auslande." *PrPr* pt. 1, July 16, 1924, p. 4; pt. 2, July 19, 1924, p. 4.

Michelis, Cesare G. De. 1973. *Il futurismo italiano in Russia 1909–1929*. Bari: De Donato.

Míšková, Alena. 1992. "Zánik a vzkříšení Pražského lingvistického kroužku" [Extinction and Resurrection of the Prague Linguistic Circle]. (To appear.)

Misteli, Franz. 1882. Review H. Paul *Principien der Sprachgeschichte;* 1880. *Zeitschrift für Völkerpsychologie und Sprachwissenschaft* 13, 376–409.

————. 1887. "Studien über die chinesische Sprache." *Internationale Zeitschrift für allgemeine Sprachwissenschaft* (Techmer's Zeitschrift) 3, 27–91.

Morkovin, Vadim. 1971. "Obščestvo Dostoevskogo v Prage" [Dostoevskij Society in Prague]. *Československá rusistika* 16, 165–171.

Moholy-Nagy, László. 1922. "Constructivism and the Proletariat." *Moholy-Nagy,* ed. by Richard Kostelanetz, 185–186. New York: Praeger 1970. [Originally in *MA,* May 1922.]

Mukařovský, Jan. 1923. *Příspěvek k estetice českého verše* [A Contribution to the Aesthetics of Czech Verse]. Praha: Filosofická fakulta University Karlovy. (Práce z vědeckých ústavů, 4.)

————. 1929. Review J. V. Sedlák *K problémům rytmu básnického. LF* 56, 378–384.

————. 1933. "Kultura jazyka—Rozhovor s Janem Mukařovským" [Language Culture—A Conversation with Jan Mukařovský]. *Rozhledy po literatuře a umění* 2, 1, 2–5.

————. 1940. "O jazyce básnickém" [On the Language of Poetry]. *SaS* 6, 113–145.

————. 1946. "Postavení a úkoly inteligence v národním životě" [Place and Tasks of Intelligentsia in National Life]. *Rudé právo* January 9, 1946, p. 1.

————. 1947. "F. X. Šalda, kritik národního života" [F. X. Šalda, A Critic of National Life]. *Tvorba* 16, 233–237. (April 2, 1947.) [Quoted from Mukařovský 1948a, 1, 321–336.]

————. 1948a. *Kapitoly z české poetiky* [Chapters on Czech Poetics]. 2nd, enlarged edition. Praha: Svoboda. 3 vols.

————. 1948b. "Inteligence v socialismu" [The Intelligentsia in Socialism]. *Lidové noviny* vol. 56, no. 119, p. 1. (May 22, 1948.)

————. 1951. "Ke kritice strukturalismu v naší literární vědě" [On the Critique of Structuralism in Our Scholarship]. *Tvorba* 20, 964–966. (Oct. 4, 1951.)

————. 1985. *O motorickém dění v poezii* [On Motor Activity in Poetry]. Praha: Odeon. [Posthumous edition of a 1926/27 manuscript.]

Mulligan, Kevin, ed. 1990. *Mind, Meaning and Metaphysics*. The Philosophy and Theory of Language of Anton Marty. Dordrecht: Kluwer.

Nejedlý, Zdeněk. 1921. *Otakara Hostinského esthetika* [Otakar Hostinský's Aesthetics]. Vol. 1. Praha: Laichter.

————. 1938. "Kolem Mejercholda" [Around Meierhold]. *Praha/Moskva* 2, 1937/38, 342–344.

Nerlich, Brigitte. 1990. *Change in Language: Whitney, Bréal, and Wegener*. London: Routledge.

Neumann, Stanislav Kostka. 1925a. [Reply to] "B. K." *Reflektor* 1, no. 4, p. 15.

————. 1925b. [Reply to] "K. V." *Reflektor* 1, no. 4, p. 15.

————. 1925c. "Romanu Jakobsonovi" [Reply to Roman Jakobson]. *Reflektor* 1, no. 14, p. 14.

————. 1938a. "Zrušení divadla Mejercholdova" [Liquidation of Mejerhold's Theatre]. *Lidová kultura* Feb. 2, 1938, no. 2, unpaginated. [Signed: -n]

————. 1938b. "Prohlášení" [Statement]. *Lidová kultura* 2, no. 14, unpaginated. [Unsigned.]

Nezval, Vítězslav. 1932. *Skleněný havelok* [The Havelock of Glas]. Praha: Borový.

————. 1933. *Zpáteční lístek* [Return Ticket]. Praha: Borový.

————. 1934a. "O surrealismu" [On Surrealism]. [Quoted from his *Dílo*, vol. 25, 144–149; Praha 1974.]

————. 1934b. "Surrealismus v ČSR" [Surrealism in Czechoslovakia]. [Quoted from his *Dílo*, vol. 25, 69–78; Praha 1974.]

————. 1936. *Praha s prsty deště* [Prague with the Fingers of Rain]. Praha: Borový.

————. 1958. *Pražský chodec* [The Street Walker of Prague]: [. . .]. Praha: Československý spisovatel. (His *Dílo*, vol. 31.)

————. 1959. *Z mého života* [From My Life]. Praha: Československý spisovatel.

Nosek, Jiří. 1965. "Soupis uveřejněných prací [. . .] Bohumila Trnky" [List of B. Trnka's Published Works]. *Prague Studies in English* 11, 69–83.

Novák, L'udevít. 1933/34. "Fonologia a štúdium slovenčiny" [Phonology and the Study of Slovak]. *Slovenská reč* 2, 1933/34, 97–107, 143–157, 161–171.

Novák, Pavel. 1990. "Konstanty a proměny Havránkových metodologických postojů (se zvláštním zřetelem k jeho pojetím marxistické orientace v jazykovědě) [Invariants and Variants in Havránek's Methodological Positions, with Special Reference to his Marxist Orientation in Linguistics]. *Slavica Pragensia* 34, 21–38.

Novikov, M. 1938. "Organisační činnost ruských učenců v ČSR" [Organizational Activity of Russian Scholars in the Czechoslovak Republic]. *Zapiski naučno-izsledovatel' skogo ob'edenija pri Russkom svobodnom universitete* 8, 47–52.

———. 1952. *Ot Moskvy do N'ju-Jorka* [From Moscow to New York]. New York: Izd. imeni Čexova.

———. 1957. "Russkie emigranty v Prage" [Russian Emigrés in Prague]. *Novyj žurnal* (New York) no. 49, 243–256.

Novotný, František. 1920. Untitled gloss on Saussure's *Cours*. *LF* 47, 253.

Nyrop, Kristoffer. 1916. "Zvuk i ego značenie" [Sound and Its Meaning]. *Sborniki* 1, 61–71. [Vladimir B. Šklovskij's translation from K. Nyrop *Grammaire historique de la langue française*, vol. 4, 3–14, Copenhagen 1913.]

Oertel, Hanns. 1902. *Lectures on the Study of Language*. New York: Charles Scribner's Sons and London: Edward Arnold.

Olbracht, Ivan. 1931. "Jazykový zmatek" [A Linguistic Mess]. *Literární noviny* 5, 1930/31, no. 12, July 1931, pp. 3–4. [Quoted from his *O umění a společnosti*, Praha: Československý spisovatel, 1958, pp. 110–111.]

Olivová, Věra. 1957. *Československo-sovětské vztahy v letech 1918–1922* [Czechoslovak-Soviet Relationships in the Years 1918–1922]. Praha: Naše vojsko.

Osthoff, Hermann and Karl Brugmann. 1878. *Morphologische Untersuchungen auf dem Gebiete der indogermanischen Sprachen*. Theil I. Leipzig: Hirzel.

Otáhal, Milan. 1986. "The Manuscript Controversy in the Czech National Revival." *Cross Currents* 5, 247–277.

Ozenfant and Jeanneret [Amedée Ozenfant and Le Corbusieur]. 1922. "Le Purisme." *Život* 2, 8–15.

Parnis, A. E. 1987. "Rannie stat'i R. O. Jakobsona o živopisi—vstupitel'naja zametka" [R. Jakobson's Early Essays on Art—An Introductory Remark]. In Jakobson 1987a, 409–413.

Paul, Hermann. 1886. Review H. Schuchardt *Über die Lautgesetze;* 1885. *Literaturblatt für germanische und romanische Philologie* 7,1,1–6.

Peterson, Mixail Nikolaevič. 1922. "Lingvističeskoe Obščestvo pri Moskovskom Universitete" [Linguistic Society at Moscow University]. *Naučnye izvestija—Akademičeskij centr Narkomprosa*, vol. 2: *Filosofija, literatura, iskusstvo*, p. 287. Moskva.

Poètika. Sborniki po teorii poètičeskogo jazyka. Petrograd: 18-aja Gosudarstvennaja tipografija. 1919.

Poggioli, Renato. 1937. "Il collettivo." *L'Omnibus* (Florence) Aug. 21, 1937, p. 7.

———. 1962. *Teoria dell'arte d'avanguardia*. Bologna: Il Mulino. (Saggi, 34.)

Sources and References

Polivanov, E. D. 1916a. *Konspekt lecij po vvedeniju v jazykoznanie i obščej fonetike,* čitannyx in 1915–1916. . . . Čast' I. [Introductory Lectures on Linguistics and General Phonetics, Read in 1915–1916. . .; Pt. I]. Petrograd: Tipografija A. È. Kollins.

————. 1916b. "Po povodu 'zvukovyx žestov' japonskogo jazyka" [On Sound Gestures in Japanese]. *Sborniki.* . . 1, 31–41. [Also in *Poètika* 27–36.]

————. 1918. "Formal'nye tipy japonskix zagadok" [Formal Types of Japanese Riddles]. [Quoted from Polivanov 1968.]

————. 1932. Review Jakobson 1929a. *Slavia 11,* 141–146.

————. 1960. "*Slovar' lingvističeskix terminov* E. D. Polivanova" [ed. by V. P. Grigor'ev]. *Voprosy jazykoznanija* 1960, no. 4, 112–125.

————. 1968. *Izbrannye raboty.* Stati po obščemu jazykoznaniju [Selected Works— Articles on General Linguistics]. Ed. by A. A. Leont'ev. Moskva: Nauka.

————. 1980. "Rifmologija Majakovskogo." *Izvestija Akademii nauk SSSR—Serija literatury i jazyka* 39, 153–162. [Published by A. A. Leont'ev.]

Polívka, Jiří. 1921. "Aleksej Aleksandrovič Šachmatov (1864–1920)." *Nové Atheneum* 2, 186–192, 228–240.

————. 1922. "Kn. N. S. Trubeckoj: Etnické základy ruské kultury." *Národopisný sborník českoslovanský* 15, 97–102.

Pomorska, Krystyna. 1968. *Russian Formalist Theory and Its Poetic Ambiance.* The Hague: Mouton.

————. 1977. "N. S. Trubeckoj o perevode ego knigi *Evropa i čelovečestvo*" [N. S. Trubetzkoy on the Translation of His Book *Europe and Mankind*]. *Rossija/Russia* 3, 230–237.

————. 1981. "Majakovskij i vremja: K xronotopičeskomu mifu russkogo avantgarda" [Majakovskij and Time: On the Chronotopic Myth of the Russian Avant-Garde]. *Slavica Hierosolymitana* 5/6, 341–353.

————, E. Chodakowska, H. McLean, and B. Vine, eds. 1987. *Language, Poetry and Poetics.* The Generation of the 1890's: Jakobson, Trubetzkoy, Majakovskij. Proceedings of the First Roman Jakobson Colloquium [. . .]. Berlin: Mouton de Gruyter.

Porzeziński, Viktor. 1910. *Einleitung in die Sprachwissenschaft.* Übersetzung aus dem Russischen von E. Böhme. Leipzig: Teubner. [Originally in Russian 1907.]

Postnikov, Sergej Porfirevič, ed. 1928. *Russkie v Prage 1918–1928.* Praga: Volja Rossii.

Potexin, I. I. 1949. "Zadači bor'by s kosmopolitizmom v ètnografii" [Tasks of the Fight With Cosmopolitism in Ethnography]. *Sovetskaja ètnografija* 1949, 2, 7–26.

Prosenc, Miklavž. 1967. *Die Dadaisten in Zürich.* Bonn: Bouvier.

Puni, Ivan. 1919[1975]. "Die Erschaffung des Lebens." [In the exhibition catalogue] *Ivan Puni (Jean Pougny) 1892–1956,* Haus am Waldsee: Berlin [. . .] 1975. [No pagination. Originally in Russian in *Iskusstvo komuny* (Petersburg), no. 5, Jan. 5, 1919.]

———. 1923. *Sovremennaja živopis'o* [Contemporary Painting]. Berlin: Frenkel'.

Puškarev, S. G. 1983. "O russkoj èmigracii v Prage (1921–1945)" [On Russian Emigration in Prague (1921–1945)]. *Novyj žurnal* (New York) no. 151, 138–146.

Rádl, Emanuel. 1922. "Úkol filosofie v československém státě" [The Task of Philosophy in the Czechoslovak State]. *Česká mysl* 18, 17–23; 65–71.

Raeff, Marc. *Russia Abroad: A Cultural History of the Russian Emigration, 1919–1939.* Oxford University Press.

Raynaud, Savina. 1982. *Anton Marty, filosofo del linguaggio:* Uno strutturalismo presaussuriano. Roma: La Goliardica Editrice.

———. 1990. *Il Circolo Linguistico di Praga (1926–1939).* Radici storiche e apporti teorici. Milano: Pubblicazioni dell'Università Cattolica.

Riasanovsky, N. V. 1964. "Prince N. S. Trubetzkoy's *Europe and Mankind.*" *Jahrbücher für die Geschichte Osteuropas* N. F. 12, 207–220.

———. 1967. "The Emergence of Eurasianism." *California Slavic Studies* 4, 39–72.

Ripka, Hubert. 1935. "Východní pakt" [Eastern Treaty]. *Země sovětů* 4, 1935/36, 15–17.

Ripellino, Angelo Maria. 1950. *Storia della poesia ceca contemporanea.* Roma: D'Argo.

Robinson, M. A. and L. P. Petrovskij. 1992. "N. N. Durnovo i N. S. Trubeckoj: Problema Evrazijstva v kontekste "Dela slavistov" (Po materialam OGPU — NKVD)" [N.N.D. and N.S.T.: The Problem of Eurasianism in the Context of the "Slavists' Plot"—On the Basis of Materials from OGPU-NKVD]. *Slavjanovedenie* 1992, no. 4, 68–82.

Romanu Jakobsonovi — Pozdrav a díkůvzdání [For Roman Jakobson—Salute and Thanks]. Spolek posluchačů filosofie. Brno 1939.

Ronen, Omry. 1991. "Zaum' za predelami avangarda" [*Zaum'* Outside the Confines of the Avant-garde]. *Literaturnoe obozrenie* 1991, 12, 40–43.

Rothstein, Robert A. 1975. "The Linguist as a Dissenter: Jan Baudouin de Courtenay." *For Wiktor Weintraub* [. . .] on the occasion of his 65th birthday, ed. by Viktor Erlich et al., 391–405. The Hague: Mouton.

Rudy, Stephen. 1978. *Jakobsonian Poetics of the Moscow and Prague Periods.* Doctoral dissertation, Yale University.

———. 1986. "Roman Jakobson: A Brief Chronology." In *Roman O. Jakobson, 1896–1982,* pp. 5–15. Institute Archives and Special Collections, MIT.

————. 1987. "Jakobson-Aljagrov and Futurism." In Pomorska et al., 277–290.

————. 1990. *Roman Jakobson 1896–1982: A Complete Bibliography of His Writings.* Berlin: Mouton de Gruyter.

Rutkoff, Peter M. and William B. Scott. 1983. "The French in New York: Resistence and Structure." *Social Research: An International Quarterly of the Social Sciences* 50, 185–214.

Rypka, Jan. 1924. *Beiträge zur Biographie, Charakteristik und Interpretation des türkischen Dichters Sábít.* (Filosofická fakulta University Karlovy; Práce z vědeckých ústavů, 8.)

————. 1936. "La métrique du Mutaqérib épique persan." *TCLP* 6, 192–207.

————. 1943. "O překládání a překladech z perštiny a turečtiny" [On Translating and Translations from Persian and Turkish]. *SaS* 9, 96–114.

Šalda, F. X. 1927. "Inteligence a demokracie" [Intelligentsia and Democracy]. *Tvorba* 2, 1927/28, 225–231. [Quoted from his *Soubor díla,* vol. 22, pp. 260–265. Praha: Československý spisovatel 1963.]

Sandfeld-Jensen, Kr. 1915. *Die Sprachwissenschaft.* Leipzig: Teubner. (Aus Natur- und Geisteswelt, 47.)

————. 1930. *Linguistique balkanique: problèmes et resultats.* Paris: E. Champion.

Sapir, Edward. 1925. "Sound Patterns in Language." *Language* 1, 37–51.

Šapir, M. I. 1990. "Kommentarii" [Annotations]. In Vinokur 1990, 256–365.

————. 1991. "Materialy po istorii lingvističeskoj poètiki v Rossii; konec 1910-x - načalo 1920-x godov)." *Izvestija Akademii nauk SSSR– Serija literatury i jazyka* 50, 1, 43–57.

Saussure, Ferdinand de. 1976. *Cours de linguistique générale.* Paris: Payot. [Originally 1916.]

Savickij, Petr Nikolaevič. 1921. "Evropa i Evrazija. Po povodu brošjury kn. N. S. Trubetskogo *Evropa i čelovečestvo.*" [Review Trubetzkoy 1920]. *Russkaja mysl'* (Sofija) no. 1–2, 119–138.

————. 1929. "Les problèmes de la géographie linguistique du point de vue du géographe." *TCLP* 1, 145–156.

————. 1933. *Šestina světa. Rusko jako zeměpisný a historický celek* [One Sixth of the World—Russia as a Geographical and Historical Whole]. Praha: Melantrich. (Výhledy, 16.)

Schleicher, August. 1850. *Die Sprachen Europas in systematischer Übersicht.* Bonn: H. B. König.

Schmidt, Johannes. 1872. *Die Verwandtschaftsverhältnisse der indogermanischen Sprachen.* Weimar: Böhlau.

Schmidt, Wilhelm. 1926. *Die Sprachfamilien und die Sprachenkreise der Erde*. Heidelberg: Carl Winter.

Schuchardt, Hugo. 1884. "Majmačinskoe narečie" [The Majmačin Dialect]. *Russkij filologičeskij vestnik* 12, 318–320.

———. 1900. *Über die Klassifikation der romanischen Mundarten*. Probe-Vorlesung gehalten zu Leipzig am 30. April 1870 [. . .]. Graz: K. k. Universitäts-Buchdruckerei Styria.

Schwyzer, Eduard. 1914. "Genealogische und kulturelle Sprachverwandtschaft." In *Universität Zürich, Festgabe zur Einweihung der Neubauten* [. . .]. *Philosophische Fakultät I*, pp. 133–146. Zürich: Schulthess.

Sechehaye, Charles-Albert. 1908. *Programme et méthodes de la linguistique théorique*. Psychologie du langage. Paris: Champion.

Sedlák, Jan V. 1929. *K problému rytmu básnického* [On the Problem of Poetic Rhythm]. Praha: Filosofická fakulta University Karlovy.

Seifert, Jaroslav. 1966. "Chvíle s Jaroslavem Seifertem" [A Moment with Jaroslav Seifert]. *Literární noviny* 15, no. 39, p. 1. (Sept. 24, 1966.) [Interview by A. Jelínek.]

———. 1981. *Všecky krásy světa*. Příběhy a vzpomínky. [All the Beauty of the World: Stories and Reminiscences]. Toronto: 68 Publishers.

———. 1984. "Un entretien avec Jaroslav Seifert." *Le Monde* Dec. 11, 1984, pp. 1 and 4. [Interview by Zagorka Zivkovic; originally in Swedish.]

Sériot, Patrick. 1992. "La double vie de Trubetzkoy, ou la clôture des systèmes." (To appear.)

Seznam přednášek, které se konati budou na c. k. české universitě Karlo-Ferdinandově v Praze v zimním běhu 1909/1910 [List of Lectures to Be Held at the Imperial-Royal Karl-Ferdinand-University in Prague in the Winter Term 1909/1910]. [Praha 1909.]

Sgall, Petr. 1951a. "Stalinovy práce v jazykovědě a pražský lingvistický strukturalismus" [Stalin's Works on Linguistics and Prague Linguistic Structuralism]. *Tvorba* 21, 674–676. (July 1951.)

———. 1951b. "Stalinovy články o jazykovědě a pražský lingvistický strukturalismus" [Stalin's Articles on Linguistics and the Prague Structural Linguistics]. *SaS* 13, 1–11.

———. 1956. "Ještě k otázkám strukturalismu" [One More Word on Questions of Structuralism]. *SaS* 17, 181.

———. 1983. "Semantics and Pragmatics from a Praguian Viewepoint." *Theoretical Linguistics* 10, 277–281.

Šíma, Josef. 1922. "Reklama" [Advertisement]. *Život*, vol. 2, ed. by J. Krejcar, pp. 102–103. Praha: Umělecká beseda. (Dec. 1922.)

Simeonov, Boris. 1976. "Nikolaj Sergeevič Trubeckoj v Bolgarii" [N. S. Trubetzkoy in Bulgaria]. *Bolgarskaja rusistika* 3, no. 2, 43–45.

————. 1977. "N. S. Trubeckoj v Bolgarii—dokumenty" [N. S. Trubetzkoy in Bulgaria—Documents]. *Balkansko ezikoznanie / Linguistique balkanique* 2, 4, 5–12.

Skalička, Vladimír. 1935. "Zur mitteleuropäischen Phonologie." *ČMF* 21, 1934/35, 151–154.

————. 1948. "Kodaňský strukturalismus a 'Pražská škola' " [Copenhagen Structuralism and the Prague School] *SaS* 10, 135–142.

————. 1950. "Stalinův článek a naše jazykovědná tradice" [Stalin's Article and Our Linguistic Tradition]. *Tvorba* 19, 718.

————. 1951. "Ke kritice strukturalismu" [On the Critique of Structuralism]. *Tvorba* 20, 1011–1012.

————. 1953. "Les travaux de J. V. Staline sur la linguistique et la linguistique orientale." *Archiv orientální* 21, 1–7.

Šklovskij, Viktor Borisovič. 1914. *Voskrešenie slova* [The Resurrection of the Word]. [Quoted from *Texte der russischen Formalisten*, ed. by Wolf-Dieter Stempel, pp. 2–17. München: Fink, 1972.]

————. 1916. "O poèzii i zaumnom jazyke" [About Poetry and the Zaum' Language]. *Sborniki*. . . 1, 1–15. [Also in *Poètika* 13–26.]

————. 1917 "Iskusstvo kak priem" [Art as a Device]. *Sborniki*. . . 2, 3–14. [Also in *Poètika* 101–114.]

————. 1919a. "Potebnja." *Poètika* 3-6. [Originally in *Birževye vedomosti*, Dec. 30, 1916.]

————. 1919b. "Svjaz' priemov sjužetosloženija s obščimi priemami stilja" [The Connection of Devices of Sjuet-Composition with General Devices of Style]. *Poètika* 1, 15–150.

————. 1923a. *Xod konja*—Sbornik stat'ej [The Knight's Move—A Collection of Articles]. Moskva-Berlin: Gelikon.

————. 1923b. *Zoo ili pis'ma ne o ljubvi* [*Zoo, or Letters not about Love*]. Berlin: Gelikon.

————. 1926. *Tret'ja fabrika* [The Third Factory]. Berlin: Artel' pisatelej "Krug."

————. 1940. *O Majakovskom* [On Majakovskij]. Moskva: Sovetskij pisatel'.

— 1983. "Gorod našej junosti" [The City of Our Youth]. In *Vospominajia o Ju. Tynjanove—Portrety i vstreči*, ed. by V. A. Kaverin, pp. 5–37. Moskva: Sovetskij pisatel'.

Šklovskij, Vladimir Borisovič. 1917. "O ritmiko-melodičeskix opytax prof. Siversa" [On Prof. Sievers' Rhythmic-melodic Experiments]. *Sborniki*. . . 2, 87–94.

Sljusareva, Natalija A. and V. G. Kuznecova. 1976. "Iz istorii sovetskogo jazykoznanija. Ruskopisnye materialy S. I. Bernštejna o F. de Saussure" [From the History of Soviet Linguistics. S. I. Bernštejn's Manuscript Materials on F. de Saussure]. *Izvestija Akademii nauk SSSR—Serija literatury i jazyka* 35, 5, 440–450.

Šmeral, Bohumír. 1920. *Pravda o Sovětovém Rusku* [Truth about the Russia of the Soviets]. Praha: Ústřední dělnické nakladatelství.

Soboleva, Elena Vladimirovna. 1983. *Organizacija nauki v poreformennoj Rossii.* [Organization of Science in Russia Since the Period of Reforms]. Leningrad: Nauka.

Sokolov, N. 1908. "Opredelenie i oboznačenie granic russkix govorov" [Description and Delimitation of Russian Dialect Boundaries]. *Trudy Moskovskoj dialektologičeskoj komissii* 1, 1–16.

Soloviev, A. V. 1959. "Serge Karcevski." *Histoire de l'Université de Genève.* Annexes. Historique des facultés et des instituts 1914–1956, pp. 106–108. Genève: Librairie de l'Université.

Sommerfelt, Alf. 1922. "Un cas de coup de glotte en Irlandais." *Bulletin de la Société Linguistique* 23, 7–14.

Součková, Milada. 1976. "The Prague Linguistic Circle: A Collage." In Matejka 1976, 1–5.

Sovětská diskuse o základních otázkách jazykovědných. Soubor diskusních statí z listu Pravda a z časopisu Bol'ševik. [Soviet Discussion About Basic Linguistic Questions. A Collection of Discussion Articles from the Newspaper Pravda and the Magazine Bol'ševik.] Praha: Rovnost. 1951.

Špet, Gustav G. 1922/23. *Estetičeskie fragmenty* [Esthetic Fragments]. Peterburg: Kolos. 3 vols. (Vol. 1, 1922; vols. 2 and 3, 1923.)

————. 1927. *Vvedenie v ètničeskuju psixologiju* [Introduction to Ethnic Psychology]. Moskva: Gos. akademija xudožestvennyx nauk.

Sprondel, Walter M. 1981. "Erzwungene Diffusion. Die 'University in Exile' und Aspekte ihrer Wirkung." In *Geschichte der Soziologie: Studien zur [. . .] Identität einer Disziplin,* ed. by Wolf Lepenies, vol. 4, pp. 176–200. Frankfurt/M.: Suhrkamp.

-ss- [A. Isačenko?]. 1935. "Logische Syntax." *PrPr* May 23, 1935.

Stangl, Kurt. 1951. "Gustav Wilhelm Becking." *Die Musik in Geschichte und Gegenwart. Allgemeine Enzyklopädie der Musik.* Vol. 1, 1487–1489. Kassel: Bärenreiter.

Steiner, Peter. 1978. "Jan Mukařovský's Structural Aesthetics." In *Structure, Sign, and Function,* by Jan Mukařovský, pp. ix–xxxix. Yale University Press.

————, ed. 1982. *The Prague School: Selected Writings, 1929–1946.* University of Texas Press.

————. 1984. *Russian Formalism: A Metapoetics.* Cornell University Press.

————. 1988. "Gustav Špet et l'Ecole de Prague: Cadres conceptuelles pour l'étude de la langue." In *Centres et périphéries: Bruxelles - Prague et l'espace culturel Européen;* pp. 81–94. Bruxelles: Editions Yellow Now.

Stepanskij, Aleksandr Davidovič. 1987. *Istorija naučnyx učreždenij i organizacij dorevoljucionnoj Rossii* [History of Academic Institutions and Organizations in Pre-revolutionary Russia]. Moskva: Mosk. gos. istoriko-arxivnyj institut.

Štern, Jan. 1950. "Strážce jazyka mateřského" [The Guardian of the Mother Tongue]. *Tvorba* 19, 680.

Štoll, Ladislav. 1966. O tvar a strukturu ve slovesném umění [Form and Structure in Literature]. Praha: Československý spisovatel.

Stolz, Benjamin and Jindřich Toman. 1993. "Philologia Militans: N. S. Trubetzkoy and R. Jakobson on Old Church Slavonic Legacy." In *American Contributions to the 11th International Congress of Slavists,* ed. by Robert A. Maguire and Allan Timberlake, pp. 414–424. Columbus, Ohio: Slavica.

Striedter, Jurij. 1989. *Literary Structure, Evolution, and Value: Russian Formalism and Czech Structuralism Reconsidered.* Harvard University Press.

Stumpf, Carl. 1873. *Über den psychologischen Ursprung der Raumvorstellung.* Stuttgart. [Reprint: Ansterdam: Bonset, 1965.]

————. 1907. *Zur Einteilung der Wissenschaften.* Berlin: Verl. d. Königl. Akademie der Wissenschaften. (Aus den Abhandlungen der Königl. preuss. Akademie der Wissenschaften vom J. 1906.)

Suess, Eduard. 1892. *Das Antlitz der Erde.* 2nd ed. Wien: Tempsky.

Superfin, G. G. 1967. "O neopublikovannom nasledii N. S. Trubetskogo" [On N. S. Trubetzkoy Unpublished Materials]. In *Tartuskij gos. universitet. Materialy XXII. naučnoj studenčeskoj konferencii,* vol. I, *Poètika, istorija literatury, lingvistika,* pp. 179–182. Tartu.

Suvčinskij, Petr. 1922. "Tipy tvorčestva—Pamjati A. Bloka" [Types of Creation—In Memory of A. Blok]. *Na putjax* (Sofija), 147–176.

Švácha, Rostislav, ed. 1990. *Devětsil—Czech Avant-Garde Art, Architecture and Design of the 1920s and 30s.* Museum of Modern Art Oxford and Design Museum London. [Exhibition catalogue.]

Swiggers, Pierre. 1990. "Une lettre de Vilhelm Mathesius à Antoine Meillet." *Philologica Pragensia* 33, 201–203.

Syllaba, Theodor. 1986. *Jan Gebauer.* Praha: Melantrich.

Szporluk, Roman. 1981. *The Political Thought of Thomas G. Masaryk.* Boulder: East European Monographs.

Tarde, Gabriel. 1890. *Le lois d'imitation.* Paris: F. Alcan.

Sources and References

————. 1895. *La logique sociale*. Paris: F. Alcan.

Tasteven, Genrix. 1914. *Futurizm. (Na puti k novomu simvolizmu)* [Futurism: On the Way to a New Symbolism]. Moskva: Iris.

Teige, Karel. 1925. "Konstruktivismus a likvidace 'umění' " [Constructivism and the Liquidation of 'Art']. *Disk* (Brno), no. 2, spring 1925, 4–8.

————. 1927. "Slova, slova, slova" [Words, Words, Words]. *Horizont* 1, no. 1–4. [Quoted from *Avantgarda známá a neznámá*, vol. 2: Vrchol a krize poetismu, ed. by Š. Vlašín, pp. 331–354. Praha: Svoboda, 1972.]

————. 1938. *Surrealismus proti proudu*. (Dvě polemické kapitoly.) [Surrealism against the Current. Two Polemic Chapters.] Praha: Surrealistická skupina. [Printed at the author's expense.]

Titunik, I. R. 1976. "Between Formalism and Structuralism: N. S. Trubetzkoy's 'The Journey Beyond the Three Seas' by Afonasij Nikitin as a Literary Monument." In Matejka 1976, 303–319.

Toddes, E. A., A. P. Čudakov and M. O. Čudakova. 1977. "Kommentarii [Annotations]." In *Poetika—Istorija literatury—kino*, by J. N. Tynjanov, pp. 397–572. Moskva: Nauka.

———— and M. O. Čudakova. 1981. "Pervyj russkij perevod 'Kursa obščej lingvistiki' F. de Sossjura i dejatel'nost' Moskovskogo lingvističeskogo kružka" [The First Russian Translation of F. de Saussure's 'Course of General Linguistics' and the Activity of the Moscow Linguistic Circle]. *Fedorovskie čtenija* 1978, 229–249. Moskva: Nauka.

Toporov, V. N. 1990/91. "Nikolaj Sergeevič Trubeckoj — Učenyj, myslitel', čelovek" [NST—Scholar, Thinker, Man]. *Sovetskoe Slavjanovedenie* 1990, no. 6; 1991, no. 1.

Toman, Jindřich. 1979. "Logic, Epistemology, and Prague Phonological Ideas." *Studies in Diachronic, Synchronic and Typological Linguistics—Festschrift for Oswald L. Szemerényi*, ed. by B. Brogyanyi, 869–883. Amsterdam: Benjamins.

————. 1981. "The Ecological Connection: A Note on Geography and the Prague School." *Lingua e stile* 16, 271–282.

————. 1984. *Roman Jakobsons ideologisches Lexikon*. Unpublished. Universität Regensburg. 148 pp.

————. 1985a. "Hašek's Early Critics." *Language and Literary Theory*, ed. by B. A. Stolz et al., pp. 577–584. Ann Arbor: Michigan Slavic Publications.

————. 1985b. "Wort, Bild und Objekt: Das Werk des tschechischen Surrealisten Jindřich Heisler." *Pantheon—Internationale Zeitschrift für Kunst* 43, 165–170.

————. 1986. "Linguists in Avant-Garde Institutions: Observations on the Group-Dynamics of the Prague Circle." In *Cercle Linguistique de Prague: Son Activité, Ses Prolongements*, ed. by N. Stangé-Zhirovova and J. Rubeš, 105–125. Université Libre de Bruxelles, Section de Slavistique.

———. 1987a. "A Marvellous Chemical Laboratory . . . and Its Deeper Meaning: Notes on Roman Jakobson and the Czech Avant-Garde Between the Two Wars." In Pomorska et al. 1987, pp. 313–346.

———. 1987b. "Trubetzkoy before Trubetzkoy." *Papers in the History of Linguistics: Proceedings of the 3rd International Congress of the History of Language Sciences,* [. . .], ed. by Hans Aarsleff et al., pp. 627–638. Amsterdam: Benjamins.

———. 1991. "Nationality as Choice—Baudouin de Courtenay's Individualistic Approach." *Cross Currents* 10, 47–56. Yale University Press.

———. 1992a. "Karel Čapek and/vs. The Prague Linguistic Circle." *For Henry Kučera: Studies in Slavic Philology and Computational Linguistics,* ed. by Andrew McKie et al., 365–380. Ann Arbor: Michigan Slavic Publications.

———. 1992b."Karel Čapek, Karl Kraus, and Moral Philology." *On Karel Čapek,* ed. by M. Makin and J. Toman, 87–108. Ann Arbor: Michigan Slavic Publications.

———. 1992c. "Opredeljajuščie obrazy myšlenija N. S. Trubeckogo" [Guiding Images of N. S. Trubetzkoy's Thought]. *Vestnik Moskovskogo gosudarstvennogo universiteta,* Serija 9: Filologija, 1992, no. 5, pp. 13–36.

———. 1992d. "Without a philosopher we won't get anywhere"—An unpublished letter by N. S. Trubetzkoy to Dmitrij Čiževskij. *Prehistory, History and Historiography of Language, Speech and Linguistic Theory,* ed. by B. Brogyanyi, 113–130. Amsterdam: Benjamins.

———, ed. 1994. *Letters and Other Materials from the Moscow and Prague Linguistic Circles. 1912–1945.* Ann Arbor: Michigan Slavic Publications. (Retrospects, 1.)

———. "Dada Well Constructed: K. Teige's Early Rationalism." *Umění* (Prague) 43 (to appear).

Trávníček, František. 1950a. "Akademik Marr a jeho směr v jazykozpytě" [Academician Marr and his Approach to Linguistics]. *NŘ* 34, 1–6.

———. 1950b. "Stalinova stat' a česká jazyková kultura" [Stalin's Article and Czech Language Culture]. *Tvorba* 19, 820.

———. 1951. *Český jazykovědný strukturalismus ve světle Stalinova učení o jazyce* [Czech Linguistic Structuralism in the Light of Stalin's Teaching on Language]. Praha: Slovanské nakladatelství.

Trnka, Bohumil. 1922. Review J. Epstein, *La pensée et la polyglossie. ČMF* 9, 1922/23, 73–77.

———. 1923. Review F. Schürr, *Sprachwissenschaft und Zeitgeist. ČMF* 9, 1922/23, 164–166.

———. 1924. "Jespersenova teorie mluvnice" [Jespersen's Theory of Grammar]. *ČMF* 11, 1924/1925, 31–39.

Sources and References

————. 1925. *Syntaktická charakteristika řeči anglosaských památek básnických* [Syntactic Characterisation of the Language of Anglo-Saxon Poetry]. Praha: Filosofická fakulta. (Příspěvky k dějinám řeči a literatury anglické, 2.)

————. 1927. "Semasiologie a její význam pro jazykozpyt" [Semasiology and its Importance for Linguistics]. *ČMF* 13, 1926/27, 40–45; 121–133.

————. 1928. "Ženevská škola linguistická" [The Geneva School of Linguistics]. *ČMF* 13, 1926/27, 199–204.

————. 1928–1936. "Pražský linguistický kroužek" [The Prague Linguistic Circle]. *ČMF* (i) 14, 1927/28, 182–186; (ii) 15, 1928/29, 173–175; (iii) 17, 1931, 256; (iv) 18, 1932, 212–213; (v) 20, 1934, 341; (vi) 21, 1935, 351; (vii) 22, 1935/36, 300.

————. 1929. "Méthode de comparison analytique et grammaire comparée historique." *TCLP* 1, 33–38.

————. 1935. *A Phonological Analysis of Present-Day Standard English.* Praha: Filosofická fakulta. (Příspěvky k dějinám řeči a literatury anglické, 5.)

————. 1937. *Pokus o vědeckou teoru a praktickou reformu těsnopisu* [An Attempt at a Scientific Theory and a Practical Reform of Short-Hand]. Praha. (Facultas Philosophica Universitatis Carolinae Pragensis, Sbírka pojednání a rozprav, 20.)

————. 1946. "Vilém Mathesius." *ČMF* 29, 3–13.

————. 1955. "Jak psáti azbukou na našich psacích strojích" [How to Render Cyrillic on Our Typewriters]. *SaS* 16, 258–259.

————. 1983. "Personal Recollections of V. Mathesius and His Circle." *Theoretical Linguistics* 10, 249–259.

Trubetzkoy, Nikolai Sergeevič. 1905. "Finnskaja pesn' 'Kulto neito', kak preživanie jazyčeskogo obyčaja" [Finnish Song 'Kulto neito' as a Remanant of a Pagan Custom]. *ÈO* 17, no. 2–3, 231–233.

————. 1906. "K voprosu o 'Zolotoj Babe'" [On the question of the 'Golden Woman']. *ÈO* 18, no. 1–2, 52–62.

————. 1908a. "Kavkazskie paralleli k frigijskomu mifu o roždenii iz kamnja (-zemli)" [Caucasian Parallels to the Phrygian Myth of Birth from Stone (Earth)]. *ÈO* 20, no. 3, 88–92.

————. 1908b. Review *Sbornik materialov dlja opisanija mestnostej i plemen Kavkaza* [Collection of Materials Describing Areas and Tribes of the Caucasus]; 1907. *ÈO* 20, no. X, 146–151.

————. 1913. "Stefan Kirovič Kuznecov (Ličnye vpečatlenija)" [Stefan Kirovič Kuznecov—Personal Impressions]. *ÈO* 25, no. 1–2, 325–331.

————. 1920. *Evropa i čelovečestvo* [Europe and Mankind]. Sofija: Rossijsko-bolgarskoe knigoizdatel'stvo.

————. 1921a. "Predislovie" [Preface]. In *Rossija vo mgle* [Russia in the Shadows], by G. D. Uèl's [Herbert George Wells], pp. iii–xvi. Sofija: Rossijsko-bolgarskoe knigoizdatel'stvo.

————. 1921b. "Ob istinnom i ložnom nacionalizme" [On True and False Nationalism]. *Isxod k Vostoku*, 71–85. Sofija.

————. 1921c. "Verxi i nizy russkoj kul'tury. (Ètničeskaja osnova russkoj kul'tury.)" [Highs and Lows of Russian Culture. (Ethnic Foundations of Russian Culture.)]. *Isxod k Vostoku*, 86–103. [Also in Trubetzkoy 1927, 21–33.]

————. 1922. "Essai sur la chronologie de certains faits phonétiques du slave commun." *Revue des études slaves* 2, 217–234.

————. 1923. "Vavilonskaja bašnja i smešenie jazykov" [The Tower of Babel and the Confusion of Languages]. *Evrazijskij vremennik* 3, 107–124.

————. 1925a. "Einiges über die russische Lautgeschichte und die Auflösung der gemeinrussischen Spracheinheit." *Zeitschrift für slavische Philologie* 1, 287– 319.

————. 1925b. *Nasledije Čingisxana*. Vzgljad na russkuju istoriju ne s Zapada, a s Vostoka. [The Legacy of Genghis Khan—A Look at Russian Culture not from the West but from the East.] Berlin. [Signed: I. R.]

————. 1925c. "O turanskom elemente v russkoj kul'ture" [On the Turanian Element in Russian Culture]. *Evrazijskij vremennik* 4, 351–377. [Quoted from in Trubetzkoy 1927a.]

————. 1927a. *K probleme russkogo samopoznanija* — Sobranie statej [On the Problem of Russian Self-understanding — A Collection of Essays]. Paris: Evrazijskoe knigoizdatel'stvo.

————. 1927b. "O gosudarstvennom stroe i forme pravlenija" [On the Structure of the State and the Form of Its Government]. *Evrazijskaja xronika* 8, 3–9.

————. 1927c. "O metrike častuški" [About the Meter of the *častuška*-songs]. *Versty* (Paris) 2, 205–223.

————. 1929a. "Zur allgemeinen Theorie der phonologischen Vokalsysteme." *TCLP* 1, 39–67.

————. 1929b. "Proposition 16: Jede Gesamtheit..." In *Actes...*, 17–18.

————. 1929c. "Pis'mo v redakciju" [A letter to the editors]. *Evrazija* (Paris) no. 7, p. 8. (January 5, 1929.)

————. 1930. *Polabische Studien* [Polabian Studies]. *Sitzungsberichte der Akad. der Wissenschaften in Wien, Philos.-historische Klasse*, vol. 211, 4.

————. 1931a. "Die phonologischen Systeme." *TCLP* 4, 96–116.

————. 1931b. "Phonologie und Sprachgeographie." *TCLP* 4, 228–234.

————. 1931c. "Lettre sur la géographie de la déclinaison." In Jakobson 1931a, 51–52.

————. 1933. "La phonologie actuelle." *Journal de Psychologie* 30, 227–246.

————. 1935a. "O rasizme" [On Racism]. *Evrazijskie tetradi* vol. 5. [Quoted from Jakobson 1975.]

————. 1935b. Statement in the panel "Il problema delle parentele tra i grandi gruppi linguistici." *Atti del III congresso internazionale dei linguisti, Roma* [. . .] *1933*, pp. 326–327. Firenze: Monnier.

————. 1936. "Essai d'une théorie des oppositions phonologiques." *Journal de psychologie normale et pathologique* 33, 5–18.

————. 1937a. "Nová kniha o indoevropské pravlasti" [A New Book about the Indo-European Homeland]. *SaS* 3, 105–108.

————. 1937b. "Myšlenky o problému Indoevropanů" [Thoughts About the Problem of the Indo-Europeans]. *SaS* 3, 191–192. [Summary.]

————. 1937c. A letter to the Prague Linguistic Circle. *SaS* 3, 63–64.

————. 1939a. *Grundzüge der Phonologie*. Prague. (*TCLP* 7.)

————. 1939b. "Gedanken über das Indogermanenproblem." *Acta Linguistica* 1, 81–89.

————. 1958a. "Autobiographische Notizen von N. S. Trubetzkoy—mitgeteilt von Roman Jakobson." In *Grundzüge der Phonologie*, by N. S. Trubetzkoy, pp. 273–288. Göttingen: Vandenhoek and Ruprecht.

————. 1958b. "Mysli ob indoevropcjskoj probleme" [Thoughts About the Indo-European Problem]. *Voprosy jazykoznanija* 1958, 1, 65–77.

————. 1987a. *Izbrannye trudy po filologii* [Selected Works on Philology]. Moskva: Progress.

————. 1987b. "Mysli ob indoevropejskoj probleme" [Thoughts About the Indo-European Problem]. In Trubetzkoy 1987a.

————. 1991. *The Legacy of Genghis Khan*, and Other Essays on Russia's Identity. Ed., and with a postsrcipt, by Anatoly Liberman. Ann Arbor: Michigan Slavic Publications. (Michigan Slavic Materials, 33.)

Tylová, Milena. 1990. "Bibliograficky soupis publikovanych prací akademika Bohuslava Havránka [A Bibliography of Published Works by Academician Bohuslav Havránek]. *Slavica Pragensia* 34, 309–358.

Ušakov, Dmitrij Nikolaevič. 1913. *Kratkoe vvedenie v nauku o jazyke* [A Brief Introduction into the Science of Language]. Moskva: V. S. Spiridonov.

——— and N. Sokolov. 1914. "Kratkij očerk vozniknovenija Moskovskoj Dialektolog-ičeskoj Komissii i ee dejatel'nosti za pervoe desjatiletie (1904–1914)" [A Brief Sketch of the Origin of the Moscow Commission for Dialectology and its Activity during the First Ten Years (1904–1914)]. *Trudy Moskovskoj Dialektologičeskoj Kommissii* 3, 19–30. [Authors listed in this order.]

———. 1922. "Moskovskaja Dialektologičeskaja Komissija" [Moscow Commission for Dialectology]. *Naučnye izvestija—Akademičeskij centr Narkomprosa.* vol. 2: *Filosofija, literatura, iskusstvo,* pp. 287–289. Moskva 1922.

——— and I. G. Golanov. 1927. "Kratkij očerk dejatel'nosti Postojannoj Komissi po Dialektologii Russkogo Jazyka za 12 let (Janvar' 1914 g.—janvar' 1926 g.)" [A Brief Outline of the Activity of the Permanent Commission for Dialectology of the Russian Language [...] (January 1914—January 1926)]. *Trudy Komissi po Dialektologii Russkogo Jazyka* 9, 1–12. [Authors listed in this order.]

Vachek, Josef. 1933. "Pražský linguistický kroužek" [The Prague Linguistic Circle]. *ČMF* 19, 1933, 203–204

———, ed. 1964. *A Prague School Reader in Linguistics.* Indiana University Press.

———. 1966. *The Linguistic School of Prague.* An Introduction to Its Theory and Practice. Indiana University Press.

———, ed. 1970. *U základů pražské jazykovědné školy* [At the Origins of the Prague Linguistic School]. Praha: Academia.

———. 1982. "Vilém Mathesius." In Mathesius 1982, 455–463.

——— and Libuše Dušková, eds. 1983. *Praguiana:* Some Basic and Less Known Aspects of the Prague Linguistic School. Amsterdam: Benjamins. (Linguistic and Literary Studies in Eastern Europe, 12.)

Václavek, Bedřich. 1929. "Nový člověk a nová kultura" [The New Man and the New Culture]. *Index* (Brno) 1929, no. 2, 1–3.

Vallier, Dora. 1987. "Intimations of a Linguist: Jakobson as a Poet." In Pomorska et al., 291–304.

Vančura, Vladislav. 1932. "Poznámka ke sporu o básnický jazyk" [A remark on the controversy about standard language]. *Rozhledy po literatuře a umění* 1, 25–26.

———. 1934. "Jazyková kultura." *Listy pro umění a kritiku* 2, 433.

———. 1935. Untitled contribution in "K diskusi o řeči ve filmu" [A discussion on language in film]. *SaS* 1, 40–42.

Veltruský, Jiří. 1980/81. Drama as Literature. Lise: Peter de Ridder. (PdR Publications in Semiotics of Literature, 2.)

———. "Jan Mukařovský's Structural Poetics and Estehtics." *Poetics Today* 2, 117–157.

————. 1987. "Structure in Folk Theater: Notes Regarding Bogatyrev's Book on Czech and Slovak Folk Theater." *Poetics Today* 8, 141–161.

Vernadsky, George. 1968. "P. N. Savickij (1895–1968)." *Novyj žurnal* (New York) no. 92, 273–277.

————. 1970. "Iz vospominanij" [From My Life]. *Novyj žurnal* (New York) no. 100, 196–221.

Viel, Michel. 1984. *La notion de 'marque' chez Trubetzkoy et Jakobson.* Un épisode de l'histoire de la pensée structurale. Paris: Didier-Erudition.

Vinogradov, Viktor Vladimirovič. 1975. "Iz istorii izučenija poètiki (20-e gody) [From the History of the Study of Poetics]." *Izvestija Akademii Nauk SSSR—Serija literatury i jazyka* 34, 259–272.

Vinokur, Grigorij Osipovič. 1921. "Reforma universitetskogo prepodavanija v Rossii" [Reform of Instruction at Universities in Russia]. *Novyj put'* (Riga). Nov. 20, 1921. [Signed: L. Kirillov.]

————. 1922. "Moskovskij lingvističeskij Kružok" [Moscow Linguistic Circle]. *Naučnye izvestija—Akademičeskij centr Narkomprosa.* vol. 2: *Filosofija, literatura, iskusstvo,* pp. 289–290. Moskva 1922.

————. 1990. *Filologičeskie issledovanija: Lingvistika i poètika* [Philological Investigations: Linguistics and Poetics]. Ed. by T. G. Vinokur and M. I. Šapir. Moskva: Nauka.

Vočadlo, Otakar. 1948/49. "V. Mathesius—In memoriam vědeckého organisátora." *Naše věda* 6, 161–171.

Vodička, Felix. 1972. "The Integrity of the Literary Process. Notes on the Development of Theoretical Thought in J. Mukařovský's Work." *Poetics* 1972, no. 4, 5–15.

Watkin, David. 1977. *Morality and Architecture:* The Development of a Theme in Architectural History and Theory from the Gothic Revival to the Modern Movement. Oxford: Clarendon Press.

Wegener, Philipp. 1885. *Untersuchungen über die Grundfragen des Sprachlebens.* Halle/Saale: Niemeyer.

Weil, Jiří. 1921. "Je možné proletářské umění? Debatní večer Česko-ruské jednoty 30. června" [Is Proletarian Art Possible? A Debate Evening in the Czech-Russian Union on June 30]. *Rudé právo* vol. 2, no. 154. (July 4, 1921.)

Weingart, Miloš. 1919. "Pohled na českou literaturu vědeckou" [A Look at Czech Scientific Literature]. *Nové Atheneum* 1, 1919/20, 81–94.

————. 1924. *O podstatě slovanské filologie* [On the Nature of Slavic Philology]. Bratislava. (Sborník filosofické fakulty University Komenského v Bratislavě, vol. 2, no. 26 (9).)

————. 1928. "První mezinárodní sjezd jazykozpytců a některé živé otázky současného jazykozpytu" [The First International Congress of Linguists and Some Current Questions of Contemporary Linguistics]. *Bratislava* 2, 472–482.

————. 1931. "Josef Zubatý." *ČMF* 17, 1930/31, 289–291.

————. 1932. "Na okraji knihy *Spisovná čeština a jazyková kultura*" [A propos *Standard Czech and Language Culture*]. *ČMF* 19, 1932/33, 70–78.

————. 1935/36. "Úvaha o zkoumání českého individuálního jazyka, zvláště básnického, a o t. zv. strukturalismu" [A Note on the Study of Czech Individual Language, Especially in Poetry, and the So-called Structuralism]. *ČMF* 22, 1935/36, 79–85; 365–370.

Weinhold, Karl. 1850. "Bemerkungen über den Unterricht in der deutschen Sprache und Literatur auf den österreichischen Gymnasien." *Zeitschrift für die österreichischen Gymnasien* 1, 345–350.

Wellek, René. 1976. "Vilém Mathesius (1882–1945): Founder of the Prague Linguistic Circle." In Matejka 1976, 6–14.

Winner, Thomas G. 1977. "Roman Jakobson and Avantgarde Art." In Armstrong and Schooneveld, 503–514.

Xardžiev, N. I. 1940. "Majakovskij i živopis'" [Majakovskij and Painting]. In *Majakovskij—Materialy i issledovanija*, ed. by V. O. Perec and M. I. Serebrjanskij, pp. 337–400. Moskva: Xudožestvennaja literatura.

Xlebnikov, Velimir. 1931. *Stixotvorenija 1917–1922* [Poems 1917–1922]. Leningrad: Izd. pisatelej. (Sobranie proizvedenij V. Xlebnikova, 3.)

Zelenka, Miloš. 1992. "Několik poznámek k Jakobsonově habilitaci na Masarykově univerzitě v letech 1932–1933" [Some Remarks on Jakobson's *Habiliatation* at Masaryk University 1932–33]. *Slavia* 61, 74–81.

Index

347

Index